THE FIRST LONDON THEATRE:

Materials for a History

THE FIRST LONDON THEATRE:

Materials for a History

by Charles William Wallace

BENJAMIN BLOM

London and New York

First published in the series, UNIVERSITY STUDIES,
by the University of Nebraska,
Vol. XIII, January-April-July, 1913, Nos. 1, 2, 3

First Published 1913
Reissued 1969 by
Benjamin Blom, Inc., Bronx, New York 10452
and 56 Doughty Street, London, W.C. 1

Library of Congress Catalog Card Number 68-56496

Printed in U.S.A. by
NOBLE OFFSET PRINTERS, INC.
NEW YORK 3, N. Y.

THE FIRST LONDON THEATRE:

MATERIALS FOR A HISTORY

BY CHARLES WILLIAM WALLACE

INTRODUCTORY SURVEY

The story of the first London theatre, from the date of its inception by James Burbage in 1576 to the full florescence of Shakespeare in 1599, has a human interest of its own, and at the same time furnishes a historical background of some of the intimate personal conditions that made the dramatic and histrionic achievements of Shakespeare and his associates at the Globe supreme. That story, based upon a large collection of documents, bringing us into close personal contact with Richard and Cuthbert Burbage, their father, and the life in and about the Theatre, may here be told in a brief survey of the human side as a help to the student in unraveling the voluminous records. The complete history, with other added documents, must wait yet awhile. Around the business arrangements made for building and managing the Theatre, centre the records of the Burbage-Brayne controversy, ranging over a period of nearly twenty years; and about the destruction of the Theatre in 1598, grew the voluminous documents of the Burbage-Allen litigation of 1599 to 1602, recounting their business relations from the first. It is these two interwoven series of records that the present collection presents in entirety.

The twenty-one-year lease of the grounds on which the Theatre was built, dated April 13, 1576, expired April 13, 1597. In February, 1597, two months before the expiry, James Burbage, the lessee, died, and the troubles engendered in the course of years between him and others concerning it, now fell upon his widow and administratrix, Ellen Burbage, and their sons Cuthbert and Richard.

The historical background of the conditions in which the Burbages found themselves in 1597–98 ranges from roseate hope to gray reality. They had in these twenty-one years lived through the most remarkable development of theatres, companies, and dramatic methods of all time,[1] and had been near the heart of all changes. Already theatres had come and theatres had gone. Their own, so distinctive in its soleness at first as to be called "The Theatre," was the first to rise. It was begun with high hope, and was maintained through the years under grave difficulties. The first Blackfriars theatre, which opened under Richard Farrant only a few months after the Theatre, came to an end in 1584, in a series of bitter litigations. Its complete history, based upon approximately a hundred documents found by the present writer, is related for the first time in *The Evolution of the English Drama up to Shakespeare,* above referred to.[2] An old playhouse built at Newington Butts in Southwark at some unknown date, presumably in these early days of development, was in 1599 only a memory, as shown by a contemporary record to be published later. Meanwhile, some of the old inns of London were either prohibited by the City authorities from further use

---

[1] See Wallace, *The Evolution of the English Drama up to Shakespeare* (Berlin, 1912), *passim.*

[2] It is greatly to be regretted that a Frenchman, A. Feuillerat, using information derived from me, and finding seven of these hundred Blackfriars documents, hastened to publish them in fragmentary anticipation of my complete work, and afterwards, through the public press and influence upon reviewers of my book, attempted to enlist public opinion by misrepresentation of the facts. Research is beset with many difficulties, but this is one of the things that time will set right. One needs only to lay his fragments by the side of the complete history to find the truth. A statement of the facts may be seen in *The Athenaeum,* January 4, 1913, continued from November 23.

as playhouses, or their companies were driven out of business or into the new theatres in the suburbs.

Companies in all the public theatres shifted and changed like satellites in erratic orbits about central suns. None were stable. Uncertain financial conditions, internal differences, or other theatrical troubles were the common causes. Almost every change of company can be traced to financial difficulties. More than an equal share of these troubles huddled on the backs of the Burbages in connection with the Theatre and its companies from the first. Briefly may we survey the troubled years that led up to the organization of the Burbage-Shakespeare company and the building of the Globe.

James Burbage was reared to the trade of carpenter and joiner. One of his enemies, Robert Myles, goldsmith, said of him in 1592 that "he never knew him but a po^r man & but of ſmall Credit, being by occupa*ci*on A Joyner, and reaping but A ſmall lyving by the ſame, gave it over, and became A Com*m*en Player in playes." Burbage was one of the principal actors in Lord Leicester's company, and in 1574 he and his associates obtained the first royal patent ever granted in England to a company of players. This was primarily intended as a means of protection against the constant opposition of the City authorities. Still the opposition continued, and made acting at the inns difficult. Burbage talked the situation over with his brother-in-law and others. He showed them that the erection of a building devoted solely to play-acting would be profitable. There was the constant demand of the Court for plays, and the growing demand of the public. But the opposition of the City made it necessary to find a location outside its jurisdiction. He cast about, and found such a location in the precincts of the old dissolved Hallywell priory in Shoreditch, north of the City. Here he found he could get cheaply, for only 14 *l.* rent per annum, a plot of ground, with some old buildings on it.

Old men and women agreed in the statement of Thomas Bromfield in 1600, concerning the nature of the buildings in 1576, that "they weare houſes of Offyce as A Slaughter houſe and Brewe houſe and low paulterye buyldin*ges*". Richard Hudson, a carpenter, who worked on them and helped Burbage convert them into habitable places, described them in 1600 as being in 1576 "ould decayed and ruynated for want of rep*ara*cions and the beſt of them was but of twoe ſtories hie." A man whom Burbage long employed about the Theatre, Randolph May, who knew the property all his life, likewise remembered them in 1600 as "very ſymple buyldinges but of twoe ſtoryes hye of the oúld faſhion and rotten," and adds that they were "ould houſes of office and ſome of them open that Roges and beggars harbored in them."

The principal building was a long, rickety old tile-roofed barn, eighty feet long and twenty-four feet wide, built of timber, one end used as a barn by Hugh Richards of Coleman street, the other end as a slaughter house by Robert Stoughton, butcher. Part of the barn served also as tenements, and one of its occupants at that time, Oliver Tilt, deposed in 1600 that "yt was lyke to have fallen downe and was ſo weake as when A greate wynd had come the tenant*es* for feare have bene fayne to goe out of yte." In fact, to keep it from falling down, when making it over into eleven tenements, Burbage had it cross-beamed and strengthened and shored up by the carpenters, Bryan Ellam and his son-in-law Hudson, as they testified, to the Theatre, which was built wholly new only a few feet from it.

Such was the uninviting site, just adjoining Finsbury Fields, chosen for the first London theatre, the cradle of the young English drama. But Burbage was a builder, a planner, and saw possibilities in it. The buildings could be renovated, repaired, made decent, even habitable, and the rent from them would pay back the annual expense of the lease. If a theatre could be built, the income from it would be clear profit. The plan was alluring. So on April 13, 1576, James Burbage secured a lease of the property from the owner, Gyles Alleyn, for twenty-one years at 14 *l.* a year, plus a "fine" or bonus of 20 *l.*, with provision for a ten-year extension if Burbage should expend 200 *l.* on buildings and repairs aside from the cost of building his proposed theatre, and with further provision that such building as he should erect for a playhouse might be taken down and removed by him within the period contemplated by the lease. For the performance of his part in the agreement, Allen gave Burbage a bond of 200 *l.*

Burbage lacked money. Some dozen men who knew him then declare that he was not well-to-do, and some of them testify that he was not worth 100 *l.*—an apparent minimization. His brother-in-law, John Brayne (or Braynes), whose sister Burbage had married, was stirred with enthusiasm at the speculative prospects of the project. Brayne was a prosperous grocer in Bucklersbury, near Grocers Hall, well thought of in London, believed by his friends to be worth at least 500 *l.,* and commonly reputed to be worth 1000 marks. Whether urged by Burbage, on the representation that the building of the theatre would not cost over 200 *l.* and that the profits would be great, as witnesses for the Braine faction in 1590–92 testified, or whether, seeing large hopes in the project, Brayne urged his brother-in-law to let him share with him, as the Burbage faction claimed, Brayne did at any rate join with Burbage in a plan to build and conduct the Theatre on equal shares of expenses and profits, and appears even to have agreed, since he had no children, to leave his half interest at death to Burbage's children, as represented in the Chancery bill of 1588.

The new venture was entered upon with high hopes. Burbage raised all the money he could, even mortgaging the new lease to a money-lender for all he could get on it. Brayne sold his stock of groceries to Edward Collyns for 146 *l.* and his house to the elder Collyns for 100 *l.* The entire proceeds of 246 *l.* he put into the building of the Theatre, 40 *l.* of it going into iron-work alone. It was said by some of his friends afterwards that he borrowed still more, that he spent, some said, 500 *l.,* some 600 *l.,* some 700 *l.,* and that Burbage did not spend over 50 *l.* One of the most partisan of the witnesses, Robert Myles, himself later litigiously interested in the Theatre by executorship, even says in 1592 that Burbage admitted he spent less than 100 *l.* and further reports Brayne as saying Burbage spent but 37 *l.* in money, and furnished timber to the value of 50 *l.,* charging sometimes 6 *d.* for a groat's worth of stuff. But Myles was Burbage's deadly enemy. He adds that Brayne sold all he had to raise money, some 600 *l.* to 700 *l.,* pawned his clothes and also his wife's, ran in debt, he and his wife worked as laborers in finishing the building to save the hire of two workmen, while Burbage, if he worked at all, was paid laborer's wages.

On the other hand, Henry Beth, a lawyer of Lincoln's Inn, who had drawn many papers for both Brayne and Burbage, who was familiar with their business, and who had at various times examined their account-books and taken notes from them, deposed at the same time that Brayne's share in the first cost of the Theatre, as he himself had confessed in 1582, was 239 *l*. 6 *s*. 6 *d*. That would make the total first cost to both parties about 480 *l*. Unable to raise sufficient money otherwise, they began acting plays in the building before it was finished, and used the proceeds to complete it. Later they spent more money on it, enough to make a total of approximately 700 *l*. It was the common impression among their friends and neighbors that the Theatre cost about 1000 marks (666 *l*.), and that Brayne paid the most of it. And even Henry Lamman, whose own evidence as well as that of John Allen reveals him as proprietor of the Curtain theatre, after some years of intimate business relations with Burbage and Brayne in managing both the Theatre and the Curtain, gives this as his understanding of the facts. Whoever may have been responsible for raising the funds, it turns out at any rate that each bore the burden equally. That they shared profits equally is also testified by many persons, among the number being Henry Johnson, " gatherer " at the Theatre, who handled all the money, and John Alleyn, one of the actors, an elder brother of Edward Alleyn.

No written agreement appears to have existed between Burbage and Brayne at first. Burbage owned the lease, and Brayne had spent much money on the property. In accordance with their general understanding, Burbage was willing to assign one half of the lease to Brayne. Accordingly, on August 9, 1577, an assignment was drawn up by William Nicoll, the scrivener, whose evidence we have on it. But Burbage did not seal and complete it, because the original lease was still in pawn for a loan to build the theatre. Therefore, on May 22, 1578, Nicoll drew up a bond between them, binding Burbage in 400 *l*. to make over one half of the lease. This bond was sealed and delivered by Burbage, and was in 1590-92 introduced as evidence in court. Nevertheless, Burbage never did make the assignment. The lease remained in his name to its termination, nearly twenty years later.

Within a month or so after the above bond for assignment, the brothers-in-law fell out over the receipts, Brayne charging Burbage with indirect dealing. Robert Myles even says that Burbage had had a false key to the cash-box made by a smith whom he names as one Braye, of Shoreditch, and that he stole money thus from Brayne and from his fellow-actors, also sometimes put money in his bosom, and even confessed his peculations, during these first two years. All of which we may properly discount upon full acquaintance with Myles. The dissension was serious enough to require an arbitration of their interests, which they referred by agreement to two friends, John Hill and Richard Turner. While the arbitrators were considering their claims, Burbage and Brayne went to the office of the scrivener Nicoll to have him draw up papers. There Brayne accused Burbage of wronging him, saying among other things that he had spent three times as much as Burbage on the Theatre. In the midst of their altercation, Burbage struck Brayne with his fist, "and ſo they went together by the ears," says Nicoll, "In ſomuch that this deponent could hardly part them."

On July 12, 1578, just following the quarrel, Hill and Turner signed and sealed the articles of arbitrament, and Burbage and Brayne each gave the other a bond of 200 *l.* to perform the conditions imposed. By the terms of the arbitrament, concerning which the direct testimony of John Allen and Ralph Myles in 1592 is particularly valuable, Burbage and Brayne were to be considered as equal partners in the lease, buildings, and profits. The lease could be mortgaged only by both joining in the mortgage. Then the rents and profits were to go to paying off such mortgage. Next, out of the weekly plays, the debts of both parties for the Theatre were to be paid, and meanwhile out of the Sunday plays Brayne was to have 10 *s.* a week and Burbage 8 *s.* a week. Next, all profits of weekly plays, after payment of the above theatre debts, were to go wholly to Brayne, until he should be paid the amount spent in excess of Burbage's expenditure. Thereafter, they were to share equally.

The failure of one party or the other to perform the arbitrament was the cause of bitter contention and long litigation for the next twenty years both within the family and without. Moreover, the part of the agreement relating to Sunday plays could not be carried out in full. The City had long insisted on allowing no plays or other recreations on Sunday, and the city records contain many orders prohibiting them. Finally, to stop the practice, Burbage and Brayne were indicted at the Peace Sessions of Middlesex (the record is well known) for acting plays on the Sabbath, the specific performance of Sunday, February 21, 1580, being cited, since a specific charge was necessary, and those before and after being referred to only in general terms. On April 12, 1580, the Lord Mayor complained to the Lord Chancellor of disorders at a play at the Theatre on the preceding Sunday, mentioning that he had begun action against the players, but that, finding the Privy Council had it in hand, he left it to them. These actions and repeated City orders at least interrupted if they did not wholly prohibit their playing on Sundays, thus preventing that part of the arbitrament from being fulfilled,—a point that Burbage's second question to Ralph Myles, April 26, 1592, aimed to establish, but without getting an answer.

Debts were not immediately wiped out. Brayne in fact had gone into debt heavily on his own account, and either before or during the building of the Theatre he had made a deed of gift of his property to save it from creditors. This was a favorite method of Brayne (and others) when heavily indebted. Sometimes he made the deed of gift to William Thompson, his brother-in-law, who had married his wife's sister, sometimes to John Gardner, sometimes to one Ashburnham, or to some one else. For example, in 1579, he made such a deed to Thompson, to save himself from a judgment of 25 *l.* 10 *s.* 1 *d.* in favor of John Hynde, haberdasher, which had been placed in the hands of the bailiff to execute. Also in other cases, not directly connected with the theatre, he took similar action, and left Burbage and his other securities to settle the debt. He got most deeply into debt, some 800 *l.* to 900 *l.*, by building the George Inn, in Whitechapel, to which, rather than to the Theatre, many of the financial difficulties that involved the Theatre seemed traceable, as Burbage, attorney Bett, former bailiff James, John Hynde and others in their depositions of 1591-92, indicate.[3]   In 1597, Brayne and Burbage were indebted in another sum of 5 *l.* 13 *d.* to John Hynde, the haberdasher.   On the afternoon of June 23, about two o'clock, Burbage was arrested for the debt in Gracious street as he was on his way to a play at the Cross Keys there, and was able to free himself only by at once paying the Sergeant at Mace the whole amount.

In spite of the apparent general prosperity of the Theatre, laudly complained of by the puritanical in pulpit, pamphlet, and City orders, the partners could not get out of debt.   On September 26, 1579, through the intermediacy of a money-broker, John Prynne, and by mutual agreement of the partners, Brayne and Prynne got of John Hyde, grocer, 125 *l.* 8 *s.* 11 *d.*, for which James Burbage at the same time signed a mortgage of the lease in security for one year.   At the end of the year, the amount was not paid, and the mortgage was accordingly forfeited to Hyde on September 27, 1580.   Then Hyde, as he relates, agreed with the proprietors to extend the loan, on condition that they pay him 5 *l.* a week until all should be paid.   This they carried out for only four or five weeks, and the mortgage was again forfeited. Thereby, Hyde became legal owner of the lease of the Theatre. By agreement he allowed Burbage and Brayne to continue the business.   But he was greatly dissatisfied with the results, as he received no profits from it.   He threatened to put them out, and thereupon in June, 1582, arrested Burbage, who, upon payment of 20 *l.* and the signing of a bond to appear at Hyde's house at an hour's notice to be subject to his action, was allowed to go on.

---

[3] Numerous documents—enough to fill a small volume—have been found by the writer in different courts concerning the George Inn, of Whitechapel, relating its troublous early history from the first.   They are of no immediate interest beyond showing the financial relations of Brayne, Burbage, and Myles in the business, through which the interests of the Theatre were jeopardized, as here sufficiently observed for the present.

But Burbage complained to Hyde that Brayne took to his own use the money received at plays, and refused to deliver any of it to him or to Hyde. Whereupon Hyde appointed a servant or agent with Burbage to dismiss and put out Brayne from the Theatre. As he could not get rid of Brayne, however, he appointed them to collect and deliver 5 *l.* weekly, thinking thus to pay himself with the profits. But by this means Hyde was able to collect only 20 *l.* to 30 *l.* Brayne never at any time paid any sum on the mortgage.

Meanwhile in 1582, during a bitter suit by Edmond Peckham against Gyles Allen over the ownership of the grounds on which the Theatre stood, Peckham tried to get possession by force, and James Burbage, whose life was on one occasion endangered in protecting the property against Peckham and his servants, was compelled to hire men and to keep them on the premises day and night to guard the Theatre and defend his rights. As Cuthbert Burbage related in 1600, it was for his father's expense in this that he withheld 30 *l.* of the rent from Allen, which remained an item of contention and dispute for sixteen years. Two men employed during the whole period of the Peckham siege, Randolph May and Oliver Tilt, gave in 1600 a graphic notion of the situation. As a result of the annoyance, plays were stopped, Burbage lost money, and his company, the Earl of Leicester's servants, who had played there from the first, was broken up. That was the end of Leicester's company in London. Their last recorded performance was *A History of Telomo* at Court on February 10, 1582[-83].[4] After the Peckham trouble, deposed attorney Bett, Brayne seemed not to care for the Theatre, and said if the profits would not redeem the lease, it might go.

The breaking up of Leicester's company was the beginning of a readjustment of all the London companies. The principal men who caused this condition by leaving the Theatre were Robert Wilson, the dramatist, Richard Tarleton, the famous comedian, John Laneham, and William Johnson. In March, 1583, with the

---

[4] For a list of plays at Court, see the present writer's *Evolution of the English Drama up to Shakespeare* (1912), 199–225.

help of Edmond Tylney, Master of the Revels, who assisted in selecting the actors by appointment of her Majesty, a new company was formed around this nucleus, consisting of twelve of the best actors of London, under her Majesty's patronage, called the Queen's Servants.[5] Thereafter they wore her livery and were given the rank of grooms of the chamber—the first instance of such recognition by royalty.[5] I shall later publish in extenso a license granted by the City to the Queen's men, dated 28 November, 1583, wherein we learn for the first time that the twelve chosen actors were "Roberte Willson, John Dutton, Rychard Tarleton, John Laneham, John Bentley, Thobye Mylles, John Towne, John Synger, Leonell Cooke, John Garland, John Adams, and Wyllyam Johnson," and that their playing places were to be "at the Sygnes of the Bull in Busshoppesgate streete, and the synge of the Bell in gratioustreete and nowheare els w[th]in this Cyttye," for the time being. This company was thereafter the favorite at Court until its dissolution about 1591. Its leader was Robert Wilson, to whom payments for their Court performances were regularly made. The principal rivals of it were the Admiral's and the Chamberlain's men, at the Curtain and the Theatre, as we now find.

It has hitherto been supposed that the Queen's men acted at the Theatre. No document to that effect is known. The new evidence, moreover, indicates that they did not, and that Burbage was not connected with them.

Before the organization of the Queen's players, Burbage had already taken steps. He was a good organizer, and was not without support at Court. Around the remnants of the Leicester's company still remaining with him after the Peckham trouble of 1582, Burbage appears to have reorganized, under the patronage of Lord Hunsdon, cousin to the Queen. Lord Hunsdon's players are first heard of at Court at the following Christmas season of 1582–83. Then, in a well known account of the City's trouble with players in 1584, dated June 18, preserved in *Lansdown MSS*.

---

[5] See the account in Stowe's *Chronicle* (ed. Howes, 1615) under 1583; also contemporary records in Collier, I, 247.

41, the Recorder of London reported that "the owner of the Theatre"—by which he could have meant no one else than Bur- bage—declared he was Lord Hunsdon's man.

The support accorded to Burbage at Court is significant to the next two steps with reference to companies and theatres. It is further stated by Recorder Fleetwood that "Upon Sonndaye my Lo [*i. e.*, Lord Mayor] fent ij Aldermen to the Court for the fuppreffing and pulling doune of the Theatre and Curten All the LL agreed therevnto faving my Lord Chamberlen [Lord Charles Howard, 1583–85] and m^r vizch [Sir Christopher Hatton, 1577– 1602] but we obteyned a lre to fuppreffe theym all/" Yet no such order was executed. Then on July 4, 1858, Lord Howard was made Lord Admiral, and Lord Hunsden succeeded him in the office of Lord Chamberlain. Within the next three months, it was thought advantageous for Burbage and Brayne to make an alliance with Henry Lanman, proprietor of the Curtain, which stood adjoining to the Theatre property. The notion was, that the Curtain should serve as an "easer" to the Theatre, as it was put. Accordingly, as Laneman and others deposed in 1592, an agreement and bonds were signed for a term of seven years, dated Michaelmas, 1585, whereby Burbage and Brayne were to have one-half the profits of the Curtain and Theatre, and Lane- man the other half. Three months later, during the Christmas season of 1585–86, the Lord Chamberlain's men and the Lord Admiral's played at Court together. Also, in 1590, as John Allen deposed, the Admiral's men were under Burbage at the Theatre.

It would seem that, from 1583, Lord Hunsdon's men (called the Lord Chamberlain's after 1585) acted at the Theatre, and the Admiral's at the Curtain for about two years, and that in 1585 the two companies and their theatres were united under one management. It is well known that the company with which the Burbages and Shakespeare were associated in and after 1594 was the Lord Chamberlain's, and it appears now that the beginnings of that illustrious company go back to 1582–83, when Leicester's company split on the Peckham rock. A further word will be said when we come to the next reorganization of companies as the result of another split at the Theatre in 1590–91.

In 1582–83, Burbage made extensive improvements in the property. Near the Theatre he built a house for his own use, mainly out of new materials, at a cost of 200 *l.* On the evidence of Ellam and Hudson, carpenters, he either then or some time before repaired the other buildings, shored up the old long barn to the Theatre, grounselled, cross-beamed, dogged together and strengthened it, so that it was fit for use as tenements. He converted the barn into eleven tenements, which he rented to poor people at 20 *s.* per annum, according to the statement of Giles Allen in Star Chamber, in 1602. That the poor people thus housed were a hardship on the parish, as Allen complained after nearly twenty years of their residence there, one may have leave to doubt, when one remembers that wandering rogues and vagabonds previously harbored there. That Burbage improved the old mill-house and other buildings and got considerable rent from them is apparent. The income from the houses probably paid in full the annual rent of 14 *l.* on the Theatre grounds, leaving Burbage his own residence rent-free.

The above expenditures on improvements, amounting to about 220 *l.*, were in fulfilment of the agreement to spend 200 *l.* on improving the property, besides building the Theatre, within the first ten years, in consideration for which the landlord was to grant a ten-year extension of the lease. But when 1585 came round, and Burbage brought the new lease for Giles Allen to sign, trouble was engendered between them which lasted the rest of Burbage's life.

When Burbage and the scrivener brought Allen the new lease, in the presence of his later witnesses, Philip Baker, John Goldborn, Henry Johnson, and others, he refused to sign it on the ground that it was "not verbatim agreeable with the ould lease," which Burbage told him was the fault of the scrivener's, not his. Then Allen wanted time to consider it. Upon Burbage's refusal or demurrer, Allen said he would take leave. So he pocketed the lease, and never did sign it. A verbatim copy of the 1585 lease, incorporating the substance of the 1576 lease, is preserved in the suit of Allen *v.* Street, 1600. It closes with a special provision for Allen and his family to have a "room" or box at the Theatre free to see plays at any or all times according as he might wish.

Allen's real reason for not signing lay in his objection to the playhouse and his desire for more money. He claimed also that Burbage had not spent 200 *l*. in improvements. So on November 20, 1585, Burbage had the property viewed by three experts in building, former workmen there, Bryan Ellam, William Botham, and William Clerke, who estimated his expenditures on buildings, aside from the theatre, at 220 *l*., and so entered and signed their verdict in Burbage's account-book. Still Allen refused on the evidence to grant the extension. Meanwhile, Burbage made still other improvements, and on July 18, 1586, he had six appraisers value his expenditures, Brian Ellam, John Griggs, William Botham, William Clarke, Thomas Osborne, and Richard Hudson, all practical builders and later important witnesses, who found he had spent 240 *l*. in the last three to five years. This likewise they entered and signed as their appraisement in Burbage's account book. But Allen remained obdurate.

Meantime, Brayne became heavily involved in debt, mainly, it seems, through building the George Inn in White Chapel with Robert Miles, goldsmith, at an expense of 800 *l*. to 900 *l*. as already noticed. He put all his property into the hands of others by deeds of gift to defraud creditors, and absented himself for a time, as also did Miles, so that when the bailiff went to levy on their goods and arrest them, they could not be found.

Under this state of affairs, Brayne died in August, 1586, charging Miles with being the cause of his death. In fact, he died from certain "stripes" Miles had given him, as is brought out in the depositions of Burbage *v*. Brayne in 1591–92. His will, which it is not necessary to publish, an old one, dated 1578, and proved Aug. 10, 1586, makes no mention of the Theatre. At the suit of the widow and executrix, Margaret Brayne, Miles was tried for murder at the coroner's inquest. Yet Miles and Brayne had been close friends, and after this event, the widow and Miles were equally close friends even to her death some ten years later, Miles becoming then her sole legatee. Miles claimed that Brayne at death owed him 500 *l*., and the widow declares in her will that she owed him more than all she possessed and expressed her life-long gratitude to him.

After the death of her husband, Margaret Brayne made life at the Theatre during the rest of her existence more exciting than profitable. She received her share from the Curtain for a time, and also from the Theatre for a while. When she had about 30 *l.* from the Theatre, Burbage suddenly cut her off from further income in the business, say John Allen, Ralph Miles, John Hyde, and others who took sides later against Burbage. Also, shortly after Brayne's death, the mortgagee, John Hyde, and his father-in-law George Clough, tried to oust Burbage from the Theatre, and put in Clough. But by something in the agreement with Burbage they could not—even when they falsely represented, as Hyde admits, that Hyde had sold Clough the forfeited lease, and Clough brought or threatened suit against Burbage for possession.

Then in the early part of 1587 began a long series of litigations between the widow Brayne and James Burbage. Miles backed her with money, and threatened to spend all he had, if need be, in order to win against Burbage. Also, in 1587, John Gardner died, to whom Brayne had made over some of his property by deed of gift, and the executors likewise sued Burbage. Still he held the fort. In 1588, he in turn sued the widow. And so for the next ten years the contest raged between them—always with Burbage as victor, supported by the decisions of the Court.

Both Burbage and the widow Brayne went to see Hyde again and again in the matter of assigning them the lease. Each wanted it, but Hyde assured them that he would deliver it, not to one of them only, but to both of them, whenever they paid him the rest of the 125 *l.* he had loaned on the Theatre, together with interest. Finally, he said he would wait no longer, and would deliver it to the one who should first pay him. Hyde says that Burbage sundry times wanted him to convey the lease to his son Cuthbert, but Hyde was loth to do it, without the widow's consent. Yet meanwhile Hyde was, as he admits, planning to sell the lease to his father-in-law Clough and one Middlemore.

In June, 1589, Burbage and his son Cuthbert appealed to Walter Cope in the matter. Cope was gentleman usher to the

Lord High Treasurer of England, and in that important post had great influence. He was intimate with every high official of the realm, and later himself became one of the powerful men of England under James I. Cuthbert Burbage, a young man of only twenty-two years, according to his own deposition, was then and for some years later employed by Cope as his "servant," probably as clerk in some department of the Treasury. Upon the request of Cuthbert and his father, Walter Cope wrote a letter to John Hyde suggesting that Cope might be of service to Hyde with the Lord Treasurer sometime, if he would be so good as to convey to Cuthbert Burbage the lease of the Theatre. So Hyde did it. He said afterwards, as Bett testified, that if it had not been for Cope's letter he would not have sold to Cuthbert, but to Clough and Middlemore, who very much wanted it. It was a close shave for the Burbages—and possibly for the future drama.

Cuthbert Burbage entered into this arrangement to save his father from the ruin of debts incurred by him and Brayne. He was sorry afterwards that he did it, for otherwise, he said, he might have used his suit to better purpose for his advancement by Cope, as was done by some of his fellows who had not been in service with Cope so long as he had been.

Hyde had owned the lease absolutely, by virtue of the forfeited mortgage, and held it as his, he declares, during the years after the forfeiture. He had a right therefore, later disputed unsuccessfully in the courts, to sell it or otherwise dispose of it at his own pleasure. It was necessary for Cuthbert to borrow most of the money to shoulder the burden. It was proved that the money was either his own or was borrowed by him. How much he paid is not sure. His opposing litigants in 1591–92 claimed it was but 30 *l.*, but Hyde himself indicates that it was practically the whole of the 125 *l.*, with interest. The lease was accordingly assigned to Cuthbert Burbage and the purchase completed in his name on June 7, 1589, in the presence of Henry Bett, attorney, and others. Still his father continued to manage the Theatre, and the business went on pretty much as before. But the Theatre itself was Cuthbert's. And just here, with this infusion of blood, begins the history that brought about the Globe, of which Cuthbert Burbage was a principal owner until his death in 1636, forty-seven years after this fateful venture. It is the accident rather than the essential that makes careers. And by this circumstance, conditions arose which not only shaped the careers of Cuthbert and Richard Burbage, but also made a Shakespeare possible.

Meanwhile, the controversy between widow Brayne and James Burbage raged. By Cuthbert's purchase, he was drawn into it, and then Richard also was made a party to the various suits. On November 4, 1590, the widow had obtained the court's order for a sequestration of the property, granting her the moiety claimed, until the case could be heard. But on the 13th, Cuthbert got that order stayed, and was granted instead the Court's order for both parties to perform the terms of the arbitrament of 1578—which, of course, he knew was impossible for the widow, and amounted in effect to a decision against her. Nevertheless, three days later, November 16, 1590, she and Robert Miles, his son Ralph, and their friend Nicholas Bishop assembled themselves and took a copy of the order to the Theatre to force James Burbage to perform its terms. It was on a play day, just as the people were beginning to come to see the performance. The parties concerned, and others then present, notably John Allen, afterwards related graphic portions of the scene that ensued.

When the invaders arrived in the Theatre yard, James Burbage put his head out of the window, and a lively exchange of epithets followed. Then Burbage came down. He told Miles that that Court order was but a piece of paper fit for base soilure, and called him a knave and a rascal; and named the widow as "murdering whore." She and her supporters were determined none the less to carry out their purpose "to ftand at the doʳ that goeth vppe to the galleries of the faid Theatre, to take & Receyve for the vfe of the faid Margarett, half the money that fhuld be gyven to come vppe into the faid Gallaries at that doʳ."

By that time, Mrs. Burbage, accompanied by her younger son Richard, then about nineteen or twenty years old, arrived on the scene, and "charged them to go out of her grounde, or elles fhe wold make her fone breake ther knaves heades, and fo hottelie

rayled at them." She and Richard declared in effect to the
Brayne contingent "that yf they did tarye to heare the playe as
others did, they fhuld, But to gather any of the money, that was
gyven to go vpon, they fhuld not." The Burbages thereupon, not
receiving assent, with violence thrust them from the door,
threatening "that yf they dep*ar*ted not from that place, they wold
beate them away." "And fo indede," one of the beaten enemy,
Nicholas Bishop, afterwards related, "vpon fome wordes vttered
by the faid Robert Myles to the faid Burbages wyffhing them to
obey the faid Order, the faid Ry. Burbage & his mother fell upon
the faid Robert Myles & beate him w^t A broome ftaffe calling
him murdring knave and other vyle and vnhoneft wordes."

Then Nicholas Bishop put in a word for the widow, whereupon, as he naïvely relates, "the faid Ry Burbage fcornfully &
difdainfully playing w^t this depo*nen*^{tes} Nofe, fayd, that yf he delt
in the matter, he wold beate him alfo, and did chalendge the feild
of him." A life-size portrait of the future great actor.

About that time, Cuthbert Burbage came home, and with "great
& horrible othes" declared he would keep, against any court
order, what he had paid for, and hotly threatened them and bade
them get hence.

Meanwhile, some of the actors had arrived on the scene. John
Alleyn, brother of Edward Alleyn, relates that upon his arrival
he "found the forefaid Ry. Burbage the youngeft fone of the
faid James Burbage there w^t a Broome ftaff in his hand, of whom
when this depo^t afked what fturre was there, he anfwered in
laughing phrafe hew they come for A moytie, But q*u*od he (holding vppe the faid broome-ftaffe) I have, I think deliv*e*red him
A moytie w^t this & fent them packing." Another study for a
painter with a proper sense of the situation. And the father
said that if his sons would be ruled by him, they would the next
time provide pistols loaded with powder and hempseed to shoot
them in the legs.

John Alleyn, though only Burbage's servant, as he says, also
remonstrated in behalf of the widow, and appealed to conscience.
Burbage did not exactly bid conscience be condemned nor tell
Alleyn in precise words that

"Thus conscience does make cowards of us all,"

but he said things that meant as much and swore as Alleyn understood, by "God's blood," and other great oaths, "that he cared not for any Contempt, & yf there were xx contempt*es* & as many Iniunc*c*ions he wold w*t*ftand & breake them all before he wold lofe his poffeffion."

Other disturbances were caused by Miles and Margaret Brayne at the Theatre or at the home of the Burbages. James Burbage's own account of this one differs materially from the accounts by his opponents, and lacks the picturesqueness and piquancy they give it.

The above quarrel and John Alleyn's interference in it led to the withdrawal of the Admiral's company from the Theatre, of which John and Edward Alleyn were principal members. Eight days after the trouble, namely, on November 24, 1590, John Alleyn went to the Theatre to have a settlement with Burbage for money due to him and his fellows. His testimony furnishes us the first known evidence that the Admiral's men acted at the Theatre. Burbage refused to pay the amount claimed, and John then "told him that belike he ment to deale w*t* them, as he did w*t* the po*r* wydowe," and threatened that "yf he did, they wold compleyne to ther lorde & M*r* the lord Admyrall and then," Alleyn continues, "he in a Rage litle Reverencing his hono*r* & eftate, fayd, by a great othe, that he cared not for iij of the beft lord*es* of them all." This talk, says Alleyn at the close of his second deposition, was in the tiring room of the Theatre, in the presence of James Tunstall and others of the Admiral's men,— who then or soon after quitted the Theatre and went across the Thames to Henslowe's theatres under the management of John and Edward Alleyn.

Within a fortnight after the *mêlée* at the playhouse door, and four days after the tiring-house quarrel with John Alleyn, namely, on November 28, the widow Brayne, backed by Miles, had James Burbage and his sons Cuthbert and Richard arrested for contempt of the Court of Chancery's order, and on January 30 Cuthbert appeared in court to save his bond given thereon to the sheriff of

London. It is around this alleged contempt of November 16, 1590, when the trouble at the theatre door occurred, that the litigation of the parties and numerous court orders and depositions centred for the next two or three years.

In the midst of the Court's long investigation, in the latter part of April, 1593, Margaret Brayne died, before a decision was reached. By her will, dated April 8 and proved May 3, 1593, she left all the property she had to Robert Miles as executor and sole legatee, and said that not even that could repay him. She specifically bequeathed him the moiety she claimed in the Theatre, and, as a matter of course, he fell heir to the litigation that he had already taken so active a hand in for her. Near the close of the same year 1593, Miles accordingly filed a bill of revivor, and carried the case on till May 28, 1595, when the Court of Chancery hung it up by sending him to the Common Law for relief. That practically ended the case, which had no solid foundation in law or equity, and never would have come into court except for Miles's spite against Burbage and his determination to back the widow at all costs. Such a case could have no standing in the Common Law, and consequently Miles appears never to have attempted to introduce it there, even after the Chancery's suggestion to try it.

During the long litigation, great question was made as to costs and profits to Burbage and his late partner Brayne. In July, 1591, Burbage again had the property viewed, by Ellam, Hudson, Clerke, and others, as they testified on February 25, 1592, and it was found by the viewers that he had spent 240 *l.* or at least 230 *l.* for new buildings and repairs, aside from the Theatre. Besides, between January 1 and February 25, 1592, Burbage or his son Cuthbert, as Hudson and Ellam, the workmen, testified, had spent 30 *l.* to 40 *l.* in repairs on the Theatre. On September 30, 1591, attorney Henry Bett, of Lincoln's Inn, deposed that he had often seen and copied out the accounts between Burbage and Brayne. Burbage's books showed expenditures of 220 *l.* for buildings near the Theatre, 230 *l.* for rent and repairs of the Theatre, 220 *l.* 13 *s.* 4 *d.* for bonds, debts, etc., paid since Brayne's death. One half of all these amounts were due to Burbage from

Brayne. Besides, Brayne's estate still owed Burbage 135 *l.* 1 *s.* received by Brayne out of the Theatre, as acknowledged by a note in Brayne's own hand.

Burbage's profits were variously estimated. Robert Miles, in his usual exaggerating fashion, estimated in 1592 that Burbage's half-interest in the Theatre had produced him 2000 *l.* in the preceding eight or nine years. The estimate of Gyles Allen eight years later, in his Court of Requests Answer in 1600, that Burbage had made a profit of 2000 *l.* on the Theatre, is based upon this earlier estimate by Miles, with whom he was bound in a common enmity toward Burbage, and is therefore of no value. Ralph Miles put it at about 100 *l.* a year, and John Alleyn estimated it at 100 *l.* to 200 marks a year. Henry Laneman's statement should be most nearly correct. He was proprietor of the Curtain, and from 1585 to 1592 had half the profits of the Theatre and Curtain, and Burbage, or he and Brayne, had the other half. Laneman says that in that period Burbage had received profits of 100 marks to 80 *l.* a year. And there we may leave it. Even at the most extravagant estimate the profit was modest. Eighty pounds a year then would have purchased about the same necessities of life as 300 *l.* today. For money then, as I find from an extensive search among original records of prices of the time, contrary to the usual exaggerated supposition, would purchase from 3½ to 4 times the same value of necessities as now.

No attempt can be made here to disentangle the complicated relations of the various companies and playhouses to each other. Companies shifted greatly. As already observed, the Admiral's men, headed by John and Edward Alleyn, appear to have withdrawn from the Theatre soon after the events above related. Thereafter, the Burbages and the Alleyns belonged to rival companies. The Alleyns united with Henslowe at the Rose and Newington Butts, where the Admiral's company, Lord Strange's company (called in 1593-94 Lord Derby's), Lord Pembroke's, and Lord Sussex's men are heard of in the course of the next few years.

It was by these companies of the Henslowe-Alleyn régime that some of Shakespeare's early plays were acted. Nor is it yet known that Shakespeare was associated with the Burbages prior to 1594, when, some time after the death of Lord Strange, Earl of Derby, which fell on April 16, 1594, another reorganization of companies was effected. Thereby Edward Alleyn became permanent head of the Admiral's company, and at the same time certain men of the late Lord Derby's company, namely, William Kempe, Thomas Pope, John Heminges, Augustine Phillipps, and George Bryan, united with Richard Burbage and William Shakespeare in the reorganization or formation of that illustrious permanent company under Lord Hunsdon, known throughout the rest of Elizabeth's reign as the Lord Chamberlain's company and thereafter for the next forty years as the King's players. With this company Shakespeare was associated from 1594 to the close of his dramatic career some twenty years later. The first notice of his connection with it is contained in the official record of payment of 20*l.* by the Treasurer of the Chamber "To William Kempe William Shakeſpeare & Richarde Burbage ſervauntes to the lorde Chamberleyne" for two comedies acted at Court on December 26 and 28, 1594. According to a letter from Lord Hunsdon to the Lord Mayor in their behalf, October 8, 1594, this company was then acting at the Cross Keys in Gracious street, where James Burbage may have had a company in 1579, when he was arrested on his way to a play there, as above noticed. Their principal playhouses after 1594 appear to have been the Theatre and the Curtain up to the close of 1598, when they set about building the Globe. We have the contemporary evidence of John Marston that *Romeo and Juliet* was acted at the Curtain about 1598. The joint management of the Theatre and the Curtain by the Burbages and Henry Laneman from 1585 to 1592 may have been extended in such way that members of the company owned shares. It is known that at least one of them, Thomas Pope, at the date of his death in 1603, still owned one share in the Curtain, and that even as late as 1623, John Underwood, at his death, owned a share in the Curtain.

As the period of Barbage's lease of the Theatre property was drawing to a close, it became necessary for him to provide for the future. The landlord, Gyles Allen, was not disposed to renew the lease on any equitable terms. The City's authorities had from the first been opposed to theatres. From 1417 onwards, their records are strewn with orders against mummings, disguisings, maskings, interludes, plays, players, and finally theatres, all of which I hope in due course to publish. They had at all times done what they could to expel the companies from their precincts. At the close of 1595, James Burbage provided against opposition of both landlord and City by purchasing for theatrical purposes, at the rather high price of 600 *l.,* a part of an old cloister building in the Blackfriars liberties, almost in the heart of the City, but free from its jurisdiction. The purchase was made probably by Christmas, 1595. The earliest information about Burbage's purchase and his proposed new theatre is contained in a letter from Lord Hunsdon, who was disappointed at not getting a chance at it himself, addressed to Sir William More, the recent owner, under date of January 9, 1596, as published by the present writer in *The Evolution of the English Drama up to Shakespeare.* The deed was signed a month or so later, February 4, 1596. On the back of the counterpart in the *Loseley MSS.,* signed by James Burbage, is the important note that possession was given the same day. Burbage paid only 100 *l.* down. He and his sons Cuthbert and Richard, on the preceding day, February 3, had given their recognizance to George More, son of Sir William, for the other 500 *l.,* which I find was paid off in full on July 23, 1597. Then on July 30, 1596, Burbage mortgaged to Lord Cobham for 28 *l.* a little piece of the property that adjoined Cobham's mansion, and on October 12 of the same year, he mortgaged all the rest of the grounds and buildings to Edward Vaughan for 200 *l.* This was probably to raise money for making the old priory over into a theatre, which he proceeded almost at once to do. The mortgage to Vaughn was paid in full on March 11, 2 James I (1605).

After completing the above transactions in 1596, and only a short time before his death, Burbage took steps to protect his very considerable estate against any possible claims or contingencies that might arise, by making a deed of gift to Cuthbert of all his personal property, and another deed of gift of the Black-

friars to his second son, Richard—a transfer which was made
much of in Robert Miles's attack on the estate in 1597, and in
Gyles Allen's great suits against Cuthbert and Richard in 1599
to 1602, and which also, forty years later, caused great suits
among Burbage's grandchildren, with serious but unsubstantiated
charges of fraud against Cuthbert and Richard for depriving
their mother and their two sisters, Alice and Eleanor, of their
due portions. All these and many other new records on the
Blackfriars will be published by the present writer in dealing
finally with their relations to dramatic and theatrical history.
The brief mention here given them is necessary to the understanding of other matters in hand.

Also by the close of the year 1596, shortly before his death,
James Burbage and his son Cuthbert had taken up with Allen
the question of renewing the lease on the Theatre. Allen was
unwilling, and made many objections and excuses. The elder
Burbage frankly told him that if the lease were not renewed, he
would remove the Theatre and take advantage of Allen's bond,
as one of Allen's own witnesses, John Goborne, testified on May
23, 1600. Finally, after much delay, a draft of a new lease was
drawn up for them by Robert Vigerous, of the Middle Temple,
who in 1600 testified to the nature of it. It was agreed, he says,
that the lease should extend for another ten years (but Cuthbert
Burbage, John Goborne and others on both sides say twenty-one
years) at the rent of 24 *l.* a year, an increase of 10 *l.*, and the
payment of a disputed claim of 30 *l.*, all of which Burbage was
willing finally to yield to, rather than lose the desired extension.
Various witnesses testified that there was then no proposal to
limit the use of the Theatre as a playhouse to only five years
of the period, with requirement that it should then be converted
into some other use, as Allen later claimed. That lease was never
completed. James Burbage was engaged in the negotiations and
was likewise just in the midst of making the old Blackfriars
cloister building over into the second Blackfriars theatre, the one
of famous Shakespearean memory, when, in February, 1597, he
died. Then came the burden of both the Theatre and the new
Blackfriars upon the shoulders of his sons Cuthbert and Richard.

Almost immediately in 1597 Robert Miles, executor and sole legatee of the late Margaret Brayne, unable to make out a successful case at the Common Law, to which the Court of Chancery had referred him in 1595, brought suit in the Court of Requests against Cuthbert, Richard, and Ellen Burbage, their mother, as administratrix—cunningly joining Gyles Allen with them as co-defendant—claiming a moiety of the Theatre, and charging fraudulent transfer of the estate to the sons to defeat him and other creditors of their dues—a charge made in vain by him and later by others. Miles estimated the value of the goods on which the widow had taken out administration papers to be 1000 *l.*, and claimed that 600 *l.* was due to him—all of which may be passed as unreliable. On May 9, 1597, the Court of Requests ordered that his bill should be compared with his bill of revivor of 1593 that was still hung up in Chancery, with the intention of dismissing it if both dealt with the same matter. But on the 27th of May, Miles's attorney was able to get an order that the case should be retained and the defendants should be required to file their answers. No further records in the case are extant, but it is apparent on the face of it that the suit could not succeed.

With the death of their father, followed two months later, on April 13, 1597, by the expiration of the lease on the Theatre grounds, it grew desperately clear to Cuthbert and Richard Burbage that they must have the question of a permanent playhouse settled if they were to maintain the business that had for over twenty years been the support and income of the family. Cuthbert now took up the interrupted negotiations with Allen, who, with old age and prosperity upon him, was inclined to dictate his own terms, and showed himself of an uncompromising and contentious nature. Allen found new excuses for delay. Cuthbert wanted to extend the lease for another period of twenty-one years, claiming some right under the former arrangement for an extension. Allen, however, demanded the 30 *l.* which he claimed was still due him for arrearages, required the increased rent of 24 *l.* a year, and made other hard conditions. He drew up the draft of a lease, but Cuthbert refused it as unreasonable in its covenants. Finally Allen yielded, on condition that the

Theatre should be used as a playhouse but five of the twenty-one years, and should then be converted into tenements. This slow and partial consent was wrung from him after some two years of conference.

Meanwhile, Allen permitted the continuance of the Theatre by receiving rent therefor in 1597 and 1598. This sort of tenure was precarious. The lessor might on any rent day refuse to accept further payment, and thus close the playhouse. The Burbages were continuing simply under his sufferance, and were at his mercy. Allen himself declares in his Star Chamber suit of 1602, that he had intended to tear the Theatre down and convert its materials to his own use. But he kept this purpose secret, and led the Burbages to believe that he would renew the lease, on the terms above stated. Cuthbert long demurred to the exorbitant terms, but after many conferences finally agreed, even yielding to the heavy condition, related by attorney Vigerous in 1600, of paying a fine or bonus of 100*l.* for the lease. Accordingly, Cuthbert Burbage prepared a lease, engrossed on parchment and provided with wax ready for sealing, which, from the testimony of Vigerous, he appears to have taken to Allen at his home in the country, at Haseley, Essex. Then at the final conference in London in Michaelmas, 1598, a hitch occurred over security.

Cuthbert offered his brother Richard as security for the lease. But Allen "misliked" the notion, and would not accept him. This was only another of Allen's excuses for not granting. the lease. Thereupon, the negotiations were broken off, with some heat on both sides. This final conference took place at the George Inn in Shoreditch,[6] near the Theatre (not the George Inn of

_____

[6] There were several George Inns of London at that time. The one in Shoreditch (a long distance from the one built by Brayne and Miles in Whitechapel) stood near the Theatre on or near Gyles Allen's estate, and was the place where he stopped whenever he came to town, year after year, to collect his rents. Various depositions, as by Bett, Gascoyne, Hynde, and James on the one in Whitechapel, and by Baker, Goborne, and Johnson on Allen's frequenting the one in Shoreditch and the conferences there held with the Burbages, suffice to prevent confusing the two. See previous note on the voluminous documents relating further to the one in Whitechapel.

Whitechapel, in which Brayne, Burbage, and Miles were in-volved), in the presence of Allen's principal witnesses, John Goborne, Henry Johnson, and Thomas Nevill, whom Allen had summoned for the occasion, in Michaelmas term, 1598. "And the Christmas next after," say both Goborne and Johnson, "the faid Theatre was pulled down and Carried away."

Documentary declaration of the plans and purposes of the Burbages during the weeks that intervened between this final conference and the following Christmas is at present lacking. Their acts alone furnish us with evidence, and these we can read with some understanding from the outcome.

After the final conference with Allen, the Burbages had good reason to fear his purposes. Accordingly they decided to antici-pate him, and thus save themselves, by tearing the Theatre down and using its materials elsewhere, as they had before warned him they would do. By a provision in the original lease of April 13, 1576, the lessee had the right, upon certain conditions, to remove the building at pleasure. This they now purposed to do. They could at least save the timbers and use them in setting up a new theatre, if a suitable site could be found. They conferred with some of their associates, notably William Shakespeare, John Heminges, Augustine Phillipps, Thomas Pope, and Will Kempe, and arrangements were made whereby definite plans could be carried out. The story of that enterprise is related by the writer in a separate work presenting the complete history of Shake-speare's theatres, the Globe and the Blackfriars—on the basis of new documents, several mentioning Shakespeare in connection with the site of the Globe—with some account of the dramas acted there, up to 1642. It was agreed that they should unite in forming an organization, altogether novel in theatrical affairs, whereby they should constitute themselves into a company not only to act plays, but to build and own a theatre on the basis of what is termed in law a joint-tenancy. The Burbage brothers had the materials of the Theatre and their experience to con-tribute. They were willing to furnish half the materials, risk half the expense of building anew, and share half the profits, if these their theatrical associates were willing to undertake the

These five were thus joined with the Burbages in the
e. It was a rare combination, consisting of the great-
st, the best actors, and the most experienced managers
of the time. Neither the Burbages nor their associates can have
had much ready money by them, both from the circumstances of
the partnership and from the statement of the Burbage family
thirty-five years later, that they had to take up the money at
interest, which lay heavy upon them for many years.

The young company was fortunate in finding a site for their
new building. Southwark was the common resort for sports.
There bear-baiting, bull-baiting, and other diversions had long
been practised. It had become a popular theatrical centre since
the building of the Rose there in 1587 by Henslowe, and the
Swan in 1594–5 by Langley. On the Bankside just north of
Maiden lane, on the same side of the street as the Rose and
within stone's throw to the east of the Rose, lay a waste piece
of ground, formerly used as a lay-stall or dumping ground, and
this they fixed upon. It had two little old two-room shacks on it.
The owner was Sir Nicholas Brend, who was living in the parish
of St. Mary Aldermanbury, where both Heminges and young
Coudell were living, within a few doors of Shakespeare's residence at the corner of Monkwell and Silver streets. As everybody knew everybody else in the little parish, we may be sure
that Heminges and Shakespeare were acquainted with the lawyer
and large landowner, who, being a fellow after his own heart and
head, and having accordingly married to suit himself secretly and
contrary to his father's wishes, had at first been disinherited but
had finally, by the death of the elder Brend a few months before,
just come into possession of a large inheritance. Brend was a
member of the Inner Temple, and was most likely present at the
Grays Inn performance of *The Comedy of Errors* by the Burbage-Shakespeare company, December 28, 1594, as one of the
Templarians, who were invited and present in large numbers.

The uninviting lay-stall in Southwark, which had only location
to recommend it, was a part of Sir Nicholas Brend's new possessions, and it is quite likely that his near neighbors, Heminges
and Shakespeare, or one of them, opened negotiations with him

for the company. He wanted 14 *l.* 10 *s.* a year for it—only 10 *s.* more than the original rent of the grounds on which the Theatre had been built. So they struck a bargain, and Brend agreed to lease the grounds to the company for twenty-one years, with term to begin on Christmas day, 1598. This arrangement must have been very near Christmas time, for the company at once took possession, although the lease was not made out and signed until after the holidays, February 21, 1599.

Having decided to remove the Theatre, and having fixed upon a site for rebuilding it, the company acted quickly. The holiday season, when everybody was making merry, was opportune, for they would less likely be interfered with by the land-owner. Accordingly the Burbages, having employed Peter Street as their superintending carpenter, proceeded with ten or twelve other men on December 28, three days after the beginning of their lease on the new site, to wreck the Theatre. These were all carpenters and laborers, enough to do the work with speed. We are not told whether Shakespeare and the rest were present. Probably they were, for the occasion was important, and promised some excitement. It is not likely that their playing before the Queen two nights before, and their preparation of another Court performance for New Year's night kept them away. Even Mrs. Burbage, mother of Cuthbert and Richard, was there as an interested spectator, and a considerable crowd assembled.

The land owner, Gyles Allen, came to town but occasionally from his fine country estate, the manor of Haseley, Essex. But he clearly expected some such action by the Burbages, and so had left a power of attorney with John Goborne, one of his tenants near the Theatre, to stop any action they might take. This representative and Henry Johnson, who likewise acted for Allen, at once hastened to the scene of operations and ordered them to stop. Perhaps the Burbage faction used a little finesse if not indirection with them, or perhaps Goborne and Johnson used a little indirection afterwards in their depositions, for they claimed that the men in charge explained that they meant only to take the present building down and set it up again on the same grounds—which is manifestly untrue, for both Goborne and Johnson knew personally, as we have seen, that the Burbages had no further lease on those grounds. So the work went ahead, and in a short time they had removed all the timbers across the Thames to the new site just north of Maiden lane in Southwark, thus anticipating Allen in his own purpose to tear the Theatre down and use its materials, who in the Court of Requests suit of 1600 claimed that they took advantage of his absence from town to accomplish their sudden and secret purposes. The whole proceeding was almost as sudden and precipitate and complete as the work of a band of Hallowe'en pixies, and was probably entered into with a similar sense of humor pervading their more serious determination.

Then followed great suits at law and equity. Giles Allen immediately in the following term, Hilary, 1599, began a suit, first recorded in Easter following, in the Queen's Bench, nominally against Peter Street, the head carpenter, but in fact against the Burbages, in the course of which the unexecuted lease of 1585, incorporating substantially the original lease of 1576, is quoted verbatim, and the history of the tenure of the property is related from 1576 to 1599. Allen estimated the value of the Theatre at 700 *l.*, and claimed also 800 *l.* damages.

In the following January, 1600, Cuthbert Burbage brought suit for relief in the Court of Requests, and that Court stopped Allen's proceedings in the Queen's Bench, first by an injunction, April 10, 1600, and finally by decree of October 18, 1600. It was a tremendous suit. The pleadings found by Halliwell-Phillips, and particularly the voluminous depositions unearthed by me and now first printed, furnish a gray background for the history of the new Globe and the Shakespearean drama. Allen lost his case, and by the final decree of October 18, 1600, was forbidden ever again to bring suit on the tearing down of the Theatre.

Still Allen persisted. He was of a prominent family, brother of the former Lord Mayor of London, and was not to be beaten. Proud, wealthy, defiant, angered at the outcome, and humiliated by Cuthbert Burbage's having him arrested for contempt of Court during the preceding suit, thus disgracing him in Essex, and binding him over in a bond of 200 *l.*, Allen then almost immediately after the adverse decision, in the next term, Hilary,

1601, sued Cuthbert in the Queen's Bench on the same matter under the subterfuge of breach of agreement. This, too, could not but fail.

Allen had a further grudge to square, because William Smith, of Waltham Cross, who had testified in favor of the Burbages in the Requests suit, was, as he claimed, the real prosecutor against him, and had furnished Burbage all the money for carrying on the litigation. Still determined on his course of annoyance and possible ruin to the new Globe and the Burbage-Shakespeare company there, Allen next brought suit in the Star Chamber, still on the same matter, but under the shifted charges of riot, perjury, etc. That it likewise failed is sufficiently indicated by Sir Francis Bacon's opinion upon it, referred to in the demurrer of Hudson and Osborne, June 12, 1602. His charge that Cuthbert and Richard Burbage had threatened to stab some of his witnesses for testifying in the Requests suit and that by such intimidation he lost that suit, may be taken to be as devoid of fact as his charges of riot, perjury, suborning of witnesses, and forgery of a court record prove to be. The final decree in Star Chamber is lost. This ended Allen's litigation, and finally closed the long and turbulent history of the first London theatre.[7]

Just prior to its demolition, the Theatre was not only a bone of contention between lessor and lessee, but was also under ban of the Queen, according to the well-known order of the Privy Council, 28 July, 1597, requiring that it and the Curtain should "be plucked down." It is noteworthy that this order, unexecuted by the City authorities, to whom it was directed, is the last known notice concerning the Theatre in connection with plays there. The Theatre was closed but not yet torn down when *Skialetheia*

---

[7] Several other suits involving Giles Allen, the Earl of Rutland, Cuthbert Burbage, Francis Langley, and others, in the Court of Exchequer, Court of Wards, Star Chamber, etc., relate *inter alia* to certain property held by Cuthbert in 1597 and later, but they have no bearing upon the Theatre, besides mere location, as presented for example in the depositions of Mary Hobblethwait, Leonard Jackson, John Rowse, etc., extracts from which may be seen in Halliwell-Phillips, *Outlines*, I, 352–53. Those of any importance on the subject will find their due place in the final presentation.

was entered on the Stationer's Register for publication, September 15, 1598, and is there mentioned thus:

"   .   .   .   .   .   .   but see yonder
One, like the unfrequented Theatre,
Walks in dark silence and vast solitude."

Moreover, as already mentioned, according to John Marston's *Scourge of Villainy,* Satire XI, entered September 8, 1598, a week earlier than *Skialetheia,* the Burbage-Shakespeare company was about that time acting *Romeo and Juliet,* not at the Theatre, but at the Curtain, which likewise had not been " plucked down ' according to order. Here the company probably remained until the completion of the Globe, about the following May, 1599, according to a record I have found mentioning it, in connection with Shakespeare, as " de novo edificata."

The important new state of affairs, whereby Cuthbert and Richard Burbage on the one side and Shakespeare, Heminges, Phillipps, Pope, and Kempe on the other were formed into a company that should endure to the end of their lives, swinging the drama during the next fifteen years into the highest prominence ever attained in the world, and opening up a history that will be read with interest to the end of time, claims our full attention in certain other works on Shakespeare and his theatre, to which the present collection of records forms the gray background. Had the Brayne-Miles contention succeeded, the new company would not have come into being, and if Allen's legal onslaughts on the Burbages had not failed, their company must have suffered great danger if not ruin.

The changed tone of the dramatic products of Shakespeare and his associated actors fairly synchronizes with the business difficulties in their new enterprise—the wasteful, vicious suits of Allen, the almost immediate withdrawal of Kempe in 1599, the restrictions upon their acting, the successful rivalry of the children actors under the Queen's patronage, the Essex conspiracy of 1601 in which they were involved, and death that took off two of their number, in 1603 and 1605. The thought of possible disruption of a life-enterprise could not have been the least of cares that weighed upon Shakespeare and his fellows. The ominous note struck that shuddered through their lives, and the sharp heel of tragedy trod loud across the boards of the Globe. Not less than the rest but more sensitively, perhaps, did Shakespeare feel it, and he recorded the common tragic sense that was upon them all in the very themes chosen for enactment. Prior to the Globe enterprise, his plays had been on the sunnier side. *Henry V,* the first new play at the Globe, was the last clear note of untrammeled life for many years. Then came the treachery and misguided statesmanship in *Julius Caesar,* the vanquishing of idealism in the play of *Hamlet,* and the whole series of tragic interruptions of noble aspirations in the plays that range down the years to those more placid days when, about 1608–9, doubt and discord and threatened disaster were safely weathered. The following documents, aside from the history they hold, show in this regard some of the mere business conditions that made Shakespeare possible, and some of the difficulties that wrought in him supreme achievement.

The materials for a history of the Shakespearean theatre and drama grow apace. After the labors of Malone, Chalmers, Collier, and Halliwell-Phillips in their life-long searches for documentary evidences, it was gradually thought that the end was reached. The field long lay almost fallow, until about ten years ago, when the present writer took it up, with the result that vast new sources have been opened that enrich dramatic and theatrical history. Today no department of research is looked to with larger expectations. By the encouragement of the better sort, in spite of annoyances from a narrow circle, the scholar's dream of bringing all these materials into a complete corpus may be realized. I am glad to be the inspirer of scholarly research, and have given help freely to many worthy students, whose work I heartily welcome. But my researches have unfortunately attracted . also another sort, an envious few, who find out by one means or another what records I have examined or am having prepared for examination, and then proceed to " discover " a document here and there for hasty publication. Such but hinder scholarship, divide and confuse the public. It is easy for them to "leaf" through a set of records when once the way is pointed out either publicly or privately.

It is but fair, therefore, to other scholars as well as to myself to say that the field I have opened is now fairly worked out. There remain, of course, innumerable details to complete, and the slow process of correlating and presenting the materials in permanent and useful form. On a conservative estimate, approximately three million records have been searched under my direction, in public, private, and municipal archives. Most of these had not previously been examined. I have reasons to believe that I have now reached all documents of first importance in the public archives and among the London City records for the Tudor-Stuart period of stage-history. The more varied and interesting field of private, provincial, and continental archives, which should yield valuable results, invites earnest students, to whom I shall be glad to give help and encouragement. This announcement of the state of research will prevent any duplication of results by others, and should enable any investigator to choose a line of direction that will not lead him into conflict with work thus done and now preparing for publication. I shall be pleased to give information to any scholar who is engaged in a serious piece of work contributive to knowledge in this department of research.

The present collection of records on the Theatre is a fair example of some of the materials gathered for publication on other Shakespearean theatres, as the Globe, Blackfriars, Whitefriars, Swan, Fortune, Hope, Red Bull, Cockpit, Salisbury Court, etc. Others already published by the present writer, relating to theatres, dramatists, etc., may be seen in *University Studies* for 1905, on *Shakespeare;* 1908, on *The Children of the Chapel at Blackfriars 1597–1603;* 1909, *Three London Theatres of Shakespeare's Time* (twenty-eight documents on Red Bull, Fortune, and Bear Garden); 1910–11, *Shakespeare and his London Associates* (fifty-six documents). Others may be seen in *Globe Theatre Apparel,* Taylor *v.* Heminges (privately printed, August, 1909); *The Times,* London, October 2 and 4, 1909, on *Shakespeare and the Globe* (the Ostler-Heminges documents); *The*

Times, March 28, 1913, *A London Pageant of Shakespeare's Time* (with Burbage and Rice as speakers and Anthony Munday as author, from the City archives); *Harper's Magazine,* March, 1910, on a signed deposition by Shakespeare, and his life in London; *Century Magazine,* August and September, 1910, on Shakespeare's Globe and Blackfriars; *Shakespeare-Jahrbuch,* 1910, on Gervase Markham, Dramatist, and thirty-nine defendants, chiefly actors; *Keyzar v. Burbage* (privately printed, 1910); *Englische Studien,* 1911, on the Swan, Jonson, Nash, etc. (with bibliography of documents published from the Court of Requests, p. 344); and especially *The Evolution of the English Drama up to Shakespeare,* a volume dealing with over 500 records (Berlin, 1912).

The principal documents in the present collection are the voluminous depositions, which bring us into intimate touch with the people and events they deal with in connection with the Theatre. These were discovered by the writer and his devoted wife a few years ago in the course of a complete search of the proceedings of the Court of Requests, and the equally unknown Town Depositions of Chancery. The uncalendared records of these two enormous classes for the period of my research, in the reigns of Elizabeth, James I, and Charles I, had not before been examined since they were filed away three centuries ago, and were prepared for inspection at my request. Such materials as they contain in any way elucidating the history of the drama and stage, and of dramatists and actors, I now have and shall in due course publish, as soon as the task can be completed of bringing together the results with all related matters from various other original sources in a permanently useful form. The complete series of documents arising out of the trouble in different courts over the two events of building the Theatre in 1576 and of tearing it down in 1598 here follow.

CHRONOLOGICAL ARRANGEMENT OF DOCUMENTS

[The documents are printed in the following chronological order. None have previously been published in extenso, with the exception of five court orders printed by Collier. Documents hitherto known are indicated in head-notes or foot-notes. Those belonging to the present writer's researches are here marked with an asterisk (*). The total list comprises ninety-nine documents, some of them grouped in sets, according as the originals are fastened together or separate. With reference to other documents, see *Introductory Survey.*]

PAGE

*1588, Burbage *v.* Braine, Chancery, Bill and Answer, on agreements between Burbage and Braine, concerning the Theatre...................................... 39

*1588–9, Feb. 17, Court order referring bill and insufficient demurrer to Dr. Carew.......................... 46

*1590, May 21, Court order referring case to Dr. Caesar; head-note on cross-bill.......................... 46

*1590, Nov. 4, Court order on sequestration of the Theatre.. 47

*1590, Nov. 13, Court order to stay sequestration and fulfil abitrament 48

*1590, Nov. 28, Robert Miles's affidavit, on contempt by the Burbages 49

*1590–91, Jan. 30, Personal appearance of Cuthbert Burbage on bond 49

*1590, Dec. 8, Brayne *v.* Burbage. Depositions ex parte Burbage by John Hyde and George Clough............. 50

*1590–91, Feb. 16, Brayne *v.* Burbage. Depositions by James and Cuthbert Burbage on charge of Contempt....... 57

1590–91, March 23, Brayne *v.* Burbage. Court order, referring above depositions on Contempt to Dr. Caesar.. 64

1591, April 24, Burbage *v.* Brayne. Defendant's demurrer referred to Dr. Carew.......................... 64

*1591, June 15, Burbage *v.* Brayne. Widow's demurrer referred to Dr. Carew.............................. 65

1591, July 20, Brayne *v.* Burbage. Court order transferring consideration of depositions on contempt from Dr. Caesar to Dr. Hone.............................. 66

*1591, October 12, Brayne *v.* Burbage. Hone reported; case now referred to Dr. Legg and Dr. Stanhope......... 66

*1591, Nov. 13, Brayne *v.* Burbage. Dr. Legg and Dr. Stanhope report they must examine John Hyde and Ralph Miles on the Cause, and Nicholas Bishop and John

Allein on the contempt. Whole case re-referred to Legg and Stanhope, to try out in full. Hence case in their hands and they examined many witnesses...... 67

*1591, Sept. 30, to 1592, Feb. 25, Brayne *v.* Burbage. Depositions ex parte Burbage by Henry Bett, Gyles Allen, Brian Ellam, Richard Hudson, William Clerke...... 68

*1591, Sept. 30, to 1592, July 24, Burbage *v.* Brayne. Depositions ex parte Burbage by Henry Bett, Ellen Gascoyn, John Hynde, William James................. 78

*1592, Jan. 29, to Feb. 12, Brayne *v.* Burbage. Depositions ex parte Brayne by Nicholas Bishop, John Alleyn, Ralph Miles, John Hyde 92

*1592, Feb. 21, to May 6, Brayne *v.* Burbage. Depositions in cross-examination ex parte Burbage by John Hyde, Nicholas Bishop, Ralph Miles, John Alleyn......... 109

*1592, July 29, Brayne *v.* Burbage. Depositions ex parte Brayne by John Griggs, Edward Collyns, Robert Miles, Henry Laneman, William Nicoll............. 127

*1593, April, Will of Margaret Brayne................... 153

*1593-4, Feb. 11, Miles *v.* Burbage. Court order referring to the death of Margaret Brayne, and allowing a Bill of Revivor by Miles, her executor................. 155

*1594-5, March 14, Burbage *v.* Miles and Miles *v.* Burbage. Court order to hear case....................... 155

1595, May 28, Miles *v.* Burbage. Decree referring the case to the Common Law............................. 156

*1597, Miles *v.* Burbage. Court of Requests, Bill of Complaint attacking the Burbage estate............... 158

*1597, May 9, order by Court of Requests to compare Miles's bill with his former bill in Chancery................ 162

*1597, May 27, order retaining Miles's bill in Requests, and requiring the defendants to answer............ 163

1599-1600, Allen *v.* Street, Coram Rege, containing proposed lease of Theatre of 1585 and incorporating substance of lease of 1576......................... 163

1600, Jan. 26 to April 27, Burbage *v.* Allen, Court of Requests Proceedings, Bill, Answer, and Replication.

Suit for relief in equity against Allen, re-stating the
history 181

*1600, April 10, Court order; injunction against Allen to
stay his proceedings in the Queen's Bench against
Peter Street 205

*1600, April 22, Court order, on injunction, examination of
witnesses, and the hearing of the cause............. 205

*1600, April 26, Depositions ex parte Allen, by Philip Baker,
John Goborne, Henry Johnson.................... 206

*1600, May 15, Depositions ex parte Burbage, by Richard
Hudson, Thomas Bromfield, Thomas Osborne, Wil-
liam Furnis, William Smythe, Randolph May, Oliver
Tilt 223

*1600, May 23, Depositions in Burbage's cross-examination
of Allen's witnesses, Henry Johnson and John
Goborne 243

*1600, June 2, Affidavit of Allen as to additional witnesses.. 251

*1600, June 11, Affidavit of Cuthbert Burbage that Allen has
broken court order of May 31, by causing the Common Law suit against Street to be joined up......... 252

*1600, June 11, Order of Sir Julius Caesar, Master in Re-
quests, for arrest of Allen....................... 252

1600, August 14, Country depositions at Kelvedon, Essex,
ex parte Allen by Robert Vigerous and Thomas Neville 253

*1600, Oct. 1, Depositions ex parte Allen by Robert Miles
and Ralph Miles.................................. 259

*1600, Oct. 9, Appearance of Allen...................... 266

1601, Jan.–Feb., to 1602, summer. Allen *v.* Burbage, Court
of Queen's Bench, on breach of agreement, recounting much of the history of the Theatre, with part of
lease of 1576.................................... 267

1602, Allen *v.* Burbage and others, Court of Star Chamber,
Bill, and three Answers, on tearing down the Theatre,
&c. 275

*1602, Allen *v.* Burbage and others, Court of Star Chamber,
examination of Richard Lane, deputy register of

the Court of Requests, on the previous suit of 1600
in Requests 290

[NOTE.—In printing the documents, signs of contraction are expanded
into italics. Where no sign of contraction occurs, the shortened form is
retained, except in the case of Latin documents, which are expanded in
full, the Roman type showing in all cases what letters stood in the
original. There is, therefore, no uniformity in spellings or expansions.
The transcripts have been carefully proof-read against the originals before
putting them into type, and the correction of the printed proofs has been
generously carried through by the Editor of the *Studies,* during my
absence in Europe. The object has been to be faithful to the originals in
word and letter, and thus to make this publication of the documents of
lasting value.]

BURBAGE V. BRAYNE

Chancery Proceedings, Series II, 222/83.

[Bill and Demurrer. Date at upper left-hand corner of Bill all decayed
away, except the final "8" and the right edge of the "8" just before it,
giving the date as 1588. As the first order of the Court was in Hilary
(February 17), 1588-9, the suit was filed in the preceding term of
Michaelmas, 1588.

The entire left third of the Bill and the left half of the Demurrer rotted
away. Officially repaired at my request, 1908. (See further, note at close
of Demurrer.) Bill originally about 22 inches wide and 17 inches long;
Demurrer originally about 15 × 9.

In the following transcript, the first number inserted within the brackets
indicates the line; the second number, the approximate number of inches
missing at the beginning of that line.]

BILL

[158]8

To the right Honorable Sᵣ Xpofer Hatton Knight
Lord Chancellor of England

[Humblie complaining fheweth] to yoᵣ good Lordfhipp James
Burbedge of [Hallywell] in [Shordiche Crypple gate London]
gentleman Cutbert Rychard Alce and Ellen Burbedge the Children of the faid James and Ellen his wief That wher yoᵣ faid
Orator [James Burbage was poffeffed of a leafe granted by]

one Giles Allen gent in or about the xviij. yere of the Reigne of
the Queenes moſt Excellent Matie that now ys of and in certaine
decayed Barnes vacant ground and garden plott*es* ſcituat & [being
in Haſlywell in Shordiche aforeſaid for a] terme of Certeyn
yeres yet [to endure] for [a yearly] rent of xiv^{li} to be quarterly
paied and in the ſaid Leaſe did promyſe and Coven*a*nte to and
wth the ſaid Giles Allen to build in & vpon the demiſed [prem-
iſſes 4—3] buildings for Tenement*es* to be errected vpon the
premiſſes the ſome of two hundrethe pound*es* and the ſame to
be done and fyniſhed by a certain tyme [5—9] for the Accom-
pliſhm^{t} wherof the ſaid James yor ſaid Orator was conſtrayned
to borrowe dyvers ſomes of monye and to impawne his ſaid
[leaſe 6—8] buildinge and erectinge of a plaie howſe or Theatre
& other the buildings for Tenement*es* as is aforeſaid.   The w^{ch}
one John Brayne Late of White [Chappel 7—9] he practiſed
to obteyne ſome intereſt therin, preſumynge that he might eaſelie
compaſe the ſame by reaſon that he was naturall brother [to your
ſaid Orators wife 8—9] diuers ſomes of monye) he made meanes
to yor ſaid Orator James Burbedge, that he might haue the
Moietie of the aboue named Theatre & [9—9] that in conſidera-
c*i*on therof he would not only beare and paie haluf the chardg*es*
of the ſaid building*es* then beſtoed & therafter to be beſtoed
[10—9] yor Orato^{rs} aforſaid her Children ſhuld haue the ſame
Moietie ſo to him to be conveyed and aſſured, making ſemblaunce
that his induſtrie was [11—9] child*ren* of his ſiſter as is aforſaid/
Wherupon yor ſaid Orator James Burbedge did become bound
to the ſaid Braine in 400^{li} [12—9] effect That yor ſaid Orator
ſhuld at the requeſt of the ſaid John Braine his executo^{rs} or
aſſignes convey to him the ſaid John Braine his [executors or
aſſigns 13—9] to be errected vpon the p*re*miſſes demyſed by the
ſaid Giles Allen to yor ſaid Orator/ wth ſutch Coven*a*nt*es* and
warranties as yor Orator might [14—9] Leaſe made by the ſaid
Giles Allen was then or therafter ſhuld be chardged wth by any
acte then done or therafter to be done by yor [ſaid Orator 15—9]
monye borrowed by yor ſaid Orator as by the ſame obligac*i*on and
condic*i*on more at Lardge yt doth and may appere./   And after
the [16—9] amountinge vnto exceedinge chardg*es* about the ſaid

building*es* then of habilletie to fupport the fame and havinge gotten yor faid Orator to be bound [17—9] to redeeme the faid Leafe nor had wherwth to p*r*ocied in thofe manner of building*es* wherein he had procured yor Orator to enter into [18—9] chardge any fomes of monye growen due for the faid building*es* nor paie the Moietie of the rent aforfaid but wth yor Orato^{rs} monye the profitt*es* [19—9] welth of the faid Brayne before, beinge con- ferred and weyed wth the coft*es* vpon the faid Inn by him beftoed after yt manyfeftlie appered And [20—8] and fynifhinge of the faid building*es* to his gret hinderaunce as is well to be proved. And after for that yor faid Orator James Burbedge had no bond [21—8] foe by him to be receved out of the p*r*emiffes from thenfforthe vpon the faid building*es* & maintenance therof he the faid Brayn and the faid James Burbedge yor [faid Orator 22—7] Arbitrem^t of certaine Arbitrato^{rs} who thervpon according to the^r faid fubmiffion did delyver vp An Award or Arbitrem^t in wright- ing, dated about the [xxth] yere [23—7] John Braine fhuld not be comprifed wthin the compafe of the faid Arbitrement but that afwell by force therof as by vertue of the faid Arbitrem^t yor faid Orator [24—7] Theatre and building*es* and of the Moietie of the profitt*es* therof whenfoeuer the faid Braines would dem*a*und the fame wth futch exception of Act*es* as is aforfaid [25—7 with] wch Arbitrem^t yor faid Orator did content himfealf and did p*er*mitt and fuffer the faid John Braine to receve the moietie of the p*r*ofitt*es* of the faid Theatre and [26—7] one his p*a*rte. But the faid John Braine being a verie fubtell p*er*fone and confeder- ating him fealfe wth one Rob*er*t Myles of Londo*n* Gouldfmithe
Tomfone of [27—7] thei might impouerifhe yor faid Orato^r and to depryve him of his intereft and tearme for yeres in the faid Theatre and building*es* and to bring him into the daunger [28—7] fame he the faid Braine not meaning to gyve the faid Moietie nor his intereft therin to yor faid Orato^{rs} the Children aforfaid nor the Leafe of the faid Geordge [29—6] the Moietie of the p*r*ofitt*es* of the p*r*emiffes as is aforfaid the wch p*r*omife was made afwell before as after the faid Arbitrem^t made as is aforfaid. but practifing to depryve [30—6] againe made a deed of gift to the faid Tomfon and therby did gyve and graunt to him all his

goodes & chattels wherof he was then or therafter fhuld be
poffeffed. wherby yor [31—6] for the Recoverie of the bond of
200^{li} to hym forfeited by the faid Braine for the not performynge
of the faid Arbitrem^t nor to levie the fame out of his goodes &
chattells [32—6] againft the bodie of the faid Braine for the
fame the wch during his lief he was Loathe to do for that he was
his brother in Lawe as is aforfaide. The benefitt [33—6] the
faid Tomfone, the faid Braine for the mayntenance of his faid
frawde & devices procured the executo^{rs} or adminiftrato^{rs} of the
faid Tomfone to conveye to the faid Robert [34—6] fo graunted
to the faid Tomfone by the faid Braine wth the Leafe of the faid
Inn called the Geordg alfo at his owen deathe or not longe before he
fearinge [35—6] ample conveyaunce of all his goodes & Chattells
wch he then had to the faid John Gardiner & to others to the
intent that he or thei by force therof fhuld or might enter into
[36—6] or other the premiffes or that the faid Myles by vertue
of the fame deed of gift made to the faid Tomfone fhuld challendge or demaunde the fame or to incurr the daunger [37—6]
in the tyme of his ficknes & not longe before his death promifed
confeffed and agreed wth yor faid Orator James Burbedge and
his faid wief in the prefence [38—6] of the faid Myles That
afwell the Moietie of the premiffes and all matters whatfoever
concerning the faid Theatre and buildinges and his moietie therin
to be affured & [39—6] had receved of & by the premiffes as
namelie the Leafe of the George in Whitechappell were and
fhuld be and remaine yf he died (for that he had no children and
for [40—6] premiffes) to yor Orato^{rs} the Children aforfaid
whofe advauncem^t he then feemed gretlie to tender And further
promifed to yor faid Orato^r that his faid bondes fhuld be [41—6]
of yor faid Orator James Burbedge. And after the faid John
Braine died in A° 1586. by meanes wherof Now So yt ys yf
it may pleafe yor Honor the [42—6] adminiftracion of the goods
of her faid Late hufband the wch fhe practifed then to haue) by
the faid John Gardener and Robert Myles by reafone y^t thei
claymed the fame goodes & chattells [43—6] conveyaunces)
vnder the cullor of a will fuppofed to be made by the faid Braine
longe before the faid conveyaunces fo made to the faid gardiner

and Tomſon, the wch is ſuppoſed to be raſed [44—6] that any
ſutch will ſhuld be maynteyned or produced. yet by vertue therof
and being therin nominated to be executo^r to her ſaid huſband/
ſhe now as executor goethe about to arreſt yor ſaid [45—6] pretending that he did not performe the ſaid Arbitrem^t (as in truthe
he did) and for the ſaid bond of 400^ll pretending that yor Orato^r
hath alſo forfeited the ſame as in truthe he hath not. And
[47—6] ſaid huſband denying that her ſaid huſband made
any ſutch promiſſes as is aforſaid ether for the cancelling
or conveying of the premiſſes to yor orators aforſaid And
the ſaid Robert Myles by [48—6] then to ſue yor ſaid Orato^r
James burbedge for the ſaid bondes but hath entered into
and vpon the ſaid Theatre & buildinges & troublethe yor
Orators & his tenantes in the^r peaceable poſſeſſion [49—6] bothe
the yſſues & profittes therof by vertue of the Conveyaunces made
to him therof. And the Adminiſtrato^rs of the ſaid John Gardener
who deceaſed in A° 1587 to whom the ſaid bond [50—6] made
to the ſaid Gardener demaunde & go about to ſue yor ſaid Orato^r
James burbedge for the ſaid two ſeuerall bondes. And amongeſt
them by reaſone of multiplicitie of [51—6] ther conveyaunces,
& ſomtyme denying the ſame to be good) thei do all ioyne
together to impriſone yor ſaid Orato^r James burbedge therby
to enforce him to yeld to ther requeſtes And [52—6] imperti-
nent acciones only to procure him to gret chardges & to his im-
poveriſhem^t for euer, the rather becauſe by thes devices he can
not haue the ſaid 200^ll due to him by the ſaid [53—7] Braine.
In tender conſideracione of the premiſſes And for that the ſaid
Margarett Braine Robert Myles and   Gardiner the
Adminiſtrato^r of the ſaid John Gardner [54—7] ſaid Leaſe ſo
being mortgaged & forfeited as is aforſaid and haue the ſaid
Leaſe to them reconveyed, do now demaunde the ſame moietie &
will not permitt the Children aforſaid [55—7] all the ſaid
promiſſes the wch now yor ſaid Orato^rs are vnhable to do by
reaſone that the ſame promiſſes were done in ſecrett & in the
preſence only of the ſaid Robert [56—7] or gone beyond the ſeas
ſo that yor Orato^rs can not haue ther Teſtemonye in the premiſſes
by wch meanes yor ſaid Orato^r James Burbedge is w^thout [57—7]

the faid bond*es* or to enforce the*m* to cancell the fame nor the
childre*n* aforfaid by the ordinarie courfe of the commo*n* Lawe
aforfaid can not procure the [58—7] the p*re*miffes fo p*ro*mifed
to the*m* by the faid John Braine. the wch to do the faid Braine
was bound in confcienc to foe p*er*formed and that the faid bond*es*
fhuld [59—7] done by the faide John Braine & by yor faid Orato^r
James burbedge ioynctlie in contradiction of the matters conteyned in the faid bond & Arbitrem^t fo [60—7] not be p*er*formed
yf thei or any of them had lawfull interest therin/ as thei haue
not. May it therfor pleafe yor Honor to graunt to yor faid
[61—7] directed to the faid Margarett Braine Rob*er*t Myles
&   Gardener commaunding them and everie of the*m*
p*er*fonallie to appere in the Court of Chançerie [62—6] then
and ther to make aunfwer to the p*re*miffes And further to com-
mand the faid Margaret Braine Rob*er*t Myles & Gardener to
[63—7] other the^r faid Conveyaunc*es* fo to them made only to
p*er*turbe yor faid Orators as is aforfaid, to the end the fame may
be then [64—7] and abide such further order as to yor honor
fhalbe thought to agree wth equitie & confcienc. And all yor faid
[65—7] in all felicetie.

ffraunc*es* Morgan   [attorney]

ANSWER AND DEMURRER

[Date and whole left half of
this skin mouldered away]

> [The Joint and feveral aunfwere & demurrer of]
> M*a*rgaret Brayne wydowe and Robt [Myles twoe
> of the defendantes to the Bill of] Complainte of
> James Burbeidge and other [   ]

[1—7] the faid Bill of Complainte is very vntrue and infuffi-
cyent in the [2—7] contryued of fet purpofe to put the faid def^{tes}
to wrongffull [3—7] that he the faid Complayn*a*nt might fhadowe
his bad and vnconfcionable [4—7] defend^{tes} fhalbe Compelled to
make any ffurther Aunfwere to [5—7] and infufficyency therof
nowe and at all tymes [6—7] faieth that the faid Compl^{tes} in ther

tedious and vntrue bill do [7—6] faid Gyles Allen vnto the faid Complaynantes neither what [8—6] vnto the faid Complayantes as in the faid Bill is alfo fet downe [9—6] Certaine date or tyme of any fuch bonde wherein he and [10—6] hundreth poundes to abyed a Certaine awarde and arbitrament [11—6] when they yeelded vpp any fuch arbitrament. And ffurther fetteth [12—6] wth this def^t Robert Myles, and John gardyner who is not nowe [13—6] neither doth the faid Comp^l fet fforth any fufficyent Confideracion [14—6] of the faid leaffes in the faid Bill mencyoned vpon the Children of the [15—6] The faid Margaret Braine the other defendant beinge his wief w^thout [16—6] and divers other in the faid Bill mencyoned over tedyous to be Recyted. The [17—6] of this honorable Courte yf they or either of them fhalbe Compelled [18—6] fufficyent bill. And for the infufficiency therof thei pray to be difmyffed owt of this honorable Courte [19—6] wrongfully fufteyned

Scott   [attorney]

[The preceding Bill and Demurrer, in a badly damaged state, were discovered by me among the Chancery Proceedings at the Public Record Office in the summer of 1908, and on August 7, while still registered as "kept out" on my name, they were sent to the official in charge of the Repairing department. Before they got back to me, about a fortnight later, a Mrs. Stopes learned of their existence, and applied for them. (The dates of these events, I may say, are recorded in the official registers of the Public Record Office.)   I informed her at once that they were still at the Repairing department on my name, told her their contents, since she was curious to know, referred her to the court orders connected with them, and gave her my purpose of complete publication in extenso. Fortunately for scholarship, I did not tell her of the more important records, the voluminous depositions. Her assumed "discovery" of the Bill, Demurrer, and some of the court orders, later referred to in her amateurish first effort at theatrical history in the *Fortnightly Review*, July, 1909, is only one of several "coincidences," some of them of a graver nature, that have occurred during the last few years since I opened this field of research, as mentioned in the Introductory Survey.]

BURBAGE V. BRAYNE

Chancery, Decrees and Orders, 30 & 31 Elizabeth, Hilary, vol. 1588 " A," 485; also 1588 " B," 449.

xvij° die ffebruarij [1588–9]

James Burbage and others ⎱ fforafmuche as this Courte was this
—— p^ltes Margaret Brayne ⎰ prefent daye informed on the p^les
widowe Robte Miles and ⎱ behalf that the def^tes haue put in a
John Gardyner def^tes ⎰ very infuffycient demurrer to the
p^les bill of complainte w^thout fhew-
ing any good or fuffycient caufe
therof It ys therefore ordered that the confideracion of the faid
bill and demurrer be referred to m^r Dr Carewe one of the M^rs
of this Courte To thend he may Reporte vnto this courte whether
the fame demurrer be fuffycient or not, if not Then a *Subpoena*
ys awarded againft the def^tes w^thout further mocion to anfwere
directly to the p^les bill of Comp^l and to all the materyall point*es*
thereof And the defend^tes Attorney ys to be warned hereof

BRAYNE V. BURBAGE.

Chancery Decrees and Orders, vol. 1589 " A," 610; also in 1589 " B," 597. Easter, 32 Elizabeth (1590).

[While Dr. Carew was carrying out the order of February 17, 1588–9, in the case of Burbage *v.* Brayne, a cross-bill was filed by the widow and Myles, to which the Burbages filed a demurrer. Unfortunately, both bill and demurrer in this suit of Brayne *v.* Burbage are missing, but the Court's orders are preserved. Both cases run parallel, and were taken together by the Court. Hence we have orders and depositions from this date on to the death of the widow in 1593, sometimes under the title of Burbage *v.* Brayne, sometimes under Brayne *v.* Burbage.]

xxj° die Maij [1590]

Margaret Brayne p^l James ⎱ fforafmuchas this Courte was this
Burbage Cuthbert Burbage ⎰ prefent day informed on the de-
and Richard Burbage de- ⎱ fend^ts behalf that the def^tes haue
dend^tes ⎰ put in an Jnfufycient demurrer to
the p^les bill of complainte w^thout

fhewinge any good or fuffycient cawfes thereof It ys therefore
ordered that the confideracion of the faid bill and demurrer be
Referred to Mr Dr Cefarr one of the M^{rs} of this courte To thend
he may Reporte vnto this Courte whether the fame demurrer be
fuffycient or not If not then a *Subpoena* ys awarded against the
def^{tes} to aunfwere directly to the p^{les} bill of complainte and to
all the materyall pointes thereof. And the def^{ts} Attorney ys to
be warned when the *premeffs* fhalbe confidered of

BRAYNE *v.* BURBAGE

*Chancery Decrees and Orders, vol. 1590 "A," 109; also in
1590 "B," 113. Michaelmas, 32 & 33 Elizabeth (1590).*

Mercurij iiij^{to} die Novembris [1590]

Margaret Braynes exec of
John Braynes deceaffed p^l
James Burbage and Rich-
ard & Cuthbert Burbage
def^{tes}

fforafmucheas this courte was this
prefent daye enformed by Mr Scott
being of the p^{les} Councell That fhee
havinge exhibited A bill into this
Co^{rt} against the def^t for and concernyng the moyety of the Theater
and other ten*ementes* wch the faid James Burbage was by an
agreem^t had betwene him and the p^{les} late hufbande to affigne
to thexecuto^{res} adminiftrato^{res} or affignes of her faid hufband and
to fuffer him and them to enioye yt for and duringe the whole
terme to come in a leafe made of the faid Theate^r or of the
grounde wherevpon yt ftand*es* and of other the *premiffes* to the
faid James Burbage by one Gyles Allyn He the faid James Burbage hathe not only put in an yll demurrer to that bill wch hathe
bene overruled by order of this co^{rt} But alfo dothe by himfelf &
thother def^{tes} take awaye the whole gayne and benyfytt of the
faide Theate^r and other premiffes from the p^l Albeyt fhee and
her hufband haue bene at very great charg*es* in buylding thereof
to the fome of vj C^{li} and did for A tyme enioye the moyety of
the *premiffes* accordinge to the trewe meanynge of the faid
agreem^t It ys therefore ordered That yf the def^{tes} fhall not by
this daye fenight fhewe vnto this courte good caufe to the con-

trary Then A Sequestracion fhalbe graunted of the moyety of all the yffues and profyttes of the premiffes vntill the matter fhalbe here heard and determyned or otherwife ordered by this co[rt]

[The above order was first printed by J. P. Collier, modernized throughout, in his *Memoirs of the Principal Actors* (Shakespeare Society, 1846), p. 8.]

BRAYNE *v.* BURBAGE

Chancery Decrees and Orders, vol. 1590 "A," 145; also in 1590 "B," 150. Michaelmas, 32 & 33 Elizabeth (1590).

Veneris xiij° die Novembris [1590]

Margaret Brayne wid p[l] James Burbage Cutberd Burbage and others def[tes] } fforafmucheas vpon the openynge of the matter this prefent daye by M[r] S[r]ieaunt Harrys beinge of the def[tes] Councell and feakinge for ftaye of A fequeftracion prayed by a former order on the p[les] behalf and alfo vpon the hearinge of M[r] Scott beinge of the p[les] councell what he could faye touching the caufe It feemed vnto this co[rt] That there was an Arbytrament heretofore made betwene the p[les] late hufband & the faid James Burbage the xij[th] daye of July in the xx[th] yere [1578] of her Ma[ties] Raigne by one Richard Turnor & John Hill touching the fame matter w[ch] ys nowe agayne brought in queftion And that nether of the partyes did nowe fhewe any fuffycyent caufe wherefore the fame Arbytram[t] or awarde fhould not be performed It ys therefore ordered That the faid award or Arbytram[t] fhalbe well and truly obferved and performed accordinge to the teno[r] & trewe meanynge thereof Afwell by the p[l] and all claymyng from by or vnder her As alfo by the def[tes] and euery of them and all claymynge from by or vnder them or any of them And the faid order for fequeftracion fhalbe ftayed

[The preceding order caused a tremendous row at the Theatre, and gave occasion for many of the later depositions in the case. Three days after the order, namely, on Nov. 16, 1590, Margaret Braynes, Robert Myles, his son Ralph, and Nicholas Bishop went with this order to the Theatre, and attempted to stand at the door and take the money for entrance to the play. But Richard Burbage and his mother beat Myles off with a broom-staff, and drove them all away, after a furious quarrel by all parties concerned. Then, a fortnight later, Myles and his faction had the Burbages up for contempt of Court, as shown in the next order. The whole story is told with graphic details in the course of the numerous depositions.]

BRAYNE *v.* BURBAGE

Chancery Decrees and Orders, vol. 1590 " A," 270; also in 1590 " B," 280. Michaelmas, 32 & 33 Elizabeth (1590).

xxviij die Novembris [1590]

Margaret Braynes vid p¹ ⎤ Robert Miles made othe that the
James Burbage and others ⎬ faid Burbage and Cutbert Bur-
defendauntes   ⎦ bage haue broken an order made
in this Courte, the xiij^th of Novem-ber laft. Therefore an att*achment* is awarded againft the faid parties to the fherif of Midd*lefex*.

Idem, vol. 1590 " A," 317; also in 1590 " B," 327.

Sabba*ti* xxx° die Januarij [1590–91]

Margaret Brayne wid p¹ ⎤ The faid def^t hathe this pre*fent*
Cutbert Burbage def^t   ⎦ daye made his per*fonall apparaunce

in this co^rt vpon an att*achment* for faving of his bond made to the fherif of london

BRAYNE *v.* BURBAGE.

Chancery Town Depositions, Bdl. 218, No. 93. Michaelmas, 32 & 33 Elizabeth (1590).

INTERROGATORIES.

Articles vpon the parte and behaulf of James Burbadge and Cuthbert Burbadge and others Defend^tes to John Hide grocer And Georg Cloughe gentelma*n* Againſt Margaret Braine Widdoe Compl^t.

1 **Impr***imis* whither did one John Brayne the huſband of the Compl^t, and one John Prynn broaker, take vp, borrowe and owe to yo^u about the xxvj daye of Septemb A° 1579 the ſome of — 125^li 8^s 11^d./ yf thei did: then, whither did the ſaid James Burbadge the defend^t about the ſame tyme, Mortgadge and convey to yo^u the ſaid John Hide, the Leaſe, and all his title therin, of and in the Theatre, and other edifici*o*ns in Hallywell, in the Countie of Mid-d*le*ſex, the wch he had of one Giles Allen and Sara his Wief vpon Condicon/ That yf the ſaid ſome of 125^li 8^s 11^d were Repaid to yo^u or yor aſſignes w^thin xij Monethes & one daie, next enſuing after the ſaid ſeptemb^r in A° 1579 by The ſaid James Burbadge, that then yo^u ſhuld Reconvey to him the ſaid Leaſe and Theatre, and other the *p*remiſſes againe. And whither was not the ſaid Leaſe and other bond*es* made by Giles Allen, for the enioying Thereof, Deliuered into yor hand*es* and poſſeſſion, at the tyme of the ſaid Conveyaunc ſealed by the defend^t/ wth and by the conſent and appointm^t of The ſaid John Braine yea or no

2 **Item** whither was not the ſaid Leaſe and the ſaid James Burbadge the defendant*es* title theirin, abſoluteli forfeited and loſt to yo^u, for the nonpayement of the ſaid 125^li 8^s 11^d, according to the tyme lymyted for the payem^t Thereof, & to the effect of the ſaid deed of Mortgadge, And whither did yo^u not repute and accompt yor ſealf, to be therby Rightfull owner of the ſaid Leaſe and title of this defend^t James Burbadge yea or no

3 It*em* whither was not this defend^t, for yor better fecuretie, bound to yo^u Ioyntlie wth the faid Braine and Pryne, in abond of 200^{li} wth Condic*i*on endorfed, afwell for the repaym^t of the faid mony at the faid tyme appointed, as for the p*er*formance of the Cove-n*antes* and for p*er*forming The faid mortgadge yea or no And whither did the faid Brayne or prynn p*er*forme the fame/

4. It*em* were yo^u not offended, that the faid Burbadge and Braine, did not repaie yo^u The faid 125^{li} 8^s 11^d And did you not Threaten, to put the faid Burbadge out of poffeffion of the faid Theatre, and building*es,* for that yo^u receyved no p*ro*fitt therby: And did not yo^u arreft thervpon the faid Jeams Burbadge, by p*ro*ces out of her Ma^{tes} bench, about June in A^o 1582 And whither did not he ther vpon come to yor howfe wth the officer or balie, that had him vnder arreft, Ahd whither did not yor wief in yor abfence, accept of xx^{li} paid then to her, to yor vfe by the faid defend^t, And did fhe not difchardge the faid defend^t, from the faid Bailie, vpon Condic*i*on that the faid defend^t, fhuld come To yo^u when yo^u fent for him, to take order in the p*re*miffes. And whither did not he repaire to yo^u accordinglie, And whither was he not conftrayned to gyve yo^u, newe bond*es* wth a fuertie, for The forthcomyng at yor howfe, of this defend^t, at an howers warning to be fubject to yor actions.

5 It*em* did not The faid defend^t complayne to yo^u, that the faid Braine had Receyved and gotten into his hand*es,* agret porc*i*on of money levied in the faid Theatre, at the playe tymes, And that he would catche what he could, And That the faid defend^t could not enforce him, to delyver any p*ar*te therof neyther To this defend^t, nor to yo^u towardes an agreem^t wth yo^u in the premiffes/ yea or no/

6. It*em* did not yo^u thervpon, fend yor fervaunt*es* to Chardge the faid Braine not to deale any further wth any thinge, concerning the faid Theatre, Except he would deliuer to yo^u, The mony he Re-ceyved: And did yo^u not appoinct one of yor fervant*es* with the faid James Burbadge, as in yor faid Right, title and intereft, to

difchardge, difmife and put out the faid John Braine, from the faid
Theatre yea or no.

7. **Item** whither were yo^u not conftrayned, by reafon the faid Braine
would not dep*arte* wth the mony he had Receyved, to appoinct one
of yor fer*vauntes* and this defend^t, to gather vp. v.^{li} weekelie,
during the tyme of plaies; thinking by that meanes, to have paid
yor fealf out of the Theatre, for that yo^u fawe that the faid Braines,
was fo Badd a fellowe: And howe mutche mony Receyved yo^u by
That rate, to yor remembraunce, and was it aboue xxx.^{li} yo^u fo
receyved; or les./yea or no

8. **Item** During thes payeme^{tes} whither held yo^u ftill The faid Leafe
in yor Hand*es,* And whither did the faid Braine afterward*es* paie
yo^u any other or more mony, then that wch was brought to yo^u
weeklie out of the faid Theatre. yea or no.

9. **Item** whither did not yo^u, after the death of the faid Braine, and
after the receipt*es* abouefaid, faie, that yo^u had fett ouer and
affigned the faid Leafe, and bond*es* to Cloughe yor father in Lawe,
& whither did not he fue the faid James Burgadge, and the faid
Pryne Thervpon, after the death of Braine And whither did
not the faid Cloughe, go about to put out The faid defend^t out of
the faid Theatre, yea or no after Braines his death and whither
did not Burbadge tell yo^u, that he could not accomplifhe futch
order, as the faid Cloughe or yo^u had fett downe, and prefcribed
to him, for the redemption of his faid Leafe yea or no

10 **Item** whither did not m^r walter Cope, attendant vpon the Lord
Trea*furer*, write his le*ttere*s to yo^u, & therby earneftly entreate,
that yo^u would fell to his fervaunt Cuthbert Burbadge, yor title
and intereft of the faid Leafe the rather, for that he might help
to difcharge his father out of manie trobles, wch the faid Braine
& his faid father, might haue fufteyned about conveyaunc*es* &
bond*es,* made by them, about the faid Theatre, when was the faid
le*ttre* written to yo^u. And what conteyned it as yo^u rememb^r

ii **Item** Whither did not yo⁰ thervpon make an agreemᵗ wᵗʰ the ſaid
Cuthbert, for yoʳ ſaid Leaſe and title. And whitheʳ were yo⁰ paid
the mony by him agreed vpon, at his handₑs & by his appoinctemᵗ.
And whither did yo⁰ convey to him accordinglie the ſaid Leaſe.
And whither by all this ſpace, did the executors of the ſaid Braine
paie to yo⁰ any mony for the premiſſes. yea or no.

DEPOSITIONS

Ex parte Jacobi Burbage

Octauo Dec 33 E. Regine

Jo. Hide of London grocer of thage of lviij yeres or theraboutₑs
ſworn &c. i. Interrogatory That true it ys one Jo Brayne late
huſband of the Comp. and one Jo. Prynne a Broker did take vp,
borow and owe vnto hym this dpᵗ about the xxvj day of Sept 1579.
the ſome of 125ˡˡ 8ˢ 11ᵈ. or thereaboutₑs as this dpᵗ rememberₑth
and he doth alſo well know & rememberₑ that the ſaid James burbage the now def did about the ſame tyme morgage and convey
vnto hym this depᵗ the leaſe and all his title therin of and in the
Theatre and other buyldingₑs in Halliwell in the Comitatu of
Middleſex the wᵒʰ he had of one Gīles Allen and Sara his wief
Vppon Condicion to this effect that if the ſaid ſome of one hundred xxvˡˡ were repaid to hym this dpᵗ or to his aſſignes wᵗʰin
twelve monethes and one day next enſewing after the ſaid September 1579 by the ſaid James burbage That then he this Depᵗ
ſhuld reconvey to hym the ſaid James the ſaid leaſe and Theatre
and other the premiſſs agayne And as he rememberₑth the leaſe
and other bondes made by Giles Allen for the enjoying therof
were deliverₑd in to his handₑs and poſſeſſion at the tyme of the
ſaid conveyaunce ſealed by the def. wᶜʰ was donne wᵗʰ the conſent
and appoyntmᵗ of the ſaid Jo Brayne./

2 That not only the ſaid leaſe but the ſaid James burbage the Def
title therin was abſolutely forfeited and loſt to hym this Deponᵗ
for the none paymᵗ of the ſaid ſome of 125ˡˡ — 8 — 11. or theraboutₑs according to the tyme lymyted for the paymᵗ thereof and
to theffect of the ſaid dede of morgage And he this dpᵗ did

accompt and repute hymſelf to be therby rightfull owner of the ſaid leaſe and title therin of the ſaid James Burbage

3 That the def for this dp^{tes} better ſecurite ſtode bound to hym this dep^t ioyntly wth the ſaid brayne and Pryne in a bounde of 200^{li} (as this dep^t rem*ember*eth) wth condic*i*on indorſed aſwell for the repaym^t of the ſaid money at the tyme appoynted as for the p*er*formaunce of the Couen*ant*es and p*er*formyng the ſaid morgage wch Brayne and Pryne nor either of them did p*er*forme

4 Tɜat true it is he was offended that the ſaid burbage and Brayne did not repay hym the ſaid ſome of 125^{li} 8^s 11d   And did thervpon threaten to put the ſaid burbage out of poſſeſſion of the ſaid Theatre. and buyldi*n*g*es* for that he this dep^t rec*eived* no proffit thereby and thervpon did cauſe the ſaid James burbage to be arreſted by proces out of her ma^{tes}   Benche about June as he rem*ember*eth 1582.   And the ſaid James Bur: did thervpon come to this dp^{tes} houſe wth the officer or bailif that had hym arreſted and this dp^{tes} wief in his abſense did accept of xx^{ll} paid vnto her to his this dp^{tes} vſe by the def   And the ſame def was thervpon either by hym this dep^t or his wief but preciſly by whether of them he doth not nowe rem*ember* diſcharged from the bailif vpon Condic*i*on that he the ſame def ſhuld come vnto hym this dp^t when ſoeuer he the ſame dep^t did ſend for hym to take order in the premiſſ*es*.   And the ſaid def did accordingly repaire vnto hym and did geue vnto hym this Dep^t new boundes wth a ſurety for his furthcoming to this dp^{tes} houſe at an houres warning to be ſubiect to his this dp^{tes} acc*i*ons./

5 That true it is the Def burbage did complayne vnto hym that the ſaid brayne had rec*eived* and gotten in to his hands a g^t porcon of money levied in the ſaid Theatre at the play tymes and that he wold catch what he cold and that he the ſame def cold not enforce hym to d*e*li*ver* ay part therof neither to hym the ſaid def nor vnto hym this dp^t toward*es* an agrem^t wth hym this Dep^t in the premiſſ*es*.

6. That he thervpon did fend his Servantes to chardg the faid Brayne
not to deale ay further wth ay thing concerning the faid Theatre,
except he wold deliver vnto hym this dp^{t} the money he received.
And this deponen^{t} remembereth that he did appoint one of his
Servantes wth the faid James burbage as in his this dep^{tes} right
title and intereft to difchardg difmyffe and put out the faid Brayne
from the faid Theatre/

7. That by reafon the faid braine would not departe wth the money
he had received he this dep^{t} was conftreyned to appoynt one of his
Servantes and the faid Ja. Burbage the def to gather vp v^{li} wekely
during the tyme of playes thinking by that meanes to haue p^{d} hym
felf wth the proffites of the Theatre ffor that he faw the faid
Brayne to be fo bad a fellow   And this dp^{t} by that rate did receive
in money to the fome of xx or xxx^{li} as he remembereth./

8 That during the faid paym^{tes} he held ftill the faid leafe in his
handes.   And depofeth that the faid Braine did not afterward
pay vnto hym this dp^{t} ay other or more money than that wch was
brought to hym wekely out of the Theatre as aforefaid

9 That after the death of the faid Braine and after the receptes as
aforefaid he did fay and gaue it out in fpech that he had fet ouer
and affignced the faid leafe and bondes to one George Clough his
this dp^{tes} ffather in lawe but in truth he did not fo neither did the
faid Clough to this dp^{tes} remembrance and as he thinketh few the
faid James Burbage and the faid Pryne or either of them after
the death of the faid Brayne.   But this dp^{t} thinketh that the faid
Clough his father in law did go about to put the faid def out of
the Theatre or at left did threaten hym to put hym out   And as
this dp^{t} remembereth the faid burbage did tell hym that he cold
not accomplifh fuch order as he this dep^{t} and his faid ffather in
law Clough had fet downe and prefcribed to hym for the redempcion of his faid leafe

10 That m^{r} Walter Cope being Attendaunt vpon the Lord Treafaurer

did write his le*tte*res to hym this dp^t thereby intreating hym that
he wold fell to his the fame m^r Copes S*erva*nte Cuthber burbage
his title and interest of the faid leafe the rather for that he might
help to difcharg his father (meaning the def) out of may
[=many] troubles wch brayne and his faid ffather might haue
fufteyned about conveyaunc*es* and bond*es* made by them concerning the Theatre And to this dp^tes beft rem*embrance* the fame were
the effect of the content*es* of the faid le*tte*res   But the certeyne
tyme when the fame le*tte*res were fo written he rem*embereth* not/

11 That he did thervpon make an Agrem^t wth the faid Cuthbert for
his faid Leafe and title and interest therein and was truly paid the
mony by hym agreed vpon at the hand*es* of the fame Cuthbert and
by his appoyntm^t and this dp^t did convey vnto hym the faid leafe
accordingly.   And depofeth that by all this fpace   Thexecuto^rs
of the faid Braine did not pay vnto hym this dep^t ay one peny for
the *premiffes*.   And more this dp^t faith not in this matter/

                    pro burbage

Die & Anno pred*ictis*

George Clough of London Clotheworker of thage of xlviij or
therabout*es* fworn &c 1. 2. 3. 4. 5. 6. 7. & 8.   *Jnterrogatories* he
cane not depofe

9 That on a tyme but certenly how long fithens he rem*embereth*
not. one Jo Hide of London grocer who had maried this dp^tes
wief*es* daughter told hym this dp^t y^t he had certeyne mony owing
vnto hym by one burbage and one brayne as this dp^t rem*embereth*
and y^t for his fecuritie of the paym^t thereof he had af*fi*gned vnto
hym a leafe of the Theatre and told this dp^t that he cold not haue
his money p^d and therfore requefted hym this dp^t being his father
in law to go vnto the faid burbage to demand of hym the money
he owed hym and to fay that he had affigned ouer the faid leafe
to hym this dp^t   And this dp^t. thervpon went diuers and fondry
tymes to the faid burbage and rec*eived* money of hym due to the
faid Jo Hide wherof he made vnto the fame Jo Hide an Accomp.

from tyme to tyme as he rec*eived* the fame but to how moch the fame moni*es* did a mount vnto this dp^t remembereth not. Neither did he at ay tyme to his rem*embrance* feue the fame James burbage or one Js. Prynne concerning the faid Leafe nor went about to put the now def out of the Theatre nor ay thing ell*es* to that Jnt*errogatory* canne depofe nor more faith in this matter

[Signed]   George Cloughe

BRAYNE *v.* BURBAGE (CONTEMPT)

Idem. Bdl. 221, No. 12. Hilary, 33 Elizabeth (1591).

Interrogatories to be mynyftred on the p*a*rte and behalf of Margaret Braines widowe Compl^t againft James Burbage & Cuthb*er*te Burbage defend^tes vpon contempt

1 **Inprimis** whether were you Cuthbert Burbage pr*e*f*e*nte at the Chauncery Barr the xiij of Nouember 1590 the Court ther beinge moved by yor owne Councell m^r Seriant Harris to ftay and Order before granted vpon a Sequeftracion of the Moytie of the Theatre at the fute of Margaret Brayns the nowe Compl^t. Againft yow and others And wheth^r did not yow them wth the Confent of your faid Councell Caufe and order to be fett downe for to p*er*forme the Arbitram^t made and Ordered by Richard Turner and John Hill betwene the faid James Burbage & John Braines the hufband of the nowe Complain^t Dated the xij of Julie in the xx^th yere of her Maties reigne yea or no/

2 **Item** whether do yow James Burbage and Cuthb*er*t Burbage knowe of your owne knowledge or otherwife haue hard fay that one Robert Myles wth divers others vpon the xvj^th of Nouember laft paft did come in the behalf and in the name of the Nowe Compl^t to the nowe dwellinge howfe of the faid James Burbage your ffather and ther did demande of yow both the p*er*formance of the faid Award accordinge to the faid Order And wheth^r did not yow both then fay that yow would not ftand to anie fuch

order and that the Court of Chancery fhould not Cofen yo^w Cuthbe*rte* of your right yea or no, and what was ye fpeaches yow both
then vfed

3 **It***em* whether did not yow James borbadges faye or fpecke thes
wordes in this interrog*atory* foloinge or worde*s* to that Efecte
Cuthbe*rte* Burbage yo^u heard the faid James your ffather fay that
he would not obay the faid Order and threaten the faid Robe*rte*
Myles to beate him of the grounde and that he cared not a tord
for Confcience wth other odious termes and what was the wordes
your ffather and yow then vfed to the faid Robe*rte* Myles
Declare the whole truth therein

4. **It***em* whether do yow James and Cuthbe*rte* Burbage know the
faid Margaret Braines the nowe Comp^{lt}. wth divers other pe*r*fons
accompanyinge wth her fithence the Order made came to the
Theatre and ther Demanded of yow and your ffather and of the
ten*antes* fuch rent*es* as were due and behinde for the Moitie of
the theatre and all fuch fomes of money as were then dewe accordinge to the f*ai*d Arbitrement made as beforefaid and whether did
yow fay or here your ffather fay or both y^t the faid Compl^t had
nothinge to do ther and that yow would not obay the faid order
and ffurther faid that yf fhe or any for her or in her behalf came
any more vpon the faid ground yow would beate them from the
fame and did not yow both vfe her wth moft vnfemely and bad
fpeaches   Declare yor knowledge therin

5 **It***em* wheth^r did yow Cuthbe*rte* Burbage vpon the xxixth of
Nouemb^r nowe laft Come into the howfe of one Henrie Bett*es* in
Shordich wher the faid Robt Myles then chanced to be and ther
in fcoffinge manno^r did afke him when he would Come againe to
the Theatre for any more Rent in the Comp^{tes} behalf and whether
did not yow fay then that yf he did Come anie more abought anie
fuch matter he fhould be thorowghly payed home notwthftandinge
the faid Order or word*es* to the like effect and what was the
wordes yow then vfed to him towchinge the fame. fpeake to your
knowledge

6 It*em* wheth[r] did yow James Burbage heare or knowe of any Order to be made in the chancery the xiij[th] of Nouemb[r] 1590 vpon a moticion made by m[r] Seriante Harris beinge of yo[r] councell for a ftay of a fequeftracion of a moity of y[e] Theatre and other the tenem[tes] and wheth[r] haue yow both done you[r] beft endever to p*er*forme the faid Arbitram[t] & Order made as aforefaid yea or no

Scott [Attorney]

DEPOSITIONS

> Re*ff*onfio Cuthberti Burbage vnius defend*entum,* ad a*rticulos* Margarete Braynes vid*uae* fup*er* Contempt*um* ut afferitur capt*a* per Henr*icum* Johnes in Cancellar*ia* Ex*ami*natorem./

Cuthbert Burbage f*erva*unt to Walter Cope efquier gentleman vfher to the lorde Treaforer of England/ of the age of xxiiij yeres or therabout*es* fworn and ex[d] the xvj Daye of ffebru*ary* in the xxxiij yere &ct To the firft Int*errogatory* that he was p*re*f*ent* at the Chauncery Barre the xiij daye of November laft paft 1590 when M[r] Serieant Harrys did move the co[r]te on the behalf of this depo[tes] ffather to ftaye an Ordre w[ch] was before graunted by the fame/ vpon A Sequeftrac*ion* of the one Moytie of the houfe or building called the Theato[r] in Shordyche/ w[th] out Bifhops gate London/ at the Sute of the now compl*ainant*/ At w[ch] tyme and moc*ion* the co[r]te ordered/ that an Arbytryment made by R*ychard* Turno[r] & Jo. Hill named in this Int*errogatory* betwene James Burbage this depo[tes] faid ffather and Jo. Braynes deceffed late hufband to the now compl*ainant* in Julye in the xx[th] yere of her Ma[tes] Reign/ fhuld be p*er*formed & fulfylled by ether fydes/

To the 2. that it is true indede/ that Robert Myles named in this Interr*ogatory*/ and others w[t] him came to this depo[tes] ffathers dwelling houfe in Hallywell by Shordiche vpon or about the xvj day of November/ aforefaid/ for & in the name of the now comp[l] as he faid/ and Demaunded Rent/ and the p*er*performa*n*ce of the faid Award according to the faid Ordre/ and what anf*wer* this depo^tes said ffather made vnto him he saith he Remembreth not/ but this depo^t. made him answer/ that he shuld haue no Rent ther he wold sufficientlie answer the co^rte the cause why/ when he were called/ and w^t all told him that Braynes nor his wyef had no right there/ ffor it was his this depo^tes & he had boght it w^t his owne proper money as they well knewe/ And vtterlye denyeth that he said/ that he wold not stand to any suche order & that the Co^rte of Chauncery shuld not Cosyn him of his right/ Nor any word of suche vnreuerend/ & vnduetyfull speche

To the 3. that when the said Myles came to this defend^tes fathers house as aforsaid in the last former Interrogatory he came in suche rude & exclammable sort/ as indede his said ffather threatened to sett him away of his ground/ yf he wold not go his waye quyetlie/ And saith that true it is he this depo^t heard not his said ffather saye/ nor vtter vnto him any suche ymperyous Wordes/ as that he wold not obey the said Ordre/ Nether did ether this depo^tes said ffather/ nor he this depo^t threaten to beat the said Myles/ Nether did he this depo^t hear his said father vtter any suche an vnreuerend & vnsemelye worde of Conscience/ as is so malycyouslye & vngodlie sett down in this Interrogatory/

To the 4. that he cannot certenlye depose/ what answer or spech this Depo^tes said ffather made or vttered to the comp^l at any tyme she came to him/ or to the Theater/ for any Rent or other Demaunde/ concerning the moytie of the same/ for he did not heare the same/ Or at the least he did [not] hede the same/ And what answer this depo^t made to her/ and the said Myles he hath deposed before/ And so saith still/ that/ nether she nor any by or vnder her/ haue any thing to do ther/ ffor it is this depo^tes right/ & none ells/ And otherwyse to this Interrogatory he saith he cannot depose/

To the 5. that true it is/ he this depo^t sins he was serued w^t the said Attachem^t/ chaunced to mete the said Robert Myles at one Henrye Bettes house by Shordiche Church/ where the said

Myles began*n* to Gybe & Scoffe this depo^t/ concerni*n*g moche of the matters depending in Sute betwene the said comp^l/ and this depo^{tes} said ffather & him this depo^t/ and that she shuld haue this & that And this depo^t told him/ that nether he nor she could do more then Justice bidd them/ and that he was sure/ the right was in him this depo^t/ and therfor wished him to deale no furth^r in the matter/ nor to come againe to Demaunde any Rent there/ ffor yf he did/ this Depo^t wold paye him truelie/ But wth out that/ that he added these wordes/ vizt/ notwthstanding the said Ordre/ for he sayd it not/

To the 6. that for his own p*a*rte he can say no more/ then he hath before said/ And this for his true ans*w*er to the said Inter-rogatories/

[Signed] Cuth: Burbadge.

James Burbage of Hallywell in Shordiche w^tout Crypple gate London gentlema*n* of the age of lx yeres or therabout*es* sworne and exd the Daie and yere aforesaid &ct To the first Interroga-*tory*. That he doth thinke/ ther was suche an order sett down in the Co^rte of Chauncerye for the stay of the said Sequestracion/ at the moc*i*on of Mr Serieant Harrys/ in the behaulf of this depo^t and of his sone Cuthbert Burbage/ for to that end/ this Depo^t and his sayd sone gave him iust Instrucc*i*ons of the matter/ and accordinglie this Depo^{tes} Counsell opteyned the same/ And saithe that at that tyme/ at the moc*i*on of ther counsell/ ther was an ordre sett downe/ that the Arbitrym^t & Award wch was made & ordred/ betwene this depo^t and Jo. Braynes deceased the husband of the now comp^l/ by Rychard Turno^r & Jo. Hill named in this Int*er*rogatory shuld be p*er*formed & done/ and this Ordre was made in Julye in the xx yere of her Maties/ Reigne/ and w^{ch} ·this Depo^t for his p*a*rte hath performed/ as farre as in him hath layne/ as he verelie beleveth/

To the 2. that true it is/ Robert Myles named in this Int*er*rogatory w^t ij^o other p*er*sons w^t him whose names he knoweth not/ in

Novemb^r laſt paſt the certen Daye he now remembrethe not/ did
in the behaulf of the now comp^l come to this Depo^{tes} Dwelling
houſſe nere the Theater in Shordiche/ and there did demaund
firſt of this depon^{tes} ſone/ the moytie of the ſaid Theatre & the
Rentes of the ſame to her vſe/ and of the performance of the ſaid
Award/ and what anſwer this Depo^{tes} ſaid ſone made him
thervnto/ he cannot certenly tell But he ſaithe/ that this Depo^t
being w^{t}in the howſe/ hearing A noyce at the do^r/ went to the
do^r/ and ther founde his ſone the ſaid Cuthbert and the ſaid Myles
ſpeaking lowde together/ And aſking what the matter was/ the
ſaid Myles did as afore Demaund the moytie of the ſaid Theatre/
and the Rent therof/ and the performance of the ſaid Award on
the Comp^{ltes} behalf and then this Depo^t told him/ that/ the
Ordre did not warrant any ſuche demaund of Rent nor of any
moytie of the ſaid Theater/ And for the performance of the ſaid
Award/ he told him that he this Depo^t for his parte could not
performe it better/ then he had done/ And then the ſaid Myles
ſayd/ that by the ſaid Award the moytie of the Theater/ & the
Rent therof are to be had & Receyved by & to the vſe of the ſaid
comp^l/ So it was indede qd this depo^t/ before Jo. Braynes himſelf & he this depo^t/ Did after the making of the ſaid Awarde/
Joyne in A graunt to one Henry Laynmann gent/ of the one
Moytie of the ſaid Theater & of the proffittes and comodities
growing therby for certen yeres yet enduring/ as by the Dede
yerof maye appere/ and bound them ſelf in g^t bondes for the
performance therof/ And further ſaith that long after the ſaid
Arbytryment and award & before the graunt made to the ſaid
Laynman the ſaid Braynes the comp^{ltes} ſaid huſband did procure
this depo^t to morgage the leaſe of the ſaid Theatre for the ſome
of Cxxv^{li} & od money to one John Hyde of London grocer/ for
one yere/ & after that for another yere/ w^t A proviſo that for
the none paym^t of the ſaid ſome at A daye/ the ſaid leaſe to be
forfettyd/ wch was forfetted accordinglie by the none paym^t of
the money. So as then the ſaid Hyde was fullye and abſolutelye
poſſeſſed therof/ to diſpoſe of the ſame at his will and pleaſur/
by wch meanes/ he this depo^t doth verelie take it/ that the ſaid
Arbytryment/ and award was determyned & diſſolued/

To the 3. that true it is, he for his owne part did neu*er* faye that he wold not obey the Ordre of the chauncerye/ But he this depo[t] being nerely vrged and dared by the faid Myles/ w[t] g[t] threates & wordes that he wold do thys/ and could do that/ to the vndoing and g[t] Dyfgrace of this depo[t] and his fone he this depo[t] told him/ that/ it was too moche to face him fo on his owne grounde/ & that he knew/ he could not anf*w*er it/ And that yf he wold not leave his Rayling & quyetlye dep*a*rte/ he this depo[t] wold/ fend him away/ w[t]out that/ that ever this depo[t] did ever fay or thinke the vnreu*er*end word*es* fett down in this Int*errogatory* again[t] Confcience furmyfed by the faid Myles to be vttered by this Depo[t]/ at that tyme/

To the 4. that true it is/ the faid comp[l] accompanyed w[t] the faid Myles and others came to the faid Theater to the Ten*antes* therof/ and there verye ymperyoufiie fyns the faid Order/ did chalendge & Demaunde Rent*es* of the fame as due vnto her for the moytie of the fame/ according to the faid Arbytryme*nt*/ And anf*w*er was made vnto her/ and them that came w[t] her/ both by the faid ten*antes* and Cuthbert this depo[tes] fone/ that fhe had nothing to do there/ and that they neu*er* knew her to haue any interelt in the fame/ But what the fubltance of ther talke was then betwene them/ he ca*n*not Depofe ffor he was not pre*f*ent therat/

To the 5. that he ca*n* fay nothing but by heare faye

To the 6. that he can*n* fay no more in effecte/ then he hath before faid to the firlt Int*errogatory*/ Nor more faith to all the faid Int*errogatories*/

[Signed] By me James Burbage

BRAYNE *v.* BURBAGE

Chancery Decrees and Orders, vol. 1590 "A," 456; also in 1590 "B," 455. Hilary, 33 Elizabeth (1590–91).

xxiij die Marcij [1590–91]

Margaret Brayne widowe playntif Cutbearde Burbage James Burbage def^{tes}	Whereas the def^{tes} haue bene ex- amyned vpon Interrogato^{res} at the p^{les} fuyte towchinge the breache of an order made in this Courte be-

twene the faid par^{ties}: It is ordered by the Right worfhip^{ll} the M^r of the Rowll*es* that the Confider-ac*i*on of theire examynac*i*ons be Referred to Mr Docto^r Cefar one of the M^{rs} of this Courte To thende he maye Confider and Re-porte to this Courte whether the faid def^t or eyther of them haue Committed anye Contempte or not That further order maye be taken therevppon accordinglye And the faid def^{tes} or theire At-tornes are to be warned when the pr*e*miffes fhalbe fo con-fidered of/

[The above order was first published, modernized throughout, in Collier's *Actors* (*n. s.*), p. 9.]

BURBAGE *v.* BRAYNE

Chancery Decrees and Orders, vol. 1590 "A," 493; also in 1590 "B," 497. Easter, 33 Elizabeth (1591).

Sabb*a*ti xxiiij^{to} die Aprilis [1591]

James Burbage p^l Margaret Brayne & Robte def^t	fforafmuche as this co^{rt} was this pr*e*f*e*nte daye enformed on the p^{les} behalf That the faid def^{tes} hathe

in A very fryvolous and Infuffy-cynt demorrer to the p^{les} bill wthout fhowinge any good caufe thereof   Therefore the confyderac*i*on of the faid bill and de-morrer ys Referred to Mr Dr Carewe one of the M^{rs} of this Co^{rt}

To thend he maye confyder and report to this co^{rt} whether the
faid demurrer be fuffycynt or not yf not Then A *subpoena* ys
awarded againft the def^{tes} to make A p*er*fect and dyrect aunfwere
to the p^{les} bill of Comp^l and to all the materyall poynt*es* thereof
And the def^{tes} Attorney ys to be warned when the p*remi*ffes
fhalbe fo confydered of

[The above order, modernized in spelling, was printed by J. P. Collier
in his *Actors* (*u. s.*), p. 9.]

BURBAGE *v.* BRAYNE

*Chancery Decrees and Orders, vol. 1590; " A," 720; also in 1590
" B," 725. Trinity, 33 Elizabeth (1591).*

Martis xv^{to} die Junij [1591]

James Burbage p^l
Margaret Brayne
Myles def^t

fforafmuche as this co^{rt} was this
p*re*fente daye enformed on the p^{les}
behalf That the faid defte hathe
put in an Infuffycyent demorrer to
the p^{les} bill wthout fhewing any good caufe thereof   Therefore
the confyderac*i*on of the faid bill and demorrer y*s* Referred to
Mr Dr Carewe one of the M^{rs} of this co^{rt} to thend he maye confyder and reporte to this co^{rt} whether the faid demorrer be fuffy-
cyent or not yf not Then A *fubpoena* ys awarded againft the def^t
to make p*er*fect and dyrect aunfwere to the p^{les} bill of Comp^l and
to all the materyall poynt*es* thereof   And the def^{tes} Attorney ys
to be warned when the p*remi*ffes fhalbe fo confydered of/

BRAYNE *v.* BURBAGE

Chancery Decrees and Orders, vol. 1590 "A," 818; also in 1590 "B," 831. Trinity, 33 Elizabeth (1591).

xx° die Julij [1591]

Margaret Brayne ⎫ fforafmuche as Mr Dr Cefarr one
widowe p^l ⎪ of the M^rs of this Courte to whofe
Cuthberte Burbage ⎬ confideracion the def^tes examina-
and James Bur- ⎪ cions vpon Interogatories towch-
bage defend^tes ⎭ inge the breache of an order made
in this Courte was referred can not
nowe attend the fame It ys therefore by the Right worfhipfull
the M^r. of the Rowles ordered that Mr Dr Hone one other of the
M^rs of this Courte fhall confider afwell of the fame contempte
As alfo heare and end the cawfe in queftion betwene the faid
parties yn this Courte, yf he can yf not that then he certifie into
this Courte afwell what he fhall finde towchinge the faide contempte As alfo his opinion of the faid cawfe And by whofe
defalt he can not end the fame wherevpon fuche further order
fhalbe taken therein as to this Courte fhalbe thought meete.

[The above order, modernized throughout, was first printed in Collier's *Actors (u. s.)*, p. 10.]

BRAYNE *v.* BURBAGE

Chancery Decrees and Orders, vol. 1591 "A," 16; also in 1591 "B," 18. Michaelmas, 33 & 34 Elizabeth (1591).

Marti xij° die Octobris [1591]

Margaret Brayne ⎫ Vpon the opening of the matter this pref-
wid p^l ⎪ ente daye by M^r S^rieant Harrys being of
James Burbage ⎬ the def^tes councell and comynge to fhowe
and Cutbart Bur- ⎪ caufe wherefore an attachm^t fhould not
bage df^tes ⎭ be awarded againft them vpon A reporte lately made by Mr Dr Hone one

of the M^{rs} of this co^{rt} of a contempt fuppofed to be comytted
on the def^{tes} behalf It ys thought meete and fo ordered by this
courte That no advantage or further proceeding fhalbe had vpon
that reporte But that Mr Dr Stanhope and Mr Dr Legg two of
the M^{rs} of this courte fhall confyder and reporte to this co^{rt}
whether the def^{tes} or either of them haue comitted any contempt
or not in breache of A former order Layd to theire charge vpon
whofe reporte fuche order fhalbe peremptoryly taken w^{th}out
further delaye as to this co^{rt} fhall be thought meete

BRAYNE *v.* BURBAGE

*Chancery Decrees and Orders, vol. 1591 " A," 151; also in 1591
" B," 163.   Michaelmas, 33 & 34 Elizabeth (1591).*

xiij° die Novembris [1591]

Margaret Brayne
widowe   p^l
James Burbage &
Cutbert Burbage
def^{ts}

Vpon the opening of the matter in vary-
ance to the right worfhipfull the M^r
of the Rolles by Mr Scott on the behalf of the faid p^l after the Ryfing of
the courte It appered that before this
tyme the confyderacion of the caufes
was Referred to Mr Dr Stannop and Mr Dr Legg two of the
M^{rs} of this co^{rt} who haue heard the caufe and the councell on
bothe partes and haue made A reporte in wryting vnder bothe
theire handes being in hec Verba By order of the xij^{th} of october laft wee haue had the councell on bothe partyes before vs and
entring into the confyderacion of the contempt comytted to vs to
examyne them Wee doe fynde that wee could not well proceede
to examyne them before John Hyde of London grocer and Raphe
Myles of London Sopemaker were examyned towching the caufe
and one Nicholas Bufhop and John Allen vpon the contempt in
the Interrogatoryes againft the faid def^{tes} pretended wherevpon
yt was concented by Councell on bothe fydes That the courte
would be pleafed to geve aucthoryty vnto vs to geve othe vnto

all thefe partyes to aunfwere to fuche Interrogatoryes on ether fyde to be mynyftered as by theire councell Learned fhould be mynyftered vnto them and vpon theire depofycions wee maye better proceede to examyne the pretended contemptes As by the fame Certyficate maye appere It ys ordered That the matter be agayne Referred to the faid Mr Dr Stannop and Mr Dr Legg and aucthoryty ys geven vnto them by this co^{rt} to call all the faid perfons named in the faid Certyfycate or reporte and to examyne them vpon theire othes vpon fuche Interrogatoryes as ys mencioned in the faid reporte To thend this co^{rt} maye the better be enformed towching the faid fuppofed contempt/

[Thus the whole case was placed in the hands of the two Masters in Chancery, Dr. Legg and Dr. Stanhope, to be heard and determined. Accordingly, they examined many witnesses during the succeeding year. It is not practicable to arrange the depositions in exact chronological order, because some of the five following sets of them were taken concurrently with others. They are here placed, therefore, in the order in which they were filed by the Court, the depositions of Hyde, Myles, Bishop, and Allen, mentioned in the above report, coming next to the last, and their cross-examinations in behalf of the Burbages, last, in the series of examinations in this case.]

BRAYNE *v.* BURBAGE

Chancery Town Depositions, Bdl. 226, No. 9, Michaelmas 33 and 34 Elizabeth (1591).

INTERROGATORIES

William Clerk iur*atus*
25 Feb 1591 cor*am*
Mat Carew

Articles to be myniftered vpon the parte and behaulf of James Burbage and Cuthbert Burbage Defend^{tes} againft Margaret Braines the executrixe of John Braynes Complaynante, to Giles Allyn gentelman, Bryan Ellame, Richard Hudfone, [*John Greges,*

William Botham, (stricken out)] Wm Clarke, Henry Bett gen-*tleman* ſcryven*er.*

.1. **Imprimis** Whither did yo^u knowe John Braines whileſt he lyved. And whither do yo^u knowe the *parties* plaintife and defendaunt*es*. And how longe haue yo^u knowen them.

.2. **Item** whither did James Burbage the one of the defend^{tes} take a Leaſe of yo^u of certaine void ground & decaied Tenementes in Hallywell, wheron the Theatre is now builded. And whither did John Brayne at the enſealinge of the ſaid Leaſe or at any tyme before, make ſute or require of yo^u to be ioyned with the ſaid Burbage in the ſaid Leaſe. Or to make the ſame in truſt to the ſame Burbege to his the ſaid Braines vſe. Yea or no.

.3. **Item** what fyne or Jncome did the ſaid Burbege paie or bynd him-ſealf to paie to yo^u for the ſaid Leaſe. And how mutch therof is to yo^u paid And how mutch is v*n*paide. And whither did the ſaid John Braines paie to yo^u any *parte* therof Or promyſe to paie yo^u any p*arte* therof. And whither did yo^u alwaies repute the ſaid Burbedge to be yor Ten*a*nte only of ye premiſſ*es* Yea or no. And what rent did yo^u receyve for the *premiſſes* before yo^u demyſed the ſame to Burbag

4. **Item** whither did Braines at any tyme paie to yo^u any rent for the ſaid Theatre and *premiſſes* by yo^u demyſed to the ſaid Burbege. And whither was ther not owinge vnto yo^u ſix yeres before the death of the ſaid Braines more or leſe the ſome of the fyftie and one poundes or therabout p*arte* of wch ſaid ſome beinge for the ſaid fyne, & p*arte* for Arrerag*es* of Rent, And who p^d yo^u the ſame/

5. **Item** whither did yo^u vewe the new buildinges and the Repracions done by the ſaid Burbage vpon & in certaine decayed howeſes houlden of m^r Allyn in Hallywell, To what ſome of mony did yo^u eſtymate the ſaid building*es* and Rep*ar*acions. Or what ſome or ſomes of monye do yo^u knowe or haue herd ſaye that the ſaid Burbage did beſtoe in the ſaid New building*es* & in the decayed

howſes adioyninge to the ſaid Theatre & vpon the Repairyng of
the Theatre   And whither did John Braine or his executor beſtoe
or laie out any mony theron or paye any thinge toward*es* the ſaid
Building*es* or Rep*a*raci*o*ns, yf he did, How mutche did he diſburſe
or paie/   And whither was ther iij^{xx}x^{li} [= 70 *l.*] beſtoed on the
Theatre ſince Braines death   yea or no

.6. **Item** what ſome of monye hath the ſaid Burbage diſburſed in
Repayringe of the Theatre more then Brayne did Joyne wth him
in allowaunce of the ſame Rep*a*raci*o*ns, And how know yo^u the
ſame.   And what Bondes wherin the ſaid Braines & Burbage were
ioyntlie bound, hath the ſaid Burbage paid and diſchardged
ſythenc the deathe of Braines   And to what vallewe do the ſaid
Bond*es* arriſe vnto.   And whither did the ſaid executrix ioyne wth
him in the payem^t therof.   And what other ſomes of monye hath
he paid wherof the moitie ought to haue byne p^d by Braines or
his execuo^{rs} as yo^u knowe or haue herd.   And how knowe yo^u
the ſame

.7. **Item** whither was ther any Arbitrem^t made betwen the*m* about
the endinge of the controverſies moved betwen them for the p*ro*-
fitt*es* of the Theatre.   And whither was the Arbitrem^t obſerved.
And what ſome of mony did the ſaid Burbage dem*a*unde of
Braines by force of the ſaid Arbitrem^t.   And how know yo^u the
ſame.

.8. **Item** whither do yo^u knowe or haue herd ſaye That the ſaid Burbage had Mortgaged forfeited & loſt his ſaid Leaſe to one John
Hyde grocer,   And whither did the ſaid Hide arreſt the ſaid Burbage vpon pourpoaſe to haue removed him fro*m* thence/   And
whither haue yo^u herd or did yo^u knowe of yor owne knowledge
that Cuthbert burbedge the other defend^t did pourchaſe and buy
wth his p*ro*per monye the ſaid Leaſe of the Theatre of the ſaid
Hide.   And to his owne vſe onlye.   yea or no

.9. **Item** what haue yo^u herd the ſaid Hyde confeſe and ſaie towchinge ſutch ſomes of monye as he receyved at the Theatre.   And
whither haue yo^u herd him ſaye That he neuer made any agreem^t

wth Braine nor Burbage the father for the reconveyinge of the ſaid Leaſe to them. And that the ſomes of monye by him Receyved, were the profitt*es* of the Theatre And not for the mony lent vpon the Leaſe, nor for the redemption therof / nor for vſurye for the forbearinge of his monye. yea or no

NOTE TO THE EXAMINER.

[This note is attached in front of the interrogatories, but belongs chronologically after them as here placed.]

> A brief noate for the eaſe and ſpede of the examiner, ſhewinge how many Articles are to be obiected, to eache p*ar*tie to be exa*m*in*e*d on thes Articles & whervnto thei can aunſwer.

Impr*im*is to m^r Allen the firſt. ſecond, third, & fowerth. onli for him

Item. to Brian Ellam Richard Hudſon [*John Griges Carpenters W*^m *Botham Ralf Bett*es (stricken out)] & Wm Clarke plaiſterers firſt & fyſt.

Item to Henry Bett, &   Gall ſcriven*er*, 1. 6. 7. 8. 9.

[All the above witnesses were examined except Gall the scrivener. Their depositions now follow.]

DEPOSITIONS.

> Ex parte Jacobi Burbage et Cuthb*er*ti Burbage defen*dentum* verſus Margaret*am* Brayne vid*uam* q*u*erentem Teſte exa*m*inator*e* p*er* Henr*icum* Johnes in Cancellar*ia* Exa*m*inatorem/

Henrie Bett, of the pariſhe of St Leonardes in Shorditche, in the Countie of mid*dleſex* gentelma*n* of the age of xlij yeres or therabout, ſworne and exa*m*in*e*d the laſte daie of September in the xxxiij^{tl} yere of the reigne of o^r Sovereigne Ladie Queen Elizabeth by vertue &c

1. To the firft Interr.　That he knewe John Braine when he was lyvinge, and that he knowethe the *parties* Defendant*es* and Com-playn*a*nte, & hath knowen them thes xiiij yeres & vpward*es*

2. 3. 4. To the ij. iij and iiij Interr*ogatories* he can not depoafe

5. 6. To the v and vj Jnterr. he depoafethe and faiethe, That he was not prefent, when the buildinge, latelie errected by James Burbege or his affignes, nere the Theatre were vewed/ but beinge in Com-panye wth the vewers therof, thei did eftimate the chardge thereof, to arrife to 220^{ll} & vpward*es* the wch matter certaine worckmen alfo affermed ; who did acknowledge that they had receyved a good p*a*rte therof, fortheir wo^{r}kmanfhip and other thinges ; wherof, they alfo affermed, that nether Braines, nor his executo^{rs}, did paie to them any thinge. but what fome of monye certainelie, the faid James Burbege did beftoe, ether vpon the new buildinge of the Theatre, or vpon the repayringe of the fame, this depon^t knowethe not of his owne knowlege, nor what monye he hath paid, fince the deathe of Braine, but by the accompt*es* of the faid Bur-bege, the wch this depon^t hath often feene and coppied out, yt it fett dowen.　That the faid Braine and his executo^{rs}, did owe to him the moitie of 220^{ll} beftoed as is aforefaid.　And the moitie of 230^{ll} paid by the faid Burbege for rent, and for repayring of the Theatre and the moitie of 220^{li} 13^s 4^d, paid by the faid Burbege, for the difcharginge of bond*es* debt*es,* and other exfpences, fynce the deathe of Braine, befides the fome of 135^{li} 1^s. the wch the faid Braine, by a noate vnder his owne hand, confeffethe to haue receyved out of the Theatre, and to be accomptable for the fame ; but whither the faid accompt*es,* payem^{tes} & demand*es* of the faid James Burbege, be true or falfe, he faiethe he knowethe not ; but he faiethe, that he is verie fure that the noate, that the faid John Braine hath fett downe, for the receipte of the 135^{li} 1^s, is the pr*o*per hand writinge of the faid Braine : And more to thes Interr he faiethe not/

7 To the vij Interr*ogatory* he faiethe, That ther was an Arbitrem^t made, betwene Braine & Bvrbege in writinge, afwell for the certaine difpoafinge, of the p*rofittes,* levied in the Theatre and Tenem^{tes}, as in directing the faid Braine, when, and how, fuch fomes of monye, as he the faid Braine had difburfed, aboute the buildinge the faid Theatre, fhuld be to him paid : for the certaintie wherof, this depon^t referrethe himfelf to the faid arbitrem^t, only he faiethe, that nether the faid Braine nor his executrix the now comp^l haue obferved the fame, nor by their owne fpeches and affirmac*i*ons, neuer will p*er*forme the faid arbitrem^t, and further to this Interr*ogatory* he can not depoafe of his owne knowledge/

8. 9. To the viij and ix Interr*ogatory* he depoafethe and faiethe, That the faid James Burbege wth the confent of John Braine did mortgadge the Leafe of the Theatre, to one John Hyde the wch was to him forfeited, who did thervpon arreft the faid Burbege intendinge (as this depon^t takethe it) to take the advauntadge therof, and to expell the faid Burbege and Braine, and to that end did fend one of his fervaun*tes,* to collecte and gyve order, that futch monye, or the beft p*ar*te therof, as was receyved at the Theatre, fhould be brought and paied to him, and becawfe he did not receyve futch fomes of monye, in that wife, as was to his likinge, he the faid Hyde gave order to George Cloughe, father in Lawe to him the faid Hyde, to demaunde his monye, or to remove the faid Burbege out of the Theatre, by wch meanes, the faid Cloughe did go to the faid Theatre, and threatened to remove the faid Burbege fro*m* thence, fynce the deathe of the faid Braine (as this depon^t remembrethe) And this depon^t further faiethe, that for a fome of monye the certaintie wherof he rememb^{r}eth not, the faid Hyde, did fell his title in the faid Leafe, to Cuthbert Burbege one of thes defend^{tes}, at the payem^t of p*ar*te wherof, this depon^t was prefent, at ij feverall tymes, the wch monye fo paid to the faid Hyde, was the p*ro*per monye of the faid Cuthbert (as this depon^t is p*er*fwaded) and he beleeveth it, the rather, for that the faid Cutbert did then declare, that he was faine to borrowe p*ar*te therof the wch he affermed he would not haue done, but only to haue

redemed and deliuered his father, from many encombraunc*es*, whervnto he and Braine, had rune them fealues into, about the faid Theatre, at wch tyme the faid Hyde likewife affermed, that yf one m^r Coape, had not written to him about the faile therof, to the faid Cutbert, that he never fhould haue had it, for that one m^r middelmor & his father in Lawe Cloughe, were importinat wth him for the fame/ And further to this Jnterr*ogatory* he can not depoafe, favinge that he well remembrethe, that the faid Hyde, hath often confeffed and fworne to this depon^t that the mony by him Receyved at the Theatre was in his owne right, and nethe^r for intereft, nor by waye of Compofition of his principall debt, but what he now will fweare or afferme this depon^t knowethe not/ nor further faiethe to all the faid Jnterr*ogatories*/

[Signed]   Per me Henricu*m* Bett

Gyles Allen of Hafelye in the Counte of Effex gent*leman* of the age of lviij yeres or therabout*es* fworn and ex^d the thirde daye of November in the yere aforefaid &c To the firfte Int*errogatory*. that he did verye well knowe John Braynes deceffed named in this Int*errogatory*./ And knoweth all the p*arties* p^{ltes} and Defend^{tes}/ And faith that he knewe the faid Jo. Braynes fondry yeres before he dyed/ And hath knowen the p*arties* to this Sute about viij or x yeres/ but yong Burbage he hath not knowen but about ij° or iij yeres/

To the 2. that about xiiij or xv yeres paft as he now Reme*m*breth James Burbage one of the now deffend^{tes} did take A leafe of this depo^t for the, terme of xxj yeres of fome of the then voyd ground & Ruynous tenem^{tes} w^tin the p*recinct* of Hallywell nere Shordych/ vpon part wherof the playing place called the Theater/ now ftandeth./ And faithe that nether the faid Jo. Braynes/ nor any other for him did ether make Sute to this depo^t at any tyme before the enfealing of the faid leafe, to be Joyned w^t the faid James Burbage in the faid leafe, nor to make the faid leafe, in truft to the faid James Burbage, to the vfe of the faid Braynes/ But faithe/ that in verye trothe the faid leafe was fuewed for/ by the faid Burbage & not ment any way to the faid Braynes

To the 3. that he cannot now Remember how moche for an Incombe or ffyne for the faid leafe he did receyve or was to Receyve of the faid James Burbage/ But he thinketh he had fome therof in hand/ and A bonde for the paym^t of the reft/ not fullye yet difcharged/ the certenty how moche yerof was payd in hand/ and yet is vnpayd/ he cannot certenlye depofe/ for that the faid Bonde is now remayning at his houfe in the cuntrye/ Of wch ffyne or Jncome the faid Jo. Braynes paid no penny to this depo^t for any thing he can Remember/ nor promyfed to paye this Depo^t any part therof/ And faith that he never reconed or reputed any perfone or perfones whatfoever as his tenant of the premiffes fyns the making of the faid leafe but onlye the faid James Burbage/ And faith that the Rent wch this Depo^t receyved for the premiffes before the making of the faid leaffe to the faid James Burbage/ was as he thinketh about xiiij^{li} by yere/ Marye he faithe that fyns the making of the faid leafe/ Cuthbert Burbage the faid James Burbage fonne/ did paye this Depo^t Rent for the faid premiffes how often he Remembreth not/ faying vnto this depo^t/ that then he was this Depo^{tes} tenant of the premiffes/ by reafone he had [*Redemned the faid leafe his ffathers intereft thereof* (stricken out)] the faid leafe/ But fhewed no affignem^t or other Conveyance to this depo^t made vnto him of the fame

To the 4. that he doth not Remember that the faid Johne Braynes payd this Depo^t Rent at any tyme/ for the faid premiffes/ And faith that he cannot tell when the faid Braynes dyed/ But he faithe that he well Remembreth that about vj yeres now paft/ ther was owing this Depo^t partlie for part of the faid ffyne or Jncome/ and partlie for arrerages of Rent for the faid premiffes/ about ffyftie poundes & vpwarde of the w^{ch}/ fo moche as was payd yerof was payd by the faid James Burbage & his affignes for any thing he now Remembreth/ But he faith ther is remayning & vnpayd of the fame, the fome of xxx^{li}/ at this daye/ Vpon the reft of the Jnterrogatories he is not ex^d/ by the direccion of the parties Defend^{tes} And more he faith not/

[Signed] Gyles Aleyn

Bryane Ellam of Silverftreete london Carpinter of the age of lviij yeres or therabou*tes* fworne and ex^d the xxv daye of ffebruarye in the yere aforefaid &c   To the firft J*nterrogatory* that he did knowe Jo. Brayne whille he lieved/ And knoweth all the p*a*rties p^l and Defend^{tes}/ and hath known them about xiiij or xv yeres/

To the 5. that he was one emong*es* others/ that of late yeres did view the new building*es* and the rep*a*racions fett vppe & done by the now Defend^{tes} or of one of them of dyvers decayed howfes and Roomes in hallywell by Shordiche wthout Biffhops gate london/ taken of Mr Allen menc*i*oned in this J*nterrogatory*.   And faith that they were viewed twice/ And faith that in ther Judgem^t, the faid new building*es* and rep*a*racions in all manner of work*es* of the fame/ could amount to no leffe then about the fome of CCxl, or CCxxx^{li}/ the charge wherof for any thing this Depo^t doth know or then did heare/ was the faid defend^{tes}/ or one of them/ And fo hath this Depo^t and the reft of the viewers therof fett Down/ vnder ther handes/ and markes in A memorand*um* therof made in the defend^{tes} booke in Julye laft paft/ as by the fame maye appere/ And further faith that the faid defend^{tes} or one of them haue beftowed in further building & Rep*a*racions of the Theater there [*& other the houfes in hollywell aforefaid* (stricken out)] w^{t}in this vj or vij weekes paffed/ to the value of xxx or xl^{li} as this depo^t dothe eftymate the fame/ And for any coft & charges beftowed vpon the p*r*emiffes or vpon any part therof/ ether by the forefaid Jo. Brayne deceffed before he dyed/ or by his Wyfe the now comp^l fins his deceffe/ he faith he can fay nothing/ Only he Reme*m*breth that the faid Braine being p*a*rtener (as he tooke him) w^t James Burbage now one of the defend^{tes}/ of & in the premiffes/ payd this depo^t for fome work wch this depo^t did vpon the fame p*r*emiffes before he dyed the fome of xl^s, [*at fondrye tymes* (stricken out)]/ at the leaft xiiij yeres paffed/

Vpon the reft of the J*nterrogatories* he is not ex^d by the dyreccion of the faid defend^{tes}/ or of one of them/

                              [His mark] /K

Rychard Hudſon of Puddyng lane london Bricklayer of the age
of xxxj yeres or therabout*es* ſworne and ex^d the daye & yere
aforeſaid &c To the firſt J*n*ter*r*ogatory. That he did know Johne
Brayne deceſſed named in this J*n*ter*r*ogatory/ And knoweth all
the p*a*rties p^l and defend^{tes}/ And ſaith that he knewe the ſaid Jo.
Brayne about ij° yeres before he dyed/ And hath knowen the
comp^l and the defend^{tes} about A doſen yeres/

To the 5. that he was one emong*es* others/ that in Julye laſt paſt/
did S*u*rvey and view the new building*es* and the rep*a*racio*n*s done
by the now defend^{tes} or by one of them/ in & vpon certen decayd
houſes & places in hallywell nere ſhordiche wthout Biſhops gate
london/ And ſaith that in ther Judgem^t they could recone it to no
leſſe then CCxl^{li} or theraboute*s*/ as by A memorand*um* vnder
ther hand*es* and mark*es* written in the defend^{tes} Book of the
ſame/ may more plainely appere/ And further ſaith that the ſaid
defend^{tes} or one of them haue ſins that view beſtowed in further
building & repairing of the Theater or playhouſſe there/ wherin
he this depo^t was one of the workmen/ to the value of xxx^{li} or
theraboute*s*/ And ſaith that he ca*n*not tell what ſome of money
the ſaid Brayne/ in his lyf tyme or his wydow the now comp^l
ſins his deceſe paid for or towardes the building or Repayring of
the ſaid Theater/ and other the p*r*emiſſes/ But he ſaith that he
did heare ſaye, that the ſaid Brayne/ and James Burbage now
one of the defend^{tes} were p*a*rteners together of the ſame Theater
& other the p*r*emiſſes/

Vpon the reſt of the J*n*ter*r*ogatories he is not ex^d by the dyrec-
ci*o*n of the defend^{tes} or of one of them./
                    [Signed]   Richard hudſone

Willi*a*m Clerke of Mugwellſtreete w^tin Cripple gate london
plaſterer of the age of lxxij yeres or theraboute*s* ſworne & ex^d
the daye and yere aforeſaid &c To the firſt J*n*ter*r*ogatory. that
he did not know Jo. Brayne named in this J*n*ter*r*ogatory/ nor
his wydowe the now Comp^l and of the ij° defend^{tes} he knoweth

but James Burbage the ffather/ and hath known him about xiij
or xiiij yeres/

To the 5. that he was one emong*es* others, that at the Requeſt
of the ſaid James Burbage, did in Julye laſt paſt view the new
building*es* and rep*a*racions of certen decayed howſes in hallywell
nere ſhordiche/ w*t*out Biſſhops gate london/ holden of one M*r*
Allen there/ and they did judge in ther conſcience that the
charges of the ſame did amount to no leſſe then CCxl*li* at the
leaſt/ as they did then vnder ther hand*es* and m*a*rk*es* ſett down
the ſame in A Memorandu*m* wrytten in the defend*antes* booke
as may appere by the ſame/ And to the reſt of this Jnterro*gatory*
he ſaith he ca*n*not certenlye depoſe/

Vpon the reſt of the Jnterro*gatories* he is not ex*d* by the direc-
c*i*on of the defend*tes* or of one of them/

[His mark] +

BURBAGE *v.* BRAYNE

*Idem, Bdl. 226, No. 10. Michaelmas, 33 and 34 Elizabeth, and
Trinity, 34 Elizabeth (1591–92).*

[Two skins of Interrogatories, one of them being for Hynde alone,
attached to seven paper sheets of depositions.]

INTERROGATORIES

Jurata coram me
Thoma Legg 8° Maij 1592
Willms James Jurat*us*
25° Julij 1592 cora*m* Jo. Hone

> **Articles to be** mynyſtred to Ellyn Gaſcon late,
> wief of W*m*. White [*James Norman* (stricken
> out)], Henry Bett, [*John Meade, Thomas Rum-
> ney* (stricken out)], John Hynde and others
> vpon the parte and behaulf of James Burbadge
> Complaynan*te* againſt Margaret Brayne widdoe,
> and Robe*rt* Myles Gouldſmythe defend*tes*.

1. **Imprimis** did yo^u knowe John Braines whileſt he lyued. And whither do yo^u knowe the parties plaintife & defend^tes And how longe haue yo^u knowen them.

2. **Item** what ſome of monye did the ſaid John Braines and Robe*rt* Myles owe to Noble, or White. And for what cauſe was the ſame due. And whither was yt for Tymber and certaine worcke & frames errected in the Inn called the George in whitechappell. And whither did the plaintif Burbage become a ſuertie for the ſame. Yea or no.

3. **Itm** did not the ſaid Braines and Myles promise to the ſaid white. That he ſhuld diſpoaſe haue and hould a Myll howſe ſcituat in the ſaid Inn vntill he had levied the ſaid debt at v.^li yerlie. Or els that the ſaid White ſhuld haue the rent of v.^li yerlie out of the ſame Myll howſe. And whither did the ſaid Myles and Braines ſpeake to yo^u to entreat the ſaid White to accept the ſame. And how came yt to paſe that the ſaid white had nether the Mylhowſe nor rent.

4. **Item** was not the ſaid white offended therw^th. And did not he thervpon take out p*roces* to Impriſone the*m* and ther ſureties. And whither did the ſaid defend^tes entreate the Compl^t to become bound in a Recognizance or ſtatute for the true payem^t of the mony accordinge to an order then taken. And whither did the ſaid white aſſigne and ſett ouer to the Compl^t & to one Garden*er* the Bonde of the ſaid Myles, wth a le*tt*re of Attorney to ſue them yea or no. And who now hath the ſame bond & le*tt*re of Attorney. And whither did the defend^tes p*romi*ſe to diſchardge the p^l therof

5 **Item** whither do yo^u knowe the hand writinge of the ſaid John Braine. And of Robe*rt* Myles. And whithe^r is this le*tt*re here pre*ſ*ente the proper hand writinge of the ſaid Myles. And what ſome of mony did the ſaid Myles and Braines, or Myles him ſelf, ſhewe yo^u in ther Accompt*es* or confeſe that the plaintif did

owe to them, as paid by them for him to one John Hynd. And whither did thei or any of them declare to yo[u], that the plaintif had paide to them or any of them all ſutch ſomes of mony as had byn paid to the ſaid Hynd for him. And whither did Thomas Rumney ſubſcribe this Bill as witnes that the mony therin expreſſed was paid for the diſchardge of the ſaid Myles. yea or no. And what can yo[u] Roger Saunders ſaie therin

6. **Itm** whither is this Bill of Accompt the proper hand of John Braine. And whither was the ſame written after the Award made betwen the p[lt] and the ſaid Braine. And what haue yo[u] herd the ſaid Braine ſaye concerninge the ſaid Arbitrement. And whither did he accompt the ſame to be diſſolued, & not to be performed. And what reaſon had he ſo to ſaie And whither is the ſome of monye therin expreſſed that w[ch] the defend[tes] do challendge as laid out vpon buildinge of the Theatre by John Braine more then the plaintiſe beſtoed. Yea or no.

7. **Item** what and how manye deedes of giftes haue yo[u] knowen or haue herd That John Braine hath made of his goodes and Chattells. To whom haue the ſame byne made. How longe ſythen, and for what conſideracion. And whither were ther any ſutch made ſythence the date of the ſaid will & Teſtament of John Braine. And whither did the ſaid Margarett Braine notw[th]ſtandinge the ſaid deedes of gift, and will, go about to take letters of Adminiſtracion of the goods and Chattells w[ch] apperteyned to her ſaid Huſband. And what was the cawſe ſhe proceded not therin as yo[u] thincke And whither do yo[u] thincke that yt was the meaninge of Braines at his deathe, to make Myles a witnes of his Wil and laſt Teſtament. Yea or no.

8. **Item to what** vallewe or ſome of monye doth the bondes appere to arriſe vnto, the w[ch] Burbage hath diſcharged ſythence the deathe of Braines wherof the ſaid defend[t] ought to haue paid a Moitie. Or what ſome of monye haue yo[u] herd, that the ſaid Burbadge hath paid, or is to paie for Braines, ſythenc his deathe.

And what may he inſtlie clayme in yor conſcience of her towardes the ſame. Or what may ſhe duelie challendge of him the Compl^t by reaſone of the Theatre. declare yor knowledge therin, And whither haue yo^u herd ther differences or Accomptes betwene them. Yea or no.

9. **Item** how longe is yt ſynce That the ſaid Braines and Myles did abſente them ſeaulues for their Credito^{rs}. And how mutche monye did thei then owe. And whither were thei ſo indebted for any cawſe concerninge the Theatre. to yor knoweledge or as yo^u haue herd.

10. **Item** what ſome of monye did Braines confeſe to yo^u that he re-ceyved out of the Theatre. And whither did he ſaie that the ſame did arriſe to a greter or leſſer vallewe, then that wch he laid out, about the buildinge of the ſaid Theatre. And whither do yo^u thincke, that Braine did rune into Bondes and Credite for thinges about the ſaid Theatre, and imployed the monye he receyved ther, about other affaires. And that he neuertheles imputed that the ground of his hinderance and loſe, was by the Theatre and the buildinge therof

11. **Item** what thinge or matter Materiall do yo^u knowe or can yo^u declare concerninge the ſomes of monye by Braine diſburſed aboute the Theatre in his lief tyme Or by her the defend^t ſythence his death. Or of or concerninge the will of the ſaid Braines. And the deedes of gift by him made. And for what vſe or pourpoaſes the ſame were made. And who maynteyneth the ſutes of the ſaid Margaret, And for what conſideracion. declare yor knoweledge therin. And how often to yor knoweledge is the ſaid Robert Myles indighted for comon Imbarracie & Adultri or as yo^u haue herd, And whither was he called before the Coroners Inqueſt for the death of Braine. Yea or no/

NOTE TO EXAMINER

[This note is attached in front of the interrogatories to the previous set of depositions, No. 9, in this same bundle 226, but belongs to the present set filed just after it and numbered 10.]

A Briefe noate for the eafe & fpede of the Examiner, fhewing how many Articles are to be obiected to each partie, to be examined one thes Articles, & wherto thei can aunfwer.

+ Imprimis to Ellyn Gafcone. 1. 2. 3. 4.
Item to James Norman. 1. 2. 3. 4. 5. 6. 7. 11.
+ Item to Henry Bett. 1. 2. 3. 4. 5. 6. 7. 8. 9. 10. 11.
+ Item to [*John Mead* (stricken out)] Mr William James. 1. 5. 6. 7. 9. 11.
Item to [*Thomas Ramey* (stricken out)] and Rogr Saunders. 1. 5.

[Of the above witnesses, only those were examined against whose names the examiner placed a cross, as will be seen by comparing with the depositions themselves.]

INTERROGATORIES TO HYNDE

John Hind Juratus
24 Julij 1592
Edw Hank

Interrogatories to be miniftred vnto John Hinde on the behalf of James Burbage Plaintif againft Margaret Braine widdow and Robert Miles bear Clerk def

Impr. whether did you John Hinde knowe one John Braine in his lief
1. tyme, and whether do you now know the partie plaintif James Burbage yea or noe./

Itm whether did you John Hinde about xiij yeares paft in Anno 1579.
the xxiijth of June abowt twoe of the Clock in the afternoone
2. fend the Sherif his Officer vnto the Crofkeys in gratious ftreet

being then the dwelling howſe of Richard Ibotſon Cittizen and Bruer of London, and ther by vertue of *precept* to attache the bodie of this Complaynᵗ, for the ſome of ffyve poundes one ſhillinge and a pennye wᶜʰ yoᵘ John Hinde had Recouered for coſtes & Charges in lawe againſt the ſaid John Braine & the ſaid Complᵗ by a Niſi prius out of Maᵗᵉˢ Benche at Weſtmin*ſter* tried in the guildhall in London, And whether did this Complᵗ James Burbage ſatiſfie and paie vnto the ſaid Officer the ſaid ſome of vˡˡ. Iˢ. Iᵈ. to yoʳ vſe, And whether receaued yoᵘ the ſaid money of the ſaid Officer yea or noe/.

DEPOSITIONS

Ex parte Jacobi Burbage q*uerentis* ver*ſus* Margareta*m* Brayne vid*uam* et Robe*r*tum Myles de-*fendentes* Teſte exami*nature* per Hen*ricum* Johnes in Cancellari*a* Exami*n*atorem/

Henry Bett of the p*ariſhe* of Sᵗ Leonardes Shorditch, in the Countie of Midd*leſex* gen, of the age of xlij yers or theraboute, ſworne and exa*min*ed the Laſte daie of Septembʳ, A° 1591 in the xxxiijᵗˡ yere of the raigne of our Sovereigne Ladie Quene Eliz &ct,

1 To the firſt Interrogatorie, that he hath knowen the Complᵗ. James Burbege, about xiiij yers, and hath knowen the ſaid Robeᵣt Myles, and Margaret Braine the defendᵗᵉˢ, as longe, and that he well knewe John Braine whilſt he lyved, by the ſpace of many yeres

2 To the ſecond iij and iiij Interr and to the matters in them Conteyned, this deponᵗ faith. That he the ſaid John Braine or Robeᵣt Myles, or both of them, were indebted to one Noble a Carpenter, for a frame for a howſe, & certaine tymber beſtoed about the Inn, called the George in white Chappell, the certaine ſome wherof he remembrethe not, the wᶜʰ debt one Wᵐ white demaunded of them, by reaſone that he had taken to wief, the executrix or Adminiſ-

tratrix, of the goods of the ſaid noble, And did ſue the ſaid Braine for the ſame, in her Ma^{tes} co^{rt} called the kinges benche, in wch action the ſaid Burbege the Compl^{t}, became baile, wth others; and therin were overthroen & condempned/ whervpon aſwell the ſaid Braine, as the ſaid Myles, did entreate this depon^{t}. to travell to the ſaid white, who was then this depon^{tes} Landlord, to take ſome reaſonable order therin, & by the appointm^{t}, of the ſaid Braine & Miles, this depon^{t}. did offerr to the ſaid white, the rent of a Myll howſe, beinge v.^{li} p*er* ann*um,* or therabout; errected in the ſaid Inn, to be yerlie paid to the ſaid white vntill the ſaid debt, were levied, wherby the ſaid Burbege might be diſchardged of the ſame debt; the wch aſwell the ſaid Miles, as the ſaid Braines, p*ro*miſed alwaies to do, and to ſaue him the ſaid Burbege harmeles therin, but for that the ſaid v^{li}. rent, nor the ſaid myll howſe were not conveyed, ouer, to the ſaid white; nothinge was then done nor any concluſion made in the matter. by wch meanes the ſaid White, did afterwardes pourſue the ſaid Braine and Burbege, wth others, the ſuerties in the ſaid action, & had ſome of them at the laſt in priſone. But for that the ſaid Braine was then dead; an order was taken by the ſaid White, wth the ſaid Margaret Braine, and wth Burbege and one Gardener, that thei ſhuld be bound in a ſtatute, or Recognïſaunce to the ſaid white, for the paym^{t} of a certaine ſome of monye, at certaine tymes appointed, in reſpecte of the ſaid debt; the wch bond was ſo made, and the bonde wherin the ſaid Myles and Braines, or one of them was firſt bound in vnto the ſaid noble, for the monye for the ſame frame, was aſſigned and ſett ouer wth aucthoretie, fro*m* the ſaid white, to the ſaid Burbege, and the reſt, to ſue the ſaid Myles for the ſame yf in caſe he did not yeld ſome monye for the ſame frame, for that the ſame came only to his handes, after the death of Braine, the wch bond and aucthoretie (as this depon^{t} hath herd ſaie) was de- liuered tu the ſaid Myles by the ſaid margaret, to p*re*vent the ſaid Burbege therin, and further herin he ſaiethe not

To the v Interro*gatory* this depon^{t} ſaiethe, That the le*t*tre or writinge p*ro*duced & to him ſhewed at the tyme of this his examinac*i*on, is the proper hand writinge of the faid Rob*er*t Miles written to the faid Burbege, the now Compl*t*. this he knowethe to be true, for that he this depo*t* at the requeft of the faid Burbege, who was moved therat, did go to conferr w*th* the faid miles, about the matters therin./ who did then confeffe, that the fame was his hand, & thate he did dem*a*unde, the Moitie of the xxvj*li* x*s* i*d*. of the faid Burbege/ paide to the faid John Hynd in the Interr named/, by force of a pr*e*cept and execuc*i*on laid on him the faid Myles as a fuertie for Braines, yt beinge alfo, the debt of the faid Burbege; acknowledginge alfo, that he had receyved vj*li* of the faid Burbege toward*es* the faid moitie, but at what tyme the faid letter was written, this depon*t* remembrethe not, but he thinckethe yt was fince the dethe of Braine, and this depon*t* further faiethe That in the life tyme of the faid Braine, the faid Myles and Braines, reafoning together about dyvers matte*rs*, in ther accomp*tes*, befor this depon*t*, he the faid Myles did chardge the faid Braine that he had fufteyned dyvers troubles, for him, and recited his trouble for the faid debt, At w*ch* tyme, the faid Braine did then afferme, before the faid Miles, That he for his p*a*rte had paid to the faid Miles, to fatiffie Hynd, the one half of the faid monye paid to Hynd & that Burbege, who*m* he called his brother, had fatiffied the other half alfo, and thervpon he pr*o*duced a Booke of Reconing*es* betwene them importinge afmutche, the w*he* the faid Miles, did not then contradict, but rather confeffed, only reporting and ftanding vpon his trouble, for the fame. and more in this matter he now remembrethe not, but refferrethe him felf to his examinac*i*on taken in that matter in London.

To the vj Interr this depon*t* faiethe, That the noate and fomutch of the writinge therin vndefaced now pr*o*duced and to him fhewed, at the tyme of this his exa*mi*nac*i*on, is the pr*o*per hand writinge of John Braine, the w*ch* he well knowethe, for that he had often fene him write, and that he knowethe that Burbege did demaunde the fame fomes of monye, in the faid noate, confeffed to be by him the faid Braine Receyved, beinge 135*l* i*s* w*th* other fomes afterwardes by him Receyved, the w*ch* he refufed to yeld, aunſweringe in the preſence of this depon*, to the ſaid Burbege, that he would deteyne the ſame towardes the payem* of that ſome of monye, by him laide out, towardes the firſt buildinge of the Theatre, the w*ch* the ſaid Braine, confeſſed in A° 1582 to be but 239*ll* — 6*s* — 6*d* for his p*arte* in all/ And all be it, the ſaid deteyner, was contrarie to the award, w*ch* was made betwene them in that matter, yet he affermed, that he neyther could nor would p*er*forme the ſame award: all this matter this depon* knowethe to be true, for that he hath byne often tymes required, by both the ſaid p*ar*ties, to heare ther differences, and to write ſuch matter as thei thought fitt to be equall betwene them, and further in this matter he ſaiethe riot ſaving that he beleevethe that the noate and name of Rumneys, p*ro*duced, to be the p*ro*per hand wryting of the ſaid Rumney/

To the vij Interr he ſaiethe, That yt was a Comon thinge, w*th* the ſaid John Braine, to make deed*es* of gifte of his good*es* and Chattelles, the reaſone was as this depon* taketh yt, to p*re*vent his Credito*rs* aſwell before buildinge of the Theatre, as ſince, for he beinge redie to be impriſoned for debt he would prepare ſutch ſafetie for his good*es,* as he could/ by thoſe deed*es,* who [sic] ſomtyme were made to one Tomſon, and ſomtyme to one Garden*er,* and as this depon* hath herd to one m*r* Aſhebournham, and others: but the reaſon whi thei do not challenge the ſame good*es,* accordinge to their gift*es,* this depon* knowethe not, and he further ſaiethe, that he is perſwaded in his conſcience, that yt was not the meaninge of the ſaid Braine at the tyme of his deathe, to make any will, nor to call Myles then, to be a witneſs therof, for that at his deathe (as this depon*. hath herd it credeblie reported) he charged Miles w*th* his deathe, by certaine ſtripes geven him by Miles who was afterwardes, called by the ſute of the ſaid Margeret, befor an enqueſt held by the Crowner for the Countie of Midd*lesex,* for the enquirie therof. and alſo for that the ſaid Braine did walke at libertie, w*th* the ſaid Miles by licence of ther Credito*rs,* by force of certaine tollerac*i*ons to them made, and otherwiſe.

To the viij Interr and to all the matters in it conteyned, he can fay no otherwife than he hathe faid and depoafed, beinge exam-ined vpon the parte and behaulf of the faid Burbege, beinge defend[t] at the fute of the faid Margaret Braine, favinge that he thinckethe, that Braine, did Receyve more monye by a grete fome then he laid out in the Theatre, and that yt could not be his vndo-inge for he beleevethe, that he was not of fuch abillitie, as the faid Miles reputethe him to haue byne, before the buildinge of the Theatre, the rather for that he had made one or more deedes of giftes of his goodes, ether before, or in the tyme of the buildinge therof and further to this Interr faieth not

To the ix he faiethe That true it is he this depo[t] at the Requeft of the faid Brayne did write certaine peticions, for the fame Braine and Myles, to crave favore at ther Credito[rs] handes, to whom thei did owe about viij or ix C[li], the w[ch] was not (as he takethe it) for any matter concerninge the Theatre, but for Matters concern-inge the Inn called the george in white chappell/ and more to this Int he faith he can not certainlie depoafe/

To the x and xj articles this deponent faieth, That Braine would never plainlie declare, how mutch he had receyved concerning the Theater, for that he alledged, yf the trve vallew and fome; were knowen that yt would hardlie be allowed him but yt feemed by his taulke, that he had gayned & receyved a grete deale of monye, more then he had difburfed: But after that certaine futes were moved betwen one M[r] Peckham, and Giles Allen, about the in-tereft and title of certaine Land in Hollywell, wherof the Theatre was parcell, the faid Braine did take and keepe the moft parte of that he did receyve contrarie to the forefaid arbitrem[t], and femed to be careles of the fame Leafe, the rather, for that yt was mort-gaged; and would often tymes confeffe, that yf the faid Leafe might not be redemed wth the profittes therof, that yt fhould neuer be redemed for him/, and made careles and inconvenient bar-gaines, about the faid leafe, after it was mortgaged; and faith that befor the faid Leafe was conveyed to Cuthbert Burbege, the faid

John Braine died, after whofe death the faid Margaret did take
vp fome monye at the plaie howfe, called the Curtine, but by what
right or by whofe fufferaunce, fhe fo receyved the fame, this depon[t]
knowethe not, and to that poinct of thes Interr about the mayntenance of the faid Margaret Braine in thefe futes, this depon[t]
faiethe, That he can fay nothinge but he hath heard yt reported,
that the faid Myles hath made great boaft, that it is he, that will
maynteyne and defend her herin, al be it fhe did procure his trouble before the coroners enqueft and did impute to him the deathe
of her hufband, and procured him to be indighted as a comon
barreter, but of his owne knoweledge herin, he knoweth nothinge,
nor further, Matter to thes Interr to his prefente remembraunce
can declare/

　　　　　　　　　　　　[Signed]　Per me Henricū Bett.

Elene Gafcoyne wyfe of Percyvall Gafcoyne of london peawterer
of the age of l[tie] yeres or theraboutes/ fworn and exd the viij
Daye of Maye in the xxxiiij yere &ct
To the firft/ Interr/ that fhe knew Jo. Braynes deceffed/　And
knoweth the now comp[l] James Burbage/ And knoweth Margarett
the faid Jo. Braynes wydow, and alfo Roberte Myles, the nowe
defend[tes] in this caufe/ and faith that fhe hath knowne the now
comp[l] James Burbage about a dozen or xiij yeres and the faid
wydow braynes about the fame fpace/ but for the other defend[t]
Myles/ fhe faith that fhe hath not known him but about x yeres/

To the 2. Int. that as fhe dothe Remember/ the faid Brayne &
Myles did owe to this depo[tes] late hufbande Noble/ the fome of
xx[li] or theraboutes vpon ther bonde/ and when the faid Noble
dyed/ the faid debt grew due to her fecond hufband Whyte in the
right of this depo[t]/ as Executrice of her hufbandes/ Nobles will/
And faith that the faid money grew due for Carpentrye wo[r]ke at
the Jn w[t]out Allgate called the George/ w[ch] money/ being vnpayed in her hufband Whytes dayes/ the faid whyte caufed the
faid Brayne to be arefted for the fame/ and then vpon compoficion and a daye fixed for the paym[t] therof/ James Burbage the

now comp¹/ and one Gardener were furetyes for the paymᵗ of the fame/ and of more money wᵗ all/

To the 3. that fhe doth well Remember/ that ther compoficion for the paymᵗ of the faid debt to the faid whyte was vˡˡ by yere/ till the fame debt were fullye payd/ But out of what place/ or thing/ it was to be payd/ fhe faith fhe doth not fo Remember/ And to the reft of this Jnt fhe faith fhe cannot depofe/

To the 4. that true it is bothe fhe this depoᵗ and her faid hufband Whyte made many Jorneys from ther houffe in Sᵗ Johnes ftreet to the place called the Theater beyond Shordiche/ to the faid Brayne/ for the faid money/ but had it not wᵗ the wᶜʰ this depoᵗᵉˢ faid hufband Whyte was moch offended/ and in the end fewd the faid Suretyes for the fame/ Whervpon the faid Brayne & his furetyes did compound the matter wᵗ the faid Whyte/ & for the performaunce of ther compoficion/ they became bound to the fame Whyte ether in A Statute or Recognifaunce/ But whether her faid hufband Whyte/did affigne & fett over to the faid James Burbage/ or to any ells, the bond wherin the faid Brayne and Myles ftood firft bound for the paymᵗ of the money wᵗ A lettre of Attorney to few them thervpon/fhe faith fhe cannot certenlye depofe/ Nor more can fay to this Jnt/
Vpon the reft of the Jnterrogatories fhe is not exᵈ/ by the direccion of the faid James Burbage the now comp¹/

[Her mark] ⚔

Johne Hynde of london haberdaffher/ of the age of lxiiij yeres or theraboutes fworne and exᵈ the xxiiij daye of Julye in the yere laft aforefaid &ct

To the firft Jnt myniftred vnto him/ that he knew Johne Brayne/ named in this Jnt whille he lieved/ and knoweth James Burbage the now comp¹

To the 2. that true it is he this depoᵗ about xiij yeres paft/ wᶜʰ as he thinketh was in Anno Dni/ 1579. and as he taketh it/ about

the xxiij[th] Daye of June in the after noon/ did caufe one Saun-
ders/ then one of the Se[r]iaunt*es* at mace to the Shyreff of london/
or his yeomen/ to arreſt and attache the body of the now comp[l]
as he came down Graces ſtreet towardes the Croffe Keys there/
to a Playe/ for the ſome of fyve pounds & xiij[d]/ the w[ch] this
depo[t] by Ordre of lawe had before that Recovered for charges
in Sute of law againſt the ſaid Johne Brayne/ and the now comp[l]/
by a niſi prius tryed in the Guilde Halle/ london And the ſaid
Saunders did accordinglie execute his p*r*ecepte, vpon the bodye
of the ſaid comp[l]/ And whether it was that daye/ or how ſoon
after/ he doth not now Reme*m*ber/ the ſaid Saunders came to
this depo[t]/ and payd vnto him/ the ſaid ſome of v[ll] xiij[d] in diſ-
charge of the ſaid Recou*e*rye/ And this is as moche as he ca*n*
ſaye to theſe Jnt/

[Signed] by me John Hynd

Will*i*am James of Chapell Iſode in the Countie Dublyn w[t]in the
Quenes Ma[tes] Realme of Jreland/ gent of the age of xlj yeres
or therabout*es* ſworne & ex[d] the xxiiij daye of July in the yere
aforeſaid &ct

To the firſt Jnt. that he did knowe John Braynes deceſſed named
in this Jnt And knoweth all the p*ar*ties p[l] and defend[t]/

To the 5. that he doth think he knoweth the hand wrytinge of
the ſaid Jo. Braynes/ p*ar*tlie by waye of wryting of his owne
name to ſome Acquitta*n*ce or Acquitta*n*ces/ made to this depo[t]/
And p*ar*tlie for that about Anno 1579 he ſaw the hand of the ſaid
Jo. Brayne to a dede of gyft p*r*oduced by one Will*i*am Thomſon
of Ratcliffe before this depo[t] when he was the lord wentwo[r]ths
bayliffe of his Mano[r] & lib*er*tyes of Stebneth/ this depo[t] being
then to extend the good*es* of the ſaid Jo. Braynes/ at the Sute of
one Jo. Hynde/ for xxv[ll] x[s] i[d] debt & damag*es* or therabout*es*
Recou*e*red againſt the ſaid Jo. Brayne/ w[ch] Dede of gyft (as this
depo[t] then took it) was made by the ſaid Braynes to the foreſaid
Will*i*am Thomſon/ that maryed the ſaid Braynes wyves Siſter/

rather of purpoſe to defeat and defrawde the ſaid Execution/ and others that afterwardes came againſt him/ then of troth or true meaning/ And therfore this depoᵗ wold not allowe of the ſaid dede/ But to the handwryting of Robert Myles/ he knoweth it not And more or further to this Jnt. he ſaith he cannot depoſe

To the 6. that he doth verelie think in his conſcience/ that the Bill of Accompte ſhewed to this depoᵗ in a Booke of Reconinges at the tyme of this his Examinacion/ is the proper handwryting of the ſaid Jo. Braynes/ But whether the ſame Bill was written after/ or before any Awarde paſſed betwene them/ he ſaith he can not tell/ Nor more can ſaye to this Jnt./

To the 7. that he cannot tell/ nether hath he heard of any mo Dedes of Gyfte that the ſaid Jo. Brayne made to any other perſone or perſones of his goodes and chattells other then he hath before ſaid in the 5. Jnt. And to the reſt of this Jnt. he ſaith he cannot depoſe/

To the 9 that he cannot tell how long it is ſyns/ that the ſaid Jo. Braynes/ and the foreſaid Robert Myles did abſent them ſelfes from ther Creditoʳˢ/ nor how moche money they owed ther Creditoʳˢ/ nor how ther debt grew/ But he ſaith that he well Remembreth that in Anno 1582 or theraboutes/ he this depoᵗ being Bayliff of the Manoʳ and libertyes aforeſaid/ ther was Dyrected vnto him/ at the Sute of one Anne Wilbram wydowe/ one Execucion of an Cˡⁱ debt againſt the body of the ſaid Jo. Braynes/ But after long travell and ſerche made for the ſaid Jo. Braynes/ he this depoᵗ nor any vnder him could fynde him/ by reaſone wherof/ he this depoᵗ was dryven to make his Retoʳne of non eſt inventus/ And further ſaith that about A° xxvᵗᵒ of her ſaid Maᵗᵉˢ Reigne/ ther was another Execucion Directed vnto him/ againſt bothe the ſaid Jo. Braynes/ and the foreſaid Robert Myles at the Sute of one Jo. Banberye gentleman for lxxxˡⁱ debt/ by vertue wherof this depoᵗ was not onlye to extend ther goodes but alſo to attache ther bodyes/ but by reaſon they both abſented

them felf*es*/ he this depo^t made the lyke Reto^rne for ther bodyes as aforefaid/ But inquyred of ther good*es* to that value/ and certifyed the fame accordinglie/ And what other fome or fomes of money they owed to any other perfone or perfones at that tyme/ other then he hath before faid/ he faith he knoweth not but he thought them to be gretly in debt for that Braines afterward told him this depon*ent* that they had a proteccion vnder Sr Water Waler knight/
Nor more can*n* faye to this Jnt./

To the reft of the Jnt. this depo^t faith that he can*n* fay nothing Nor more faith in this matter/

[Signed] W James

BRAYNE *v.* BURBAGE

Idem, Bundle 228, No. 11, Hilary, 34 Elizabeth (Jan.–Feb., 1591/2.).

[One skin of interrogatories, with a small paper note pinned to it, *ut infra*. Skin good, down to Interrogatory 12; bad from there on, some portions nearly illegible. Skin thonged to 12 large sheets of paper, usual deposition size, bearing signed depositions, *ut infra*.]

INTERROGATORIES.

Intergatories to be miniftred on the p*ar*te & behalf of Margarett Braynes widowe Complaynant agaynft James Burbage Cuthbert Burbage & others defendant*es*

1 **Imprimis** whether doe ye knowe the p*ar*tye playntif, & the p*ar*ties defendant*es* yea or no, Yf fo then, whether doe ye knowe of any fute Comm*en*fed by the faid Margarett Braynes againft the fayd defendaunt*es* of & Conceareinge her tytle vnto the moitye of the Theato^r and all the howfes, and other land*es* and tenementes therevnto belong*ing* in the p*ari*fhe of Saynte Leonard*es* in Shordyche in the Countye of Midlefex, yea or no.

2 **Item** whether doe ye knowe of your owne knowledge, or have heard faye, that divers Controverfies and Contentions weare betweane the fayd James Burbage and one John Brayne the late houfbande of the fayd Complaynant nowe difceafed touchinge the fayd theato^r. And whether did not they fubmitt themfelves vnto the arbitrament of Certayne perfones for the pacificatione of all matters betweane them. And whether did not the fayd arbitrators awarde that the fayd James Burbadge hys executo^rs and affignes fhoulde enioy the one moitye of all the profittes of the premiffes And the fayd John Brayne hys executo^rs and affignes fhoulde enioye the other moitye of the proffettes yea or no.

3 **Item** whether did not they alfo awarde that yf occafione fhoulde be to morgage the premiffes for the borrowinge of money to pay debtes or for the perfourmeinge of any neceffarye thinge Concearneinge the Theato^r, that then bothe they fhoulde ioyne in morgage, and the money comminge and ryfinge of the profittes of the faid Theato^r to goe to the redemptione of the faid morgage yea or no.

4 **Item** wheather did not the faid James Burbadge and the fayd John Brayne accordinge to the faid arbitrament morgage the fayd Theato^r and other the premiffes vnto one John Hyde Citizen and Grofer of London for the fome of one hundrede twentye and fyve poundes or there aboutes to be repaid at a Certaine day and tyme in the fayd morgage lymitted ye or no.

5 **Item** whether was the fayd Theato^r and other the premiffes forfatid vnto the fayd John Hyde yea or no, for that he was not payed hys money at fuche dayes and tymes as was by the faid morgage agreaed vppon Yea or no.

6 **Item** what fomme or fommes of money was payd vnto the fayd John Hyde by the faid John Brayne and the faid James Burbadge in the lyf tyme of the faid John Brayne before the forfature of

the premiffes and what fomme or fommes of money was left
vnpayed at the tyme of the death of the faid John of the aforefayed fomme, for the wᶜʰ yt was morgaged for & what ys paid
fythens his death.

7 **Item** whether did not the faid John Hyde often tymes faye vnto
the faid John Brayne and the faid James Burbage and vnto the
now Complainant and to others that if he were payde his monye
that was dewe and confideracion for the forbering of hit that he
woulde never take any advantage of the faid forfature/

8 **Item** whether did not the faid John Hide promiffis vnto the faid
Complainant that yf he were payde his monye that then he woulde
affure the premiffes vnto the faid Complainant and vnto the faid
James Burbage becaufe he had hit from the hufbonde of the faid
Complainant and the faid Burbage and nowe by the death of her
hufbonde his parte belongeth to the faid Complainant and the
rather to for [sic] that he was payde all his monye favinge
Thyrtye poundes or thereaboutes in the life of the faid Brayne/

9 **Item** whether did not the faid Margarett Brayne offer to paye
the faid thyrtye poundes vnto the faid John Hyde if he woulde
reaffure the premiffes over to her and if he woulde fo doe fhe
woulde be bounde to convaye over a moitye therof vnto the faid
James Burbage in faying that althowgh Burbage woulde defeate
her of her righte yet fhe woulde not fo deale with him And what
aunfwer made the faid John Hide thervnto/

10 **Item** whether did not the faid James Burbage of purpofe detayne
the proffites of the premiffes in his one handes of purpofe to make
a forfature vppon the morgage ye or no And whether did not
the faid James after the death of Braynes vtterly denye the faid
Complainant to receaue any more proffites of the premiffes Contrary to the Arbitramente wherby the faid John Hyde was not
payde his monye accordinge to the faid Arbitramente with the
proffites of the premiffes as oughte to haue binne by the awarde/

11 **Item** whether did not the faid James Burbage intreate the faid
John Hide to convaye the premiffes vnto Cutbarde Burbage his
fonne of porpofe to defeate the faid Complainant of her moyetye
in the premiffes ye or no, if fo then whether did not the faid John
Hyde faye that fhe fhowlde haue her moyetye before he woulde
convaye the premiffes excepte both the faid James and the faid
Cutbarde woulde promiffe that fhe fhoulde haue her moyetye and
righte at there handes.   ye or no/

12 **Item** whether did not the faid James and Cutbert often tymes
promiffe the fayd Complaynaunt that fhe fhoulde have her moitye
in the premiffes, and for that purpofe he fuffered her to enioye
yt and after putt her mofte vnconfcionablye from yt./.

13 **Item** whearas there was an order the thirteanthe of November in
the two & thirtythe yeare of the Queanes M^{tes} raigne made in
the Chauncerye betweane the faid James Burbage Cuthbert Burbage & others defendantes and the faid Margarett Braynes Complaynant that eche partie and their affignes fhoulde performe an
arbitrament made Concearneinge the premiffes, and wheather did
not the fayd Margarett Braynes fo^r her parte come divers tymes
to the theato^r & other the premiffes to entreate the fayd James
Burbage and the fayd Cuthbert Burbage that fhe might enioye
he^r moitye of the premiffes accordinge to the arbitrament & order
thearin taken and what weare the fpeaches of the faid James,
Cuthbert & Richard Burbage therevnto to your remembraunce,
And what do you knowe thearin fpeake yor wholl knowledge/

14 **Item** what fomme or fommes of money or other profittes hathe
the faid James Burbage and Cuthbert Burbage receeved for the
Theator and other the premiffes fithens the laft accompte or
reconeinge made betweane the fayd John Braynes & James Burbage to your knowledge or remembraunce, and what you knowe
thearin, fpeake yor wholle knowlege And what yo^u thinke the
faid John Braynes beftowed in buildinge of the Theator [for his

p*arte*] and what money is dewe vnto him by any of the Burbages
to yor knowledge

Scott [Attorney]

[Pinned to this skin of Interrogatories is a slip of paper addressed to
Mr. Henry Jones, examiner, by Dr. Legg, Master in Chancery, as follows:]

Mr Jones Mr Dr Stanhope & I are defyrous that yow take y^e
exam*i*nacons of fuch witnefes wch fhall be fent to yow in a caufe
betwen widowe brayne pl. & two burbadges defendant*es*.

[Signed]   Tho Legge

[On the upper left corner of skin is the note of three of the four examinations, as follows:]

Joannes Hyde iuratus
  29 Januarij 1591
Radulphus Myles iurat/
  29 Januarij 1591
          Tho Legge
Nicholaus Bifhopp iuratus
  29 Jan*uarij* 1591
          Tho Legge

DEPOSITIONS

> Re*f*ponfio Nicho*l*ai Biffhoppe ad ar^{los} Margarete
> Braynes q*uerentis* verf*us* Jacobu*m* Burbage et
> Cuthb*er*tum Burbage defen*dentes*/ p*er* ordinem
> Curie capt*a* p*er* Henr*icum* Johnes in Cancellar*ia*
> Exa*m*inatorem/

Nicho*l*as Biffhope of the pa*ri*fhe of whyte chapell w^tout Allgate
london Sope maker/ of the age of xxxij yeres or theraboute*s*
fworne and ex^d the xxix daye of Januarye in the xxxiiij yere
& ct^r

To the firft Jnt. that he doth know all the p*arties* pl*aintif* and
defend^{tes}/ And knoweth ther is Sute betwene the faid p*arties*/

for and concerning matter of the Theater at Hallywell/ the par-
ticularitie wherof he knoweth not/

To the 2 that he doth knowe ther was fome Sute betwene James
Burbage one of the now defend^{tes}/ and Jo. Brayne deceffed
the late hufband of Margarett Brayne/ in matter concerning the
faide Theater/ And to the reft of this Jnterrogatory he faith he
cannot depofe/

To the 3 that he is ingnorant

To the 4 that he is ingnorant

To the 5 that he is ingnorant

To the 6 that he is ingnorant

To the 7 that he can fay nothing

To the 8 that he can fay nothing

To the 9 that he can fay nothing

To the 10 that he can fay nothing

To the 11 that he can fay nothing

To the 12 that he is ingnorant

To the 13 that he doth Remember he hath fene fuche an ordre as
in this Jnt. is mencioned/ for the performance of fuche an Arby-
tryment/ And doth know that the faid Margaret Braynes w^t one
Robert Myles came at feuerall tymes to the faid Theater & namely
vpon one of the playe dayes and intreated James Burbage one of
the now defend^{tes} that fhe might enioye her Moytie of the
premiffes according to the Awarde/ and Ordre of the Chaun-
cerye/ And the anfwer wch James Burbage made therunto/ was

that before fhe fhuld haue any thing to do there/ fhe fhuld fhewe
good ordre for it/ and then the faid Myles fayd that he had a
fufficient ordre of the Chauncery for the fame/ & fhewed him
fome papers/ and then the faid James Burbage called his Rafcall
& knave/ and fayd that before he wold lofe his poffeffion/ he wold
make xx contempt*es*/ and then/ the wyfe of the faid James/ and
ther yongeft fone called Rychard Burbage/ fell vpon the faid
Myles & beat him and drave both him and the comp¹ away/ faying
that yf they did tarye to heare the playe as others did/ they
fhuld/ but to gather any of the money/ that was gyven to [*come
in* (stricken out)] go vpon/ they fhuld not/ And faith that Cuthbert Burbage the other of the defend^tes was not there/ to his
Remembraunce/

To the 14. that he [is] vtterlye ingnora*n*t/ Nor more can faye to
all the faid Jnterr*ogatories*/

                                   [Signed]   Nicholus Byfhop

John Allen of the parifhe of St Buttolles wth out Bifhops gate
london Jnholder of the age of xxxv yeres or y*er*about*es* fworne
and ex^d the vj^th daye of ffebr*uary* in the yere aforefaid & ct^r.
To the firft Jnt that he doth knowe all the p*ar*ties plaintif &
defend^tes named/ And knoweth of the Sute betwene the faid
comp¹/ and the faid defend^tes concerni*n*g her tytle in the moytie
of the place called the Theater and of the houfes and tenem^tes
longing to the fame/ in S^t leon*ardes* parifhe in Shordiche nere
london/

To the 2. that he doth knowe that whille the now compl^tes late
hufband Brayne lyved/ the originall of the faid Sute and contro-
u*er*cyes began betwene him & James Burbage the one of the now
defend^tes/ for & about the inter*e*ft & tytle wch the faid Brayne
had in the faid Theater & p*re*miffes/ And faith that he hath
crediblie heard/ and beleveth to be true, that for A quyet end &
order to be had in the faid Sute & co*n*trovercie then betwene
them/ they did fubmitt themfelf*es* to the Arbytryment & Award

of indyffrent ffrendes/ and that they made and Award in the fame betwene them/ the certentye wherof he knoweth not/ But he hath heard it fayd/ that they Awarded the one half of all the profittes growing by & of the faid Theater to the faid Brayne his executo^rs & affignes/ and the other half to the faid James Burbage/ his executo^rs and affignes/

To the 3. that he is ingnorant

To the 4. that he hath heard James Burbage the one of the now defend^tes faye & affirme/ that he and the faid Johne Brayne did Morgage the faid Theater and the forefaid premiffes/ to John Hyde named in the Jnt/ vpon the fome of one hundreth twentie and fyve poundes or theraboutes/
To the 5. that he hath hearde both the faid James Burbage/ and the now comp^l faye & afferme that the faid Morgage fell forfetted to the said Hyde/ for the not repaym^t of the faid Cxxv^ll at the daye fixed for the repayment therof/ by the faid Morgage/

To the 6. that he is ingnorant

To the 7 that he can fay nothing

To the 8. that he can fay nothing

To the 9 that he can fay nothing

To the 10. that he doth think in his confcience/ that the faid James Burbage did detayne the profittes of the premiffes in his own handes of purpofe/ that the faid morgage fhuld be forfetted/ And after the death of the faid Jo. Brayne/ did vtterlye deny/ that the now comp^l fhuld receyve & have any more benefitt or profitt of the fame/ contrarye to the forefaid Awarde/ So as therby the faid Hyde was not payd his money w^t the proffyttes of the premiffes/ as it was truelie ment and intended by the faid Award/

To the 11. that he can fay nothing

To the 12. that he knoweth not whether the ſaid defend^{tes} did promiſſe the comp^l that ſhe ſhuld haue the Moytie of the profitt*es* of the p*r*emyſſes/　But he ſaith that he well knoweth that ſhe had for a tyme, her p*a*rte in the p*r*emiſſes and did enioye it/ but how afterwardes ſhe was put from it/ he ſaithe he knoweth not/ otherwyſe then as he thinketh/ by the wrongfull dealing of the defend^{tes}/ w^t her/

To the 13. that he doth knowe/ that after the compl^{tes} huſband Brayne dyed/ And y^t Sute followed afterward*es* betwene her then wydowe/ and the ſaid defend^{tes} co*n*cerni*n*g her tytle by her huſband*es* death to the one half of the profittes of the ſaid Thea-ter/ in the Chauncerye/ the ſaid Co^rte of Chauncerye made an Ordre/ that aſwell the defend^{tes} as the ſaid comp^l ſhuld on ether of ther p*a*rtes/ p*e*rforme the Arbitrym^t & Award wch had bene made before that/ betwene the ſaid Jo. Brayne/ and the ſaid James Burbage/ wch was/ as is beforeſaid/ that ether of the ſaid Jo. Brayne/ and James Burbage/ ſhuld by even porc*i*ons devyde the proffitt*es* and be*n*efitt Ryſing by the vſe of the ſaid Theater/ betwen them/ ther executo^rs and aſſignes/ And ſaithe that he hath ſene the ſame comp^l w^t one Myles come Dyvers tymes to the ſaid Theater/ & hath deſyred the ſaid defend^{tes}/ that according to the ſaid Arby-trament & Ordre of the Chauncerye/ ſhe might take Receyve and enioye her Moytie of the ſaid profitt*es*/　And the ſaid defend^{tes} and one other of the ſaid James Burbage ſones called Ry. did raylle vpon the comp^l/ and the ſaid Myles & w^t vyolence Drave them out/ [*And ſayd that they wold not leave the poſſeſſion of the* (stricken out)] ſaying that ſhe ſhuld haue no Moytie there/ And then this depo^t/ being there/ did as a ſervaunt wiſhe the ſaid James Burbage to [*take hede* (stricken out)] haue A con-ſcience in the matter ſaying vnto him/ that he him ſelf knew that the woma*n* had A right in the ſame by her huſband/ and y^t it was her huſband*es* welthe that builded the Theater/ as every bodye knoweth/ and he then did anſ*w*ere/ hang her ho^r qd he/ ſhe getteth nothing here/ lett her wyn it at the Com*m*en lawe/ and bring the Shiref w^t her to put her in poſſeſſion/ and then he wold tell her more of his mynde/ Then this depo^t told him that thoughe he overreached her hufband being but a plaine & fymple man/ yet fhe being enforced to feke remeadye againft yo^u/ hath the Chauncerye being the highest co^rte and A co^rte of confcience on her fyde and hath an Ordre out of the fame to haue her moytie therof/ Confcience qd he/ god*es* blood what do yo^u tell me of Confcience/ or Ordres/ No qd this depo^t/ Remem*b*er yor felf well/ ffor yf my lord Chauncello^r/ make an Ordre againft yo^u/ yo^u were beft to obey it/ otherwyfe it will prove A contempt/ and then yo^u fhall purches my lord Chauncello^{rs} Difpleaf*ure*/ and he made anf*were* that he cared not for any contempt/ faying/ that yf ther were xx co*n*tempt*es*/ and as many Jniu*n*ccions he wold w^tftand them all/ before he wold lofe his poffeffion/ And further faith that/ when this Depo^t about viij Daies after came to him for certen money wch he deteyned from this depo^t and his fellowes/ of fome of the Dyvydent money betwene him & them/ growing alfo by the vfe of the faid Theater/ he denyed to pay the fame/ he this depo^t told him that belike he ment to deale w^t them/ as he did w^t the po^r wydowe/ mean*in*g the now comp^l/ wifhing him he wold not do fo/ for yf he did/ they wold com- pleyne to ther lorde & M^r the lord Admyrall/ and then he in A Rage litle Reu*er*encing his hono^r/ & eftate/ fayd/ by a great othe/ that he cared not for iij of the beft lord*es* of them all/ And further faithe/ that at the tyme when the comp^l and the faid Myles Requyred (as is beforefaid) her Moytie of the faid Theater & p*r*emiffes this depo^t found the forefaid Ry. Burbage the yongeft fone of the faid James Burbage there/ w^t A Broome ftaff in his hand/ of whom when this depo^t afked what fturre was there/ he anf*w*ered in laughing phrafe hew they come for A moytie/ But qd he (holding vppe the faid [*ftaff of that ftuck in the* (stricken out)] broomes staff) I haue, I think deliu*er*ed [*them* (stricken out)] him A moytie w^t this & fent them packing/ and then this depo^t fayd vnto him & his ffather/ that the faid Myles might haue an Acc*i*on againft the faid Rychard/ Tufche qd the father/ no J warra*u*nt yo^u but where my fone hath now beat him hence/ my fones/ yf they wilbe Rueled by me/ fhall at ther next com*in*g pro-

vyde charged Piſtolles wᵗ powder and hempſede/ to ſhoote them
in the legg*es*/   But to his Reme*m*bra*n*ce he ſaw not Cuthbert the
other defendᵗ there/

To the 14. that he knoweth not whan the laſt Accompte was made
of the profittes of the ſaid Theater betwene the ſaid James Bur-
bage/ and the ſaid Jo. Braynes/ But he ſaithe/ that for theſe v.
yeres he verelie thinketh that the ſaid James Burbage hath Receyved at the leaſt of the p*ro*fitt*es* of the ſaid Theater & other the
p*re*miſſes to the ſame belonging/ an hundreth poundes or CC
m*ar*k*es* by yere/ for his owne ſhare/   And more he ſaith not to
all the ſaid J*n*terr*ogatories*/

[Signed]   Joⁿ Allein.

Raphe Myles of london Sope maker/ but free of the company of
the Gold ſmythes/ of the age of xxvij yeres or therabou*tes*
ſworne & examyned the xᵗʰ Daye of ffebruarye in the yeare aforeſaid & ctʳ   To the firſt Jnt that he doth knowe all the p*ar*ties pˡ
and defendᵗᵉˢ And knoweth that ther hath bene & yet is Sute &
co*n*trau*er*cye betwene them/ for the one half & Moytie of the
Place called the Theater at Shordiche nere london/ & of the
howſes & tenemᵗᵉˢ longing to the ſame/

To the 2. that he hath heard by credible report/ and beleveth to
be true that ther was co*n*trovercye and contenc*i*on/ betwene Jo.
Brayne deceſſed the late huſband of the now compˡ/ and James
Burbage one of the now defendᵗᵉˢ/ touching the ſaid Theater/
And that they ſubmitted them ſelf*es* to the ordre and Arbitryment
of certen p*er*ſones for the pacyficac*i*on therof/ to witt one John
Hill/ and Richard Turnoʳ   And that they made an Award betwene them in Julye 1578. in the xxᵗʰ yere of her Maᵗᵉˢ Reynge/
by wᶜʰ Awarde/ they ordred that the ſaid Jo. Brayne his executoʳˢ
& aſſignes ſhuld haue & enioye the one half or moytie of the
Rent*es* and p*ro*fitt*es* Ryſing and growinge of the ſaid Theater &
of the howſes & building*es* therunto belonging/ and the ſaid
James Burbage his executoʳˢ and aſſignes to haue & enioye the

other half or moytie of the premiffes/ w^t Dyvers other covenantes as by the fame Award maye more at lardge appere/ w^{ch}
this Depo^t hath redd/

To the 3. that the faid Arbitrato^{rs} did alfo award/ that yf occafion
fhuld move them to borow any fome of Money for the paym^t of
ther debtes owing for any neceffarye vfe & thing concerning the
faid Theater/ that then the faid James Burbage and the faid Jo.
Brayne/ fhuld Joyne in pawning or morgage of ther eftate &
intereft of & in the fame/ and the money that fhuld ryfe of the
Rentes and proffittes of the fame Theater & of the howfes apper-
teyning therunto/ fhuld go to the Redempcion of the faid Mor-
gage/ The wch Morgage being redemed/ and fuche debtes as then
were owing dew for & about the matter of the faid Theater being
payde/ that then the faid Jo. Brayne his executo^{rs} & affignes
fhuld take haue & enioy to his owne vfe/ all the profittes of the
faid Theater till he were fatiffyed of fuche fome of money as the
faid James Burbage was owing vnto him for and in liew of
fomoch more money lade out & defrayed by him vpon & about
the faid Theater/ then the faid James Burbage had lade out in
the fame/

To the 4. that he doth knowe/ that for the fome of one hundreth
twentie & fyve poundes/ or theraboutes/ the faid James Burbage
and John Brayne did morgage ther leafe & intereft of the faid
Theater & of the premiffes longing to the fame/ to Jo. Hyde
grocer named in this Jnterrogatory/

To the 5. that he hath heard faye/ that the faid Morgage fell forfetted to the faid Jo. Hyde/ for that the faid money was not
repayd vnto him at the dayes lymytted for the paym^t therof/

To the 6. that he hath heard the faid Jo. Hyde confeffe and affirme
after the deceffe of the faid Brayne that he was fatiffyed of all
the money wch he lent vpon the fame Theater [w^t *the intereft*

therof, in the lyf tyme of the ſaid Jo Brayne (stricken out)] ſaving the ſome of xxx^{li} or therabout*es*/ as he Remem̃brethe/

To the 7. that he hath heard the ſaid Jo. Hyde promes to the now
Comp^l the ſaid Braynes wydow ſyns her huſband dyed/ in the
pre*ſ*ence & hearing of this depo^t and others/ that yf he were payd
the money that was behynde vnpayd/ of the ſome wch he lent
vpon the ſaid Morgage/ he wold never take any advantage of
the furfetture of the ſaid Morgage/

To the 8. that he hath heard the ſaid John Hyde promiſe the ſaid
comp^l/ in the pre*ſ*ence & hearing of the foreſaid per*ſ*ones/ that
yf he were payd his money behynde vnpayd/ he wold deliu*er*
vppe the leaſe that laye forfetted in his hande/ to her & the ſaid
James Burbage/ as it was morgaged vnto him by the ſaid Burbage
& her huſband Brayne/

To the 9. that he was pre*ſ*ent w^t others/ whan the ſaid Comp^l the
wydow Brayne/ offred to the ſaid Jo. Hyde/ that yf he wold
deliu*er* vppe the leaſe vnto her/ ſhe wold make ſhyft for the
money that was behynde/ and wold be bounde to aſſure to the
ſaid James Burbage, the one half therof/ although he went about
to do her wrong in it/ Wherunto the ſaid Jo. Hyde made an-
ſwer/ that he wold not ſo do/ but whan qd he/ I haue my money/
I will deliu*er* it vppe to yo^u both/ as I had it of yor huſband &
him/ and then ſhe told him ſaying/ Mr Hyde yf yo^u do otherwyſe/
yo^u do vndoe me/ ffeare not M^{res} Brayne (qd he) I wilbe as good,
as my worde whan I am payd my money/ ffor had it not bene
for yor huſband whom I knew to be of Creditt/ I wold not haue
delt w^t the other/ or wo^{r}d*es* to this effecte/

To the 10. that he did heare ſaye ſyns the deceſſe of the ſaid
Brayne/ y^t the ſaid James Burbage did earneſtlie purſuade the
ſaid comp^l to beſtow all the money that ſhe was hable to make in
reparing and building about the ſaid Theater/ and in that reſpecte

he fuffred her A certen tyme/ to take & Receyve the one half of
the profittes of the Gallaries of the faid Theater vntill fhe had
fpent & beftowed vpon the fame/ all that fhe had Receyved and
A great deale more/ And then on a foden he wold not fuffer
her to receyve any more of the proffittes there/ faying that he
muft take & Receyve all, till he had payd the debtes/ And then
fhe was conftrayned as his fervaunt/ to gather the money/ & to
deliuer it vnto him/ and fhortlie after/ he wold not fuffer her
any waye to medle in the premiffes/ but thruft her out of all/
and fo vfeth her to this Daye/ againft Dyvers Ordres out of the
Coᵣte of Chauncerye/ in verye contempcyous fort/

To the 11. that he can fay nothing

To the 12. that he can fay no more then he hath before faid to
the xᵗʰ Jnterrogatory/

To the 13. that he doth knowe/ ther was fuch an Ordre/ & to
the fame effecte/ as in this Jnterrogatory is mencioned/ the wᶜʰ
Ordre the faid compˡ being verye willing to performe the fame/
went Dyvers tymes wᵗ fondrye her frendes and neighboʳˢ to the
now defendᵗᵉˢ/ and demaunded of them her moytie of the Rentes
and profittes of the faid Theater & premiffes according [to] the
faid Ordre/ and they did vtterlye deny fo to do/ in the hearing
of this depoᵗ and others of credit and reputacion/ the faid James
Burbage faying he wold obey no fuche Ordre/ nor cared not for
them/ Revyling the compˡ wᵗ termes of Murdring hoʳ & otherwife & chardged her & her companye to get them of his grounde/
Or elles he wold fett them of wᵗ no eafe/ At wᶜʰ tyme Cuthberde
Burbage the other defendᵗ came to them/ and then the faid
compˡ demaunded of him/ the performance of the faid Ordre/
and he made anfwer/ he wold not ftand to any fuch ordre/ and
willed her & her company to gett them thence faying thow haft
nothing to do here/ nether fhalt thow haue any thing to do here/
and fo wᵗ moche threatening and manacyng, fhe and her companye went awaye/

To the 14. that he hathe heard faye by credible reporte/ that the
faid James Burbage/ & his affignes & fervaunt*es*/ fyns the deceffe
of the faid Jo. Brayne/ hath Receyved great fomes of money/
to the value of feaven or eight hundreth pound*es*/ of Rent*es*
and proffitt*es* growing of the faid Theater and the app*ur*tynanc*es*
longing & adioyni*ng* to the fame/ & deteyneth in his & his fones
hand*es*/ afwell the comp^ltes part/ wch fhe ought to haue both by
the faid Awarde/ and ordre of the Chauncerye/ as ther owne/
to the po^r womans vtter fpoyll & vndoing/ her faid hufband
having beftowed & lade vp*p*on the fame (well known to them that
knewe him) vj or vij^Cli more/ then the faid James Burbage did/
Soas by this g^t wrong myniftered by the defend^tes to the now
comp^l/ the comp^l being indebted abrode to the value of foure
or fyve hundreth poundes/ fhe is enforced to hyde her felf/ and
to lieve in g^t myferye/ But whan the laft Accompt was made
betwene the faid Brayne and the faid James Burbage/ he knoweth
not/ But he faithe that it doth appere by the Booke of Reconi*ng*
of the proper hand wrytinge of the faid Brayne/ made betwene
him and the faid Burbage in his lyfe tyme/ that the faid James
Burbage was then in his debte of the one moytie of CCxxxix^ll
& od money/ And otherwyfe to this Jnt. he faith he ca*n*not de-
pofe/   Nor furth^r faithe in this matter/

[Signed]   p*er* me Raphe Miles

Johne Hyde of london Grocer/ of the age of lx yeres or therabout*es* fworne and ex^d the xij^th daye of ffebruarie/ in the yere
aforefaid & ct^r

To the firft Jnt. that he doth know all the p*ar*ties pl*ai*ntiff &
defend^tes named in this Jnt*er*ro*ga*tory/   And faith that he hath
heard of Sute and controu*er*sy depending betwene the faid p*ar*-
ties/ for & concerni*ng* the Theater beyond Shordiche w^thout
Biffhops gate london/ the certentye of wch Sute/ he ca*n*not depofe

To the 2. that he did heare fay/ that in the lyfe tyme of John

Brayne deceffed/ the late hufband of the now comp¹ ther was
fome contencion/ and controuercye betwene him and James Burbage one of the now defend^tes Concerning the faid Theater/
But what end the fame contencion took/ he faith he is ingnorant

To the 3. that he is ingnorant

To the 4. that true it is/ the faid James Burbage and the faid
John Brayne did Joyntlie Morgage the intereft they had in the
faid Theater to this depo^t vppon & for the fome of Cxxv^ll as he
doth now Remember or theraboutes/ to be repayd at a yeres end
as [this deponent] doth now call to mynde/
To the 5. that for nonpaym^t of the faid money they forfetted the
faid Theater to this depo^t/ and fo remayned forfetted vnto him
feuerall yeres/

To the 6. that nether the faid James Burbage/ nor John Brayn
payd vnto this depo^t any part or parcell of the faid money ether
before the faid forfetture/ nor long after it was forfetted/ Nor
how moche was left vnpayd of the fame at the death of the fame
Jo. Brayne/ Nor how moche therof hath bene payd fyns his
deathe/

To the 7. that it is verye truc/ that he this depo^t/ did many and
fondrye tymes tell bothe the faid Jo. Brayne/ the faid James Bur-
bage/ the now comp¹/ and others her ffrendes/ that yf he this
depo^t were payd his money that was behynde due [and fome
reafonable confideration] for the forbearing therof/ that he wold
never take any advantage of the faid forfeture/

To the 8. that it is true indede/ he this depo^t did dyvers tymes tell
the now comp¹/ that yf he were payd his money/ he wold make
over the faid Theater to her and the faid James Burbage by caufe
her hufband & the faid Burbage did Joyntlie Morgage it vnto him/
And this anfwer he this depo^t made vnto the faid comp¹, fondrye
yeres/ and at the laft he told her that fyns he had forborne his

money ſo long/ he could do it no more/ ſo as they that came firſt to paye him/ ſhould haue it of him/ as he doth now Remember/

To the 9. that it maye be the ſaid compˡ did offer this depoᵗ the money behynd vnpayd vnto him/ of the ſaid Morgage/ ffor ſhe came many & often tymes vnto him concerning the ſame/ but in troth he doth not Remember ſhe made him any ſuche offer/ But he ſaith that yf ſhe had/ and had performed the ſame/ he wold rathʳ have put it over vnto her/ then to the ſaid Burbageſ/ ffor that ſhe did greatlie complayne vnto him/ that James Burbage did her wrong/ & ſoght to put her from it/ And ſaith that to his Remembrance/ he did not heare her ſaye that yf this Depoᵗ did put it over to her/ ſhe wold be bounde to convey the one Moytye of it to the ſaid James Burbage/ And otherwiſe to this *Jnterrogatory* he ſaith he cannot depoſe/

To the 10. that he can ſay no more/ but that he did heare ſaye/ yᵗ the ſaid James Burbage after the death of the ſaid Jo. Brayne/ dyd denye/ the compˡ to receyve any of the profitteſ of the ſaid Theater/

To the 11. that true it is/ the ſaid James Burbage was ſondrye tymes in hand wᵗ this depoᵗ, that vpon the paymᵗ of the money behynde and ſome conſideracion for the forbearing therof/ he this deponᵗ ſhuld convey over the premiſſes to his ſone Cuthbert Burbage/ and this depoᵗ was verye loth ſo to do/ wᵗʰout the conſent of the compˡ/ And at the laſt he and his ſone brought to this depoᵗ A lettre from one Mʳ Cope one of the Lord Treaforoʳˢ gentlemen/ the ſaid Cuthberteſ Mʳ/ that he this depoᵗ wold at his Requeſt and as he might be able to do this depoᵗ any frendſhip or pleaſure in any his occaſiones to his lord & Mʳ/ ſhuld convey over his intereſt of & in the premiſſes to his ſervaunt Cuthbert Burbage the ſone of the ſaid James vppon the paymᵗ of ſuche money as was due vnto him & vnpaid/ and vpon ſome conſideracion for the forbearing of it/ And this depoᵗ (partlie at the faid gentlemans Requeft/ and partlie at inftant entreatye of the faid James Burbage & his faid fone) did indede vppon the confideracions aforefaid convey over the premiffes to the faid Cuthbert/ But whether this depo^t faid vnto them that he wold not fo do/ except the comp^l had her moytie in the fame/ or not/ he doth not Remember/ But he well Remembreth/ that he wiffhed the faid Burbages to do the comp^l no wronge/ her hufband was dead/ & had left her in g^t lack/ and that he did vndoe him felf/ by entring in the doinges of the Theato^r/ and they faid/ & many tymes haue faid/ that they wold do her no wronge/

To the 12. that true it is, the faid Burbages did promes this Depo^t that took what was the compl^{tes} right & due to haue/ that fhe fhuld haue it at ther handes

To the 13. that he can fay nothing

To the 14. that to the firft poynt of this Jnterrogatory he faith he can fay nothing/ And to the fecond poynt of the fame he faith/ that he doth thinke that when the faid Braynes entred into the Accion of the faid Theater/ he was wo^{r}th fyve hundreth poundes at the leaft and by commen fame wo^{r}th A thowfand markes/ and A man well thoght of in london/ And this depo^t verelie thinketh he beftowed the fame/ or the moft part therof vppon the fame Theater/ to his vndoing/ And to the laft poynt of this Jnterrogatory he faith he cannot depofe/ And more he faithe he cannot faye to all the faid Jnterrogatories/

[Signed] per me John Hyd grocer

BRAYNE *v.* BURBAGES

Idem, Bundle 228, No. 10, Hilary and Easter, 34 Elizabeth (Feb., April, May, 1592).

[Four skins of interrogatories—one to John Hyde, one to Nicholas Bishop, one to Ralph Miles, and one to John Allen—thonged in this order to the depositions, which are incorrectly arranged in the following order— Bishop, 2½ sheets, Miles, 3 sheets, Allen 2, Hyde 1.

The following transcripts are arranged, however, in the chronological order in which the depositions were taken, which is also the order of the interrogatories—Hyde, Bishop, Miles, Allen—the interrogatories to each being placed immediately before the answers to it, as the more convenient.

These four depositions, taken in behalf of the Burbages, are in effect the cross-examination of the plaintiff's four principal witnesses.]

INTERROGATORIES TO HYDE

Articles to be miniſtred to John Hyde Citezein and grocer of London as followeth.

ex *parte* Jacobi Burbage
et Cuthberti Burbage.

Impr whether are you John Hyde examined in the Courte of Chauncerye in and vpon the Queſtions and to theſe matters following, or to Articles to theſſecte thereof, And whether haue yow declared yor knowledge and conſcience therein yea or no.

Bothe how and of whome yow had the Leaſe of the Theater to yow conveyed/ And vpon what conſideracion And that before yow did grauntt the ſame to Cuthbert Burbage yow did repute the ſame to be yor owne duringe the ſaide Leaſe.

And that yow did not compounde wth John Brayne for yor title in his life tyme, And that yow did at noe tyme receyve moneye of him by force of anye ſuche Compoſition And that yow at noe tyme ment or had cauſe to deale wth the ſaide John Brayne for the ſaide Leaſe or anye *parte* thereof, nor wth any other on the behalf of the plaintyfe or any for her.

DEPOSITION OF JOHN HYDE

Reſponſio Joha*nn*is Hyde ad ar^los Jacobi Burbage et [Cuthberti] Burbage/ defen*dentum* ver*ſus* Brayne vid*uam* q*uerentum* [per] ordinem Cur*ie* capt*a* per Henr*icum* Johnes in Canc[ellaria] Exa*m*inatorem/

[This heading stricken out by the clerk on rearranging the depositions for filing.]

Johne Hyde of london grocer/ of the age of lx yeres or ther-aboutes sworne and ex^d the xxj daye of ffebruary in the xxxiiij yere & ct^r To the first Jnterrogatory That he hath bene ex^d twyce alredye before now in this Co^{r}te in the matters in controuercye betwene the comp^l & the now defend^{tes}/ that is to saye/ first in the substance of the Cause/ and secondlye now of late vpon matter of contempte alledged by the comp^l against the defend^{tes}/ wherin he thinketh he hath sayd truelye/ according to his con-science knowledge & Remembrance/

To the 2. that one Prvne A Broker/ was the first man that offred the lease of the Theater in morgage to this depo^t/ and after he had broght this depo^t acquainted w^t James Burbage/ and one Jo. Brayne/ he the sayd James Burbage & Brayne did Joyntlye/ morgage to this depo^t the said lease for one Cxxv^{ll} or yeraboutes and Joyntlie they and the said Prvne as he Remembreth did entre into bonde to this depo^t for the Redempcion therof/ at A daye/ but it was forfetted to this depo^t/ at the least v or vj yeres [first written *vij or viij yeres*] or theraboutes as he Remembreth in wch space/ he this depo^t did repute the same leasse to be his owne during the yeres therin then to come/

To the 3. that after the said leasse became forfetted to him this depo^t/ Jt was agreed on both sydes/ that yf the said Burbage and Brayne or ether of them/ did pay this depo^t v^{ll} A weke/ till all the foresaid Morgage money were payd/ w^t some reasonable con-sideracion for the forbearing of it/ that then they shuld haue ther lease againe/ wch they performed by the space of iiij^{or} or v. weekes after/ but they performed no more/ and so suffred ther lease to be ones againe forfetted to this depo^t/ And saithe that in troth he this depo^t did never compounde w^t the said Brayne for the right and interest this depo^t had in the said lease by the said forfetture at any tyme/ in the lyfe tyme of the sayd Brayne/ nor ever receyved any money of him to his Remembrance vpon any suche composicion/ And to the rest of this Jnterrogatory/ he

faith/ that he can say no more in effecte/ then he hath heretofore
depofed & fayd on the ·compltes behaulf in the matter of the faid
contempt/ Nor further can fay to thefe Jnterrogatories/

[Signed]   per me John Hyde

INTERROGATORIES TO NICHOLAS BISHOP

> **Interrs** to be mynyftered vpon the parte and
> behaulf of James Burbage and Cuthbert Bur-
> bage to Nycholas Bifhop, accordinge to an order
> made the xiij of Nouembr A° xxxiij° Rne in a
> cawfe betwene Margaret Brayne pl & the faid
> Burbages defendtes.

1. **Inprimis** whither are you fervaunte to Raphe Myles: And whither
   haue you feene An Arbitremt wch one Hill and one Turner did
   make, betwen one John Brayne, and the faid James Burbage,
   about the Theatre. And what doth the faid Margaret Brayne
   clayme therby to yor knoweledge. And whither do the players
   of enterludes, vfe to plaie in the faid Theatre vpon the fabothe
   day yea or no

2. **Item** who placed you to be a Collector at the faid Theatre, at that
   tyme when Robert Myles did place Collectors at the doares of the
   faid Theatre, vnder the cullor of an order made in the Chauncerie, That afwell the partie pl as thes defendtes fhould performe the aforfaid Arbitremt. And what were you appoincted
   to collect. Whither did the pl. at that tyme fhewe fourth
   the faid Arbitremt, Or require thes defendtes to performe the
   fame. And whither did thes defendtes require her to fhowe her
   auctoretie fhe had, and the fame Arbitremt. And whither did
   thei the faid defendtes offerr to the pl. that yf her aucthoretie were
   fufficient, to Collect the profittes of the faid Theatre, that thei
   would admitt her quietlie fo to do. What aunfwer was made
   therto, And who made the faid aunfwer. And whi did fhe refufe
   to fhew furthe any aucthoritie for her doinges to yor knoweledge.

3. **Item** wherin do you knowe that thes defendtes or any of them,
   hath committed any contempt, againft the Court of Chanceri or

againſt any order made in the ſaid Covrt. And wherin do yo^u knowe that the p^l hath performed the Arbitrem^t, And wherin haue the defend^{tes} broken, or not performed the ſaid Arbitrem^t. to yor knowledge.

4. Item whither haue yo^u herd Robert Myles report that the Theatre was his, And that he had moſt right thervnto And that he would pull the ſaid defend^{tes} out of the ſaid Theatre by the eares. What ſome of mony hath he, or his ſonne Raphe Myles reported that the ſute againſt thes defend^{tes} had coſt him or them, And what ſome haue thei ſworne to ſpend, for the removinge thes defend^{tes} from the Theatre.

5 Item what title or promyſe of title in the ſaid Theatre haue yo^u herd the p^l to make to the ſaid Robert or Raphe Myles. And what haue yo^u herd them boaſt thei ſhuld gayne therby. And whither do yo^u thincke in yor conſcience, that Robert Myles or Raphe Myles ſhall haue ſome intereſt or profitt out of the Theatre in Lieu of ther chardges and travell after the ſame ſhalbe recovered from the defend^{tes} yea or no.

6. Item whither did yo^u at ſuch tyme as Robert Myles or the p^l place Collecto^{rs} at the doores of the Theatre as is aforſaid heare James Burbage ſaye thes wordes. Conſcienc. Godes bloud what tell yo^u me of conſcienc or orders Or thes wordes. I care not for any contempt. Or thes wordes, I care not for iij of the beſt Lordes in England. yf yo^u did heare them, then who was by and preſente when yo^u herd thoſe wordes. And to whom were thei ſpoken. And whither were thos wordes ſpoken to the playntif yea or no And whither was ſhe preſente when Myles did ſo often tymes come to the Theatre to demaund a moitie of the profittes therof yea or no.

DEPOSITION OF NICHOLAS BISHOP

Reſponſio Nicholai Biſſhoppe ad ar^{los} Jacobi Burbage & Cuthberti Burbage verſus Margaretam Brayne viduam capta per Henricum Johnes in Cancellaria Examinatorem per ordinem Curie/

Nycholas Biſſhoppe of the pariſhe of whytechapell wᵗout Allgate
london Sopemaker/ of the age of xxx yeres or theraboutes ſworne
and exᵈ the vjᵗʰ Daye of Aprill in the xxxiiij yere & ctʳ To the
firſt Jnt myniſtred vnto him/   That he was never ſervaunt to
Raphe Myles named in this Jnt. but was & is now his partener/
And ſaith that he hath ſene ſuche an Award or Arbitryment But
who made the ſame/ he now remembreth not/ but he doth Re-
member/ it was about the matter of the Theatre/ And ſaith that
by the ſame Awarde/ Margarett Brayne the now compˡ doth
clayme to haue of right the one Moytie or half of the profittes
growing by the vſe of the ſaid Theatre/ and of all ſuche Rentes
as do ryſe of ſuche tenemᵗᵉˢ & howſes longing to the ſame/ wᶜʰ
profittes do ryſe by reaſon of the wekelie playes & interludes that
are vſed to be playd there/

To the 2. that he was requeſted by the ſaid Margaret Brayne and
Robert Myles/ the ffather of the ſaid Raphe Myles/ to go wᵗ them
to the Theater vppon A playe daye/ to ſtand at the doʳ that goeth
vppe to the gallaries of the ſaid Theater/ to take & Receyve for
the vſe of the ſaid Margarett/ half the money that ſhuld be gyven
to come vppe into the ſaid Gallaries at that doʳ/ according to the
foreſaid Award/ & an order made thervpon by the coʳt of
Chauncerye/ Requeſting this depoᵗ in very earneſt maner/ to
reſiſt no violence or other wᵗſtanding of him ſo to do/ that ſhuld
be made to or againſt him in ſo doing/ by the ſaid Burbages/
At wᶜʰ tyme for the better aucthoᵉ of the ſaid Margarett ſo to do/
ther was ſhewed fourth in the hande of the ſaid Myles to the ſaid
Burbages both the ſaid Arbitrymᵗ/ and Ordre of the Chauncerye/
and requyred the ſaid Burbages to ſuffre the performance therof/
But true it is/ the ſaid James Burbage & his wyfe & his ſone
Rychard Burbage did wᵗ vyolence thruſt this depoᵗ/ and the ſaid
Margarett/ and Robert Myles awey from the ſaid doʳ going vppe
to the ſaid Gallaries/ wᵗ vehement threates & manaſſing/ that yf
they departed not from that place/ they wold beate them away/
And ſo indede vpon ſome wordes vttered by the ſaid Robert
Myles to the ſaid Burbages wyſſhing them to obey the ſaid Ordre/

the faid Ry. Burbage & his mother fell vpon the faid Robert
Myles & beate him w^t A broome ftaffe calling him murdring knave
w^t other vyle and vnhoneft wordes at wch tyme the faid James
Burbage told the faid Robert Myles/ that he had but A paper/
wch he might wype his tale w^t/ and rather then he wold lofe his
poffeffion/ he wold committ xx contempt^{tes}/ And by caufe this
depo^t. fpake then fomewhat in the favo^r. of the po^r womman/
that fhe did nothing then but by aucthoritie of the faid Ordre/ the
faid Ry. Burbage fcornfully & difdainfullye playing w^t this depo^{tes}
Nofe/ fayd/ that yf he delt in the matter/ he wold beate him alfo/
and did chalendge the field of him at that tyme/ And the caufe
why the faid Robert Myles kept faft in his hand the faid Ordre/
was/ for that the faid Burbages wold haue torne the fame in
peeces/ yf they had had the fame/ in ther handes/ And otherwyfe to this Jnt he faith he cannot depofe/ then he hath before
now depofed on the part & behalf of the faid Margarett Brayne/

To the 3. that in his Judgem^t/ the faid Burbages haue committed
g^t contempt againft the co^{r}t of Chauncerye afwell at this tyme as
before in not performing the faid Awarde/ & fulfylling the fame
Ordre/ And that the faid Margarett hath in his Judgem^t performed the Ordres of the faid Co^{r}te/ and wold be glade of the
performance of the faid Awarde/

To the 4. that he never heard the faid Robert Myles faye that the
Theatre was his/ or that he had great right therinto/ Or that he
wold pull the faid Burbages out of the Theater by the eares/
But he faithe/ that he hath heard the faid Robert and Raphe Myles
faye/ that they had lade out A g^t deale of money for the faid
Margarett in this Sute/ but how moch in particuler/ he did not
heare them faye/ And to the reft of this Jnterrogatory he faith
he can fay nothing/

To the 5. that he never heard the faid Margarett Brayne open or
declare/ of any Tytle or promiffe of Tytle/ the faid Robert &
Raphe or ether of them fhuld haue of her/ of & in the faid

Theater/ Nor ever heard them or ether of them boaſt/ what
they ſhuld gayne therby/ by any graunt from the ſaid Margarett/
But he ſaith that he doth think in his conſcyence/ that the ſaid
Robert Myles/ is like to haue ſome Recompence/ or ſome intereſt
from her therof/ yf ſhe recover againſt the ſaid Burbages/ for
his charges & travell vſed for her in this Sute/ as this depoᵗ
thinketh in his conſcience/ he is worthie to haue in Equitie/
To the 6. that he can ſay no more/ then he hath before ſaid/ to
the ſecond Jnterr/ And more he ſaith he cannot ſaye in this
matter then he hath now/ & before this tyme ſayd on the parte
& behaulf of the ſaid Margarett Brayne/

[Signed]   Per me Nicholas Byſhopp

INTERROGATORIES TO RALPH MYLES

Interrogatorˢ to be mynyſtered to Raphe Myles
of Londone ſoapemaker accordinge to an order
made the xiij daye of Nouember Aᵒ xxxiijᵒ Rⁿᵉ
in the cawſe Betwene Margaret Braine pˡ and
James Burbage and Cuthberte Burbage defendᵗᵉˢ

1 **Item** whither do yoᵘ knowe, or haue yoᵘ herd, ſeene and read an
Arbitremᵗ that was made by one Hill and on Turner betwen
James Burbage on the one parte And John Brayne on the other
parte concerninge the Theatre, And what title therby, was geven
to John Braine & his executoʳ in the ſaid Theatre to yoʳ
knowledge,

2. **Item** whither do yoᵘ knowe or haue yoᵘ herd, That in the ſame
Arbitremᵗ yt is expreſſed, That the mony collected at the Theatre
ſhuld be to the vſe and for the paymᵗ of ſuch debtes, as ether the
ſaid Brayne, or the ſaid Burbage ſhould rune into, about the
buildinge or repayringe of the ſame Theatre. And that before
thoſe debtes were paide that the ſaid Braine nor his executoʳˢ
ſhuld haue nor enioy the ſame or the profittes therof, only xˢ by
the weeke excepted to be defaulked for the ſaid Braine out of

the faid profitt*es,* for fuch plaies as fhould be fhewed vpon the
fondaies only. And whither do thei vfe to plaie on the fondaies
ther, yea or no.

3 **It*e*m** whither haue yo^u feen herd or rede That in the fame Ar-
bitrem^t it is alfo expreffed. That yf the faid Braine or the faid
Burbage or both of them, had occafion to vfe any mony for any
thinge concerninge the faide Theatre or for the paym^t of any debt
made for or about any matter towching the fame, That then yt
fhould and might be Lawfull for the faid Burbage to mortgadge
or fell the Leafe to hym made for the levying of fuche needfull
mony. And whither was the faid Leafe of The theatre, mortgaged
accordinglie to John Hyde grocer wth confent of the faid Brayne.
And whither was yt to him forfeited for none payem^t of the
money fo borrowed, yf it were, then what title in yor Judgem^t
hath the faid John Braine or his executrix the p^l. to the faid
Theatre or to the profitt*es* therof & how much therof is fhe in
right to haue to yor knowledg.

4. **It*e*m** whither do yo^u knowe or haue yo^u herd y^t the faid Braine,
fythenc the makinge of his will, wherby he did appoincte the p^l
to be his executrix hath & did make a deed of gifte of all his
good*es* & Chattells: to on Tomfon, or to yor father, or to one M^r
Afhbournha*m*. or to one John Gardyner. And whither did thei
or any of them by vertue therof clayme the good*es* & Chattells
of the faid Brayne. and his title in the faid Theatre. yea or no.
And what is the cawfe whi thei nor none of them do now fhew
forth the fame but conceale the faid deed or deed*es* of gifte to yor
knoweledge.

5. **It*e*m** whither did the p^l. and Robert Myles yor father place Col-
lecto^{rs} at the doares of the Theater, vnder the cullor of an order
made in the Chauncery that afwell the p*a*rtie playntife as thes
defendant*es* Burbage fhould p*e*rforme the Arbitrem^t aboue faid.
ffor what pourpofe were the faid Collecto^{rs} fo placed at the
Theatre And whither did the p^l then and ther fhewe fourth the
faid Arbitrem^t and offerr to p*e*rforme the fame to thes defend^{tes}

And whither did the faid defend^tes or any of them require to fee the aucthoretie the p^l had to place any collectors ther, And whither did fhe fhewe her aucthoretie. And whither hath fhe befor that tyme or fynce that tyme performed the faid Arbitrem^t. And yf fhe haue then fhewe wherin & in what poinctes fhe hath performed the fame, And in what poinctes thes defend^tes haue not performed the fame. And whither did fhe at the fame tyme require thes defend^tes to performe the fame Arbitrem^t. And what matter did fhe require them to performe conteyned in the faid Arbitrem^t.

6. Item wherin do yo^u knowe that the defend^tes haue, or any of them hath, comitted contempt againft the Court of Chaunceri, or againft any order made in the fame Court, yf thei haue then fhewe wherin.

7. Item whither do yo^u knowe, or haue herde that James Burbage on of theis defend^tes by his deed in wryting wth the advife and confent of the faid John Brayne did convey or graunte any parte of the Theatre and profittes therof to one Henry Lenman. And whither doth he yet receyve and collect and take any profittes of the faid Theatre fo graunted. And whither doth the playntiff knowe therof or that fhe knewe of the faid graunt in thee lief tyme of her faid hufband yea or no. yf fhe did knowe therof, Then whi doth fhe now clayme a Moitie of the faid Theatre of thes defend^tes.

8. Item whyther hath the p^l geven or graunted, or promyfed to gyve or graunt, to yor father, or to yo^rfealf her pretended title in the faid Theatre. Or what parte therof haue yo^u or are yo^u to haue, And what parte therof is yor father to haue, fo foane as, or after the fame fhall be recovered of the p^l, from the defend^tes. And what fome of mony did yo^u gyve to one Henry Bett, to comence futes or plaintes in the name of the p^l. againft the defend^tes or any of them for the recoverie of the faid Theatre. And by what aucthoretie or title did yo^u fo delyver monye for mayntenance of fuch futes. And whither did yo^u or yor father faie that the Theatre was his,

and that he would ſpend all that he had but he would pull the
defend^t out of the ſaid Theatre by the eares. yea or no.

9. **Item** whither did yo^u at ſuch tyme as Rob*ert* Myles and the p^l
did place Collecto^{rs} at the doares of the Theatre as is aforſaid
heare James Burbage ſaye thes word*es*: Conſcienc. Gods bloud
what tell yo^u me of conſcienc or orders. Or thes wordes. I care
not for any contempt. Or thes wordes I care not for .iij. of the
beſt Lord*es* in England. Yf yo^u did heare them, then who was
by and pre*ſe*nte when you herd theſe word*es* And to who*m* were
thei ſpoken.

DEPOSITION OF RALPH MYLES

Raphe Myles ſone of Rob*er*t Myles of Whyte Chapell pariſhe
w^tout Allgate london Bacheler/ of the age of xxvij yeres or therabout*es*/ ſworne and ex^d the xxvj daye of Aprill in the yere aforeſaid xxxiiijth &ct^r To the firſt Jnt. that he doth know and hath
ſene & redde/ an Awarde that was made by one Turno^r/ and one
Hill/ betwene James Burbage/ of the one p*ar*te and Jo. Brayne
deceſſed of the other p*ar*te/ concerni*n*g A controvercye betwene
them about the Playehouſſe called the Theater by wch awarde the
ſaid Brayne was entytled to haue the one Moytie of the Rent*es*
and profitt*es* Ryſing & comi*n*g by & of the ſame Theatre/

To the 2. that it is p*ar*cell of the ſaid Awarde/ that the money
Receyved and taken of the Rent*es* and proffitt*es* comi*n*g of the
ſaid Theatre/ ſhuld be to the vſe & for the payment of ſuche debt*es*/
as ether the ſaid Brayne/ or the ſaid Burbage were then in/ for
the building and repayring of the ſaid Theatre/ And that before
thoſe debt*es* were ſatiſſyed & diſcharged nether the ſaid Brayne/
nor the ſaid Burbage/ nor ther Executo^{rs}/ ſhuld haue nor enioye
any p*ar*te or p*ar*cell therof to his or ther owne vſe/ but onlye that
the ſaid Brayne ſhuld haue x^s by the weeke for & toward*es* his
houſe keeping/ and the ſaid Burbage to haue viij^s as he remembreth weekelye out of the ſame for & towardes his houſe keping

of the profitt*es* of fuch playes as fhuld be playd there vpon fun-
daies/ And that when the faid debt*es* were difcharged/ that then
the faid Brayne fhuld take & Receyve all the Rent*es* and proffitt*es*
of the faid Theatre/ to his own vfe/ till he fhuld be anfwered/
fuche fomes of money w*ch* he had lade out/ for & vpon the fame
Theatre/ more then the faid Burbage had done/ And then the
Rent*es* & profitt*es* of the fame/ to go in devydent equallye betwene them/

To the 3. that it is alfo p*ar*cell of the faid Awarde/ That yf the
faid Brayne & Burbage/ fhuld haue any occaf*i*on to vfe any money
nedefull to be beftowed vp*p*on the faid Theatre/ or for the paym*t*
of any money towching the fame/ that then it fhuld & might be
lawfull for the faid Burbage and Brayne/ to morgage the leafe
therof for A fom*m*e of money for that purpofe/ And faithe that
true it is, the faid leafe w*t* bothe ther confent*es* was morgaged to
Jo. Hyde grocer of london vpon the fome of one Cxxv*ll*/ as he
hath credible heard/ And y*t* by report they forfetted the faid
leafe to the faid Hyde/ for nonepaym*t* of the money lent vp*p*on
the fame/ Albeit the faid Hyde, did frome tyme to tyme promes
& beare in hand the faid Brayne in his lyfe tyme and to his wyfe
the now comp*l* fyns his deceffe the faid Braynes Executrice/ that
he wold take no forfetture of the fame/ yf he were payd his
money due/ and ordinarye confideraci*o*n for the forbearing
therof/ And therfor this depo*t* thinketh in his confcience/ that
the now comp*l* hath as great inter*e*ft in the faid leafe/ as the faid
Burbage hathe/ ffor he faithe/ that whan the faid Burbage and
his fone/ by pollycie betwene them/ did Redeme the faid leafe/
ther was no more owing to the faid Hyde/ but xxx*ll* or therabout*es*/ as the faid Hyde co*n*feffed to this depo*t*/ in the w*ch* Redempci*o*n/ the faid comp*l* had bene well hable to haue Joyned/
yf the faid James Burbage had ether fuffered her to haue had her
Moytie of the proffitt*es* of the faid Theater, as by the faid Award
fhe was to haue had/ or had gyven her warni*n*g of his intent for
the Redempci*o*n of the fame/ And further faith/ that he this
depo*t* doth well Reme*m*ber that the faid comp*l* did offer to the faid

Hyde/ in this depo^tes pre/ence/ to paye him fo moch as was behynde of his Money lent w^t confideracion therfore/ yf he wold
deliuer the faid leafe to her/ & that the faid James fhuld haue
his Moytie of the proffittes therof, afwell as fhe/ But he made
anfwer/ that as it was morgaged vnto him by both her hufband
Brayne/ and Burbage/ fo would he deliuer it vppe/ to both Burbage & her/

To the 4 that he can fay nothing

To the 5. that he can fay nothing

To the 6. that true it is/ that at fuche tyme he this depo^t & others
went at the comp^ltes Requeft w^t her to the now def^tes/ to Requyer
them to performe the faid Awarde/ as by an Ordre made in the
Chauncerye they were ordred to do/ the faid James Burbage
wyfe/ charged them to go out of her grounde/ orelles fhe wold
make her fone breake ther knaves heades/ and fo hottelie rayled
at them/ And then the faid James Burbage her hufbande looking
out at A wyndoe vpon them/ called the comp^l murdring ho^r/ and
this depo^t & the others villanes Rafcalls and knaves/ and then the
comp^l fayd vnto him/ that fhe was come to requyre of him the
performance of the award/ as the Co^rte of Chauncerye had ordred to do/ and then he cryed vnto her/ go go/ A Carte A cart
for yo^u/ I will obey no fuch ordre/ nor I care not for any fuch
ordres/ and therfor it were beft for yo^u and yor companyons to
be packing by tymes/ for yf my fone Come/ he will thumpe yo^u
hence/ W^t that in maner his fone came home/ of whome the
comp^l did alfo Requyer the performance of the faid Award, according to the faid Ordre of the Chauncerye/ and then he in verye
hotte fort/ bidd them gett them thence/ orelles he wold fett them
forwardes/ faying I care for no fuche Ordre/ the Chauncerye
fhall not gyve away what I haue payd for/ Nether fhallt thow
haue any thing to do here/ Whille I lyeve/ gett what Ordres
thow canft/ And fo w^t great & horrible othes vttered by both him

& his ffather/ that they wold do this & that/ the comp^l and her company went ther wayes/.

To the 7. that he can say nothing to any effecte

To the 8. that by the othe that he hath taken/ he knoweth of no graunt or promes made by the comp^l/ ether to this depo^t/ or to his ffather of the comp^ltes Tytle in the Theatre/ nor more can saye to that poynt of this Jnterrogatory./ And to the rest of this Jnterrogatory concerning Bett named in the same/ he saithe that he can say no more but this/ That whan (on a tyme) the said Bett at the Requeft of the comp^l did pervse her wrytinges/ he did (whan he had done and told her what everye of them concerned) require money for his paynes/ But the comp^l having none to gyve him/ she prayd this depo^t to lend her A cople of shillinges/ and this depo^t lent her the same/ and she gave Bett the same/ Whervppon the said Bett went & disclosed to the defendtes/ the whole story that he conceyved of her wrytinges/ and so hath ever syns that tyme wroght w^t them what he could/ againft the said Comp^l/ And otherwyse to this Jnterrogatory he said he cannot depose/

To the 9. that he can say nothing/ ffor he was not present at suche wordes or speeche/ Nor more can saye to any further effect to all the foresaid Jnterrogatories/

[Signed] per me Raphe Miles

INTERROGATORIES TO JOHN ALLYN

Interrogator^s to be mynyftered vpon the parte and behaulf of James Burbage and Cuthbert Burbage, to John Allyn, accordinge to an Order made the . xiij^th of Nouemb^r A° xxxiij R^ne.

1. **Imprimis** whither do yo^u knowe, or haue yo^u herd, seene or rede, an Arbitrem^t that was made betwene John Braine whileft he

lyved, and James Burbage by one Turner and Hill. What title therby was geven to the ſaid John Brayne & his executoʳˢ of and in the Leaſe of the Theatre in Hallywell made to the ſaid James, by on Gyles Allyn. And whither do yoᵘ knowe that on Henry Lenman hath or had any *parte* of the profitt*es* of the Theatre. Yf he had, then who graunted to him the ſame. And how longe is yt ſince he receyved ſuch *profittes* to yoʳ knoweledge. And how longe is he yet to receyve the ſame as yoᵘ haue herd. And whither did John Braine agree that Lenma*n* ſhould receyve yᵉ ſame

2 **Item** whither did Margaret Braine, and Robe*rt* Myles, in yoʳ preſence place Collectoʳˢ at the doares of the Theatre to collect the profitt therof, vnder the cullor of an order made in the Court of Chaunceri. That aſwell the *partie* pˡ. viz the ſaid Margaret, as the ſaid James Burbage and Cuthbert Burbage defendᵗᵉˢ ſhuld *performe* the Arbitremᵗ aboue named. And whither did the ſaid Margaret at that tyme ſhewe furth the ſaid Arbitremᵗ, or offerr to *performe* the ſame to the ſaid defendᵗᵉˢ And whither did the ſaid James Burbage require the ſame, & to ſee theʳ aucthoreti*es* thei had to place the ſaid Collectoʳˢ. yea or no. And whither did not the pˡ. refuſe plainli to *performe* the requeſt*es* of the ſaid Burbedge. Yea or no.

3. **Item** wherin do yoᵘ knowe that the defendᵗᵉˢ haue, or any of them hath comitted any contempt againſt the Court of Chaunceri, or what order hath thei or ether of them broken in Contempt of the ſame Court to yoʳ knoweledge.

4. **Item** whitheʳ hath the ſaid Myles confeſſed to yoᵘ. That he had to do wᵗʰ the ſaid Theatre, and that the ſame was his. And that he would pull the defendᵗᵉˢ Burbag*es* out therof by the eares. yea or no. And whither hath he confeſſed that he and his had more to do ther then Burbege had and that his title therof viz of the ſaid Theatre was better then Burbages. And that he had

his title from the p^l. How longe is yt fynce he vfed thes wordes to yo^u. Yf the faid Myles did not vfe thes wordes to yo^u or fuch like, then whi did yo^u tell the faid James Burbage, that he vfed fuch wordes to yo^u. And whi did yo^u require the faid James to conceale whatfoeu*er* yo^u tould to hym of the faid Myles, to the end yo^u might Lerne of the faid Myles his whole p*rocedinges* therin.

5. It*em* whither did not Raphe Myles the fonne of the faid Rob*ert* Myles, afferme to yo^u that the word*es* and fpeaches of the faid Rob*ert* were true. And what fomes of mony did thei or ether of them fweare thei would fpend to ouerthroe the faid Burbage. And what wordes hath the faid Ralphe vfed to yo^u about the faid Theater, and his or his fathers title therin to yor remembraunce/

6. It*em* whither haue not yo^u byn prefent in the lief tyme of Brayne, when he and Burbedge did delyver the one haulf of the profitt*es* collected by them at the Theatre to the aboue named Henry Lenman or his deputes. And fync his death by the faid Burbage. And whither do yo^u thincke that the faid Lenman had any right to haue fuch p*rofittes*. Yf he had whi do yo^u fweare That ye p^l hath good right and title to haue haulf the p*rofittes* collected in the Theatre/ And whither were the wordes wch yo^u alledge to be fpoken by James Burbage viz thes word*es*. (Confcienc God*es* bloud, what tell yo^u me of Confcienc, or orders. or thes word*es* I care not for iij of the beft men in England. Or that he would Committ xx contempt*es* &c) whither were thei fpoken when the faid Myles or the p^l did place Collecto^{rs} at the Gates of the Theatre by force of the order aforfaid. Or when were thei fpoken and who was p*refe*nte when thei were fpoken to yor knowledge And in what place. And whither were thei fpoken to the plaintif yea or no.

DEPOSITION OF JOHN ALLEN

Johne Allen late of the p*arifhe* of St Buttollphes wthout Bifhops gate London ffree of the company of the Jnholders of london of

the age of xxxv yeres or therabout*es* fworne and ex^d the vjth
daye of Maye in the yere aforefaid & ct^r To the firft J*nterroga-*
tory/ that he hath crediblie heard faye/ that ther paffed an Arbi-
trym*ent* or An award betwene James Burbage of the one part/
and Jo. Brayne named in this J*nterrogatory* now deceffed on the
other p*arte/* c*oncerning* the co*ntrouer*cye betwene them of the
p*ro*fitt*es* of the play houfe of the Theater/ by the wch Arbitry-
ment/ (as this depo^t did heare faye/ the one half of the proffitt*es*
of the faid Play houfe was awarded to the faid Brayne his execu-
to^{rs} and affignes/ and the other half to the faid James Burbage/
his executo^{rs} and affignes/ And faithe/ that one Henrye Laynman*n* had (and as he thinketh yet hathe & doth receive) part of
the proffitt*es* of the fame/ & fo muft till Mych*aelm*es now next
comi*ng* but by whofe graunt/ he knoweth not/ But wheth^r the
faid Brayne did confent therunto/ he knoweth not/

To the 2. that to his now Reme*m*bra*n*ce, he can fay no more, then
he hath hertofore depofed on the compl*ainantes* behaulf to the 13
J*nterrogatory.* And further faithe, that at the fame tyme whan
the faid comp^l, and the faid Robert Myles came to demaund of
the faid James Burbage & of his fone/ the p*erforman*ce of the
forefaid Arbitryment/ and ordre of the Ch*auncery* co*ncerning*
the one half of the proffitt*es* of the faid Theater/ the faid comp^l
and Myles/ femed to be readye & willing w^tout any deniall to
fhew to them/ by what aucth*o*^e they were to haue the fame/ yf
the defend^{tes} wold haue demaunded the fame/

To the 3. that he doth verelie thinke/ that the faid James Burbage
hath co*m*mitted A contempt to the faid hon*or*able Co^rte of Chaun-
cerye/ in Maner & fourme/ as this depo^t hath depofed vp*p*on
his othe before to the fame 13. J*nt*/ on the compl^{tes} behalf/ wher-
unto/ for the better proof therof/ he doth referre him felf/

To the 4. that the faid Robert Myles did at no tyme confeffe to
this depo^t/ that he had any thing to do w^t the faid Theater then
as A freind by the compl^{tes} *lett*re of Atto^rney to do for her in the

fame/ Nor ever heard him faye that he wold pull the faid James Burbage out of the fame by the eares/ Nether dyd this depo^t tell the faid James burbage or any of his fones/ any fuche tale of the faid Myles/ Nor ever byd the faid Burbag*es* or any of them to conceyle y^t he had told him or them/ any fuche word*es* of the faid Myles/ nor any fuche fpeche to that effect/ to his nowe Reme*m*bra*n*ce/

To the 5. that ther hath paffed at no tyme/ any fuche fpeche betwene the faid Robert Myles or Ra*l*phe his fone to this depo^t as are fett down in this Jnt*err*ogatory/

To the 6. that in the lyfe tyme of the faid Brayne/ this depo^t did not fee Burbage & Brayne gyve or deliu*er* the one half of the proffitt*es* of the faid Theatre/ to the forefaid Henry le*n*man*n*/ But he faith/ that he hath fene the faid Burbage paye to fome/ to the vfe of the fame le*n*man*n*/ fome money of the fame profitt*es*/ fyns the deceffe of the faid Brayne/ wch profitt*es* (as this depo^t hath heard the faid James Burbage faye) were due vnto the faid Lenma*n*n/ and that he & the faid Brayne were both bounde by wryting to paye the fame vnto him/ in confideraci*o*n that the faid lenma*n*n did graunt vnto them the one half of the proffitt*es* of the other play houfe there by/ called the Curten/ in wch half he doth thinke the comp^l is to haue her devydent w^t the faid Burbage/ afwell as her moytie of the Theater/ And fo ought fhe to haue the whole moytie of the Theater/ by the faid Arbitryment & ordre & half of the other Moytie of the p*r*ofitt*es* of the Curten/ by the Agrem^t w^t the faid Le*n*man fo long as the tyme of the fame Agreem^t is to endure/ And faith that the word*es* menconed in his former Exa*m*inaci*o*n/ to the 13 Jnt*err*ogatory fpoken by the faid James Burbage/ viz/ Confcience/ God*es* blood what tell yee me of confcience/ or Ordr*es*/ that he cared not for any Contempt/ & yf there were xx contempt*es*/ & as many Jniuncci*o*ns he wold w^{t}ftand & breake them all before he wold lofe his poffeffion/ were vttred w^{t}in the Theater yard/ whan the comp^l and the faid Myles came to defyre him to p*er*forme the faid Arbytryment & ordre/ wch he thinketh to be about A yere paſt in the hearing of one Nycholas Biſhopp/ this depo^t & others/ And the other wordes ſpoken by him/ menconed in the ſame 13 Jnterrogatory of his ſaid former Examinacion/ viz. I care not for three of the beſt lordes of them all/ were vttered by him in the Attyring houſſe/ or place where the players make them readye about viij daies nềxt after/ in the hearing of one James Tunſtall this depo^t and others/ And this for his true anſwer to all theſe Jnterrogatories/

[Signed] Joⁿ Allein

[When Dr. Legg and Dr. Stanhope were ready to make their report after considering the preceding voluminous evidence, namely, in April, 1593, Widow Bayne died, and the suit naturally died with her. But by her will, dated 8 April, 1593, and proved 3 May, following, she left her supposed interest in the Theatre and all her possessions to Robert Myles. Thereupon, as legatee and executor, Myles filed a bill of revivòr, which is lost, and the case proceeded to the end in his name.]

BRAINE *v*. BURBAGE

Idem. Bdl. 226, No. 11. Trinity 34 Elizabeth (1592).

Jo: Grigges et Robertus Myles
jurati 29 Julij 1592 coram
Jo: Hone./

> **Intergatories** to be mynyſtred on the parte and behalf of Margarett Braynes Wydowe Complaynaunte agaynſt James Burbadge, Cuthberte Burbadge, and others Defendan^{tes}./

1. **Imprimis** whether doe ye knowe the partye Complaynante Margarett Brayne, and James Burbadge, and Cuthbert Burbadge and other the Defendantes, ye or no. Yf ſo then whether doe ye not knowe one Gyles Allyne gentleman ye or no, And whether was not he ſeazed of a vacante peace of grounde a Myll howſe,

and certaine other tenem^{tes} in St Leonard*es* in the parifhe of St Leonard*es* in Sordyche in the Countye of Midlefex, ye or no

2 **Item** whether have you heard or knowen of yor owne knowledge of any Conference that was had betwene the fayd James Burbadge and . one John Brayne difceafed of the takinge of the fayd peace of vacante ground in Leafe and other the land*es* and tenement*es* at the hand*es* of the fayd Gyles Allyne, and whether did not the fayd James defyre the fayd John Brayne to ioyne wth him in takinge thearof to the intente to buylde a theato^r or a playinge howfe, and declared what greate proffitt woulde ryfe vnto them bothe by yt, yf they fo did, And what was the Aunfweare of the fayd John Brayne therevnto to your remembraunce./

3 **Item** whether did not the fayd James earneftlye intreate him to ioyne wth him in takinge of yt, otherwyfe he was not able to buylde yt, for yt woulde Cofte fyve tymes fo muche as he was worthe, And whether did not the fayd John Brayne and he agree fo to doe, And that yt fhoulde be taken at Allyns hand*es* only in the name of Burbadge, but notwthftandinge to the vfe of bothe.

4. **Item** whether was not a Leafe thearof taken accordinglye of the fayd Gyles Allyne wth Covenaunt*es* therin Conteyned to buylde the fayd Theato^r or playinge place, And whether did not the fayd James Burbadge after the takinge thearof promys the fayd John Brayne to affure him of a moitye of the theato^r and the proffitt*es* thearof after yt was buylt together wth the other land*es* and tenem^{tes}, and bounde him felf in a bonde fo to doe./

5. **Item** whether did not the fayd John Braynes (Jmmediatlye after that promyfe) make a greate fome of money to the intente to erecte & buylde the fayd howfe, and then hyred workemen provyded tymber, and other neceffaryes to builde yt wthall, and whether did not he beftowe in buyldinge therof the fomme of one thoufand Markes at the leafte for his parte and whether did not

he vtterlye forfake hys trade of livinge, the wch he had before planted himfelf in to his greate proffitte, and by the meanes of the fayd James Burbadge did forfake yt, and wholly imploye himfelf and all that he coulde make about the theato^r in fellinge all his ftocke, and was not he therby vtterlye vndone./

6 **Item** what thinke you that the faid James Burbadge beftowed for his parte, and whether was he able to beftowe the fomme of one hundred pounde, or was of fuche Credytt, that he was able to make the fomme of one hundred markes to helpe to buylde yt, & was yt not wholy donne in effecte wth the money of the fayd John Brayne, & by his Credyt, And what you knowe hearin, fpeake your knowledge./

7 **Item** when yt was buylt, and divers playes therin performed, and greate fomme and fommes of money Collected by fuche as did repayre thither to fee them, whether did not the faid Burbadge Contrary to hys owne promyfe therin, wch was that the fayd John Braynes fhoulde have half the proffitte of· all the premiffes, often tymes filche out of the Commone boxe by a Counterfayte keye to open yt, divers greate fomme & fommes of money in defraudinge of his Companyons and the faid John brayn And whether did not the faid James Burbadge often tymes hyde money in hys bofome or aboute himfelf of fuche money as was gathered, and fhoulde have bene equallye devyded betwene them, & keptt yt to himfelf & what you knowe thearin, fpeake yor knowledge or in eny other his like bad practiffes as that yo^u haue hard or knowe//

8 **Item** whether doe ye knowe of yor owne knowledge, or have hearde faye, that divers Controuerfies & Contentions weare betwene the fayd James Burbadge, & the faid John Brayne touchinge the fayd Theato^r, & whether did not they fubmitt them felves vnto the Arbitrament of Certayne perfones for the pacificacion of all matters betweane them, and whether did not the faid Arbitrato^rs awarde that the fayd James Burbadge hys executo^rs, & Affignes fhoulde enioye the one moitye of the proffittes of the

premyffes, & the faid John Brayne his executo^{rs} & Affignes fhoulde
enioy the other moitye of the proffitt*es,* ye, or no.

9 **It*e*m** whether did not they awarde alfo, that yf occafione fhoulde
be to morgage the prem*i*ffes for the borrowinge of money to paye
debt*es* for the p*er*fourminge of any neceffarye thinge concearn-
inge the theato^r, that then bothe they fhoulde ioyne in morgage,
& the money Cominge & ryfinge of the proffitt*es* of the faid
Theato^r, to goe to the redemp*ci*on of the faid morgage, ye or no

10 **It*e*m** whether did not the faid James Burbage & the faid John
Braynes accordinge to the fayd Arbitrament morgage the fayd
Theato^r & other the prem*y*ffes vnto one John Hyde Citizen &
grofer of London for the fom*m*e of one hundred twentye & fyve
pound*es* or thereabout*es* to be payed at a certayne day & tyme in
the faid morgage limitted, yea, or no.

11 **It*e*m** whether was the fayd Theato^r & other the prem*i*ffes for-
faited vnto the fayd John Hyde ye or no for that he was not payed
his money at fuche daies & tymes, as was by the fayd morgage
agreed vpon ye or no.

12 **It*e*m** what fom*m*e or fom*m*es was payed vnto the fayd John Hyde
by the fayd John Braynes & the fayd James Burbadge in the lyf
tyme of the fayd John Braines before the forfaiture of the premiffes, & what fom*m*e or fom*m*es of money was left vnpaid at the
tyme of the deathe of the fayd John Braynes, for the wch yt was
morgaged for, & what ys payed fythence hys deathe/

13 **It*e*m** whether did not the fayd John Hyde often tymes faye vnto
the fayd John Brayne & the fayd James Burbadge & vnto the
nowe Comp^l & others, that yf he weare payed his money that was
dewe, & confidera*ci*on for the fore bearinge of yt, that he woulde
neu*er* take any advantage of the fforfayture ye or no./

14 **It*e*m** whether did not the faid John Hyde promyfe vnto the fayd

Complainant, that yf he weare payed hys money that then he woulde affure the premyffes vnto the faid Complainant, & vnto the faid James Burbadge becaufe he had yt from the houfband of the faid Complainant: & the faid James Burbadge, & nowe by the deathe of her houfbande his parte belongeth to the faid Complainant, & the rather to for that he was payed all his money favinge thirtye poundes or theraboutes in the lyf of the faid Braynes, by the meanes of the faid Braynes, & what you knowe hearin, fpeake yo᷄ knowledge./

15 **Item** whether did not the fayd Margarett Brayne offer to paye the fayd thirtye poundes vnto the fayd John Hyde yf he woulde reaffure the premiffes over to her, & yf he woulde fo doe, fhe fhoulde be bounde to Convaye over a moitye thearof vnto the faid James Burbadge, in fayinge that althoughe Burbadge woulde defeate her of her right, yet fhe woulde not fo deale wᵗʰ him, & what Aunfweare made the fayd John Hyde therevnto.

16 **Item** whether did not the faid James Burbadge deteyne the proffites of the premiffes in his owne handes of purpofe to make a forfayture vpon the morgage, & therevppon to take yt againe in his owne name or to his owne vfe in the name of his chylde or freinde, ye or no, & whether did not the fayd James after the deathe of Braynes vtterly denye the fayd Complaynant to receave any more proffittes of the premiffes: Contrary to the arbitramᵗ, whearebye the faid John Hyde was not payed his money accordinge to the faid arbitramente wᵗʰ the proffittes of the premiffes as yt ought to have bene by the awarde./

17 **Item** whether did not the faid James Burbadge intreate the fayd John Hyde to Convaye the premyffes vnto Cuthbert Burbadge his fonne of purpofe to defeat the faid Complainant of her right of the moitye in the premiffes, & whether did not he procure Mʳ Cope to laboʳ in hys behalf wᵗʰ Mʳ Hyde to Convaye yt to hys fonne Cuthbert to the vfe of the fayd James ye or no, Yf fo then whether did not the fayd John Hyde faye that fhe fhoulde have her moitie

before he woulde Convaye the premiſſes, excepte bothe the ſayd James & the ſaid Cuthbert woulde promiſſe that ſhe ſhoulde have her moitie & right at their handes ye or no, & what you knowe hearin, ſpeke yoᵣ knowledge

18 **Item** whether did not the ſayd James & Cuthbert often tymes ſythence the redemption therof, promiſe the ſayd Compl*ainant,* that ſhe ſhoulde have her moitye in the premiſſes, as her houſ-bande had, & for that pur*p*oſe he ſuffred her to enioy yt for a tyme, vntill he had obteyned his pur*p*oſe, and after putt her moſte vnconſcionablye from yt./

19 **Item** what ſom*m*e or ſom*m*es of money or other pro*ffittes* hathe the ſayd James Burbadge and Cuthbert Burbadge received for the Thea-tour and other the premyſſes ſythence the laſte accompt or reconinge made between the ſayd John Braynes and James Burbadge to yoᵣ knowledge or remembraunce, and what ye knowe hearin ſpeake yoᵣ wholl knowledge and what doe ye thinke the ſaid Braines be-ſtowed in buildinge of the theatoᵣ for his p*a*rte, & what money ys owinge vnto him by any of the Burbadges to yoᵣ knowledge, and what money hathe the ſayd Burbadge beſtowed./

Scott   [attorney]

[Here ended the original list of interrogatories. Then, before witnesses were examined, questions 20, 21, 22 were added.]

20 **Item** wheather doe yoᵘ knowe that thear was an order in her Maᵗⁱᵉˢ Courte of Chauncery the xiijᵗʰ of November in the xxxijᵗʰ yeare of her highnes Reigne That Margaret Brayne pl*aintif* and James Burbadge and Cutbarte Burbade def*endants* mad the xijᵗʰ day of Julie in the xxᵗʰ yeare of her graces Reigne Betwixt the ſaid John Brayne one the one p*a*rtie And the ſaid James Bur-badge one the other p*a*rtie by Rychard Turner and John Hill Arbitratores. Confearninge the Theavter in Holloway and the pro*ffites* theareof./

21 **Item** wheather haue the ſame James Burbadge and Cutbarte

Burbadge performed and accomplifhed the faid Arebitrement
ackordinge to the faid order yea or noe/
22 **Item** in what poyntes haue the faid James Burbadge and Cutbarte
Burbadge or eyther of them or any other perfon comprifed in the
faid order broken or infringed the faid Arebitrement or order and
herein difcouer yor whole knowledge//

DEPOSITIONS

Ex parte Margarete Braynes vid*uae* q*uerentis*
verf*us* Jacobum Burbage et Cuthbert*um* Burbage def*endentes* Teſte exa*m*inat*ore* per Hen-
ricum Johnes in Cancellar*ia* Exa*m*i*n*atorem/

Johne Grigg*es* of Puddinglane london Carpinter of the age of
xliij yeres or therabout*es* fworn and ex^d the xxix daye of Julye
in the xxxiiij yere &c To the firft J*n*t*errogatory*. that he doth
knowe all the p*ar*ties p^l and Defend^t^e^s / And knoweth Gyles Allen
gent*leman* named in this J*n*t*errogatory*. And faith that the faid
Gyles Allen was owner & feyfed of A pece of voyd grounde, A
mill houfe, and other howfes or tenem^t^e^s in the parifhe of S^t
leonardes in Shordiche wth out Bifhops gate london/

To the 2. that he doth knowe that James Burbage one of the nowe
Defend^t^e^s, and John Braynes deceffed named in this J*n*t*errogatory*
the now compl^t^e^s late hufbande/ did take A leafe of the faid
Gyles Allen of the faid voyde pece of grounde & of the faid myll
houffe/ & other the faid p*remiffes*/ But what conference or
co*n*v*er*cac*i*on paffed betwene the faid James and the faid Jo.
Brayn co*n*cern*in*g the taking of the p*remiffes of the faid M^r
Allen/ or conc*er*ning what profitt & com*m*oditie wold grow vnto
them therby by building A playe houfe thervp*p*on/ he faith he
was never pryvie therof nor p*ref*ent therat/

To the 3. that he did heare it crediblye reported/ that it was
agreed betwene the faid James Burbage/ and the faid Brayne/

yᵗ the faid leafe fhuld be made in the name onlye of the fame James/ and yet to the vfe of them bothe/ and otherwyfe to this Jnterrogatory he faithe he cannot depofe

To the 4. that he cannot tell what the contentes or covenantes of the faid leafe were/ Nor more can faye to this Jnterrogatory. faving he faith that he hath heard & beleveth it is true/ that the faid James Burbage ftandeth bounde to the faid Braynes/ that during the faid leafe/ the faid Braynes his executoʳˢ or affignes fhuld haue & Receyve the one half of the Rentes & proffittes that fhuld ryfe & growe by & of the fame/

To the 5. that he doth knowe/ that vpon fuche promiffes and fpeche as paffed frome the faid James Burbage to the faid Braynes/ of the gᵗ welth and profitt that fhuld ryfe vnto them/ by buildyng A Theater or playe houfe/ & other buildinges vpon the faid voyd grounde/ he the faid Braynes being A man of gᵗ welth, and of A welthie Trade/ provided A gᵗ fome of money/ hyred woʳkmen/ provyded Tymber and all other nedefull thinges for the building of the faid Theater in fomoche/ that this Depoᵗ thinketh in his confcience he beftowed thervppon for his part what firft and laft/ the fome of one thowfand markes at the leaft/ wherby hoping of the gᵗ welth that fhuld ryfe vnto him by the fame/ he gave vppe his trade/ fold his ftocke/ his houfe he Dwelt in/ in Bucklers berye london/ & wholye ymployed all he could make towardes the faid Buildinges/ and fetting fourthe the fame/ to his own vtter vndoing at the laft./

To the 6. that he [*doth verelie thinke, that* (stricken out)] cannot certenlie tell how moche the faid James burbage beftowed for his part vppon the building of the faid Theater & other the premiffes/ But he faith that he doth thinke in his confcience/ that the faid James Burbage was not at the tyme of the firft begynning of the building of the premiffes/ woʳth aboue one C markes in all his fubftance/ for he & this Depoᵗ were familierlie acquainted long before that tyme/ and ever fyns/ So as he verelie thinketh the

ſaid James Burbage hath not in all beſtowed thervppon/ the full
value of one hundreth poundes/ but that it was the money and
goodes of the ſaid Braynes that ſett vppe & fyniſhed the ſame/
wᵗ the helpe of the profitt*es* that grewe by playes vſed there/
before it was fully finiſhed/

To the 7. that he is ingnora*n*t

To the 8. that he doth knowe/ that in the lyfe tyme of the ſaid
Johne Braynes/ ther fell out great contenc*i*on & varyaunce betwene him and the ſaid James Burbage about the profitt*es* and
the vnhoneſt p*a*rciall dealing/ of the ſaid James/ co*n*cernin*g* the
ſaid Theater/ But what end the ſame co*n*tenc*i*on tooke whill the
ſaid Braynes lyved/ he ſaith he knoweth not/ nor more can ſaye
to this J*n*terrogatory.

To the 9. that he is ingnora*n*t

To the 10. that he doth knowe that the ſaid James Burbage and
Braynes did ioyntlie morgage ther ſaid leaſe of the Theater to
one hyde A grocer of london/ but for how moch money/ or
otherwyſe/ he ſaith he knoweth not/

To the 11. that he hath heard by credible report/ that the ſaid
leaſe was forfetted to the ſaid Hyde/ for nonpaymᵗ of the money
they borowed thervppon/ both at the tyme it ſhuld haue bene
payd, and long tyme after/

To the 12. that he is ingnora*n*t

To the 13. that he is ingnora*n*t

To the 14. that he ca*n* ſay nothing

To the 15. that he ca*n* ſay nothing

To the 16. that he ca*n* fay nothing

To the 17. that he ca*n* fay nothing

To the 18. that he ca*n*not depofe

To the 19. that he can fay no more then he hath before faid/

To the 20. that he ca*n* fay nothing

To the 21. that he ca*n* fay nothing

To the 22. that he can fay nothing/ Nor more can fay to all the
forefaid Jnter*rogatories*/

[Signed]   p*er* me John Grigg*es*

Edwarde Collyns of Bucklers berye london grocer of the age of
xxxix yeres or therabout*es* fworne and ex^d the Daie and yere
aforefaid &c   To the firft Jnt*errogatory*. that he dothe knowe
all the p*arties* p^l/ and Defend^tes/ but knoweth not Gyles Allen
named in this Jnter*rogatory*/ And to the reft of this Jnter*rogatory*
he faith he ca*n*not depofe/

To the 2. that he ca*nn* fay nothing

To the 3. that he can fay nothing

To the 4. that he hath credyblie héard faye, and beleveth it to be
very true/ that the faid James Burbage one of the now defend^tes
and Jo. Braynes the comp^ltes late hufband deceffed tooke A leaffe
of the grounde wher*u*pon the playing houffe called the Theater
now ftandeth/ & of other howfes there/ but of whome they tooke
the fame/ Or what the content*es* yer*o*f is/ he faith he knoweth
not/ And further to this Jnter*rogatory* he faithe he ca*n*not
depofe/

To the 5. that this Depo^t being f*erva*unt in Bucklers berye afore-

said to one Robert Kenningham grocer/ in wch Streete the said
Jo. Braynes Dwelled also/ and of the same Trade/ he the said
Braynes at the tyme he Joyned w^t the said James Burbage in
the foresaid lease/ was reputed emonges his neyghbo^{rs} to be wo^rth
one thowsand poundes at the least/ And that after he had Joyned
w^t the said Burbage in the matter of the building of the said
Theater/ be begann to slack his own trade/ and gave him self to
the building therof/ and the chefe care therof he tooke vp*p*on
him/ and hyred wo^rkmen of all sortes for that purpose/ bought
Tymbre and all other thinges longing therunto/ and paid all/
So as in this Depo^{tes} conscience he bestowed thervp*p*on for his
owne parte the some of one thowsand markes at the least/ in
somoche as his affeccion was gyven so greatlie to the fynishing
therof/ in hope of great welth & profitt during ther lease/ that
at the last he was dryven to sell to this Depo^{tes} ffather his lease
of the howse wherin he dwelled/ for one C li/ and to this Depo^t
all suche wares as he had left/ and all that longed therunto Remaynyng in the same for the some of one Cxlvj^{li} & od money/
wherof this Depo^t did paye for him to one Kymbre an Jremonger
in london for Jron wo^rke wch the said Braynes bestowed vp*p*on
the same Theater/ the some of ffourtie poundes/ And after
wardes the said Braynes tooke the matter of the said building so
vpon him/ as he was dryven to borow money to supplye the same/
saying to this Depo^t that his brother Burbage was not hable to
help the same/ and that he found not towardes it aboue the value
of ffiftie poundes/ some parte in money/ and the rest in stuff./

To the 6. that he can say no more/ then he hath before said/ in
the last former Jnterrogatory.

To the 7. that he is ingnorant

To the 8. that he Remembreth ther fell out variaunce & contencion betwene the said James Burbage/ and as he thinketh the
said Braynes/ or his wyfe the now compleynant the wch variance
they consented that friendes shuld hear & arbytrate the same/

whervpon this Depo^t was Requeſted to say to the ſaid Arbytrato^rs
being in the Temple Churche/ what he could ſay of the habilitie
of the ſaid Braynes/ whan he & Burbage Joyned together in the
foreſaid leaſe & building of the Theater/ and this Depo^t declared
truelye vnto them/ what he could ſaye of the ſaid Braynes/ But
whether the ſaid Arbytrato^rs made any Award betwene them/
Or yf they did/ what the ſubſtaunce therof was/ he ſaith/ he
is vtterlye ingnorant/ Nor more can ſay/ to this Jnterrogatory.

To the 9. that he can ſay nothing

To the 10. that he is ingnorant

To the 11. that he is ingnorant

To the 12. that he is ingnorant

To the 13. that he can ſay nothing

To the 14. that he can ſay nothing

To the 15. that he can ſay nothing

To the 16. that he can ſay nothing

To the 17. that he can ſay nothing

To the 18. that he can ſay nothing

To the 19. that he is ingnorant/ nor more can ſay to this Jnterrogatory then he hath before ſaid/

To the 20. that he can ſay nothing

To the 21. that he is ingnorant

To the 22. that he can· fay nothing/ Nor further faith to all the
fore faid Jnterrogatoryes/

[Signed]   by me Edwarde Collyns

Robert Myles of the Parifhe of whytechapell w^tout Allgate london free of the companye of the goldfmythes of the age of lij
yeres or therabou*tes* fworne and ex^d the xxx Daye of Julye in the
yere aforefaid &c   To the first Jnt*errogatory*/ that he dothe know
the now comp^l/ And all the defend^{tes}   And knoweth alfo Gyles
Allen gentlema*n* named in this Jnt*errogatory*.   And faithe that
he doth knowe that the faid Gyles Allen was of late feyfed and
owner emong*es* other landes & tenem^{tes} w^tin the p*a*rifhe of S^t
leonardes in Shordiche wthout Bifhops gate london in & about
the late Diffolued Pryorye called hallywell there/ of A parcell of
voyd grounde/ and of dyvers other landes & tenem^{tes} p*a*rcell of
the fame Pryorye/

To the 2. that he doth knowe and was pre*f*ent at tymes whan the
faid James Burbage did earneftlie infynuate his brother in lawe
John Braynes deceffed the now comp^{ltes} late hufband/ for the
taking of A leafe of the faid Gyles Allen of the faid pece of voyd
grounde to builde the now playhouffe called the Theater thervp*p*on/ earneftlie informi*n*g him/ that it wold grow to ther co*n*-
tynuall great profitt & com*m*odytie/ through the Playes that
fhuld be vfed there everye weke/ But the faid Braynes being of
A welthie trade alredye/ and A grocer in Bucklers Burye london
& Ryche was verye lothe to deale in the matter of the faid leafe/
Notw^tftanding in the end by the co*n*tynuall p*e*rfuafion & meanes
made vnto him by the faid James Burbage the faid Braynes
Joyned w^t him in takeng the faid leafe/ But he faith/ that he
hath heard the faid Jo. Braynes many & often tymes faye/ that
the drawing of him by his brother Burbage to deale in the matter
of the faid Theater/ was his vtter vndoing/ and that he wold
never haue entred ye*r*in but by the fwete and co*n*tynuall p*e*rfua-
fions of his faid brother in law Burbage/   And for the charges
that fhuld haue bene beftowed vp*p*on the building of the fame

playe houſſe/ he this Depo^t did heare the ſaid Burbage tell the
ſaid Braynes/ that it ſhuld not excede the ſome of CC^ll/   But
this Depo^t ſaith that after the ſaid Braynes had lade out vpon
the building & Doing therof to the value (as he ſaid) of fyve
hundreth poundes or theraboutes/ he this Depo^t heard the ſaid
Braynes charge the ſaid James Burbage/ that where he made
him beleve the building therof ſhuld not excede the charge of
CC^ll/ he the ſaid Braynes had lade out fyve hundreth poundes
alredy vp*p*on the ſame/ and then this Depo^t heard the ſaid Burbage tell him/ it was no matter praying him to be co*n*tented/ it
wold ſhortlie quyte the coſt vnto them bothe/ or wo^rd*es* to like
effecte./

To the 3. & 4. that he hath heard the ſaid Braynes ſaye/ that his
Brother Burbage was the onlye meanes/ that he entred in the
taking of the ſaid leaſe/ and building of the ſaid Playe houſe/
and that yf he the ſaid Braynes wold not Joyne w^t him therin he
himſelf ſhuld never be hable to builde it/ for it wold coſt fyve
tymes ſo moche as he was wo^rthe/ And ſaithe that the ſaid
Braines told this Depo^t/ that he was advyſed to ſuffre the ſaid
Burbage to take the ſaid leaſe in his owne name and he to convey
ou*er* to him the ſaid Braynes his executo^rs and aſſignes the moytie
or half of all the profitt*es* growing by the playes & Rent*es* there/
and Burbage to haue the other moytie / [*leaft yf the ſaid Braynes
ſhuld John w^t him* (stricken out)]/ and herevpon the ſaid Burbage entred into CCCC^ll bonde to the ſaid Braynes to *p*erforme
the ſame as by the ſame bond may appere   And this the ſayd
Braynes ſayd he was advyſed to do/ leaſt yf the ſaid leaſe had
come in both ther names/ the Survyvo^r ſhuld go away wth all/
All wch or to the ſame effecte the ſaid James Burbage hath co*n*-
feſſed to this Depo^t dyvers and ſondrye tymes to be true/

To the 5. that vpon the promys & proteſtment of the ſaid James
Burbage, to the ſaid Jo. Braynes/ that he his executo^rs and
aſſeignes ſhuld during the ſaid leaſe haue & Receyve/ the one
half of the proffitt*es* that ſhuld Ryſe by the ſaid Playes there to

be vfed/ and A dyvydent or half alfo of all the Rent*es* of fuche
howfes and thinges as were graunted & were w^tin the Compaffe
of the faid leafe/ fo the faid John Braynes made a g^t fome of
money/ of purpofe & intent/ to go to the building of the faid
Playe houffe/ and thervp*p*on did provyde Tymbre/ and other
ftuffe nedefull for the building y*er*of/ and hyred Carpinters/ and
plaifterers for the fame purpofe and paid the wo^rkemen co*n*tyn-
uallye/ So as he for his part lade out of his owne purce & what
vpon Credit about the fame/ to the fome of vj or vij^C
li. [=6 or 700 *l*.] at the leaft/ And in the fame tyme feing the
faid James Burbage nothing able ether of him felf/ or by his
credit to co*n*trybute any like fome towardes the building therof/
being then to be fynifhed/ or ells to be loft that had bene beftowed
vp*p*on it alredye/ the faid Braynes was dryven to fell his houfe
he Dwelled in/ in Bucklers bery and all his ftock that was left/
and gyve vppe his trade yea in the end to pawne & fell both his
owne garment*es* and his wyves & to ren [sic] in debt to many for
money to fynifhe the faid Playe houffe/ & fo to ymploye himfelf
onlye vp*p*on that matter/ and all whatfoeu*er* he could make/ to
his vtter vndoing/ ffor he faith/ that in the latter end of the
fynifhing therof/ the faid Braynes and his Wyfe the now comp^l.
were dryven to labo^r in the faid wo^rkes/ for faving of fome of the
charge/ in place of ij° laborers/ Whereas the faid James Burbage went about his owne bufynes/ and at fometymes whan he did
take vp*p*on him to do fome thing in the faid wo^rk*es*/ he wold be/
and was allowed A workmans hyre/ as other the workmen there
had/

To the 6. that he hath heard the faid James Burbage confeffe
vp*p*on the accompt*es* and Reconi*n*g*es* had betwene him & the faid
Braynes co*n*cerni*n*g the faid leafe and the matter of the buildinge
of the faid Playehouffe/ that all the charge wch he was at/ in the
accomplifhing of the p*re*miffes from the begynni*n*g to the end did
not amount to the full value of one C^li/ wch this Depo^t verylie
thinketh to be true/ ffor he never knew him but A po^r man *t* but
of fmall Credit/ being by occupac*i*on/ A Joyner/ and reaping but

A ſmall lyving by the ſame/ gave it over/ and became A commen
Player in playes/ And further ſaith/ that he doth knowe/ that
his Credit was ſuche/ as nether merchant nor Artificer wold gyve
him Credit for the value of x^{ll} vnles his brother Braynes wold
Joyne w^t him/ being A man well knowne in london both of his
own wellth and of good credit/ And ſaith y^t he hath heard the
ſaid Braynes by earneſt othe afferme/ that all the readye money
wch his brother Burbage brought fourthe to be ymployd towardes
the building of the ſaid Theater was but about [*fyftie & od
poundes* (stricken out)] xxxvij^{ll}/ and the reſt that made vppe
about the ſome of fyftie & od pound*es* wch was in maner all that
he bore towardes the ſaid charge/ was in od peces of Tymber/
wayneſcott & ſuche like thing*es* and his own labo^r/ wherin the
ſaid Braynes told this Depo^t/ his brother Burbage made him to
allow him/ in ſome thing*es* the value of vj^d for A grote/ So as
this Depo^t knowethe y^t the whole building of the p*r*emiſſes in
effecte and the taking of the ſaid leaſe/ was done at the onlye
charge of the ſaid Braynes by his own goodes/ & credit/

To the 7. that whan the ſaid Playe houſſe was fyniſhed/ and
playes p*er*formed in the ſame/ and great ſomes of money gathered
& had of the repairers therunto the ſaid Braynes told this Depo^t
that his brother Burbage/ co*n*trarye to his faith and promes that
the ſaid Braynes ſhuld haue p*ar*te & p*ar*telyke of the ſame/ did
by the ſpace of about ij° yeres/ purloyne & filche therof to him
ſelf moch of the ſame money/ by A ſecret key wch he cauſed one
Braye A Smyth in Shordiche to make for him of the Commen
box where the money gathered at the ſaid Playes was by both ther
conſent*es* putt in/ by meanes wherof he did not onlye playe falce
w^t him the ſaid Braynes to A great value as it was thoght but
alſo Diſceyve his fellowes the Players/ And many tymes wold
thruſt ſome of the money Devident betwene him & his ſaid ffel-
lowes/ in his boſome or other where about his bodye/ Diſceyving
his fellowes of ther due Devydent/ wch was equally to haue bene
devyded betwene them/ All wch this Depo^t dothe verelie beleve
to be true/ ffor that he hath heard the ſaid James Burbage vp*p*on

fynding of the fame falce key/ confeffe fo moch in effecte to the faid Braynes/ praying him to forgyve him/ and he wold yf he lyeved make him Recompence/ faying it was the Devill that led him fo to do/ And further to this Jnterrogatory he faith not/

To the 8. that he hath bene privie and prefent at & of dyvers variances & contencions betwene the faid Jo. Braynes & James Burbage for & concerning the matters & profittes of the faid Theater/ and that they did fubmitte them felfes therin to the Award & Arbytryment of one Ry. Turnor/ and Jo. Hille/ men of great honeftye & credit/ to make a fynall end of all matters in queftion betwene them, who vppon great difcreffion and indifferiencye betwene them bothe/ having throughlye heard ther grefes/ and Demaundes did Arbitrate & Award in wryting Jndented betwene them readie to be fene that from thenfforthe the faid Jo. Braynes his executors & affignes fhuld haue/ receyve & enioye to them & ther owne vfes/ during the faid leafe/ the one half or moytie of the profittes/ that fhuld grow & ryfe by the playes to be vfed ther/ and alfo of the Rentes ffynes & other yerelie profittes of fuche other tenemtes & places there/ as fhuld yerelie grow due for the fame/ and the faid James Burbage his executors and affignes to haue alfo the other moytie of the premiffes During the faid leafe in lyke maner/

To the 9. that he doth knowe that the faid Arbitrators did alfo Award betwene them/ That yf occafion fhuld move them the faid James Burbage and Jo. Braynes to morgage the faid leafe vppon the Borowing of any fome of money to paye Debtes/ concerning the faid Theater/ that then they both fhuld Joyne in the fame morgage/ and that money coming of the proffittes of the faid Playes & the other faid Rentes and ffynes/ to go to the Redempcion of the faid leafe/ as by the faid Award may appere/

To the 10. that he doth knowe/ and fo is it confeffed by depoficions in the Chaunccerye/ that the faid James Burbage and Jo. Braynes did according to the faid Arbitryment/ having fpeciall

nede/ morgage ther faid leafe/ and the dymyfed premiffes therin
to one Jo. hyde grocer of london/ for the fome (as he Remembreth) of one Cxxv^{ll} or theraboutes payable at A certen Daye/

To the 11. that he doth knowe/ that the faid Cxxv^{ll} was not payd
to the faid Jo. hyde at his Daye/ nor long after/

To the 12. that he doth knowe that ther was payd to the fayd Jo.
hyde/ in the lyfetyme of the faid Jo. Braynes/ as the faid hyde
did confeffe to the now comp^{l}. all the faid Cth and xxv^{ll} faving
the fome of xxx^{ll} or theraboutes/ But whether it was payd
before the faid leafe was forfeitted or no he faith he cannot de-
pofe/ Nor whan or how the faid xxx^{ll} was payd/ after the
deceffe of the faid Jo Braynes/

To the 13. that he did heare the faid Jo. Braynes faye before his
deceffe many & often tymes/ that the faid Johne hyde did faith-
fullye promes vnto him that yf he were payd his principall debt/
and fome reafonable confideracion for the tyme he did forbeare
the fame/ he wold never take the advauntage of the forfetture of
the leafe/ And fyns the death of the faid Jo. Braynes, he this
depo^{t} did dyvers tymes heare the fame Jo. hyde faye to the now
comp^{l} that he wold never take any forfetture of the faid leafe yf
he might haue his money that was due behinde/ and any reafonable
confideracion for the forbearing therof/

To the 14. that he did heare the faid Jo. hyde faye and promes to
the now comp^{l}/ that yf he were payd his money/ w^{t} fome indyf-
ferent confideracion for the forbearing therof/ that he wold reaffure the premiffes to the said comp^{l} and to the faid James Bur-
bage/ in refpecte it was morgaged vnto him/ by both the compl^{tes}
hufband and the faid Burbage/ faying that he verylie tooke it/
that by the death of the compl^{tes} hufband/ his right & intereft
of & in the fame/ did belong to the fame comp^{l}/

To the 15. that he doth verie well Remember/ that on a tyme after

the deceſſe of the ſaid Braynes/ his wyfe the now comp¹ went to
the ſaid Jo. hyde and this Depoᵗ & others in her companye/ and
offered him/ to paye him the money that was behynde vnpayd/
wᶜʰ by his owne confeſſion was but xxxˡˡ/ yf he wold convey
over vnto her the ſaid leaſſe/ and that yf he wold ſo do/ ſhe wold
be bounde to aſſure the ſaid James Burbage of the moytie of all
the proffitteſ and Renteſ therof/ ſaying in verye dede/ Although
the ſaid Burbage wold & ſoght to defeat her of her right therin/
yet wold not ſhe ſo deale wᵗ him/ and then the ſaid hyde made
her anſʳ/ ſaying Whan I am payd my money/ then will I make
it ouₑᵣ to yoᵘ & burbage as yoʳ huſband & Burbage made it to
me/ or ſpeche to the ſame effecte/

To the 16. that he doth knowe that after the death of the ſaid
Jo. Braynes/ the ſaid James Burbage did deteyne in his own
handeₛ/ the proffitteₛ and Renteₛ of the ſaid premiſſes/ of purpoſe (as it was thought) that the ſaid leaſe ſhuld fall forfetted
to the ſaid hyde/ & ſo that he might take it over of the ſaid hyde
in his own name/ or in the name of ſome other to his vſe/ as it
trulie fell out after/ And ſaith that after the death of the ſaid
Braynes the ſaid James Burbage/ did vtterlye denye the comp¹
to take or Receave any more of the proffitteₛ or Renteₛ of the
ſaid premiſſes contrarye to the expreſſe meaning & Wordes of the
foreſaid Awarde & Arbitryment/ Wherby the ſaid Jo Hyde was
not payd his money according to the ſaid Arbitryment/ wᵗ the
Renteₛ and profitteₛ of the premiſſes/ as it ought to haue bene
by the ſaid Arbitryment/

To the 17 that true it is the ſaid James Burbage (as the ſaid Jo
hyde told this Depoᵗ) Did ſo laboʳ him/ what by the ſaid Burbage
wyfe/ and ſpₑciallye by lettₑres from one Mʳ Cope one of the lord
Treaſorers gentlemen/ that he ſhuld make ouₑᵣ his intereſt &
claime of & in the ſaid leaſe/ to Cuthbert Burbage the ſone of the
ſaid James Burbage/ the other now Defendᵗ/ [*to the vſe of him
the ſame James Burbage* (stricken out)]/ vppon the payment of
the ſaid xxxˡˡ & ſome further conſideracₒₙ/ meaning as this

Depo^t thinketh in his confcience/ to Defeat the comp^{lt} of her right in the premiffes/ And then the faid hyde anfred/ this Depo^t that he graunted the rather therunto for that bothe the faid James Burbage & his faid fone Did faithfullie promes him/ that the faid comp^l fhuld haue her contynuall moytie of the proffittes and Rentes of the premiffes/ wch they faithfullie promifed vnto him (as he faid) fo to do/ During the tyme of the faid leafe/ the w^{ch} (as he faid) he wold not haue done yf he had known they wold not haue lett her quyetlie haue the fame/

To the 18. that he doth well Remember/ that the faid James Burbage after the death of the faid Braines & before the Redempcion of the faid leafe did for a tyme fuffer the comp^l to take fome of the profittes of the faid Playes/ fo long as fhe was hable to laye out money/ to the neceffary vfe of the faid Playe houffe/ to the fome of xxx^{ll} or theraboutes as fhe reported/ And no longer/ Whervppon this Depo^t on the comp^{ltes} behalf both before & fins the Redempcion of the fame charged them w^t the fame/ and the faid James made him anf^r/ that fhe fhuld haue her moytie according to the faid Award/ whan all ther Debtes were payd/ and that fhe fhuld fufteyne no wrong ether at the handes of him/ or of his fone/ And likewyfe this Depo^t meeting w^t the fayde Cuthbert dyvers tymes & falling into fpeche w^t him of the faid comp^{ltes} wrong mynistred vnto her by his ffather & him in that they w^{t}held her right from her of the Theater/ he anfwered/ that for his own part he was very well contented that the comp^l fhuld haue her part of the faid Profittes/ yf his father wold agree to it/ being forye that ever he did entre into that accion/ ffor that he had both loft his tyme/ and trobled his M^r in the fame/ Whereas fome other Sute vnto his M^r/ would haue bene more profitable vnto him as had bene to fome of his fellowes that had not ferued his M^r fo long as he had and wifhed he had never Delt in it/

To the 19. that he dothe verelie thinke in his confcience that the faid James Burbage/ and his faid fone/ and ther affignes fyns the laft Accompt or Reconing had & made betwene him the faid James and the faid Jo. Braynes for the proffittes & Rentes of the Theater

& the howſes & tenem^(tes) there/ w^(ch) was about viij or ix yeres
paſt/ to his Remembrance/ haue Receyved of Rentes and proffittes
growing therby to the value of two thowſand markes at the leaſt
for his owne parte/ And ſo moche ſhuld the ſaid Braynes/ and
the now comp^(l) haue had for ther partes of the ſaid proffittes and
Rentes/ yf they had had right/ Beſydes the moytie of CCxxxix^(ll)
w^(ch) the ſaid James Burbage was to paye to the ſaid Braynes as
to one of the Credito^(rs) of money lent out & lade fourth by him
vppon the premiſſes/ and w^(ch) the ſaid James Burbage gave his
word & promes to paye him/ together w^t intereſt for the ſame/
ſo long as it ſhuld be vnpayd/ of the w^(ch) money this Depo^t heard
the ſaid Braynes ſaye A litle before his deceſſe/ that he had not
receyved one penye/ And ſhewed to this Depo^t alſo/ A bill of
xvj^(ll) debt of the ſaid James Burbage w^(ch) he was neuer payd alſo
And beſydes the moytie of the value of certen tymber lead/
Brick/ Tyle/ lyme & ſand/ left of the building of the ſaid Thea-
ter/ wo^rthe (as the ſaid comp^l affirmethe) an hundreth poundes
or an hundreth markes at the leaſt/ And further to this Jnterrogatory he cannot depoſe/ then he hath before Depoſed & ſayd/

To the 20. that he doth knowe and was preſent whan the Ordre
mencioned in this Jnterrogatory was made in the Co^rt of Chaun-
cerye/ betwene the ſaid comp^l/ and the now defend^(tes) in the
favo^r of the ſame defend^(tes)/ Albeit the ſaid def^(tes) did in g^t contempt Diſobey/ and w^t heynous preſumptyous wordes/ neclecte
& ſett the ſaid Ordre at nought/ and the Arbytryment before
mencioned allowed & confirmed by the ſame/ in all Reſpectes and
poyntes/

To the 21. that he can ſay no more in effecte/ then he hath laſt
before ſaid to the laſt former Jnterrogatory/.

To the 22. that he referreth him ſelf to certen Depoſicions of
Witneſſes taken in this co^rte of late/ concerning the manifeſt and
ſcarce tollerable contempt of the Def^(tes) & other of ther company/
againſt the ſaid Ordre/ and the ſaid Arbitrym^t/ All w^(ch) Duelye

and charitablye being confidered/ he this Depo^t Doth verylie
think in his confcience/ that the now comp^l is by this Sute vtterlye
vndone/ and Dyvers of her ffrendes hyndered that haue Relieved
her to the value of ffyve hundreth m*ar*kes/ at the leaft/   And
more to the forefaid J*nterrogatories* he faith not/

                              [Signed]   By me Robart Miles

Henry Laneman of london gentlema*n* of the age of liiij yeres or
therabout*es* fworne and ex^d the daie and yere aforefaid &c   To
the firft J*nterrogatory* that he doth knowe all the p*ar*ties of the
named comp^l and defend^{tes}/ And to the reft of this J*nterrogatory*
he faith he ca*n*not depofe/

To the 2. that he can fay nothing

To the 3. that he can fay nothing

To the 4. that he can fay nothing

To the 5. that he cannot depofe/ onlye he did heare/ that the
building of the Theater at hallywell coft A thowfand m*ar*kes/ but
who did beftowe the charge y*er*of he knoweth not/

To the 6. that he ca*n* fay no more/ but that the comen fpeche
went/ whan the faid Theater was in building that it was Braynes
money & Credit that builded the fame/ and that James Burbage
was at y^t tyme verye vnhable to Joyne therin/

To the 7. that he can fay nothing

To the 8. that he did heare of fome co*n*tenc*i*on & variance that
fell out betwene the faid James Burbage/ and the faid Jo. Braynes
after the fynifhing of the faid Theater and after that plaies were
p*er*formed therin/   And that the faid Contenc*i*on & variance was
by ther confent*es* put to the Arbitryment of certen p*er*fones/ and
that the faid p*er*fones did make an Awarde betwene them/ wher-

unto he doth referre him felf for the troth of the fame/

To the 9. that he Doth ftill referre him felf to the faid Awarde/

To the 10. that he is ingnorant

To the 11. that he is ingnorant

To the 12. that he is ingnorant

To the 13. that he is ingnorant

To the 14. that he is ingnorant

To the 15. that he can fay nothing

To the 16. that true it is/ about vij yeres now fhalbe this next
Wynter/ they the faid Burbage & Braynes having the profittes
of Playes made at the Theater/ and this Depo{t} having the profittes
of the playes Done at the houffe called the Curten/ nere to the
fame/ the faid Burbage and Braynes taking the Curten as an
Efore to their playe houffe/ did of ther own mocion move this
Depo{t} that he wold agree that the proffittes of the faid ij° Playe
howfes might for vij yeres fpace be in Dyvydent betwene them/
Wherunto this Depo{t} vpon reofonable condicions & bondes agreed
& confented and fo contynueth to this Daie/ And faith that at
the firft mocion of this agreem{t} the faid Braynes had his porcion
duelye anfwered him of the faid profittes/ and vntill he dyed/
But after his deceffe the faid Burbage began to abridge his wyfe
the nowe comp{l} of that her hufband had of the premiffes/ and
fhortlie after put her from all/ to the wch vpon fome myflike had
by this Depo{t} of the vnkynde dealing of the faid Burbage, wt the
faid Braynes wyfe, he this Depo{t} told him many tymes that he did
her wrong/ telling him that the comen fame went that it was
braynes that was at the chefe charge of the building of the faid

Theater/   And otherwyſe or more to this Jnt*errogatory* he ſaith
he cannot depoſe

To the 17. that he can ſay nothing

To the 18. that he can ſay nothing

To the 19. that he doth verelie thinke that the ſaid James Burbage
ſyns the Death of the ſaid Braynes who to this Depo^{tes} Remembraunce Dyed w^tin the firſt yere of ther compoſic*ion* and agreem^t
w^t this depo^t hath receyved & had for his parte of the proffitt*es*
of the ſaid ij° playe howſes/ one yere w^t another to this daye/
the ſome of one hundreth m*arkes* or fourſcore poundes by the
yere/   And this is all that he can ſaye to this Jnt*errogatory*/

To the reſt of the Jnterr*ogatories* he ſaith he ca*nn*ot depoſe/
Nor more ſaith in this matter/.

[Signed]   Henry lanman

> William Nicoll of london Notary publiq aged
> xliiij yeres or thereabout*es* ſworne & exa*min*ed
> the laſt daye of Julye in the yere aforeſaid &c.

To this firſt Jnterogatory that he doth knowe the ſaid Margaret
Brayne the Compl*ainant* and James Burbage one of the defend^{tes}
and hath knowen them by the ſpace of xv^{en} or xvj yeres paſt but
he doth nott (to his now remembraunce) knowe the ſaid Cutbert
Burbage or the ſaid Giles Allyn named in the ſaid Jnterogatory/

To the 2. 3. 4. & 5. Jnterogatories this Deponent ſaieth that about
fiftene yeres paſt the ſaid James Burbage and one John Brayn
Deceaſed late huſband of the ſaid Complayn*ant* came to this
Deponent to his then ſhop in the p*ari*ſhe of S^t olave in thold
Jury in london and required to have a leaſe & Coven*antes* drawen
betwene them of the moytie of certen howſes or Ten*ementes*
barne ſtable Theatre gardeins and other premiſſes wch the ſaid
James Burbage then held by leaſe of one Giles Allyn of Hal-

lowell in the Countie of midd*lefex* gent and Sara his wief fet
and being (as this deponent taketh it) at Hollowell nere vnto
ffynnefberry feild*cs* in the Countie of midd*lefex* then fhewing
vnto this deponent as he now remembreth the Copy of the faid
leafe at wch tyme the faid James Burbage and John Brayne did
declare to this deponent that though the leafe was taken in the
name only of the faid James Burbage/ yet it was ment to be
for both their vfes and therfore he the faid James Burbage was
willing to affure the one moytie of the premiffes to the faid John
Brayne/ Whervpon this deponent did drawe and engroffe an
Jndenture of leafe betwene them dated the ix^th daie of Auguft
in the xix^th yere of the raigne of o^r moft gratious foveraigne lady
that now is, to the effecte of their then agreament*es*./ W^ch leafe
fo engroffed this Deponent thinketh (to his now remembraunce)
was not fealed by the faid James Burbage/ for that the originall
leafe made to him by the faid Giles Allyn and Sara his wief was
then at pawne for money wch was borowed for the building of the
faid Theatre/ And therefore the faid John Brayne afterward*es*
about the xxij^th of may in the Twentith yere of the raigne of o^r
faid foue*ra*igne Lady did require this deponent to drawe an obligation wh*e*rein the faid James Burbage fhould be bound to the
faid John Braynes in foure hundreth pound*es* for the making
vnto the faid John Brayne his executo^rs admi*ni*ftrato^rs or affignes
a good and lawfull leafe graunt and other affuraunce of the moitie
or one Juft half of all and fing*u*ler the faid Theatre and other
the p*re*miffes graunted to the faid James Burbage by the faid
originall leafe and of all the benefit of the Coven*a*nt*es* graunt*es*
and agreament*es* comprifed in the faid leafe wch bond or obligac*i*on this deponent made and engroffed according to the agreament betwene the faid p*a*rties./. and afterward*es* the faid James
Burbage did feale and delyver as his dede the faid obligac*i*on to
the faid John Brayne in the prefence of this deponent and one
John Gardyner as by the faid obligation and tefte thereof whervnto he this deponent referreth him felf (being fhewed vnto him
at this his exa*mi*nac*i*on doth appere/ And further this deponent
faieth that fhortlie after the fealing of the faid bond there grew

fome Contenc*i*on betwene the said James Burbage and John Brayne towching the yndifferent dealing and collecting of the money for the gallories in the faid Theatre for that he well remembreth the faid John Brayne did thinck him felf much agreyved by the indyrect dealing of the faid James Burbage therein/ and coming then both together in the fhop of this deponent about bond*es* of arbitrament wch this deponent thincketh he made betwene them to abide the order & arbitrament of one Richard Turner and John hill/ they the fame James Burbage and John Brayne fell a reafoning together of the yll dealing of the faid James Burbage./. at wch tyme this deponent was prefent and doth well remember that the faid John Brayne did declare theis word*es* or the like in effect how he had left his trade and fold his howfe by the meanes of the faid James Burbage to Joyne with him in the building of the faid Theatre and that he had difburfed a great deale more money about the fame then the faid James Burbage had/ and there repeated what he had laied out and what the faid Burbage had laied out (the certen fom*m*es the deponent doth not now certenly remember) but he thincketh that the fom*m*e then difburfed by the faid John Brayne was three tymes at the leaft as muche more as the fom*m*e then difburfed by the faid James Burbage, and in the end declared fo many word*es* of the ill dealing of the faid Burbage toward*es* him in that dealing of the Theatre/ that Burbage did there ftrike him wth his fift and fo they went together by the eares Jn fomuch that this deponent could herdly p*a*rt them/ And further this deponent faieth that afterward*es* the xij^th daie of July in the faid Twentith yere of the raigne of o^r faid foue*r*aigne Lady the faid Richard Turner and John Hill did make enfeale and geve vp their award betwene the faid James Burbage and John Brayne in the prefence of this deponent and George Goffe then his apprentice as by the faid award Jndented and the Tefte therof wch was fhewed to this deponent at this his examynac*i*on doth appere/ and more to the faid Jnterogatories to his now remembrance he cannot depofe/. To the vj^th Jnterogatory this deponent thincketh that the faid James Burbage at the tyme of the taking of the faid leafe of

m^r Allyn and his wief was not able to beſtowe for his p*a*rte of
his owen money wth out Credit) the ſom*m*e of one hundred
poundes towardes the building of the ſaid Theatre for that this
deponent thincketh that he the ſaid Burbage was not then worth
a hundred poundes and as towching his credyt he thincketh it was
but ſmale/ and more he cannot depoſe/

And to all the reſt of the ſaid Jnterogatories this deponent ſaieth
he cannot depoſe otherwiſe then he hath alredy depoſed/

[Signed] p*er* me Willi*a*m Nicoll

WILL OF MARGARET BRAYNE

Commissary Court of London, Register 1592–97, p. 26.

[The will of John Braync, an old one, dated 1 July, 1578, and proved 10
August, 1586, just after his death, is also registered in this court, in the
register for 1585–92, p. 29. But as he had disposed of most of his property by deeds of gift, and the will makes no mention of theatrical interests,
no further notice need be taken of it. The widow, of course, claimed the
moiety of the Theatre as executrix.]

In the name of God Amen the eight daye of Aprill Anno 1593 in
the xxxv^th yeere of the Reigne of our ſou*er*eigne Lady Elizabeth
by the grace of god Quene of Englande ffrance and Irelande de-
fendor of the faith &c   I Margaret Braine of the p*a*riſhe of S^t
Mary Matfellon ali*a*s whitechapell in the Countie of Midd*lesex*
widdow beinge wholl in mynde ſyck of body but of a p*er*fect
memory and remembraunce laude and prayſe be given to allmightie god therefore doe make and ordeine this my preſent
writinge conteyninge herein my laſt will and Teſtament in manner
and forme followinge that is to ſaye ffirſt and principally and
aboue all thing*es* I comende my ſoule to allmightie god my maker
and to Jeſus Chriſt his ſonne my ſavio^r and redemer truſting in
and by his meritt*es* and precious blood ſheddinge to be ſaved and
to atteine liefe eu*er*laſtinge   And as concerninge the diſpoſicion
of all and ſingular ſuch my good*es* Chattles ymplement*es* and
houſhold ſtuff and other good*es* whatſoeu*er* movable and vnmov-

able which I am now invefted or wch to me is or fhalbe by any
manner of wayes or meanes howfoeu*er* app*ur*teyninge or belonging I freely and wholy geve and bequeth the fame in manner and
forme followinge   That is to faye   Item I geue and bequeth vnto
Robart Miles Cittizen and goldfmith of London in confideraci*on*
that I am greatly indebted vnto him in fuch greate fome and fomes
of money that all the good*es* I haue in the wholl worlde will
nothinge countervaile the fame all fuch intereft right propertie
claime and demande whatfoeu*er* which I the faide Margaret
Brayne haue fhould or ought to haue of in or to the one moytie
or halfe p*ar*te of the playhoufe comonly called the Theater Nere
Holliwell in the Countie of Middlefex   And alfo my mynde and
will is that the faide Robart Miles fhall haue all the benefite
proffitt and comoditie thereof any faige [sic] comynge or growinge or wch by any meanes may difcende or come by vertue of
the faide moytie or half p*ar*te of the Theater to me in Right belonginge as aforefaide   Item I geue and bequeth vnto the faide
Robart Miles all and all manner of band*es* bills fpecialties debt*es*
fom*m*e and fomes of money whatfoeuer as I now haue or wch by
vertue of any fuch band*es* or fpecialties may be gotten wonne or
obteyned or which now and here after fhall growe dewe and payable   And laftly I geue and bequeth vnto the faid Robart Myles
all and fingular my good*es* Chattalls houfhold ftuff and other of
my good*es* whatfoeuer   Item my will is in confideraci*on* p*ar*tly
of the premiffes that the faide Robart Miles fhall keepe educate
and bringe vp Katherine Braine my hufband*es* daughter of whome
I hope he wilbe good and haue an honeft care for her preferment
And I make and ordeine the faide Robart Miles fole Executor of
this my faide Teftament and laft will   It witnes whereof I the
faide Margaret Braine haue herevnto fett my hande and feale the
daye and yeres firft aboue written   fign*um* d*ic*te Margarete
Brayne   Sigillat*um* et deliberat*um* in prefencia Georgij Harrifon
fcr Nicholas Bifhop John Pattefon witneffes Burbary Bifhop and
Elizabeth Hunt/

[Proved May 3, 1593.]

MYLES *V.* BURBAGE

Chancery Decrees and Orders, vol. 1593 "B," 785. Hilary, 36 Elizabeth (1593–4).

xj° die ffebruarij [1593–4]

Robte Myles p^{lt}
James Burbage
Cutbert Burbage
and others def^{tes}

fforafmuch as this Cowrte was the prefent dayYnformed by Mr Scott beinge of the p^{ltes} councell That the Matter wherein Margarett Brayne was latelye p^{lt} againft the aboue named def^{tes} ftandinge heretofore Referred vnto Mr Dr Stanhop and Mr Dr Legg two of the M^{rs} of the Cowrte and they beinge redye to make theyr Report the fayd Margarett then p^{lt} dyed. fynce wch tyme the faid Robte Myles hath exhibited A bill and Served proces vpon the def^{tes} to Anfwere the fame to revyue the faid form^r fuyte and the orders of Referment made theirevpon in the fame ftate yt ftood at the tyme of the form*er* p^{ltes} deathe It ys therefore ordered that the fayd M^{rs} of this Cowrte fhall att the nowe p^{ltes} fuyte take the lyke confyderac*i*on as they were to doe of the Matters to them before referred at the form*er* p^{ltes} fuyte and make fuche Report thereof as by the form*er* orders made in that behalf they were appoynted to doe That fuch further order may be taken therevpon as to this Cowrte fhalbe thought meete/

BURBAGE *V.* MYLES

Chancery Decrees and Orders, vol. 1594 "A," 857; also in 1594 "B," 862. Hilary, 37 Elizabeth (1594–5).

xiiij die Marcij [1594–5]

James Burbage p^l
Robte Miles defendt

fforafmuche as the Right honorable Sr John Puckeringe knight Lorde keep*er* of the greate Seale of England was this prefent daye informed on the p^{les} behalf by M^r

Borne beinge of his Councell that the faid parties haue croffe
billes the one againft the other and that witneffes in the faid
feverall cawfes are examined and publicacion at one tyme by confente of the faid parties was longe fynce had And that the cawfe
wherein the faid Burbage ys p¹ for the moft parte Concernethe
the other And that the cawfe wherein the faid Miles is p¹ ys appointed to be heard at the Rolles Chappel on Monday the xxiij
day of May next It was therefore moft humbly defired by the
faid Mʳ Borne ffor that the matter wherein the faid Burbage is p¹
againft the faid Miles was firft comenced and is alfo Reddy for
the hearinge as aforefaide might be alfo heard together wᵗʰ the
other cawfe wherein the faid Miles is p¹ on the xxviijᵗʰ day of
May next at the faid Chappell of the Rolles It is ordered by his
Lo: that if the faid Miles fhall not by the fecond Retorne of the
next terme fhowe vnto this Courte good cawfe to the contrarye
then the faid cawfe wherein the faid James Burbage is p¹ is fet
downe to be heard on the faid xxviijᵗʰ day of May wᵗʰout further
mocion to be made in that behalfe And the faid Miles or his
Attorney ys to be warned hereof/

MYLES *v.* BURBAGE

*Chancery Decrees and Orders, vol. 1595 "A," 130; also in
1595 "B," 140. Easter, 37 Elizabeth (1595).*

xxviij die Maij [1595]

Robte Miles p¹ James Burbage and Cutberte Bur-bage defendᵗᵉˢ	The matter in queftion betweene the faide parties towchinge the moytie of the leafe of the Theator in the bill men-cioned and the proffites thereof Comynge

this prefent day to be heard in the
prefence of the Councell learned on bothe partes It was alledged
by the defendᵗᵉˢ Councell that the faid p¹ had not only a bonde of
400ˡⁱ made vnto him by the defᵗᵉˢ for the Affigninge over of the
fame moytie vnto him wherevpon a demurrer ys nowe joyned at

the comon lawe, but alſo an other bonde of 200ˡˡ made for the performance of an Arbytrament made betwene the ſaid parties wᶜʰ the ſaid pˡ pretendeth to be alſo forfyted by the defᵗ And therefore as the ſaid Councell alledged the pˡ hathe no neade of the Ayde of this Courte for the ſaid leaſe and profittes It ys therevpon thought fitt and ſoe ordered by this Courte that the ſaid pˡ ſhall proceede at the comon lawe againſt the ſaid defendᵗ vpon the ſaid bondes To thend yt may be ſeene whether the pˡ can Relive him ſelfe vpon the ſaid bondes or not But if yt fall out that the pˡ canot be Relived vpon the ſaide bondes Then the matter ſhall Receave a ſpedy heringe in this Corte And ſuche order ſhalbe geven therevpon As the equity of the cavſe ſhall Require And in the meane tyme the mattr ys Reynd[═Re-teyned] in this courte

[End of the case in Chancery. This final order, with modern spelling and wrong date of 1596 for 1595, was printed first by J. P. Collier, *Actors* (*n. s.*), p. 10.

Myles was unable to get relief at the Common Law. The secret of the matter is that the case of Widow Brayne and Myles had no foundation in either law or equity, and that it was prosecuted solely by Myles's money from the first, out of malicious enmity by her and him toward the Bur-bages. Failing in both the Chancery and the Common Law, Myles again took up the case, after the death of James Burbage in 1597, this time in the Court of Requests, as shown in the next document, to harass his widow and his sons Cuthbert and Richard Burbage.

It would have been remarkable if Shakespeare had not fused some of Myles's traits into immortal features, particularly his Shylock-like insist-ence on the pound of flesh. Such annoyances to the close business asso-ciates of the great dramatist, hindering the success of the company, can hardly have failed to leave a residuum of human experience plastic to the hand of the poet.]

MYLES *v.* BURBAGE AND ALLEN

Court of Requests Proceedings, Uncalendared, Bdl. 306.

BILL

[Bill only. No answer has ever been attached to it. Filing entry, regularly placed on back of bill, wanting. Undated; but internal evidence shows the bill was drawn early in 1597, shortly after the death of James Burbage, which fell in February. The first court-order on it is dated May 9, 1597. The suit is an attack on the Burbage estate. Having failed in his previous long litigation, Miles as executor of the late Margaret Brayne, now claims a moiety of the Theatre and 600 *l.* as due to him. Giles Allen is cunningly made co-defendant with the Burbages. It is evident on the face of it that the case could not stand in either law or equity.]

To the Quenes Moſte excellent Ma^{tle}
in her highnes courte of Requeſte

Humblye complaynyng ſheweth vnto your Moſte excellent ma^{tle} your ma^{tes} moſte faithfull ſubiect Robert Myles of London Gouldſmythe executo^r of the laſt will and teſtament of Margerette Braynes Deceaſed executrixe of the laſt will and teſtament of John Braynes her huſband allſo Deceaſed That wheras one Gyles Allen gent and Sara his wief did for a ffyne of twentye pownd*es* wherof one haulf was paid by the ſaid John Braynes and the other by one James Burbage Deceaſed by their Deede Jndented Demyſed and leaſed to the ſaid James Burbage in the eightenth yeare of the Quenes Ma^{tes} reigne Dyvers meſſuadg*es* and tennement*es* and vacant peeces of grounde in Hallowell in the countye of Myddleſexe for the terme of twenty and one yeares rendring the yearly rent of fowrtene pownd*es* in which Demyſe or leaſe the ſaid James did covenaunte to beſtowe two hundreth pownd*es* in buylding*es* in and vppon the Demyſed premyſſes Jn conſyderacyon wherof the ſaid Gyles and Sara did covenaunte to and with the ſaid James and his aſſignes that hee the ſaid Gyles and Sara and their heyres and aſſignes within tenn yeares followyng the begynyng of the ſaid

158

demyſe would make a New Demyſe or leaſe of the premyſſes to
the ſaid James or his aſſignes for one and twenty yeares to begynne att the makyng of the ſaid demyſe rendring the lyke rent as
aforeſaid and vppon the lyke covenauntes as the former demyſe
was made except as in the ſaid covenauntes is excepted for
Makyng of which ſaid leaſe the ſaid Gyles allſo became bounde
to the ſaid James in a ſome of money vnknowne to the ſaid Robert
and allſo the ſaid Gyles and Sara did further covenaunte to and
with the ſaid James and his aſſignes that att any tyme before the
end of the firſt leaſe aforeſaid the ſaid James and his aſſignes
mighte haue taken Downe and carryed awaye all ſuch buyldinges
as ſhould be buylded by the ſaid James and his aſſignes in a
gardyne and void grownd demyſed by the ſaid former leaſe excepte ſuch buyldyngs as ſhould bee buylt by the expenſe of the
ſaid two hundreth powndes And wheras allſo the ſaid James
beyng not able to buyld accordinge to the agrement made
and to his Deſire vppon the Demyſed premyſes dyd both
before and after the ſaid firſt Demyſe and leaſe ſoe taken
agree and promyſe to and with the ſaid John Braynes that
the ſaid John and his executoᵣˢ ſhould haue the bennefytte
and profyttes both of the firſt demyſe and lykewyſe of the ſecond
demyſe which was to bee made and allſo of the covenaunte and
covenauntes aforeſaid and of all other covenauntes and bondes by
the ſaid Gyles and Sara or any of them for or conſernyng the
premyſſes to the yntent and in conſyderacyon that the ſaid John
ſhould dyſburſe a moytye both of the ſaid two hundreth powndes
and of all other chardges which ſhould aryſe and growe in
buyldyngs or otherwyſe concernyng the premyſſes nowe ſoe yt
ys and yt maie pleaſe your moſte excellent maᵗⁱᵉ that ſince the firſt
Demyſe and agrement as aforeſaid the ſaid John Braynes dyd
ioyne with the ſaid James in the buyldyng aforeſaid and dyd
expend thervppon greater ſomes then the ſaid James that ys to
ſaie att leaſt fyue or ſixe hundreth powndes after which tyme
the ſaid John Did for a tyme perceyue & take proffyttes of the
moytye of the ſaid demyſed premyſſes by the aſſent of the ſaid
James as alſo by an arbitrament betwene them made by Richard

Turnar & John Hill vntill the said James did morgage the said leafe vnto one John Hide for a hundreth twentye fyue pownd*es* or therabout*es* and did forfeyte the said leafe vnto the said John Hide for non payment of thirty pownd*es* only all the which Money thirty pownd*es* excepted was paid by the said John Braynes vnto the said John Hide who allwayes made faithfull promyfe that vppon the paiem^t of the said thirty powndes and fome confyderacyon befide for the forbearyng of the money hee would affure the leafe back agayne vnto the said John Braynes and the said James Burbage and theyr affignes all the which hee was Moved vnto by the reafon that hee the said John Hide dyd know of the said agrement and ioynt expenfes and p*er*ceptyon of proffytt*es* by the said John and James before the said morgage after the which tyme the said Hide by covyne of the said James and one Cutberd Burbage his fonne contrarye to his faithfull promyfe that hee would affure the said leafe vnto the said John Braynes and to the said James Burbage not any waye takyng advantage of the said morgage did convaye the said leafe vppon paiement of the said thirty pownd*es* to the said Cutberd only to defeate the said agrement which said convaieance was fome feaven yeares agoe or therabout*es* fince which tyme the said Cutberd hath taken all the proffytt*es* of the said leafe   The which said leafe is nowe expired   And the said James Burbage is Deceafed and the said Braynes being yndetted yn the fome of fyue hundreth pownd*es* to this compl^t made his wief Margerette his executrix and Died which Margerette allfo remaynyng in the Dett as afore-faid to yor said fubiect made him to that end her executo^r and Died fithence which tyme the said Robert as executo^r to the said Margerette the executrixe of the said John Braynes hath often required the said Cutberd and Gyles and Sara to p*er*mytte and fuffer him to take Downe fuch buyldinge*s* as by the covenaunte aforefaid were to be taken downe and to allow this compl^l the moytye of the tymber and other thinges or the value of the moytye therof and allfo this compl^t hath often required the said Gyles and Sara according to the covenaunte aforefaid to make to him as executo^r of Margerette Braynes aforefaid executrixe

of the faid John a leafe of the moytye of the premyffes before
Demyfed accordinge to the covenaunte and agrement*es* aforefaid
and allfo allthoughe the faid Robert hath required the faid
Cutberd to allowe him the arrerages of the moyty of the p*r*offytt*es* of the Demyfed p*r*emyffes aforefaid receyved by the faid
Cutberd fythence the convayance therof to him Made by John
Hide aforefaid yett that to Doe they vtterly Deny contrarye to all
equitye and good confcience and Wheras allfo the faid James
had taken all the p*r*offytt*es* of the faid demyfed p*r*emyffes contrarye to the trufte aforefaid vntill thaffignement made by Hide
as aforefaid to the faid Cutberd and becaufe hee was other wyfe
yndebted to the faid Braynes in obligacyons in fixe hundreth
pownd*es* and fithence Died inteftate and one Ellen Burbage hath
taken admynyftracyon of the good*es* of the faid James and hath
gotten good*es* and chattells of his into her hand*es* amounting to
a thowfand pownd*es* refufeth to paie and allowe to this comp
the arrerages of the moytye of the p*r*offytt*es* taken by the faid
James before the faid affignem^t and allfo to paie the faid other
Dett*es* alledging fhee hath noe good*es* in her hand*es* vnadmynyf-
tred wherby yor ma^{tes} pore fubiect is likely eu*er*y waie to be De-
feated except hee maie haue fome releyf before yor ma^{tye} in this
honnorable court And forafmuche allfo as yor ma^{tes} pore fubiect
is alltogether without his remedy att the com*m*on law for the
recou*er*ye of the moytye of the p*r*offittes of the Theater & other
the land*es* and tennement*es* foe wrongfully taken by the faid
James and Cutberd Burbage by the reafon that the faid John
Braynes had noe affignem^t made vnto him of the faid leafe foe
taken by the faid James Burbage of the faid Gyles Allen allthough
yt were taken as well to the vfe of the faid John Braynes as vnto
the vfe of the faid James and foe lykewyfe of the faid bennefytte
of all the covenaunt*es* conteyned in the faid leafe and forafmuche
allfo as yor Ma:^{tes} pore fubiect hath noe remedye by the com*m*on
lawe to compell the faid Gyles Allen and the faid Sara to make
a New leafe according to his covenaunt*es* conteyned in the faid
leafe for a longer tyme allthough hee is yntereffed yn all equitye
in the fame as execuro^r vnto the faid Margerette Braynes thexecu-

trixe of the faid John Braynes who beftowed all the Coft in effect
vppon the buyldinges & ftood vppon the faithfull promas of the
faid James & Cutberd to have a moytie of the faid leafe to be
affigned and forafmuche allfo as yor Ma:^{tes} pore fubiect ys alltogether wthout his remedye vppon the faid bondes of fixe hundreth powndes as aforefaid they being made void by the connyng
practyzes of the faid James Burbage Cutbert Burbage & the faid
Ellen by attachme^{tes} & oth^r devyfe And forafmuche allfo as the
faid Gyles Allen and Sara haue bynne required to make a lease
of the moytye of the premyffes as aforefaid who hath refufed foe
to doe Jn tender confideracyon wherof Maie yt pleafe yor Ma:^{tie}
the premiffs confidred to graunte vnto yor pore fubiect yor mofte
gracyous writte of Pryvye feale to be Derected vnto the faid
Ellen Burbage Gyles Allen & Sara his wief and Cutbert Burbage
comaunding them perfonally to appeare before yor ma^{tes}. counfell
of yor highnes court of Requeftes att a certeyne tyme therin
lymytted & appoynted then and there to anfwhere the premyffes
and allfo to abide fuch order and Derectyon as fhall feme to ftand
with goode confcience And yor fubiect accordinge to his Duty
wyll Dailie praie for yor Ma:^{tes} raigne in all happines long to
raigne ouer vs To the pleafure of Allmightye God.

                                            Scott   [attorney]

COURT ORDER, MAY 9, 1597

Requests, Misc. Books, vol. 48 (Draft Order Books)

Nono die Maij [A° xxxix R^{ne} Elizabethe (1597)]

Roberte Myles compl^t Cuthbert Burbage and others defend^{tes}
vppon the mocion of m^r Walter beinge of counfaill wth the faid
defend^{tes} yt is Ordered that the Atturneis on bothe fydes conferr
the bill preferred by the plaintiff into her ma^{tes} highe Corte of
Chauncery againft the faid def^{tes} together wth his bill heare dependinge in this corte, And yf vppon reporte thereof to be made
yt fhall appeare that they bothe conteyn one matter in fubftaunce
and effecte, Then the fame matter fhalbe fromhence difmiffed/

COURT ORDER, MAY 27, 1597

Idem.

xxvij^{mo} die Maij A° p*r*edic*t*o (1597)

ffor a*f*muche as in the cau*f*e at the *f*ute of Robe*r*te Myles compl^t again*f*t Giles Allen and others defend^{tes} Mr Scott beinge of coun- *f*aill wth the *f*aid compl^t hathe this day enformed her Ma^{tes} coun- *f*aill in this corte that the p*er*fons named in the bill wch form*er*ly depended in Chaunc*er*y concerninge this cau*f*e and in the bill nowe dependinge in this corte conc*er*ninge the *f*ame cau*f*e are not all one but *f*eu*er*all and di*f*tincte Therefore vppon moc*i*on of Mr Scott afore*f*aid yt ys Ordered (notwth*f*tandinge any former Order) that this cau*f*e *f*halbe reteyned in corte to be heard in the *f*ame, And that the *f*aid defend^{tes} *f*hall make their full and p*er*fect Aun*f*weres vppon their othes vnto the *f*aid compl^{tes} bill in this corte wthout delay at their p*er*ills/

[Succeeding orders, if any, are lost. The Order Books that should have contained them are missing. It is doubtful if answers were ever made, as above ordered. In any case, they are not now extant, for we have searched the records of the Court of Requests from end to end and transcribed for publication all the theatrical documents they contain, without coming upon the answers referred to.]

ALLEN *v.* STREET

Queen's Bench, Trinity, 42 Elizabeth. (1600), m. 587.

[This suit was brought by Giles Allen nominally against Peter Street, the carpenter, but in effect against Cuthbert Burbage, for tearing down the Theatre. In the course of it, the unexecuted lease of 1585, incorporat- ing main parts of the original lease of 1576, is quoted entire. The case was stopped by the Court of Requests, first by injunction of April 10, 1600, and finally by decree of Oct. 18, 1600. See next suit. The present suit was found by Halliwell-Phillipps, who quoted extracts from it in his *Outlines,* I, 348–49, 359–60, 361–373. Allen caused the pleadings to be entered on the records, contrary to an order of the Court of Requests of May 31, 1600. See affidavit of Cuthbert Burbage on it, June 11, 1600, Sir Julius Caesar's order, of same date, for arrest of Allen for contempt, Allen's statement of the affair, in his Star Chamber suit, Allen *v.* Burbage, 1602, and the examination of Richard Lane in the same suit.]

Adhuc de Termino fancte Trinitatis Tefte J. Popham

Midd ff Memorandum quod alias scilicet Termino Pafche Anno regni
domine Elizabethe nunc Regine Anglie quadragefimo primo
coram eadem domina Regina Apud Weftmonafterium venit
Egidius Aleyn Armiger per Johannem Tanner Attornatum suum
Et protulit hic in Curia dicte domine Regine tunc ibidem quandam billam suam verfus Petrum Strete in Cuftodia Marrefcalci
&c de placito tranfgreffionis Et sunt plegii de profequendo scilicet
Johannes Dov & Ricardus Rov Que quidem billa sequitur in hec
verba ff Middlesexia ff Egidius Aleyn Armiger queritur de
Petro Strete in Cuftodia Marrefcalci Marefcalcie domine Regine
coram ipfa Regina exiftente de eo quod ipfe vicefimo die Januarij
Anno regni domine Elizabethe nunc Regine Anglie quadragefimo
primo vi & armis &c Claufum ipfius Egidij vocatum the Jnner
Courte yarde parcellam nuperi Monafterij Prioratus de Hallywell modo diffoluti Apud Hallywell in Comitatu predicto fregit
& intrauit Et herbam ipfius Egidij ad valenciam quadraginta
solidorum adtunc in Claufo predicto crefcentem pedibus suis
ambulando conculcauit & confumpfit Et quandam structuram
ipfius Egidij ibidem fabricatam & erectam vocatam the Theater
ad valenciam septingentarum librarum adtunc & ibidem diruit
divulfit cepit & abcariauit Et alia enormia ei intulit contra pacem
dicte domine Regine ad dampnum ipfius Egidij octingentarum
librarum Et inde producit sectam &c

Et modo ad hunc diem scilicet veneris proximum proft Craftinum
sancte Trinitatis ifto eodem Termino vfque quem diem predictus
Petrus Strete habuit licenciam ad billam predictam interloquen-
dum Et tunc ad refpondendum &c Coram domina Regina apud
Weftmonafterium venerunt tam predictus Egidius Alleyn per
Attornatum suum predictum quam predictus Petrus Strete per
Thomam Petre Attornatum suum Et idem Petrus defendit vim
& iniuriam quando &c Et quoad venire vi & armis ac totum &
quicquid quod eft fuppofitum fieri contra pacem dicte domine
Regine nunc preter fraccionem & intracionem in claufum predic-
tum & herbe predicte conculcacionem & confumpcionem Necnon

dirupcionem divulcionem capcionem & abcariacionem predicte
Structure vocate the Theater idem Petrus dicit quod ipse in nullo
est inde culpabilis Et de hoc ponit se super patriam Et predictus Egidius similiter &c Et quoad predictam fraccionem &
intracionem in claufum predictum & herbe predicte conculcacionem & consumpcionem necnon dirupcionem divulcionem capcionem & abcariacionem predicte Structure vocate the Theater idem
Petrus dicit quod predictus Egidius accionem suam predictam
inde verfus eum habere seu manutenere non debet quia quoad
predictam fraccionem & intraccionem in claufum predictum &
herbe predicte conculcacionem & consumpcionem idem Petrus
dicit quod predictus Egidius Alleyn dudum ante predictum tempus quo supponit tranfgreffionem illam fieri seisitus fuit de &
in predicto Claufo cum pertinentiis in quo &c in dominico suo
vt de feodo Et sic inde seisitus exiftens idem Egidius poftea &
ante predictum tempus quo &c scilicet   die   Anno
regni dicte domine Elizabethe nunc Regine Anglie   apud
Halliwell predictam in predicto Comitatu Middlefexia dimisit
conceffit & ad firmam tradidit cuidam Cutberto Burbage executoribus & Affignatis suis Claufum predictum cum pertinentiis
habendum & tenendum Claufum predictum cum pertinentiis eidem
Cutberto Burbage quidem ambabus partibus placeret reddendo
pro inde annuatim durante termino predicto quatuordecim libras
legalis monete Anglie heredibus & affignatis suis ad quatuor anni
terminos videlicet ad fefta Annunciacionis beate Marie virginis
Nativitatis sancti Johannis Baptiste sancti Michiaelis Archangeli
& Natalis domini per equales porciones virtute cuius quidem
dimiffionis predictus Cutbertus in Claufum predictum cum pertinentiis in quo &c intrauit & fuit inde poffeffionatus per quod
idem Petrus vt seruiens eiufdem Cutberti ac per eius mandatum
predicto tempore quo &c in predictum Claufum in quo &c fregit
& intrauit Et herbam in Claufo predicto crefcentem pedibus ambulando conculcauit & confumpfit prout ei bene licuit Et quoad
predictas dirupcionem divulcionem capcionem & abcariacionem
predicte structure vocate the Theater idem Petrus dicit quod
dudum ante tranfgreffionem illam superius fieri suppofitam pre-

dictus Egidius Alleyn & Sara vxor eius fuerunt coniuncte seisiti
de predicto clauso vocato the Jnner Courte dudum parcella dicti
nuperi monasterij Prioratus de Hollowell modo disoluti in dominico
suo vt de feodo Et ijdem Egidius & Sara sic inde seisiti ex-
istentes dudum ante transgressionem predictam superius fieri sup-
positam scilicet decimo tercio die Aprilis Anno regni dicte domine
Elizabethe nunc Regine Anglie decimo octauo apud Hollywell predictam in predicto Comitatu Middlesexia per quandam Jndenturam factam inter eosdem Egidium Alleyn per nomen Egidij
Allyen de Hollywell in Comitatu Middlesexia generosi & Saram
vxorem eius de vna parte & Jacobum Burbage de londonia Joyner
ex altera parte cuius alteram partem sigillis ipsorum Egidij
Alleyn & Sare vxoris eius sigillatam idem Petrus hic in Curia
profert dimiserunt clausum predictum cum pertinentiis inter alia
eidem Jacobo Burbage habendum & tenendum clausum predictum
cum pertinentiis prefato Jacobo Burbage executoribus & assignatis suis a festo Annunciacionis beate Marie virginis vltimo
elapso ante datum Jndenture predicte vsque finem & terminum
viginti & vnius annorum extunc proxime & imediate sequentem
& plenarie complendum & finiendum Et predictus Jacobus Burbage per eandem Jndenturam convenit & concessit pro se heredibus executoribus administatoribus & assignatis suis & pro quolibet eorum ad & cum prefato Egidio Alleyn & Sara vxore eius
heredibus & assignatis suis quod ipse idem Jacobus Burbage executores vel Assignati sui tam in consideracione predicte dimis-
sionis & termini annorum per Jndenturam predictam concessam
quam pro & in consideracione Maheremij laterum anglice Bricke
tegularum plumborum & omnium aliarum rerum anglice stuffe
provenientum de tenementis horreo & omnibus alijs premissis per
Jndenturam predictam dimissis ad eius aut eorum custagia &
onera infra decem annos proxime sequentes datum Jndenture
predicte impenderent & exponerent in & super edificacionem
alteracionem & emendacionem predictarum domorum & edificiorum pro melioracione eorundem vt in eadem Jndentura predicta
prefertur per prefatum Jacobum Burbage executores seu assig-
natos suos faciendas summam ducentarum librarum legalis mo-

nete Angl*ie* ad minus valore tant*i* predict*orum* vet*er*um Maherem*ij*
& r*erum* angl*ice* stuffe circa ead*em* impendend*orum* & expo-
nend*orum* Computato parcella predic*t*e sum*m*e ducent*arum* libra-
rum Et vet*er*ius p*r*edic*t*i Egidius Alleyn & Sara vxor eius convenerunt & conceff*er*unt p*r*o seip*f*is & heredib*us* executorib*us*
adminiftratorib*us* & affigna*t*is suis & p*r*o quolibet eo*rum* ad &
cum p*r*efato Jacobo Burbage executorib*us* & affigna*t*is suis p*er*
eandem Jndenturam q*uod* ijdem Egidius & Sara vel vnus eo*rum*
vel hered*es* vnius eo*rum* ad aliquid tempus vel tempora infra
decem annos p*r*oxim*e* sequent*es* datum Jndenture predic*t*e ad &
sup*er* licitam requificionem vel demand*am* p*r*edic*t*i Jacobi Burbage executo*rum* adminiftrato*rum* vel affigna*torum* suo*rum* ad
eius & eo*rum* cuftag*ia* & on*e*ra in lege fac*er*ent aut fieri cauf*ar*ent
p*r*efato Jacobo Burbage executorib*us* aut affigna*t*is suis novam
dimiffionem seu conceffionem simi*l*em conceffioni in Jndentura
p*r*edic*t*a specificat*e* omn*ium* p*r*edict*orum* Mefuagio*rum* tenemento*rum* ter*r*a*rum* fundi & soli & ceter*o*rum premiff*orum* p*er* Jndenturam p*r*edic*t*am preconceff*orum* p*r*o t*er*mino viginti & vnius anno*rum* incipiendo a die confeccionis eiufdem conceffionis sic
facie*nde*/ reddendo proinde annuatim p*r*edic*t*um annualem reddit*um* quatuor decem libra*rum* ad feita p*r*emencionat*a* & sub
tal*ibus* condicion*ibus* convencion*ibus* Articulis & agreamen*t*is
qual*es* ante & poft hanc convenc*i*onem in p*r*edic*t*a Jndentura men-
cionant*ur* & expreff*antur* & non al*iter* p*r*eter hanc convenc*i*onem
p*r*o confeccione nove dimiffionis infra decem annos & p*r*edic*t*am
convenc*i*onem p*r*o impendicione anglice the beftowinge predic*t*e
sum*m*e ducent*arum* libra*rum* prout p*er* erudit*um* concilium p*r*e-
dic*t*i Jacobi executo*rum* vel affigna*torum* suo*rum* racionabilit*er*
advif*ar*et*ur* vel devif*ar*et*ur* modo & forma p*r*edic*t*is/ Et vlterius
p*r*edic*t*i Egidius Alleyn & Sara vxor eius convenerunt & conceff*er*unt p*r*o seip*f*is heredib*us* executorib*us* & affigna*t*is suis &
quolibet eo*rum* sep*ar*atim convenit & conceffit ad [&] cum p*r*e-
fato Jacobo Burbage executorib*us* & affigna*t*is suis q*uod* licit*um*
foret eidem Jacobo executorib*us* seu affigna*t*is suis in confideraci*o*ne impendicionis & expoficionis p*r*edic*t*arum ducent*arum*
libra*rum* modo & forma p*r*edic*t*is ad aliquod tempus & tempora

ante finem predicti termini viginti & vnius anno*rum* per predict*am* Jndentur*am* concef*s*i aut ante finem predicti Termini viginti & vnius anno*rum* poft confeccionem Jndenture. predicte virtute eiuſdem Jndenture concedende ha*b*ere diruere & abcariare ad eius aut eo*rum* proprium vſum im*p*er*p*etuu*m* om*n*ia ta*l*ia edificia & omnes ali*a*s res qua*l*i*a* edificat*a* erect*a* aut suppo*s*it*a* forent anglice sett vpp in & super gardinu*m* & locis vacuis anglice the groundes per Jndentur*am* predict*am* concef*s*i*s* aut aliqua *p*arte inde *p*er predict*u*m Jacobum executores vel af*s*ign*atos* suos aut *p*ro theatro voc*ato* a theater or playinge place aut *p*ro aliquo alio licito vſu *p*ro eius aut eo*rum* Com*m*oditat*e* preter ta*l*i*a* edificia qua*l*i*a* poft hac fact*a* fuerunt virtute premif*s*o*rum* predicto*rum* racione impendicionis & expoſicionis predicte sum*m*e ducent*arum* libra*rum* abſque aliquo impedimento clam*atione* tribulaci*one* vel interrupcione predicto*rum* Egidij Alleyn & Sare vxo*r*is eius aut alte*r*ius eo*rum* aut heredu*m* executo*rum* adminiſtrato*rum* & Af*s*ign*atorum* eorum vel alicuius eo*rum* aut aliqua*rum* aliarum per*s*one vel per*s*ona*rum* in vſu anglice behalfe iure aut tit*u*lo aut *p*er remedium anglice by the meanes vel *p*rocuramentu*m* eo*rum* vel aliquo*rum* eo*rum*   Et vlterius idem Petrus Streete dicit quod predictus Jacobus Burbage virtute dimif*s*ionis predicte in tene*m*ent*a* predicta cum *p*ertinentiis intrauit & fuit inde pof*s*ef*s*ionat*us*   Et sic inde pof*s*ef*s*ionat*us* exiſten*s* idem Jacobus Burbage ad eius cuſtagi*a* & on*era* infra predictos decem annos *p*roxime sequen*tes* dat*um* Jndenture predicte impe*n*didit & expoſuit de & super edificacione alt*er*acione & emendacione tene*m*ento*rum* & edificio*rum* predicto*rum* per ip*s*um Jacobum Burbage vt prefer*tur* de & super premif*s*is faciend*i*s summ*a*m ducent*arum* libra*rum* legalis monete Angl*i*e valore tant*i* predicto*rum* veterum Maheremij & re*rum* anglice stuffe circa eadem impenſorum & expoſito*rum* accomputat*o* *p*arcella predicte sum*m*e ducent*arum* libra*rum* Et vlte*r*ius quod predictus Jacobus infra predictos decem annos *p*roxime poft dat*um* Jndenture predicte ad eius *p*ropri*a* on*era* & expenſa fabricauit & erexit sup*er* predict*a* vacua funda Structur*am* predict*am* vocat*am* the theater in narracione predict*a* specificat*am*   Et vlte*r*ius idem Petrus Streete dicit quod predict*us* Jacobus Burbage poft confeccionem Jndenture predicte & infra *predictos* decem annos *proxime* sequen*tes* dat*um* Jndenture *predicte* scil*icet* primo die Novembris anno regni *dicte* do*m*ine Regine nunc vicesimo septimo apud Hallywell *predictam* in Com*itatu* Midd*lesexia* *predicto* ad eius *propria* on*era* & cus*tagia* retinuit quendam Will*elmum* Danyell ar*migrum* nunc *seruientem* ad legem fore a concilio suo ad devis*andum* novam dimiffionem similem dimiffioni in eadem Jndentura specificate om*nium* *predictorum* mesuagio*rum* ten*ementorum* ter*rarum* fundi & soli & cet*erorum* premiffo*rum* per Jndentur*am* predict*am* preconcessorum *pro* ter*mino* viginti & vnius ann*orum* incipiendo a die dat*i* Jndentur*e* *predicte* sic vt *prefertur* faciende Et *quod* *predictus* Will*elmus* Danyell postea scil*icet* *predicto* primo die Novembris anno vicesimo septimo *predicto* apud Hallywell *predictam* in Com*itatu* Midd*lesexia* *predicto* devisauit vnam novam dimiffionem premiffo*rum* *predictorum* que quidem nova demiffis sequit*ur* in hec *verba* ff This Jndenture made the fyrst daye of November in the Seaven & twentythe yeare of the reigne of our soueraigne ladye Queene Elizabeth &c Betweene Gyles Allen of Holliwell in the Countye of Midd*lesex* gen & Sara his wyfe of the one *party* And James Burbage of london Joyner of thother *party* witneffethe That the salde Glles Allen and Sara his wyfe of one affent & confent in accomplifhing & fulfilling of a certayne Covenante conteyned & mencioned in one former Jndenture of leafe made of the land*es* & tenement*es* herafter mencioned bearinge date the thirteenth daye of Aprill Anno do*m*ini 1576 and ln the eighteenthe yeare of the raigne of our fore sayde soue*r*aigne ladye queene Elizabeth made betweene the saydę Gyles & Sara his wyfe one thone *partie* and the sayde James Burbage on thother have sett & to ffarme letten & by thes *prefentes* doe sett & to farme lett vnto the sayde James Burbage all thos two howfes or tenement*es* w[th]app*urtenances* w[ch] att the tyme of the sayde former demife made weare in the seu*er*all tenures or occupacions of Johan Harrifon widowe & John Dragon and alfo all that howfe or tenement w[th] Thapp*urtenances* together w[th] the gardyn grounde lyinge behinde *parte* of the same beinge then likewife in the occupacion of William Gardiner w[ch] said gardeyn plott dothe extende

in bredthe from a greate stone walle there wch doth inclofe parte
of the gardyn then or latlye beinge in the occupacion of the sayde
Gyles vnto the gardeyne ther then in the occupacion of Ewin
Colfoxe weaver & in length from the same howfe or tenement
vnto a bricke wall ther next vnto the feildes commonly called
ffinfbury feildes And alfo all that howfe or tenemente wth
thappurtenances att the tyme of the sayde former dimife made
called or knowne by the name of the Mill howfe together with the
gardyn grounde lyinge behinde parte of the same alfo att the tyme
of the sayde former dimife made beinge in the tenure or occupacion of the forefayde Ewyn Colefoxe or of his affignes w^{ch}
fayde gardyn grounde dothe extende in lengthe from the fame
houfe or tenement vnto the forfayde bricke wall next vnto the
forefayde feildes and alfo all thefe three vpper romes wth Thappurtenances next adioyninge to the forefayde Mill houfe alfo
beinge att the tyme of the fayde former dimife made in the occupacion of Thomas Dancafter fhomaker or of his affignes and alfo
all the nether romes wth thappurtenances lyinge vnder the same
three vpper romes and next adioyninge alfo to the forefayde
houfe or tenemente called the mill houfe then alfo beinge in the
seuerall tenurs or occupacions of Alice Dotridge widowe &
Richarde Brockenburye or of ther affignes together with the
gardyn grounde lyinge behynde the same extendynge in lengthe
from the same nether romes downe vnto the forfayde brickwall
nexte vnto the forefayde feildes And then or late beinge alfo in
the tenure or occupacion of the forefayde Alice Dotridge And
alfo so much of the grounde & soyle lyeinge and beinge afore all
the tenementes or houfes before graunted as extendethe in lengthe
from the owtwarde parte of the forefayde Tenementes beinge at
the tyme of the makinge of the sayde former dimife in the occupacion of the forefayde Johan Harryfon & John Dragon vnto a
ponde there beinge next vnto the barne or stable then in the occupacion of the right honorable the Earle of Rutland or of his
affignes & in bredthe from the forefayde Tenemente or mill houfe
to the mideft of the well beinge afore the same tenementes
And alfo all that great barne with thappurtenances att the

tyme of the makinge of the sayde former dimiſe made beinge
in the seuerall occupacions of Hughe Richardes Jnholder &
Robert Stoughton Butcher And alſo a little peece of grounde then
incloſed wᵗʰ a pale and next adioyninge to the foreſayde barne &
then or late before that in the occupacion of the sayde Roberte
Stovghton together alſo wᵗʰ all the grounde & soyle lyinge &
beinge betwene the sayde neyther romes laſt before expreſſed &
the foreſayde greate barne & the foreſaide ponde that is to saye
extendinge in length from the foreſayde ponde vnto a ditche
beyonde the brick wall next the foreſayde fieldes And alſo the
ſayde Gyles Allen & Sara hys wyfe doe by thes preſentes dimiſe
graunte & to ſarme lett vnto the sayde Jeames burbage all the
right title & interest wᶜʰ the sayde Gyles & Sara haue or ought
to haue of in or to all the groundes & soile lyeinge betwene the
foreſayde greate barne and the barne being at the tyme of the
ſayde former dimiſe in the occupacion of the Earle of Rutlande
or of his aſſignes extendinge in lengthe from the foreſayde ponde
& from the forſayde stable or barne then in the occupacion of
the foreſayde Earle of Rutlande or of his aſſignes downe to the
foreſayde bricke wall next the foreſayde feildes And alſo the
sayde Gyles & Sara doe by thes preſentes demiſe graunt & to
fearme let to the sayde Jeames all the sayde voide grounde lieynge
& beinge betwixt the foreſayde ditche & the foreſayde brich-
wall extendinge in lenght from the foreſayde brickwall wᶜʰ in-
cloſeth parte of the foreſayde garden beinge att the tyme of the
makinge of the sayde former demiſe or late before that in the
occupacion of the sayde Giles Allen vnto the foreſayde barne
then in the occupacion of the foreſayde Earle or of his aſſignes
and alſo free intire egreſſe & regreſſe in to & from all the foreſayde dimiſede premiſſes and euery parte therof aſwell to & for
the ſayde Jeames Burbage his executors adminiſtrators & aſſignes
as to & for all & euery other perſon & perſons cominge or repar-
inge to the premiſſs before demiſed or any parte therof by any
such wayes as were at the makinge of the sayde former demiſe
vſed & occupied to the said premiſſs in the right of the sayde
Gyles as alſo by such brydges & wayes as then or att any tyme

after that weare or shalbe hereafter made throughe the forefayde
brickwall into the forefayde feild*es* at all & eu*ery* tyme & tymes
convenient hereafter duringe all the tearme of yeares hereafter
graunted without any lawfull stoppe lett trouble or int*err*upc*i*on
of the sayde Gyles Allen his heres or affignes or any of them or
of any other p*er*fon or p*er*fons in his or theire behalfe right or
title or by his or theire meanes or p*ro*curement all wch p*re*miffs
before graunted are scituate lyeinge & beinge in & neere Hollowell aforefaide (excepte & referued vnto the sayde Gyles Allen
& Sara his wyfe & to theire heires & affignes & to such other
p*er*fon or p*er*fons as fhall or doe inhabite or make aboade in the
Capital Mefuage or tenement ther or any p*ar*te therof wch att the
makinge of the sayde former demife was in the occupac*i*on of
the sayde Gyles or his affignes & to & for the Ten*a*nt*es* of the
sayde Gyles wch doe & shall dwell in Hollowell aforefayde free
lib*er*tie to fetche & drawe water att the forefayde well from tyme
to tyme duringe the sayde Tearme so that they shall receyve the
com*m*oditie of the sayde well doe from tyme to tyme amonge
them ratably vpon lawfull requeft beare & paye to the sayde
Jeames Burbage his executors or affignes the one halfe of all such
Charges as shalbe layede out in & about the needfull repayring
& amendinge of the sayde well from tyme to tyme as often as
neede shall require duringe the sayde terme & alfo free ingreff*e*
& regreff*e* to & for the sayde Gyles & Sara his wyfe & there
heyres affignes executors & f*er*uant*es* & to & for the reverend
father John Scorye Byfhoppe of Hereford & Elizabeth hys wyfe
& their f*er*uant*es* & affignes into out & from the forefayde greate
garden att the tyme of the makinge of the sayde former demife
or late before that belonginge to the sayde Gyles into the forefayde feild*es* by the bridge and waye which then was therunto
vfed & occupied at all lawfull tyme & tymes duringe the termes
of yeares herevnder graunted to have & to holde all the sayde
hovfes or Ten*e*m*e*nt*es* barne gardens groundes & all other the
p*re*miffs before graunted except before excepted vnto the sayde
Jeames Burbage his executors & affignes from the day of the
makinge of this p*re*fent demife vnto the full ende & tearme of

xxj° yeares from thence next and imediatlie followinge & fully
to be compleate & endede yeildinge & payinge therefore yearelie
duringe the sayde Terme vnto the sayde Gyles Allen & Sara his
wyfe or to one of them & to the heyers & of the same Gyles &
Sara forteene pound*es* of lawfull monie of Englande att fower
fea*ſtes* or tearmes in the yeare that is to saye att the fea*ſtes* of
the birthe of our lorde gode the Annunciac*i*on of our ladye the
nativitie of St John Bapti*ſt* & St Michaell thearchangell by even
porc*i*ons And the sayde James Burbage for him his executors
Admini*ſt*rators & a*ſſ*ignes dothe Covenaunt promi*ſe* & graunt to
& with the sayde Gyles Allen & Sara ther heires & a*ſſ*ignes &
eu*er*ye of them by thes pre*ſ*entes That he the sayde Jeames Burbage his executors admini*ſt*rators or a*ſſ*ignes at his and ther owne
proper co*ſtes* & charges the sayde hou*ſe*s or ten*ementes* barne
gardens & all other the premi*ſſes* before graunted and all privies
to the premi*ſſ*s or any p*ar*te therof belonginge made or to be
made in all manner of needfull rep*ar*acions well & sufficiently
shall repare vpholde su*ſt*ayne make skoure clen*ſe* mayntayne &
amende from tyme to tyme when and so often as neede shall
require & the same so well & sufficientlye repaired clen*ſe*d
scoured and amended in the ende of the sayde terme of xxj^tle
yeares shall leave & yeild vpp vnto the sayde Gyles & Sara and
to the heirs & a*ſſ*ignes of the same Gyles & the sayde Gyles Allen
& Sara his wyfe for them & ther heirs executors & admini*ſt*-
trators doe covenant & graunt & eu*er*y of them seu*er*ally covenanteth & graunteth to & with the sayde Jeames Burbage his
executors admini*ſt*rators & a*ſſ*ignes by thes pre*ſ*entes that yt shall
or may be lawfull to & for the sayde Jeames Burbage his
executors admini*ſt*rators & a*ſſ*ignes or anie of them att anie tyme
of tymes hereafter duringe the fir*ſt* tenn yeares of the sayde
terme of xxj^tle yeares to alter change remove or take downe any
of the how*ſe*s wall*es* barne or byldinge*s* now standinge & beinge
in & vppon the premi*ſſ*s or any p*ar*te therof & the same to make
frame & sett vpp in what forme or fa*ſh*ion for dwelling how*ſe*
or how*ſe*s as yt shall seeme to the sayde Jeames Burbage his
executors or a*ſſ*ignes for the bettringe therof so that the premi*ſſ*s

& new buyldyngs hereafter to be made shall or may be reasonably
for tyme to tyme sett att a more value & greater rent then nowe
by thefe Jndentures they are set or lett for towardes the doeinge
& finifhinge wherof in forme aforefayde the sayde Gyles allen
& Sara his wyfe for them their heyers executors adminiftrators
and affignes doe covenante & graunt & euery of them seuerally
covenanteth & granteth to & wth the sayde Jeames burbage his
executors adminiftrators and affignes by thes prefents y^t yt shall
& maybe lawfull to & for the sayde Jeames burbage his executors
& affignes to haue & take to his & ther owne proper vfe & behofe
for euer all the tymber tyle bricke yron leade & all other stuffe
whatfouer of the sayde oulde howfes or buildinges wch shall come
by reafon therof and further the sayde Jeames burbage for him
hys heyres executors adminiftrators & affignes and for euery of
them dothe by thes prefentes covenante & graunte to & wth the
sayde Gyles Allen & Sara ther heires & affignes & euery of them
in forme followeinge that ys to saye that he the sayde Jeames
burbage his executors & affignes the buildings covenanted by the
sayde Jeames burbage his executors or affignes by the sayd former Jndenture to be by him or them made shall att all tymes after
the makinge therof att the coftes & charges of the sayde Jeames
his executors or affignes repaire keepe make & mayntayne from
tyme to tyme as often as neede shall bee duringe the sayde
Terme by thes prefentes graunted and all the sayd meffuages
buildings gardens tenements & other the premifs & euery parte
therof together wth the forefayde brick wall next the forefayde
feildes or annother as goode highe & fubftanciall as the same is
in the stead therof to be made sufficiently repayred made &
amended in thende of the sayde Tearme shall leave & yealde vpp
vnto the sayde Gyles Allen & Sara their heires & affignes And
further that yt shall or may be lawfull to & for the sayd Gyles
Allen & Sara his wyfe & the Survivor of them their heires &
affignes of them or any of them wth twoe or three artificers or
workmen wth them or any of them att any one tyme convenient
in euery yeare yearly duringe the sayde Terme quietlye to enter
& come into the sayde meffuages or tenements barne buildings &

all other the premiſſs & euery parte therof their to vewe searche
& se whether the reparacions therof be well & sufficiently amended
made mayntaynede kepte as the same ought to be or not So as
the same Gyles & Sara or the Survivor of them or the heirs or
aſſignes of them or either of them before such tyme as he she
or any of them shall come to vewe the same premiſſs to give to
the sayde Jeames burbage his executors or aſſignes att the premiſſs
fourteene dayes warninge therof And of the defaultes & lackes
or reparacions ther fonde beinge needfull to be repaired after the
buildinge therof to gyve monicion or warninge att the premiſſs
to the sayde Jeames burbage his executors or aſſignes or to the
inhabitors dwellers or occupiers of the premiſſs or any parte
therof for the tyme beinge to repare make & and amende all such
defaultes of reparacions needfull to be amended as shalbe ther so
founde wᵗʰin one yeare next after such warning gyven & the
sayde Jeames burbage for him his executors and adminiſtrators
and for euery of them covenanteth & graunteth by thes preſentes
to & wᵗʰ the sayde Gyles Allen & Sara ther heires executors and
aſſignes & euery of them well & sufficientlye to repayre make &
amende all such defaultes of reparacion as shalbe so fonde wᵗʰin
one yeare next after warninge therof gyven as is aforeſayde &
so from tyme to tyme as often as any such default shall happen
to be fonde & warninge or knowledge therof gyven as is aforeſayde duringe the sayde terme of one & twentye yeares to be
repayred att the proper coſtes & charges of the sayde Jeames
Burbage his executors and aſſignes and if ytt shall happen the
sayde yerelie rent of fourteene poundes to be behinde vpayde in
parte or in all ouer or after any feaſt daye of paymente therof
aforeſayde at wᶜʰ the same rent ought to be payde by the space
of xxviijᵗⁱᵉ dayes beinge lawfully aſked & noe sufficiente diſtreſſe
or diſtreſſes in & vpon the sayde premiſſs or any parte therof for
the sayde rent & arrearages therof can or may be founde or if
the some of CCˡⁱ mencioned & expreſſed in the foreſayde former
Jndenture of leaſe shall not be imployed or beſtowed wᵗʰin the
tyme therin limited & appoynted for the imployinge & beſtowinge
therof accordinge to the true intent & meaninge of the foreſayde

Jndenture of leafe or of the needfull rep*aracio*ns of the p*r*emiffs
shall not be made from tyme to tyme wthin the space of one yeere
after that lawfull warninge shalbe therof gyven vnto the sayde
Jeames Burbage his executors or affignes for the doinge therof as
is aforefayed that then or att any tyme after yt shalbe lawfull
to & for the sayde Gyles Allen & Sara his wyfe and the heirs and
affignes of the same Gyles or any of them into the sayd howfes or
tenements barne & all other the p*r*emiffs before graunted to
reenter   And the same to haue agayne retyne & repoffeede as
in his or ther former eftate   And the sayde Jeames Burbage his
exec*utors* & affignes & all other thence & therfrom vtterly to
expell putt out & amove this p*r*efent leafe or graunte or any thinge
therin conteyned to the contrary therof in anywyfe not wthftand-
inge   And moreover the sayde Gyles Allen & Sara hys wyfe for
them ther heires executors & adminiftrators doe covenant graunt
& eu*er*y of them seu*er*ally Covenaunteth to & wth the sayde
Jeames Burbage his executors adminiftrators & affignes by thes
p*r*ef*entes* that the sayde James Burbage his executors adminiftrators & affignes for the forefaid yerlye rent of fourteene
pound*es* to be payde in forme aforefayde   And vnder & accordinge to the Covenant*es* graunt*es* Chardges & condic*io*ns articles
& agreaments before declared & hereafter expreffed one the
behalfe of the sayde James Burbage his executors adminiftrators
or affignes to be p*er*formed & kepte as is aforefayde shall & may
peaceably & quietlye have houlde occupie & enioye all the forefayde howfes or ten*ementes* barne gardens groundes & all other
the p*r*emiffs before by thefe p*r*ef*entes* demifed & graunted wth
thapp*ur*tenaunc*es* (except before excepted) wthout anie lett
troble expulc*io*n evicc*io*n recou*er*y or int*err*upc*io*n of the sayde
Gyles Allen & Sara his wyfe or either of them or of the heires
executors adminiftrators or affignes of them or of any of them
or of any other p*er*fon or p*er*fons in ther behalfe right or title
or by the meanes or p*r*ocurment of them or any of them during
all the sayd terme of xxj^{tie} yeares   And further the sayde Gyles
Allen & Sara his wyfe for them there heres executors & adminiftrators doe covenante & graunte & eu*er*y of them seu*er*ally cove-

nantethe & graunteth to & with the sayde Jeames Burbage his
executors & affignes by thes pre/entes that yt shall or may be
lawfull for the sayde Jeames Burbage his executors or affignes
in confideration for the imployinge & beftoweinge of the forefayde some of CC^{li} mencioned in the sayde former Jndenture at
any tyme or tymes before the end of the sayd terme of xxj^{tie}
yeares by thes pre/entes granted to have take downe & Carrye
awaye to his & their owne proper v/e for euer all such buildinges
& other thinges as are alredye builded erected or set vpp & w^{ch}
herafter shalbe builded erected or sett vp in or vpon the gardings
& voyde grounde by thes pre/entes graunted or any parte therof
by the sayde Jeames his executors or affignes eyther for a Theater
or playinge place or for any other lawfull v/e for his or their
Comodityes (except such building*es* as are or shalbe made by
vertue of the saydc former Jndenture by rea/on of the ymployinge
& beftoweinge of the sayde some of CC^{li} wthout any stopp Clayme
lett trouble or int*err*upcion of the sayde Giles Allen & Sara his
wyfe or either of them or of the heires exec*utors* admini/trat*ors*
or affignes of them or any of them or of any other per/on or
per/ons in the behalfe right or tytle or by the meanes or pro-
curment of them & further the sayde Jeames Burbage for hym
hys executors admini/trators & affignes dothe covenaunte to &
with the sayde Gyles & Sara their heirs & affignes by thes
pre/entes that he the sayde Jeames his executors or affignes shall
not at any tyme or tymes duringe the said Terme of xxj^{tie} years
make or cause to be made out of the fore/ayd ten*ementes* w^{ch}
were att the makeinge of the sayde former lea/e in the occupacion
of the sayde John Harri/on & John Dragon into the fore/ayde
great garden then or late in thoccupacion of the sayde Gyles any
windowe or windowes but only such as shalbe made wthout any
ea/ement*es* to open without the e/peciall licence con/ent & agreament of the fore/ayde reu*er*ende ffather & Elizabeth his wyfe or
of the fore/aide Gyles & Sara or one of them or ther affigne$_5$ fir/t
had & obteyned & further that yt shall or may lawfull for the
sayde Gyles & for hys wyfe & familie vpon lawfull reque/t therfore made to the sayde Jeames Burbage his exec*utors* or affignes

to enter or come into the premiffes & their in some one of the
vpper romes to have such convenient place to sett or stande to se
such playes as shalbe ther played freely w^{th}out any thinge therefore payeinge soe that the sayde Gyles hys wyfe and familie doe
come & take ther places before they shalbe taken vpp by any others
Jn wytnes wherof both partyes to thes prefente Jndentures enter-
changeablye have putt their handes & seales the daye & yeare firft
above written./   Et vlterius idem Petrus Strete in facto dicit
quod predictus Jacobus Burbage poftea fcilicet predicto primo die
Novembris Anno vicifimo septimo predicto apud Hollowell predictam in Comitatu Middlefexia predicto novem dimiffionem
predictam sic factam adtunc & ibidem in pergamena scribi caufauit
& sic scriptam cum labellis & cera eidem dimiffioni affixis adtunc
& ibidem prefato Egidio oftendebat Et ipfum Egidium adtunc &
ibidem requifiuit ad illam sigillandum & prefato Jacobo vt factum
suum deliberandum secundum formam & effectum convencionis
predicte in predicta prima Jndentura mencionate Et quod predictus Egidius Alleyn ad hoc faciendum adtunc & ibidem penitus
recufauit Et vlterius idem Petrus Streete dicit quod predictus
Jacobus Burbage sic vt prefertur de tenementis predictis cum
pertinentiis poffeffionatus ante predictum tempus quo supponitur
tranfgreffio predicta fieri apud Hollowell predictam in predicto
Comitatu Middlefexia conceffit & affignauit tenementa mefuagia
structuram & cetera premiffa predicta ac totum ius statum &
terminum annorum sua de & in premiffis cuidam Johanni Hyde
Civi grocero londonie habenda & tenenda predicta Mefuagia ac
tenementa edificia gardina terras vocatas groundes & omnia &
singula cetera premiffa cum pertinentiis vnacum predicta Jndentura dimiffionis prefato Johanni Hyde executoribus & Affignatis
suis pro & durante refiduo predicti Termini viginti & vnius
annorum adtunc venturi & minime expirati & plenarie complendi
& finiendi virtute cuius predictus Johannes Hyde in tenementa
predicta cum pertinentiis intrauit & fuit inde poffeffionatus Et
idem Johannes Hyde sic inde poffeffionatus exiftens ante tempus
tranfgreffionis predicte superius fieri suppofite scilicet septimo die
Junij Anno regni dicte domine Regine nunc tricefimo primo apud

Hallowell predictam in predicto comitatu Middlesexia conceſſit & aſſignauit tenementa meſuagia et cetera premiſſa predicta ac totum statum ius titulum intereſſe & terminum annorum Clameum & demandam que predictus Johannes Hyde tunc habuit de & ad predicta premiſſa prefato Cutberto Burbage habenda & tenenda tenementa & cetera premiſſa predicta prefato Cutberto executoribus adminiſtratoribus & aſſignatis suis pro & durante toto reſiduo termini viginti & vnius annorum adtunc venturi & minime expirati plenarie complendi & finiendi virtute cuius predictus Cutbertus in tenementa predicta cum pertinentiis intrauit & fuit inde poſſeſſionatus per quod idem Petrus vt seruiens eiuſdem Cutberti ac per eius mandatum predicto tempore quo &c predictam structuram vocatam the Theater ibidem fabricatam & erectam diruit diuulſit cepit & abcariauit prout ei bene licuit Cum hoc quod idem Petrus verificare vult quod predicta Jndentura vltimo recitata per prefatum Willelmum Daniell sic vt prefertur diviſata facta fuit similis predicte Jndenture primo mencionate in omnibus preter dictam convencionem pro confeccione novo dimiſſionis infra decem annos & predictam convencionem pro expendicione anglice the beſtowinge predicte summe ducentarum librarum Et hoc paratus eſt verificare vnde petit Judicium si predictus Egidius Alleyn accionem suam inde verſus eum habere seu manutenere debeat &c

Et predictus Egidius Alleyn dicit quod ipſe per aliqua per predictum Petrum Streete superius placitando allegata ab accione sua predicta verſus ipſum Petrum habenda precludi non debet quia dicit quod placitum predictum per ipſum Petrum modo & forma predictis superius placitatum materiaque in eodem contenta minus sufficientia in lege exiſtentia ad predictum Egidium ab accione sua predicta verſus ipſum Petrum habenda precludendum/ Ad quod idem Egidius neceſſe non habet nec per legem terre tenetur aliquo modo reſpondere vnde pro defectu sufficientis reſponcionis in hac parte idem Egidius petit iudicium & dampna sua predicta occaſione predicta sibi adiudicari &c

Et predictus Petrus Streete dicit quod placitum predictum per ipſum Petrum modo & forma predictis superius placitatum ma-

teriaque in eodem contenta bona & sufficientia in lege exiftentia
ad predictum Edigium Alleyn ab accione sua predicta verfus
ipfum Petrum habenda precludendum quod quidem placitum
materiamque in eodem contentam idem Petrus paratus eft verificare & probare prout Curia &c

Et quia predictus Edigius ad placitum illud non refpondit nec
illud hucufque aliqualiter dedicit idem Petrus vt prius petit iudicium & quod predictus Egidius ab accione sua predicta verfus
ipfum Petrum habenda precludatur &c   Et quia Curia domine
Regine hic de iudicio suo de & super premiffis reddendo nondum
advifata dies inde datus eft partibus predictis coram domina
Regina apud Weftmonafterium vfque Jovis diem proximum poft
Octabas sancti Michaelis de Judicio suo de & super premiffis
audiendo &c eo quod Curia domine Regine hic inde nondum &c
Et quoad triandum exitum predictum inter partes predictas superius iunctum veniat inde Jurata coram domina Regina apud
Weftmonafterium die   proximo poft   Et qui nec
&c ad recogn &c Quia tam &c Jdem dies datus eft partibus
predictis ibidem &c/./
Ex

BURBAGE v. ALLEN

*Court of Requests Proceedings, 42 Elizabeth, (1600) 87/74.
Bill, Answer, and Replication.*

[The pleadings in this suit, consisting of Bill, Answer, and Replication,
and the two country depositions of Robert Vigerous and Thomas Neville
attached to them, were found by Halliwell-Phillipps, who used brief
extracts from them in his *Outlines,* I, 346, 358, 359, 361–62, 371–72. The
four great sets of paper depositions, forming the principal documents in
this great suit, however, have not hitherto been known, and were found
by the present writer in carrying out a complete search of the uncalendared records of the Court of Requests begun a few years ago. The
complete pleadings and all depositions and other records in the case are
here for the first time presented in full, and are arranged in their chronological order rather than in the order of filing. The suit was brought
by Cuthbert Burbage for relief from the preceding suit in the Queen's
Bench begun by Giles Allen, nominally against Peter Street, the carpenter,

but in effect against Burbage, as pointed out in the Bill. Part of the orders and the final decree are lost. But the Court's judgment in favor of Burbage, pronounced Oct. 18, 1600, is substantially given in the Answer of the Burbages to Allen's Star Chamber suit of 1602.]

BILL

[In dorso]
xxvj° die Januarij
Anno R Rne Eliz-
abethe &ct xlij°]

      Defend*ens* vocet*ur per*
      Nunc*ium* Camer*e*/

To the Queenes mofte excellent Matie

In all humblenes Compleyninge fheweth vnto yor mofte excellente Matie yor highnes faythfull and obediente fubiecte Cuthbert Burbage of the Cyttie of London gentl*eman* That wheras one Gyles Alleyne of Hafley in the Countie of Effex gentl*eman* was lawfullie feifed in his demeafne as of fee of and in Certayne gardein growndes fette lyinge and beinge neare Hallewell in the parifhe of St Leonard*es* in Shorditche in the Countie of Middlefex And beinge foe feifed togeather wth Sara hys wief did by their Indenture of leafe bearinge date the Thirteenth daye of Aprill in the Eighteenthe yeare of yor Maties Reigne for good Confideracions therin expreffed Amongeft other thinges demife and to fearme lette the faid gardein groundes and all proffitt*es* and Comodities therto belonginge vnto one James Burbage father of yor faide fubiecte To haue and to houlde to him the faid James Burbage his executors and Affignees from the feafte of the Annunciacion of our Ladie then lafte pafte before the date of the faide Indenture for the Tearme of one and Twentie yeares from thence nexte followinge yealdinge and payinge therefore yearelie duringe the faide tearme vnto the faide Gyles Alleyne and Sara his wyfe fourteene pownd*es* of lawfull money of Englande In and by wch faide Indenture (amongeft other Covenauntes and agreem^{tes} therin contayned) the faide James Burbage for him his heires executors and Adminiftrators and for euerie of them did Cove-

181

naunte and graunte to and wth the ſaide Gyles Alleyne and Sara
his wyfe their heires and aſſignees and eu*er*ie of them That he
the ſaide James Burbage his executors or Aſſignees in Conſidera-
c*i*on of the ſaide leaſe and Tearme of yeares and of certayne
bricke tyle lead and other ſtuffe Cominge of other Tenem^{tes} menconed in the ſaide Indenture) ſhould and would at his or their
owne Coſtes and chardges wthin Tenne yeares nexte enſuinge the
date of the ſaide Indenture ymploye and beſtowe in and vppon
the buildinge alteringe and amendinge of certayne houſes and
buildinges in and vppon the p*r*emiſſes by the ſaide Indenture
demiſed/ the ſome of Two hundred pownd*es* of lawfull money of
Englande the value of ſoe muche of the ſaide oulde ſtuffe and
tymber as ſhoulde be ymployed and beſtowed therabout*es* to be
accompted parcell of the ſaide Two hundred pound*es* And the
ſaide Gyles Alleyne and Sara his wyfe did therby Covenaunte
and graunte to and wth the ſaide James Burbage his executors
and Aſſignees that they the ſame Gyles Alleyne and Sara his wyfe
or one of them or their heires or the heires of one of them ſhoulde
and woulde at anie tyme or tymes wthin Tenne yeares next enſuinge the date of the ſaide Indenture at or vppon the lawfull
requeſte or demaunde of the ſaide James Burbage his executors
adminiſtrators or Aſſignes at his and their Coſtes and chardges
in the lawe make or cauſe to be made to the ſaide James Burbage
his executors or Aſſignees a newe leaſe or graunte like to the ſame
p*r*eſent*es* of all the foreſaide gardein grownd*es* and ſoile and of
all óther thinges graunted by the ſaide Indenture for the tearme
of one and Twentie yeares more to begynne and to take Com-
encem^t from the daye of the makinge of the ſame leaſe yealdinge
therfore the rente reſerved in the ſaide former Indenture And
vnder ſuche like Covenaunt*es* and agreem^{tes} as are in the ſaide
Indenture menc*i*oned and expreſſed (excepte this ſaide Covenaunte for makinge a newe leaſe wthin Tenne yeares and the foreſaide Covenaunte for ymployinge the foreſaide ſom*m*e of Two
hundred pound*es* Aud farther the ſaide Gyles Alleyne and Sara
his wyfe their heires executors and Adminiſtrators did therby
Covenaunte and graunte to and wth the ſaide James Burbage his

executors and Affignees that it fhoulde and mighte be lawfull to
the faide James Burbage his executors or affignees (In confidera*ci*on of the ymployinge and beftowinge of the forefaide Two
hundred pound*es* in forme aforefaide) at anie tyme or tymes
before the ende of the faide tearme of one and Twentie yeares
by the faide Indenture graunted or before the ende of the forefaide one and Twentie yeares after by vertue of the faide recited
Covenaunte to be graunted to haue take downe and Carie awaye
to his and their owne proper vfe for eu*er* all fuche buildinges and
other thinges as fhould be builded erected or fette vppe in or
vppon the Gardeins and voyde growndes by the faide Indenture
graunted or anie p*ar*te therof by the faide James his executors
or Affignees either for a Theator or playinge place or for anie
other lawfull vfe for his or their comodities w^{th}out anie ftoppe
clayme lette trouble or interrupcion of the faide Gyle**s** Alleyne
and Sara his wyfe or either of them or of the heires executors
Adminiftrators or Affignees of them or anie of them or of anie
other p*er*fon or p*er*fonnes in the behalfe righte or title or by
meanes or procurem^{t} of them or anie of them By vertue of w^{ch}
Leafe the faid James Burbage did enter into the p*re*miffs & was
therof poffeffed accordinglie and did p*er*forme all the Covenant*es*
Articles & agreem^{tes} on his p*ar*te to be p*er*formed & did alfo to
his great charg*es* erect and builde a playinge howfe called the
Theater in & vpon the p*re*miffes & afterwarde the faide firfte
tearme of Tenne yeares drawinge to an end the faide James Burbage did often tymes in gentle maner folicit & require the faid
Giles Allen for makinge a new leafe of the faid premiffes accordinge to the purporte & effect of the faid Coven*a*nte & tendred
vnto the faid Allen A new Leafe devifed by his Cownfell readie
written & engroffed wth labells & wax thervnto affixed agreable
to the Covenante before recyted wch he the faid Allen made fhew
that he would deliuer yet by fubtill devifes & practifes did from
tyme to tyme fhifte of the fynifhinge therof   After w^{ch} & before
the faid terme of one & twentie yeares were expired the intreft
of the faid terme & all benefitt & profitt that might growe by the
faid Indenture of Leafe came by good conveyaunce in the Lawe

to yo[r] faid Subiect by vertue wherof yo[r] faid Subiect was therof
poffeffed & being fo poffeffed yo[r] faid Subiect did often require
the faid Allen and Sara his wife to make vnto him the faid new
Leafe of the premiffs accordinge to the agreem[t] in the faide Indenture w[ch] the faide Gyles Alleyne woulde not denie but for
fom*me* caufes w[ch] he feigned did differre the fame from tyme to
tyme but yet gaue hope to yo[r] fubiecte and affirmed that he woulde
make him fuche a leafe By reafon wherof yo[r] fubiecte did forbeare to pull downe and carie awaye the tymber and ftuffe ymployed for the faid Theater and playinge houfe at the ende of the
faide firfte tearme of one and Twentie yeares as by the directe
Covenaunte and agreem[te] expreffed in the faide Indenture he
mighte haue done But after the faide firfte tearme of one and
Twentie yeares ended the faide Alleyne hathe fuffred yo[r] fubiecte
to contynue in poffeffion of the *premiffes* for diverfe yeares and
hathe accepted the rente referved by the faide Indenture from yo[r]
fubiecte Whervppon of late yo[r] faide fubiecte havinge occafion
to vfe certayne tymber and other ftuffe w[ch] weare ymploied in
makinge and errectinge the faide Theator vppon the *premiffes*
(beinge the cheefefte proffitte that yo[r] fubiecte hoped for in the
bargayne therof) did to that purpofe by the Confente and ap-
pointm[te] of Ellen Burbadge Adminiftratrix of the good*es* and
Chattells of the faide James Burbage take downe and Carie awaye
parte of the faid newe buildinge as by the true meaninge of the
faide Indenture and Covenant*es* lawfull was for him to doe and
the fame did ymploye to other vfes. But nowe foe it is maye it
pleafe yo[r] mofte excellent Ma[tie] that the faide Gyles Alleyne myndinge to take advantage of his owne wrongfull and vnconfcionable dealinge in not makinge the faide newe leafe fyndinge the
wordes of the faide Covenaunte to be that the faide James Burbage his executors Adminiftrators or Affignees mighte before the
end of the faide Tearme of one and Twentie yeares graunted by
the faide Indenture or before the ende of the faide one and
Twentie yeares after by vertue of the faide agreem[t] to be graunted
take downe and carie awaye the faide tymber and ftuffe vfed for
makinge of the faide Theator that therfore (in regarde yo[r] fub-

iecte truftinge to his promifes to haue a newe leafe did not take
the fame awaye at the ende of the faide tearme of one and Twentie
yeares graunted by the faide Indenture and that noe newe tearme
beinge graunted by the faide Alleyne to the faide James Burbage
or his Affignees by the wordes of the faide Covenante he hathe
not libertie to take the fame awaye afterwardes in ftrictenes of
lawe Therevppon he the faide Gyles Alleyne hathe broughte an
Accion of Trefpas in yor Maties Courte at weftmin*fter* Called the
Queenes Benche againfte Peter Streete yor fubiectes fervaunte
who by yor fubiectes direction and Comaundem^t did enter vppon
the premiffes and take downe the faide buildinge myndinge mofte
vnconfcionablie to recou*er* the value of the faide buildinge in
damages, wch mufte in [the] ende lighte vppon yor faide fubiecte
yf he fhould therin prevayle) And there dothe profecute the fame
wth all rigor and extremitie wch will tende to yor fubiec*tes* greate
loffe and hinderance excepte yor Ma^{ttes} favour and ayde in fuche
cafes vfed be to him herein extended In tender regarde wherof
for as muche as it is agaynfte all equitie and Confcience that the
faid Gyles Alleyne fhoulde (Contrarie to his Covenaunte and
agreem^{te} aforefaide throughe his owne wronge and breache of
Covenaunte hinder yor fubiecte to take the benefitte of the faide
agreem^{te} in the forefaide Indenture expreffed to take awaye the
faide tymber and building*es* before the ende of the faide one and
Thirtie yeares And for that yor faide fubiecte or his fervaunte
can Mynifter noe p*er*fecte plea at the Common lawe in barre of
the faide acc*i*on And yet in all equitie and Confcience oughte to
be releeved accordinge to the true meaninge And the faide Gyles
Alleyne oughte to be ftayed of his faide fuite Maye it therefore
pleafe yor mofte excellente Matie the premiffes Confidered/ to
graunte vnto yor faide fubiecte yor highenes writte of Privie Seale
to be directed to the faide Gyles Alleyne Comaundinge him therby
at a Certayne daye and vnder a certayne payne therin to be lymited
to be and p*er*fonallie to appeare before yor Matie in yor highenes
Courte of white Halle at Weftminfter then and there to aunfweare to the premiffes and to abide fuche further order and direction therin As to the Mafters of the faide Courte fhalbe

thoughte meete and Convenient And alfo to graunte yor Ma^tties
mofte gratious writte of Iniunction to be directed to all the Coun-
fellors Attorneys Solliciters and factors of the faide Alleyne,
Comaundinge them to Ceafe all proceeding*es* in the faide Acc*ion*
vntill the matter in equitie (wherein yor poore fubiecte humblie
prayeth to be releeued) be firfte hard before the Mafters of yor
highnes faide Courte And yor poore fubiecte will accordinge to
his bounden duetie daylie praye to god for the *pre*fervac*ion* of
yor royall Matie in all healthe and happineffe longe to reigne
ou*er* vs.

                          [Signed]   Jo: Walter   [Attorney]

ANSWER

Quarto die ffebruarij
Anno Regni Regine
Elizabethe &c xlij°/

      The anfwere of Giles Allen Gentl*eman* Defend^t to
      the Bill of Compl^t of Cuthbert Burbage Compl^t./.
The faid Defend^t faieth that the faid Bill of Compl^lt againft him
exhibited into this Honourable Courte is in the materiall p*artes*
therof verie vntrue, and is likewife (as the Defend^t by his Counfell is informed) verye vncertaine and infufficient in the lawe to
be anfwered vnto [by] the faid Defend^t for diuers and fundrie
apparaunt faultes and imp*er*fections therin Conteyned And devifed and exhibited into this Honourable Courte of malice and
evell will w^thout any iuft Caufe conceyved againfte the faid De-
fend^t to the intent thereby vniuftlie to vexe and molefte him w^th
tedious trauell beinge an aged man and to putt him to great trouble and chardges and that without any iuft Caufe or good matter
as the Defend^t hopeth it fhall appeare vnto this Honourable
Courte: Neverthelesse yf by the order of this Honourable Court
the faid Defend^t fhalbe Compelled to make any further or other
anfwere vnto the faid vntrue incertaine and infufficient Bill of
Compl^lt then and not otherwife (the advantage of exception therof
to this Defend^t nowe and all times herafter faued) for further
anfwere therevnto, and for a full and plaine Declarac*ion* of the

trueth The ſaid Defend^t ſaieth that true it is that he the ſaid
Defend^t together wth Sara his wife did by their Indenture of leaſe
bearinge Date the thirteenth daie of Aprill in the eighteenth yeare
of her ma^{ties} Raigne that nowe is for and in Conſideracion of the
ſomme of twentye powndes of lawfull money of England recited
by the ſaid Indentures to be to them in hande at thenſealinge
therof by the ſaid Jeames Burbage in the Bill of Comp^{lt} named
truelye paid for and in the name of a fine or income amongſte
other thinges did Demiſe vnto the ſaide Jeames Burbage all thoſe
twoe howſes or tenementes with the appurtenances then beinge
in the ſeuerall tenures or occupacions of Johane Harryſon widdowe and John Draggon: And alſoe all that howſe or tenemente
with the appurtenances together with the gardeine grounde lyinge
behinde parte of the ſame then beinge in thoccupacion of william
Garnett gardiner. And alſoe all that houſe or tenemente with the
appurtenances Called or knowne by the name of the mill houſe
together with the gardeine grounde lyinge behinde parte of the
ſame then beinge in the tenure or occupacion of Ewin Coleſoxe
weauer or of his aſſignes: And alſoe all thoſe three vpper Roomes
with the appurtenances nexte adioyninge to the foreſaid Mill-
houſe then beinge in the occupacion of Thomas Dancaſter ſhoo-
maker or of his aſſignes: And alſoe all the nether Roomes with
their appurtenances lyinge vnder the ſame th[r]ee vpper Roomes
and nexte adioyninge alſoe to the foreſaid houſe or tenement
Called the Myll howſe then beinge in the ſeuerall tenures or occupacions of Alice Dotridge widdowe and Richard Brackenburye
or of their aſſignes together alſoe with the gardeine grounde
lyinge behinde the ſame: And alſoe one great Barne with the
appurtenances then beinge in the occupacions of Hughe Richardes
inhoulder and Robert Stoughton Butcher (Excepte and reſerved
to the ſaid Defend^t and Sara his wife and to their heires and
aſſignes and to ſuch other perſone or perſones as then did or
ſhould inhabite or make abode in the Capitall meſſuage or tenement there or any parte thereof then or late in the occupacion of
the ſaid Defend^t, and to and for the tenantes of the ſaid Defend^t
which did and ſhould dwell in Hollowell aforeſaid free libertie

to fetche and Drawe water at the well there from time to time
Duringe the faid terme : To haue and to houlde all the faid howfes
or tenementes, Barne gardeines groundes and all other thinges by
the faid Indentures Demifed (Excepte before excepted) vnto the
faid Jeames Burbage his executors and affignes from the feaft
of Thannuncyacion of our Ladie lafte pafte before the Date of
the faid Indentures vnto the full end and terme of twentie and
one yeares from thence nexte and immeadiatelye followinge and
fullie to be Compleate and ended Yealdinge and payinge therefore yearely Duringe the faid terme vnto the faid Defend^t and
Sara his wife or to one of them and to the heires and affignes of
the faid Defend^t and Sara fourteene powndes of lawefull money
of England at foure feaft*es* or tearmes in the yeare that is to
faie at the feaft*es* of the Natiuitye of St John Baptifte, St Michaell
Tharchangell the Birth of our Lord God and Thannuncyacion of
our Ladie or within the fpace of eight and twentye Daies nexte
after eu*e*rye of the fame feafte Dayes by even porcions : And the
faid Jeames Burbage for him his executo^rs adminiftrato^rs and
affignes did by the faid Indentures Coven*a*nte with the faid De-
fend^t and Sara his wife their heires and affignes that he the faid
Jeames Burbage his executo^rs adminiftrato^rs or affignes at his or
their owne prop*e*r Coft*es* and Chardges the faide howfes or tenement*es* Barne gardeines and all other thinges by the faid Indentures Demifed in all manner of needefull rep*a*racions well and
fufficientlye fhould repaire vphould fufteyne maintaine and amende
from time to time when and foe often as need fhould require and
the fame foe well and fufficientlie repaired and amended in the
end of the faid terme of one and twentye yeares fhould leaue and
yeald vppe. And the faid Defend^t and Sara his wife Did Cove-
n*a*nte by the faid Indentures that it fhould be lawefull for the faid
Jeames Burbage his executo^rs adminiftrato^rs and affignes or anie
of them at anie time Duringe the firfte tenn yeares of the faid
terme of one and twentie yeares to alter Chaunge remoue or take
Downe anie of the howfes walles Barne or buildinges then ftandinge and beinge in and vppon the prem*i*ff*es* or anie p*a*rte therof
and the fame to make frame and fett vpp into what forme or

faſhion for Dwellinge howſe or howſes it ſhould ſeeme good to
the ſaid Jeames Burbage his executoʳˢ or aſſignes for the betteringe therof ſoe that the *premiſſes* Demiſed and the newe buildinges afterwardes to be made ſhould or might be reaſonablie from
time to time ſett at a more value and greater rente then by the
ſaid Indentures they were lett for Towardes the Doinge and
finiſhinge wherof in forme aforeſaid the ſaid Defendᵗ and Sara
his wife did Covenante with the ſaid Jeames Burbage his executoʳˢ
adminiſtratoʳˢ and aſſignes by the ſaid Indentures that it ſhould
be lawefull for the ſaid Jeames Burbage his executoʳˢ and aſſignes
to haue and take to his and their owne prop*er* vſe and behoofe
for euer all the timber tile bricke yron lead and all other ſtuffe
whatſoeuer of the ſaid ould howſes or buildinges which ſhould
come by reaſon therof. And further the ſaid Jeames Burbage
for him his executoʳˢ adminiſtratoʳˢ and aſſignes did by the ſaid
Indentures Covenante with the ſaid Defendᵗ and Sara that he the
ſaid Jeames Burbage his executoʳˢ or aſſignes aſwell in Conſidera-
c*i*on of the ſaid leaſe and terme of yeares before by the ſaid
Indentures graunted as alſoe for and in Conſideracᵢon of all the
timber bricke tile lead and all other ſtuffe comminge of the ſaid
tenement*es* barne and all other the premiſſ*es* to be had and en-
ioyed in forme aforeſaïd ſhould and would at his and their owne
Coſt*es* and Chardges wᵗʰin tenn yeares nexte enſuinge the Date
of the ſaid Indentures imploie and beſtowe in and vppon the buildinge alteringe and mendinge of the ſaid howſes and building*es*
for the betteringe therof as is aforeſaid to be made by the ſaid
Jeames his executoʳˢ or aſſignes of in or vppon the premiſſ*es* the
ſom*m*e of two hundred powndes of lawefull money of England
at the leaſte: (The value of ſoe muche of the ſaid ould timber and
ſtuffe as ſhould be imployed and beſtowed theraboutes to be
accompted p*ar*cell of the ſaid ſom*m*e of twoe hundread powndes)
and the ſame building*es* ſoe to be made ſhould at all times after
the makinge therof at the Coſt*es* and Chardges of the ſaid Jeames
his executoʳˢ and aſſignes repaire keepe make and maintaine from
time to time as ofte as neede ſhould be Duringe the ſaid terme
And all the ſaid meſſuages buildinges gardeines tenement*es* and

other the premiſſes and euerye parte therof ſufficientlie repaired
made and amended in the ende of the ſaid terme ſhould leaue
and yealde vppe. And it was further Condicioned by the ſaid
Indentures that yf it ſhould happen the ſaid yearlie rent of
fourteene powndes to be behinde vnpaied in parte or in all
after or over anie feaſte Daie of paiment thereof at which the
ſame rente ought to be paied by the ſpace of eight and twentie
Daies beinge lawefullie aſked and noe ſufficient Diſtreſſe or
Diſtreſſes in or vppon the ſaid premiſſes or anie parte therof
for the ſaide Rente and the arrerages therof Could or might
be founde; or yf the foreſaid ſomme of twoe hundred powndes
ſhould not be imployed and beſtowed w^{th}in the time and ſpace
aforeſaid accordinge to the true meaninge of the ſaid Indentures
that then it ſhould be lawefull for the Defend^{t} and Sara his wife
and to the heires and aſſignes of the Defend^{t} into the ſaid howſes
or tenementes Barne and all other thinges by the ſaide Indentures
graunted to reenter: And furthermore the Defend^{t} and Sara his
wife did Covenante with the ſaid Jeames Burbage his executo^{rs}
and aſſignes by the ſaid Indentures That they the ſaid Defend^{t}
and Sara his wife or one of them ſhould and would at anie time
w^{th}in tenn yeares next enſuinge the Date of the ſaid Indentures
at and vppon the lawefull requeſt or Demaund of the ſaid Jeames
Burbage his executo^{rs} adminiſtrato^{rs} or aſſignes at his and their
Coſtes and Chardges in the lawe make or Cauſe to be made to
the ſaid Jeames Burbage his executo^{rs} or aſſignes a newe leaſe or
graunte like to the former of all the foreſaid howſes or tenementes Barne gardeines growndes or ſoile and of all other thinges
by the ſaid Indentures graunted for the terme of one and twentie
yeares to beginne and take Commencement from the daie of the
makinge of the ſame leaſe ſoe to be made yealdinge therefore
yearelie the foreſaid yearelie rente of fourteene powndes at the
feaſtes before mencioned and vnder ſuche like Covenantes
grauntes Condicions articles and agreementes as were in the ſaid
Indentures mencioned and expreſſed and none other (Excepte
the Covenante for makinge a newe leaſe within tenn Yeares and
the Covenante for imployinge the foreſaid ſomme of twoe hun-

dred powndes: And further the Defend[t] and Sara his wife did
Covenante with the faid Jeames Burbage his executo[rs] and affignes by the faid Indentures that it fhould be lawefull to the
faid Jeames Burbage his executo[rs] or affignes in Confideracion
of the imployinge and beftowinge of the forefaid twoe hundred
powndes in forme aforefaid at anie time before the end of the
faid terme of one and twentie yeares by the faid Indentures
graunted or before the end of the forefaid one and twentye
yeares thereafter by vertue of the faid Indentures to be graunted
to take downe and Carrie awaie to his and their owne proper
vfe all fuch buildinges and other thinges as fhould be builded
erected or fett vpp in or vppon the gardeines and voide grounde
by the faid Indentures graunted or anie parte therof by the faid
Jeames his executo[rs] or affignes either for a Theatre or playinge
place or for anie other lawefull vfe for his or their Comodities
(Excepte fuche buildinges as fhould be after made by vertue of
the faid Indentures by reafon of the imployinge and beftowinge
of the faid fomme of twoe hundred powndes as the Comp[lt] in his
Bill of Comp[lt] in parte hath alledged and as in and by the faid
Indentures (wherevnto the Defend[t] referreth himfelfe more fullie
maie and doth appeare. And further the Defend[t] faieth that true
it is that the faid Jeames Burbage in the Bill of Comp[lt] named
did require the faid Defend[t] to make him a newe leafe and did
tender vnto the Defend[t] a Draught of a newe leafe written and
ingroffed as the Compl[t] hath alledged which leafe foe tendered the
Defend[t] did not make fhewe that he would deliuer it and yet did
by fubtille Devifes fhifte of the finifhinge therof as the Comp[lt]
mofte vntruelye hath alledged: but Contrarielie the Defend[t] did
vppon manie and verye iuft and reafonable Caufes and Confideracions (as he hopeth it fhall appeare vnto this Honourable Courte)
vtterlie refufe to feale and Deliuer the fame for the plaine and
true Declaracion whereof firfte the Defend[t] faith (that as he
taketh it and as he is by his Counfell informed) the Draught of
the faid leafe foe tendered vnto the Defend[t] was in manye
materiall pointes varyinge and Differinge from the leafe which
the Defend[t] and his Wife had formerlie made to the faid Jeames

Burbage and therefore in refpect that the fecond leafe fhould be
made like vnto the former and vnder the like Covenantes articles
and agreementes and noe other as before is fhewed the Defend[t]
was in noe wife (as he taketh it) either in lawe or Confcience
bounde to feale the fame: ffor the further manifeftacion of
which variances the Defend[t] referreth himfelfe to the faid Indentures of leafe and to the faid Draught of the newe leafe which
the Defend[t] fhalbe alwaies readie to fhewe forth to this Honorable Courte But yf foe it were that the Defend[t] had Contrarie to
his Covenante refufed to make the faid leafe yet hath the faid
Comp[lt] noe Caufe (as the Defend[t] taketh it) to feeke releife in
this Honourable Court for that the Comp[lt] hath diuers times
faid vnto the Defend[t] that he hath in his handes a bonde wherin
the faid Defend[t] is bounde vnto the faid Jeames Burbage in the
fomme of twoe hundred powndes for the performance of the
Covenantes in the faid Indentures vppon which the Comp[lt] hath
threatened to fue the faid Defend[t] at the Common lawe And
further the Defend[t] faith that fuch was the bad Dealinge of the
faid Jeames Burbage towardes the Defend[t] from time to time
before the time of the faid newe leafe tendered and the faid
Jeames Burbage had bene fuch a troublefome tenant vnto the
Defend[t] that there was noe Caufe in Confcience to make the
Defend[t] to yealde to anye thinge in fauour of the faid Jeames
Burbage further then by the lawe he might be Compelled to doe:
for firfte wheras the faid Jeames Burbage was bounde to paie
vnto the Defend[t] the fomme of twentie powndes for a fine for
the leafe formerlie made vnto him, the faid Jeames Burbage
neglected the paiment therof at the time appointed and longe
time after And hardelie coulde the Defend[t] after muche Delaie
and trouble by fuite in lawe obteyne the fame: And further the
faid Jeames Burbage Continuallie failed in the paiment of his
rent and never Duelie paid the fame wherby the Defend[t] was
often driven to his great trouble to goe aboute to Diftreine for
the fame and yet could not the Defend[t] that waie helpe himfelfe
for either the Dores and gates were kepte fhutt that he could
not enter to take anye Diftreffe or otherwife the matter foe

handled that the Defend^t could not finde anie fufficient Diftreffe
to fatiffie him for the arrerages therof and at the time of the
faid newe leafe tendered by the faid Jeames Burbage he the faid
Jeames did then owe vnto the Defend^t thirtie powndes for the
rent of the faid howfes and growndes Demifed vnto him which as
yet remayneth vnpaid notwthftandinge that the faid Jeames Burbage in his life time and likewife the Comp^{lt} fince his Death haue
before Diuers Credible perfonnes as the Defend^t hopeth he fhalbe
able to proue often times Confeffed the fame to be due vnto the
Defend^t. And further touchinge the repayringe of the howfes
and buildinges which the faid Jeames Burbage ought to haue repaired and maintained that was likewife by the faid Jeames Burbage much neglected; for whereas amongfte the howfes and
building*es* Demifed to the faid Jeames Burbage there was one
great tiled Timber barne of foure fcoare foote of affife in length
and foure and twentie foote of affife in breadth or verie neare
theraboutes verie fubftantiallye builte for the which the Defend^t
had formerlie receiued a rent of good value the faid Jeames Burbage did devide the fame into eleven feuerall tenementes (as the
Defend^t nowe remembereth and did lett out the fame feuerallie to
poore perfonnes for the feuerall rentes of twentie fhillinges by the
yeare to be paid by euerye tenant whoe were and are vnable to
doe anye Reparacions vppon them; for fuch was and nowe is
their pouertie that as the Def^t is informed they vfuallie begge in
the feildes and ftreetes to gett mony for the paiment of their
rentes by reafon wherof the Defend^t hath been muche blamed
and by the parifhoners there verie hardelie Cenfured that he
fhould be an occafion to bringe foe many beggers amongft them
to their great trouble and annoyance which proceeded not from
any faulte of the Defend^t but from the Covetous humor of the
faid Jeames Burbage whoe refpected more his owne Commoditie
then the good reporte and Creditt either of the Defend^t or himfelfe and the like evell Difpoficion appeareth to be in the Comp^{lt}
whoe fince the Death of his ffather hath Continued thefe poore
people there and ftill doth and yet Doth in noe wife repaire the
faid tenementes wherby they are growen in great Decaye and

are almoſt vtterlie Ruynated and are nowe by the Comp^lt vnderpropped with ſhorés to keepe them from fallinge Downe in ſtead
of Repairinge and amendinge the ſame as by the Covenante of
the ſaid Jeames Burbage ought to be done inſoemuche that the
ſaid poore people haue Complayned vnto the Defend^t that they
were ſoe Decayed both without and within that they were in
feare that they would fall vppon their heades wherbye it ap-
pearethe that the Comp^lt hath ſmale regard either of the Creddit
or the Commoditie of the Defend^t but ſeeketh onely to enriche
himſelfe by the rentes and other proffittes which he vnconſcion-
ablie receyueth for the ſame   And the ſaid Jeames Burbage & the
Comp^lt or one of them haue likewiſe heretofore placed other
poore people in other tenementes there which ſtill Continue in the
ſame which tenements are by reaſon therof ſoe Decayed that the
Defend^t ſeeth not howe he ſhall well be anſwered the ould rent
of fourteene powndes of ſuche tenantes as be of abilitie to paie
the ſame ſoe that howeſoeuer the Comp^lt hath furniſed that by
the ſaid twoe hundred powndes ſuppoſed to be beſtowed by the
ſaid Jeames Burbage his father that the howſes and buildinges
were greatlye amended and betterred (as in trueth they ought to
haue been) yet the Defend^t taketh it that he ſhalbe able to make
it appeare vnto this Honourable Court that they are rather im-
paired and in worſe plight for the beniſitt and profitt of the
Defend^t all thinges Conſidered then they were at the time when
the ſaid Jeames Burbage firſt tooke them, neither yet in trueth
had the ſaid Jeames Burbage at the time of the ſaid ſecond leaſe
tendered or anie time after (as the Defend^t hopeth he ſhalbe able
to proue to this Honourable Court) beſtowed the ſaid ſomme of
twoe hundred powndes or neare thereaboutes for the betterringe
of the howſes and buildinges demiſed neither was there anie like-
lyhood that the ſaid Jeames Burbage ſhould performe the ſame
within the time limitted by the ſaid Indentures the ſaid ſecond
leaſe beinge tendered but a verie ſhort time before the expiracion
of the ſaid terme of tenn yeares w^thin which time the ſaid ſomme
of twoe hundred powndes ſhould haue been beſtowed as before is
ſhewed for all which Cauſes the Defend^t did refuſe to ſeale the

said leafe (as he thinketh he had iufte Caufe both in lawe and
Confcience foe to Doe:) and afterwardes a little before the Death
of the faid Jeames Burbage thoroughe great labour and entreatie
of the faid Jeames Burbage and the Comp^lt and other their
ffreindes whoe often moued the Defend^t in their behalfe and the
faid Jeames Burbage pretendinge and makinge fhewe vnto the
Defend^t with manie faire fpeeches and proteftacions that he
woulde therafter Duely paie his rent and repaire the howfes and
buildinges and performe all his Covenantes as a good and an
honeft tenant ought to doe and that he would likewife paie the
faid arrerages of thirtye powndes: the Defend^t and the faid
Jeames Burbage grewe to a newe agreement that the faid Jeames
Burbage fhould haue a newe leafe of the premiffes Conteyned in
the former leafe for the terme of one and twenty yeares to beginne
after the ende and expiracion of the former leafe for the yearelie
rent of foure and twentie powndes, for the faid Jeames Burbage
in refpect of the great proffitt and Commoditie which he had
made and in time then to come was further likelye to make of the
Theatre and the other buildinges and growndes to him Demifed
was verye willinge to paie tenn powndes yearelye rent more then
formerlie he paid: And it was likewife further agreed betweene
them (as the Defend^t hopeth he fhall fufficientlie proue) that the
faid Theatre fhould Continue for a playinge place for the fpace
of fiue yeares onelie (after the expiracion of the firft terme) and
not longer by reafon that the Defend^t fawe that many incon-
veniences and abufes did growe therby and that after the faid
fiue yeares ended it fhould be Converted by the faid Jeames
Burbage and the Comp^lt or one of them to fome other vfe and be
imployed vppon the groundes Demifed wherbye the benifitt and
profitt therof after the terme of the faied James Burbage ended
fhould remaine and be vnto the Defend^t: but before that agreement was perfitted (by reafon that the faid Jeames Burbage had
not procured fuch fecurytie for the performance of his Covenantes as the Defend^t did require) the faid Jeames Burbage
Dyed: after whofe Death the Comp^lt did againe often moue and
intreat the Defend^t that he might haue a newe leafe of the

premiss*es* accordinge to the former agreement made betweene the said Jeames Burbage the father of the Comp^lt and the Defend^t, the said Comp^lt promisinge the Defend^t the paiment of the said thirtie powndes rente which was behinde in the time of the Comp^ltes father and that he would put in good securitie to the Defend^t for the paiment of the Rente Duringe the terme and the repayringe of the howses and the p*er*formance of all other Cove-nant*es* on his p*ar*te to be p*er*formed touchinge which matter there was often times Com*m*unicacion had betweene the Comp^lt and the Defend^t whoe for his p*ar*te was Contented to haue made the said lease vnto the Comp^lt whoe likewi*s*e seemed veerye willinge to haue it in such manner and vnder such Coven*an*t*es* as were formerlie agreed vppon betweene the Defend^t and the said Jeames Burbage and soe the matter was at the laste Concluded betweene the Comp^lt and the Defend^t and (as the Defend^t remembereth) a lease was Drawen accordinglie by the Comp^lt which the Defend^t thinketh he can shewe forthe vnto this Honourable Courte and yet notw^th standinge the Comp^lt founde meanes by Colourable shiftes and Delaies to Deferre the accomplishinge and execution therof from time to time   Howebeit the Defend^t hopinge that the Comp^lt had ·meant honestlie and faithfullie and to haue taken the lease accordinge to their agreement wherby the Defend^t should haue receiued the said arrerages of thirtie powndes and likewise that his howses and building*es* should haue been repaired and that he should haue been secured for the p*er*formance of the Coven*an*t*es* soe that he should not haue had such trouble and Disquiettnesse as formerlie he had founde   Herevppon the Defend^t was Con-tented to suffer the Comp^lt to enioye the premiss*es* after the first lease expired for the space of a yeare or two payinge onelie the ould rent of fourteene powndes which the Defend^t did the rather by reason that the said Jeames Burbage and the Compl^t betweene them had placed soe manie pore people there whoe were not able to paie their rent*es* that yf the Defend^t should haue taken the same into his handes he should haue beene Constreyned in pittye and Compassion to haue forborne their rent*es* to his great losse and hinderance; And further should haue beene enforced within

a fhorte time to haue turned them out of the poffeffion of the
faid tenements by reafon that they were foe greatlye Decayed that
the Defend^t muft haue beene enforced to pull them Downe and
to erecte them a newe for otherwife they Could not nor can not
be Convenientlie repaired for good and able tenantes But nowe
by the Dealinge of the Comp^lt it appeareth that he never in trueth
meant to take the leafe as he pretended but onelie fought to take
occafion when he might privelie and for his beft advantage pull
downe the faid Theatre wch aboute the feaft of the Natiuitie of
our Lord God in the fourtith yeare of her ma^ties Raigne he hath
Caufed to be done without the privitie or Confent of the Defend^t
he beinge then in the Countrie for the which the faid Defend^t
hath brought an action of Trefpas in her ma^ties Benche againft
him whoe by the Commandement of the Comp^lt was the Doer
therof which action the Defend^t thinketh he had verie good and
iufte caufe both in lawe and Confcience to profecute: for firft it
appeareth that the libertie which the faid Jeames Burbage had
by the faid leafe to pull downe the faid Theatre at anie time Duringe the terme was graunted vnto him in Confideracion onelie
of the faid fomme of twoe hundred powndes to be imployed and
beftowed by the faid Jeames Burbage vppon the howfes and buildinges that were demifed vnto him: which fomme not beinge by
him beftowed accordinglie and other Covenantes broken there
was noe Colour (as the Defend^t taketh it) either in lawe or Confcience for the Comp^lt to take awaie the fame: And further the
Defend^t could not fee by what meanes he fhould receiue anie
fatiffaction for the faid thirtie powndes of rent due vnto him
and for the loffe wch the Defend^t hath fufteyned by the not repayringe of his howfes wch amounteth to a verie great value but
onelie by the faid Theatre wch the Defend^t intended to Convert
to his vfe and therby to be recompenfed for the fame feeinge himfelfe otherwife lefte w^thout remedie by reafon that the wife of the
faid Jeames Burbage whome the Comp^lt fuppofeth to be his adminiftratrix is neither willinge nor able for ought the Defend^t
can perceiue to yeald him any fatiffaction at all; for the faid
Comp^lt hauinge (as the Defend^t is informed) gotten all or the

greateſt parte of the goodes and ſubſtance of the ſaid Jeames
Burbage into his handes and the ſaid Ellen Burbage the late wife
of the ſaid Jeames Burbage beinge a poore woman the Defend^t
[sic] verie ſubtillye Cauſed her to take the adminiſtracion of the
goodes of the ſaid Jeames Burbage to the intent that therbie and
by Colour of the ſaid adminiſtracion they might trouble and moleſt
the Defend^t and others and yet themſelues avoid the paiment of
the Debtes of the ſaid Jeames Burbage and the performance of
ſuch Covenantes and other Dueties as the ſaid Jeames Burbage
and his executors or adminiſtrato^rs ought both in lawe and Conſcience to paie and performe vnto the Defend^t and others: And
further wheras the Comp^lt ſuppoſeth that the ſaid Jeames Burbage his father did to his great Chardges erecte the ſaid Theatre
and therby pretendeth that there ſhould be the greater Cauſe in
equitie to releiue him the Comp^lt for the ſame: Herevnto the
Defend^t ſaieth that Conſideringe the great proffitt and beniffitt
which the ſaid Jeames Burbage and the Comp^lt in their ſeuerall
times haue made therof w^ch (as the Defend^t hath Crediblie hard)
doth amounte to the ſomme of twoe thouſand powndes at the leaſt:
the Defend^t taketh it they haue been verie ſufficientlye recom-
penſed for their Chardges which they haue beſtowed vppon the
ſaid Theatre or vppon anie other buildinges there had they been
much greater then they were And further the Defend^t ſaieth that
he hath Crediblie heard that the ſaid Theatre was not built at
the alone Chardges of the ſaid Jeames Burbage but that one
John Braines did defraie the greateſt parte of the Chardges
therof vppon agreement made (as the Defend^t hath heard) betweene the ſaid Jeames Burbage and the ſaid John Braines that
the ſaid John Braines ſhould haue the moyetie of the leaſe and
of the profittes therof wch becauſe he the ſaid John Braines did
not enioye accordinglie but was therin Defrauded by the ſaid
Jeames Burbage (as the Defend^t hath heard) one Robert Miles
as executo^r to the executo^r of the ſaid John Braines did exhibite a
Bill into her ma^ties highe Courte of Chauncerie againſt the Comp^lt
and the ſaid Jeames Burbage (as the Defend^t taketh it) wch ſuite
Dependinge the ſaid Comp^lt ſubtillie intendinge to Defraude both

the said Robert Miles and the Defend^t pulled downe the said
Theatre in great Contempt of the said Honourable Court and to
the great wronge and iniurye of the Defend^t, the said Compl^t
(as the Defend^t taketh it) neither yet the said Ellen Burbage
hauinge noe Colour either in lawe or Conscience soe to doe.
wthout that y^t the said Jeames Burbage did performe all the articles Covenantes and agreementes on his parte to be performed
or that he the said Jeames Burbage onely did to his great
Chardges erecte the said Theatre in manner and forme as in the
Bill of Compl^t is alledged: and wthout that y^t the interest of the
said terme & all benifitt and proffitt that might growe by the said
Indentures of lease did by good Conveyance Come vnto the
Compl^t, or that he was lawefullie possessed therof by force of any
such Conveyance made vnto him: and without that y^t the Compl^t
did often require the Defend^t and Sara his wife to make him the
said newe lease in any other manner and sort then the Defend^t
hath in his answere formerlie shewed: and wthout that y^t the De-
fend^t for any fayned Cause did Deferre the makinge of the said
lease from time to time as the Compl^t most vntruelie hath alledged: And wthout that y^t the said Ellen Burbage is the lawefull administratrix of the goodes and Chattells of the said Jeames
Burbage, or that the said Ellen Burbage did Consent and appointe
that the Compl^t should pull downe the said Theatre or that by
vertue therof (yf soe it were) the Compl^t might lawefullie pull
downe the same: And wthout that y^t the Defend^t mindeth to take
anie advantage of his owne wrongefull and vnconscionable Dealinges as the Compl^t most vntruelye hath surmised for the Defend^t
hopeth that it shall well appeare vnto this Honourable Court that
the Dealinges of the Defend^t herein haue been verie iuste and
honest and accordinge to good Conscience. And wthout y^t that
anie other matter or thinge in the said Bill of Compl^t Conteyned
materiall or effectuall in the lawe to be answered vnto by this
Defend^t and not herein sufficientlie answered vnto Confessed and
avoyded, trauersed, or denied is true, all which matters this De-
fend^t is readie to averre and proue as this Honourable Courte
shall award And therfore prayeth to be Dissmissed therof with

his reafonable Coftes and Chardges in this behalfe allreadie wrongefullie had and fufteyned./

[Signed]   Chiborne   [Attorney].

REPLICATION

xxvij° die Aprilis
Anno Regni Regine
Elizabethe xlij°

The Replicacion of Cuthbert Burbadge Compl^{te}
to the aunfwer of Gyles Allen gentleman Defend^t

The faide Compl^{te} favinge to himfelf nowe and at all times hereafter all advantages of excepcion to thincertayntie & infufficiencie of the faide anfweare for replicacon fayeth as he before in his faide bill of Compl^{te} hathe faide and dothe and will averre maynteyne & proue & euerye matter and thinge in his fayd bill conteyned to be good iuft and true in fuch forte manner and forme as therein they are moft truely fett fourth and Declared wthout that that the draught of the fayde leas tendred by the fayde James Burbage to the fayde Defend^t in the fayde bill and anfwer mencyoned was in any materiall pointe varyinge or differinge from the leas wch the fayd Defend^t & his wyfe formerlye made to the fayde James Burbage as in the fayde aunfweare is furmifed, wthout that that the fayd James Burbage did deale badlye wth the Defend^t before the tendringe of the fayd newe leas or that he the fayd James was fuch a troublefome tenant to the faid Def^tt that there was noe caufe in confcience to move the fayde Defend^t to yeild to any thinge in favour of the fayd James further then by lawe he might be compelled to doe as in the fayd Aunfweare is moft vntruely alleaged wthout that that the fayd James Burbage contynuallye fayled in the payment of his rent, and never duely payd the fame or y^t he the fayd Defend^t was often Driven to goe about to diftreine for the fame, or that the doores & gates of the houfe of the fayd James Burbage were kept fhutte that the Defend^t could not enter to take any diftres or that the fayde Def^t could not finde fufficiente diftreffe to fatiffie him for the arrerages

of the rent (if any were) as in the faid Anfwer ys fuggefted and
as towching⁰ the faid thirtie pound*es* in the faid anfwere men-
*cion*ed alledged to be dew to the faid defend^t for the rent of the
howfes and ground*es* demifed to the faid James Burbage in the
faid Anfwere fpecified this comp^lt therevnto faieth That longe
before the tenderinge of the faid newe leafe in the anfwere fpecified there was muche variaunce and Controuerfie betwene the
faid defend^t and one Edmond Peckham towching⁰ the title of the
p*r*emiffes in the faid anfwere menc*i*oned, by reafon whereof the
faid James Burbadg⁰ this Comp.^ltes father was verie muche trow-
bled and often Chardged to finde men to keepe the poffeffion of
the faid p*r*emiffes from the faid Edmond Peckham neyther could
this Comp^ltes faid father enioye the faid p*r*emiffes according⁰ to
the leafe to him made by the faid defend^t; for wch Caufes (if any
p*ar*te of the rent were vnpaide yt may be this Comp^ltes faid father
deteyned fome p*ar*te of the rent in his owne hand*es* and dyd not
pay the fame at the daies lymitted for paym^t thereof, the Certentye
of wch faid rent foe deteyned he this comp^lt knoweth not W^thout
that that the faid James Burbadg⁰ at the tyme of the faid new
leafe tendered dyd owe vnto the faid defend^t thirtie pound*es* for
rent of the faid howfes and ground*es* Or that this Comp^lt dyd
often tymes confeffe fince the deathe of the faid James Burbadg⁰
the fame to be dewe to the faid defend^t as in the faid anfwere ys
vntruly alledged. Howbeit this Comp^lt faieth that he this comp^lt
hath told the faid defend^t that if the faid Defend^t would vfe him
kindly and deale frendly wth him that then he this Comp^lt for
quietnes & frindfhippe to be had would fatiffie the faide defend^te
all fuche rent as the faide defend^te coulde reafonablie demaunde
And wheras the faide defend^t alleadgeth in his faide aunfwer that
the faide James Burbadge neglected to doe Rep*ar*acions vppon
the faide houfes and buildinges and that the faide James did devide the faide barne in the aunfwer fpecified into eleven feu*er*all
tenem^tes and did lette the fame feu*er*allie to poore p*er*fonnes for
the feu*er*all rent*es* of Twentie fhilling*es* by yeare who weare
vnable to doe rep*ar*acions vppon the fame This Compl^te thervnto
replieth and fayth that true it is that the faide James Burbadge

being poffeffed amongeft other thinges of the faide barne by vertue
of the leas to him made as aforefaid wch barne ftood & laye emptie
alonge time in the handes of the [sic] him the faide James w^thout
yeldinge him anie profitte or commoditie   And the faide James
being defirous to converte the fame for his benefitte did therfore
to his greate charges devide the fame barne into feuerall tenem^tes
as in the bill is expreffed as lawfull was for him the faide James
foe to doe as he this Compl^te taketh it   And foe muche the rather
for that he the faide James was not reftrayned by his faide leas
to builde or to converte anie parte of the premiffes to him demifed
therbie   And this Compl^te further faieth that he this Compl^te
verie well knoweth and can well and fufficientlie prove and make
manifefte to this honorable Courte, that the faide James Burbadge
hath for diuerfe yeares duringe the faide tearme beftowed & difburfed in & aboutes the reparacions of the fame tenem^tes a greate
fome of money   W^thout that that the faide tenants are foe poore
that theie vfuallie begge in the fieldes and ftreates to gette money
for the paym^te of theire rentes,   Or that that there weare anie
caufe the faide defend^te fhoulde be muche blamed or hardlie cenfured by the parifhoners   Or that the faide James refpected
more his owne comoditie then the good reporte and creditte of
the defend^te or himfelfe as in the faide aunfwer mofte flaunder-
ouflie is alleadged w^thout that alfo that he this Compl^te hathe
not fince the deathe of his faide father repayred the faide tenem^ts
or that the faide tenem^tes are growen in greate decaie or almofte
vtterlie ruinated or that there is anie caufe that the faide poore
people fhoulde complayne to the faide defend^t that the faide
tenem^tes would fall vppon theire heades as in the faide aunfwer
is vntrulie furmifed ffor this Compl^te faieth and can vearie well
proue that he this Compl^te hathe beftowed and difburfed in repayringe of the fame tenem^tes this vearie lafte yeare the fome of
twentie Markes and better W^thout that that the faide James Burbadge had not at the time of the faide feconde leas tendered or
anie time after beftowed the fomme of two hundred powndes or
neare theraboutes for the betteringe of the houfes and buildinges
demifed   Or that there was not anie likelihood that the faide

James Burbadge fhoulde performe the fame wth in the time lymitted by the faide Indentures as in the faide aunfweare is alfo
furmifed ffor this Complaynante faieth and can well and fufficientlie prove and make manifefte afwell by diuers good workemen and other perfonnes that the faide James Burbadge before
the tenderinge of the faide feconde leas to the faide defend^t did
beftowe and difburfe for the betteringe of the faide houfes and
buildinges aboue the fomme of Two hundred powndes And
therfore he the faide defend^te had noe iufte caufe to refufe to
feale the faide leas as by his faide aunfwer he pretendeth And
touchinge the newe agreem^te between the defend^te and the faide
James Burbadge in the faide aunfweare fpecified he this Complaynante therevnto fayeth That true it is that the faid James Burbage
was verie willinge to haue a newe leas for one & twentie yeares
of the premiffes from the faid Def^t vnder fuch rent, & accordinge
to fuch reafonable Covenauntes as in the former leas were conteyned, And that therevppon fpeeches & commvnicacion were
often had & paffed betweene the Def^t. and the fayd James towchinge the fame, but this Compl^t fayeth that the fayde Def^t accordinge to his owne will and direction did caufe a draughte of a
leas to be drawen wherin were inferted many vnreafonable Covenantes and agreem^tes on the parte of the faide James to be performed, And likewife the faid Defend^t required fuche fecuritie of
the faide James Burbadge for the performaunce thereof, as that
the faid James vtterlie refufed to proceade any further wth the
faid Defend^t in the faid bargaine And the faid James Burbage
wth in fhorte tyme after died. Without that that the faid James
Burbadge was willinge to paie the faid defend^t Tenne poundes
yerelie rent more then formerlie he paid Or that it was agreed
betwene the defend^t and the faid James that the faid Theater
fhoulde Contynue for A playinge place for the fpace of ffyve yeres
onelie after the firfte terme and no longer, Or that the fame after
the faid ffyve yeres ended fhould be Converted by the faid James
and this Complainant or one of them to fome other vfe and be
ymploied vppon the groundes demifed wherebie the benefitt and
proffitt thereof after that terme ended fhould remayne and be vnto

the faide defend^t as in the faid Anfweare is alfo furmifed and alleadged. Without that that this Complainant did often moue or intreate the faide defend^t that he mighte haue a newe leas of the premiffes accordinge to the former fuppofed agreem^t made betwene the faid James Burbadge and the def^t Or that this Complainant did promife to paie vnto the faide Def^t the faid fomme of xxx^li in the faid Anfweare mencioned Or that this Complainant feemed verie willinge to haue the faid leas in fuche manner and vnder fuche Covenauntes as were formerlie fuppofed to be agreed vppon betwene the defend^t and the faid James Burbadge, or that the matter was fo Concluded betwene this Complainant and the faide defend^t Or that that there was A leafe drawen accordinglie by this Complainant Or that the faid def^t was Contented to fuffer this Complainant to enioye the premiffes after the firfte leas expired for the fpace of A yere or twoo payinge onelie the olde rente of xiiij^li for fuche reafons & in fuch manner as in the faid Anfwere mofte vntrulie is fuggested and fuppofed/. Withoute that alfo that this Complainant neuer meante to take the leas of the premiffes but onelie foughte to take occafion when he mighte priuilie and for his befte advauntage pull downe the faid Theatre ffor this Complainant faieth that he was verie willinge to haue had a newe leas of the faid premiffes from the Defend^t fo as the fame leas mighte haue been made in fuche reafonable manner and accordinge to the former leas made by the Defend^t and his wief to this Comp^ltes father as aforefaid. And this Complainant doth not denie but that he hath pulled downe the faid Theatre wch this Complainant taketh it was lawfull for him fo to do beinge A thinge Couenaunted and permitted in the faid former leas to this Comp^ltes faid father made as aforefaid Withoute that that this Complainant hath gotten mofte parte of the fubftaunce and goodes of the faid James Burbadgè into his owne handes, or hath fubtillie caufed the faid Ellen Burbadge to take the adminiftracion of the goodes of the faid James Burbadg therebie to trouble and molefte the faid Defend^t and others and themfelues to avoide the paym^t of the debtes of the faide James Burbadge and the performaunce of fuche Couenauntes and other dueties as the ſaid James Burbadgᵉ his executoʳˢ or adminiſtratoʳˢ ought both in lawe and Conſcience to paie and performe vnto the defendᵗ and others, Or that the ſaid James Burbadge or this Complaynᵗ hathe made twoo thouſand poundₑₛ proffitt and bene-fitt by the ſaid theatre   As in the ſaid Anſweare is alſo alleadged And wᵗʰout that that any other matter Clauſe Article or thinge in the ſaid Anſweare Conteyned materiall or effectuall in the lawe to be replied vnto by this Complₐᵢₙₐₙₜ, and not herein or hereby ſufficiently replied vnto Confeſſed and avoided trauerſed or denied is trewe, All wᶜʰ matters he this Complₐᵢₙₐₙₜ is and will be readie to averr and proue as this honorable Courte ſhall award And praieth as before in and by his ſaid bill of Complᵗ he hath praied/

COURT ORDER, 10 APRIL 1600

Requests Misc. Books, vol. 49. (Draft Order Book, Easter 41 to Trinity 42 Elizabeth)

Tₑᵣₘino Paſche Anno Regni Rⁿᵉ
Elizₐbeth &c xlijᵈᵒ

Decimo die Aprilis [1600]

Cuthbert Burbage gentlₑₘₐn complᵗ againſte Giles Allen gentle-man defendaunt yt is Ordered vppon the mocₑon of mʳ Walter of counſaill wᵗʰ the ſaid complᵗ that an Iniunccₑon (wᵗʰout further mocₑon in that behalf to be made) ſhalbe Awarded furthe of this corte againſte the ſaid defᵗ for the ſtay of his proceedingₑₛ at the commₑn lawe in the Accₑon of treſpₐs theare dependinge, vntill this corte ſhall take further Order to the contrary, yf he the ſaid defendaunt (havinge notice of this Order in convenyent tyme) ſhall not vppon thurſday next commᵧnge ſhewe good matter in this corte in ſtay thereof/

COURT ORDER, 22 APRIL, 1600

Idem, ap. loc.

xxijᵈᵒ die Aprilis

Wheareas in the cauſe at the ſute of Cuthbert Burbage gentlₑₘₐn

205

compl^t againſte Giles Allen gent*leman* defend^t Order was pronounced vppon the xvijth of this inſtant that bothe *p*arties wth
their counſaill ſhould Attend vppon this *p*reſent day to be heard
whether An Iniunc*c*ion ſhould be in the ſame cauſe Awarded or
not, At wch dåy m^r Walter and one Chiborne beinge ſeu*e*rallye
of counſaill learned wth bothe the ſaid *p*arties Attended Accordingly, And therevppon (the matter in queſtion beinge opened vnto
her ma^{tes} counſaill in this corte) yt is by the ſame counſail ordered that the plaintif ſhall furthwth reply, And that bothe the
ſaid *p*arties ſhall examyn all ſuche witneſſes as they entende to
vſe in this cauſe by or before the ſeconde day of the next terme,
And then publica*c*ion ſhalbe therein graunted, And the ſame matter ſhalbe heard in this corte vppon the xjth day of the ſame next
terme *p*eremptorilie, And further yt ys Ordered that the ſaid
compl^t (Accordinge to thoffer of his counſaill this day made)
ſhall by or before monday next comynge put in A *p*erfect and
yſſuable plea to the def^{tes} ac*c*ion dependinge at the co*mm*en lawe,
or els in default therof ſhall take no benefit by his ſute in this
corte, wch plea (yf yt ſhalbe put in Accordingly), then the def^{tes}
counſaill dothe conſent, and yt is ſo ordered that he the ſaid def^t
ſhall ſtay his further *p*roceeding*es* at the co*mm*en lawe, vntill the
matter be heard Accordinge to this Order/

BURBAGE *v.* ALLEN

*Court of Requests Proceedings, Uncalendared, Bdl. 242. Depo-
sitions ex parte Allen, 26 April, 1600.*

INTERROGATORIES

[In dorso]
Te*r*mino Paſch*e*
xlij *Regni Regi*ne
Eliza*bethe*

Interrogatoryes to be miniſtred to the Witneſſes
to be *p*roduced on the *p*arte and behalfe of Giles
Allen gent*leman* Defend^t againſte Cuthbert Burbage Complaina*nte.*/

1./ Imprimis whether did Jeames Burbage father of the Complainante in his life time tender and Deliuer vnto the Defend^t a
Draught of a newe leafe of Certaine howfes and groundes which
were formerlye Demifed by the Defend^t to the faid Jeames Burbage requiringe the Defend^t to feale the fame: and whether is the
Draught nowe fhewed forth vnto you, the fame which the faid
Jeames Burbage Deliuered vnto the Defend^t: And whether did
not the Defend^t refufe to feale the fame; and for what Caufe to
yor rememberance did he foe refufe the fealinge therof?/ Deliuer what yowe knowe or haue heard herin.

2./ Item whether was not the Defend^t bound vnto the faid Jeames
Burbage in the fomme of twoe hundred powndes for the performance of Covenantes Conteyned in the faid leafe made by the
Def^t to the faid Jcames Burbage: and whether hath not the
Comp^lte faid that he hath the faid bond in his Cuftodye: and
whether hath not the Comp^lte of late threatened to fue the Defend^t
or to Caufe him to be fued vpon that bonde; Deliuer what you
knowe or haue heard herein./

3./ Item whether did not the faid Jeames Burbage at the time of his
Death owe vnto the Defend^t the fomme of thirtye powndes for
rent of the faid howfes and groundes Demifed vnto him by the
Defend^t: and whether doth not the faid fomme of thirtye powndes
Remaine yet vnpaid: and whether hath not the Comp^lte of late
Confeffed the faid fomme of thirtye powndes to be Due vnto the
Defend^t: Deliuer what you knowe, or haue Crediblie heard
herein./

4./ Item whether doe you knowe or thinke in yor Confcience that the
faid Jeames Burbage did within the firfte tenn yeares after the
fayd leafe made vnto him by the Defend^t beftowe the fomme of
twoe hundred powndes aboute the alteringe and amendinge of the
faid howfes and buildinges Demifed vnto him by the Defend^t: or
what fomme of money did the faid Jeames Burbage beftowe to
that purpofe w^thin that time: Deliuer the trueth what you knowe
or haue Crediblie heard herein?/

5./ It*em* whether Did the faid Jeames Burbage Duringe his life
keepe the faid howfes and buildinges in good rep*a*racions: and
whether are not the faid howfes and buildinges or fome of them
nowe growen in great Decaie: and whether hath not the Comp^lte
vnderpropped them with fhores: and whether doe they not foe
remaine: and what fom*m*e of money will it Cofte to fett the faid
howfes and buildinges in good and fufficient Rep*a*racions Deliuer
what you knowe or thinke in yor Confcience hearein: and by what
meanes as you thinke it is come to paffe that the faid howfes and
building*es* are growen foe ruinous./

6./ It*em* whether was there not an agreament had betweene the
Comp^lte and the Defend^t to this effecte: that the Defend^t fhould
make a newe leafe of the faid howfes and ground*es* vnto the
Comp^lte for one and twentye yeares from and after the expirac*i*on
of the former leafe made to the faid Jeames Burbage: and that
the Comp^lte fhould paie yearelye for the fame the fom*m*e of foure
and twentye powndes: And whether was it not likewife agreed
betweene them that the Theatre wch was erected vppon p*a*rte of
ye fayd grownd fhould Continue for a playinge place by the fpace
of fiue yeares onelye, and that then it fhould be Converted to fome
other vfe for the benifitt of the Comp^lte Duringe his terme, and
after for the benifitt of the Defend^t: And whether did not the
Comp^lte vpon that agream^t p*r*omife the Defend^t to paie him the
faid fom*m*e of thirtye powndes, and to put the howfes and buildinges in good rep*a*racions, and howe longe is it fithence fuche
agreament was made, and how longe before the faid Theatre was
pulled Downe: Deliuer the trueth what you knowe or haue heard
hearein./

7./ It*em* whether hath Ellen Burbage the late wife of the faid Jeames
Burbage any goodes or Chattells in her handes that were the
goodes or Chattells of the faid Jeames Burbage wherbye the
Defend^t maye haue recompence at her hand*es* for the faid fom*m*e
of thirtye powndes, and the breache of other Coven*a*ntes: And
whether is not the faid Ellen accompted a verye pore woman, and

not able to fatiffye the Creditors of the faid Jeames Burbage:
and whether did not the Complainante and his brother, or one
of them procure the faid Ellen to take adminiftracon of the goodes
of the faid Jeames Burbage, (the faid Comp^lte and his brother or
one of them hauinge before fecrettlye gotten the goodes of the
faid Jeames Burbage into their handes) that therbye they might
Deceiue the Credito^rs of the faid Jeames Burbage: Deliuer what
you know or haue Crediblie heard herein./.

8./ Item whether was the fayd Theatre (which was erected vpon
parte of the grounde aforefaid/ built at the alone Chardges of the
faid Jeames Burbage: or whether Did not one John Braynes
Defraye the one halfe of the Chardges therof vpon agreament
betweene the faid Jeames Burbage, and the faid John Braynes,
that the faid John Braynes fhould be partner with the faid Jeames
Burbage in the profittes therof: Deliuer what you knowe or
haue heard herein./

9./ Item what fommes of money haue the faid Jeames Burbage and
the Complainant in their feuerall times gayned by the meanes of
the faid Theatre: Deliuer the trueth what you knowe or haue
Crediblie heard herein?/

10./ Item whether were you prefent at the pullinge Downe of the faid
Theatre: and whether did you helpe to pull Downe the fame, and
by whofe Commandem^t or appointem^t did you foe helpe to take
it Downe and whome did you fee prefent at the takeing Downe
thereof: and whoe Did helpe & giue any affiftance therin, and by
whofe Commandem^t or appointment were they prefent or Did
helpe to take it downe as you knowe or haue heard?/

11./ Item whether hath not the Defend^t alwaies Dealt verye fauour-
ablie & Confcionablie wth his tenantes: Deliuer what you knowe,
or haue Crediblye heard herein: and whether are you a tenant
vnto the Defend^t and howe longe haue you foe beene?/

12./ It*em* whether did not the ſaid Jeames Burbage often times faile
in the paiment of his rent, and in the p*er*formance of other Cov-
en*antes*: and whether had not the defend* muche trouble and
Diſquietneſſe by occaſion therof: and whether did not the ſaid
Jeames Burbage place Diu*ers* verye poore people in ſome p*ar*te
of the howſes & building*es* aforeſaid: and whether did not Diuers
of the inhabitantes much miſlike therof & ſpeake ill of the Defend*
for the ſame and whether did not the Comp^lte ſtill Continue thoſe
poore people there for his owne p*ro*fitte　Deliuer what you knowe
or haue Crediblie heard herein?/.

DEPOSITIONS

> Depoſition*es* capt*ae* apud weſtmon*aſterium* xxvj^to
> die Aprilis A° Regni D*omi*ne R*egi*ne Elizabethe
> nunc &c Quadrageſimo Secundo ex p*ar*te Egidij
> Allen gen*eroſi* defend^tis v*erſus* Cuthbert*um* Bur-
> bage q^rtem./

Phillippe Baker of Clyfton in the Countye of Bedff: gen*tleman*
of the Age of ffyftye Eight yeares or there about*es* ſworne and
examyned the daye and yeare aboue ſaid depoſithe and ſaythe./

1/ Ti the ffirſte Jnterr*ogatory* this depon*en*t ſaythe he hath hard the
defendt (and oth*er*s) ſaye that the Compl*ainantes* fath*er* did in
his lyffe tyme Tender and deliu*er* vnto the defendt the Drawght
of A newe leaſe of Certayne houſes and ground*es* wch the ſaid
defend*ant* had before that tyme form*er*lye demiſed vnto him the
Compl*ainantes* fath*er*.　And that the Compl*ainantes* fath*er* did
vppon the deliu*er*ye thereof requyre the defendt to Seale and
deliu*er* the ſame accordinge to fforme of Law in thoſe Caſes p*ro*-
vided:/　And the defendt ſaid in his this depon*entes* pr*eſentes*
that he refuſed the ſame for that the Leaſe wch the Complain-
antes fath*er* ſoe tendered vnto him was not verbatim agreeable
wth the ould Leaſe before demiſed as there agreem* was to-
geath*er*./　And for that there was ſome rent behynde and vn-

payde for the premiſſˢ vppon the ould leaſe. And otherwiſe then vppon heare ſaye he ſaythe he cannot reporte for that he did not ſee the ſame leaſe tendered, nor the drawght thereof at any tyme./ And more touchinge the ſaid Jnterr*ogatory* this deponent Cannott depoſe./

2./ To the ſecond Jnterr*ogatory* this deponent ſaythe he hath hard the defendt ſaye that the Compl*ainantes* ffath*er* would ſwe him vppon A bonde of twoe hundred pound*es* for non p*er*formance of Couenant*es* But he hath not hard that the ſame bonde of twoe hundʳed pound*es* is come to the nowe Compl*ainantes* Cuſtodye, nor that the Compl*ainant* hath of late threatned the defendt to ſue him vppon the ſame bonde: And more he Cannot depoſe./

3./ To the thirde Jnterr*ogatory* this deponent ſaythe he hath hard the defendt ſaye that the Compl*ainantes* ffather did at the tyme of his deathe owe vnto him the ſome of thirtye pound*es* for rent of the Houſes and ground*es* wᶜʰ he the defendt had demiſed vnto him the pl*aintiffes* fath*er*, And the defendt ſaid that the ſame thirtye pound*es* for Rent is yett remayninge vnpayd: but he hath not hard any oth*er* ſaye ſoe, nor that Complt hath yett Confeſſed ſoe muche or any other ſome to be dwe for rent owinge in his fath*ers* tyme./ And more he Cannott depoſe./

4./ To the ffourthe Jnterr*ogatory* this deponent ſaythe he knowethe not what Coſt*es* and Charges the pl*aintiffes* ffath*er* was at in his lyffe tyme about the Alteringe and Amendinge of the premiſſes demiſed vnto him by the defendt, nor what ſome or ſomes of money James Burbage beſtowed to that purpoſe vppon the premiſſs./ And more he Cannot depoſe./

5./ To the vᵗʰ Jnterr*ogatory* this deponent ſaythe he hath hard the defendt ſaye that the Compl*ainantes* father did not keepe the ſaid demiſed premiſſs in good rep*ara*cion when he lyved./ And hath hard that ſome of them be nowe in greate decaye vnderpropped wᵗʰ Shores: but howe longe they haue bene ſoe he knowethe not,

nor what yt will Cofte to fett the houfes that be decayed in good
reparacions, nor knowethe by what meanes the premiffs are foe
growne ruynated and decayed. And more he Cannot depofe for
that he hath not bene there of purpofe to vewe the decayes
therof./

6./ To the vj[th] Jnterrogatory this deponent faythe that he was not
prefentes wth the plaintiff and defendt when there was any
Agreem[t] made and Concluded vppon betwene them onlye faythe
that about Michaellmas lafte pafte was twelue monethe the defendt
and he this deponent lyinge in An Jnne in· Shordyche Called the
George at w[ch] tyme the Complainant repayred often to talke w[th]
the defendt, And the defendt tould him this deponent that yt was
about A leafe of the premiffs that the Complainant fued to him
for :/ And that he fhould haue one to Commence after thexpiracion of the owld leafe w[ch] he the defendt had made of the premiffs
vnto the plaintiffes father : And the defendt tould him this deponent that the Complainant was Contented and did promife him
that in Confideracion of A newe Leafe in Reuercion he would
increafe the defendtes Rent ten poundes per Annum more then
yt was, and would repayre the houfes and buyldinges decayed
vppon the premiffs and would Suffer the Theater w[ch] was thervppon erected for A playe houfe foe to Contynewe for A playe
houfe the fpace of ffyve yeares onlye, and that then yt fhould be
Converted to fome other vfe for the Complainantes benefytt
duringe his terme : And after thexpireacion of his terme for the
defendtes benefytt. And that therevppon the Complainant did
promife him the defendt paym[t] of the thirtye poundes w[ch] his
ffather owght him the defendt for rent before he dyed And this
he hard by the reporte of the def[t] and not otherwife :/ And that
yt is about A yeare or better as he remembrythe fythence the faid
Theater was pulled downe./ And more he Cannot depofe touche-
inge the faid Jnterrogatory for that he knowethe not that the
Complainant Agreed wth the defendt as the defendt tould him
this deponent that he did./

7/ To the vijth Jnterr this deponent faythe he knowethe not in what
ftate the Complainantes ffather lefte his wyffe Ellen Burbage
mencioned in the Jnterrogatory And therefore knowethe not
whether fhee have in her handes goodes and Chattles of her late
hufbondes wherby the defendt maye have recompence at her
handes for the thirtye poundes he claymeth and the breach of
other Couenantes : But he fayeth that fhee is accompted A very
poore woeman. And more he cannot depofe touchinge the faid
Jnterrogatory onlye fayethe he hath hard the defendt affirme
afmuche as is in the Jnterrogatory alledged againfte the plaintiff and his brother

8./ To the viijth Jnterrogatory this deponent Can faye nothinge of
his owne knowledge : but he hath hard diuerfe of the defendtes
tenantes faye that the faid Theater was not buylded at the onlye
Charge of the Complainantes father but that one John Braynes
mencioned in the Jnterrogatory did defraye the one halfe of the
Charges thereof vppon Agreem^t betweene them that Braynes
fhould be partner wth the plaintiffes father in the profyttes
thereof./ And more he Cannot depofe./

9./10./ To the ixth and xth Jnterrogatory this deponent Can faye
nothinge

11/ To the xjth Jnterrogatory this Deponent faythe that the defendant
hath alwayes dealte well and Confcionablye wth his tenantes : w^{ch}
he knowethe to be true for that he is one of his tenantes and hath
founde him A very good Landlorde./ And more he Cannot
depofe./

12./ To the xijth Jnterrogatory this deponent faythe he thinkethe that
the Complainant doethe Contynewe fuche tenantes in the premiffs
as his father placed there and are now lyvinge./ And he hath
hard the defendt faye that the plaintiffes father fomtymes fayled
paym^t of his rent and performance of other Couenantes And
more he Cannot depofe touchinge the faid Jnterrogatory to his

nowe remembrance only he hath hard many report*es* of the defendt touchinge thofe matters menc*i*oned in the Jnterr*ogatories*./

(Signed)　　Phillip Baker

John Goborne of the p*ari*fhe of S*ct*: Leonard*es* in Shordytche in the Countye of midd*lefex* marchaunttaylo*r* of the Age of ffortye ffoure yeares or there about*es* fworne and examyned the daye and yeare abouefaid depofithe and faythe./

1/ To the ffirfte Jnterr*ogatory* this depon*e*nt faythe that James Burbage the Compl*ainantes* ffather did in his lyffe tyme (as this depon*e*nt hath hard) tender vnto the defendt the drawght of A leafe of Certayne Houfes and ground*es* w*ch* he the def*endan*t had formerlye demiffed vnto him the faid James Burbage, and required the defendt to Seale the fame newe leafe./　And as the defendt hath reported in his this depon*entes* pre*fentes* he did refufe to Seale the fame for that the Newe leafe w*ch* James Burbage did tender vnto him was not fett downe w*th* the fame woord*es* the ould Leafe was w*ch* the faid James Burbage was bound by Couenant to doe and no otherwife and the defendt refufed to Seale the faid Newe leafe for other Caufes viz for that the faid James Burbage was as he faid but A bad tenan*t* and behind w*th* his rent and had not repayred the demifed p*remiff*s accordinge to Couenant betweene them:　And more he Cannot depofe touchinge the faid Jnterr*ogatory* for that the drawght of the Newe leafe is not nowe fhewed ffoorthe vnto him at the tyme of this his exam*i*nac*io*n

2./ To the feconde Jnterr*ogatory* this depon*e*nt faythe he hath hard the defendt Confeffe and faye that he was bound vnto the deceafed James Burbage in the fome of twoe hundred pound*es* for p*er*formance of Couenant*es* Conteyned in the leafe made by him the defendt vnto the faid James Burbage:　But he never hard the Compl*ainant* faye that he had that bond of twoe hundred pound*es* in his Cuftodye, nor hath hard the Compl*ainant* threaten to put the fame or any fuch bonde in fuyte againfte the defend*ant*: And more he Cannot depofe./

3/. To the thirde Jnterr*ogatory* this depon*ent* faythe he verelye be-levethe that the faid deceaffed James Burbage did at the tyme of his deathe owe vnto the defend*ant* for rent and tharrerages of Rent Dwe vnto the defend*ant* for the houfes and ground*es* wch he held by demife the fome of thirtye pound*es*: for this depon*ent* fayth he hath hard the Compl*ainan*t Confent to paye the defendt thirtye pound*es* wch his fath*er* James Burbage did owe vnto the defendt./ And he knowethe that the faid thirtye pound*es* is yett vnpayde and more he Cannot depofe./

4./ To the ffourthe Jnterr*ogatory* this depon*ent* faythe that in his Confcience he thinkethe the faid deceaffed James Burbage did not (w^{th}ln the fpace of the firfte tenne yeares after the faid *p*remiffs weare demifed vnto him by the defendt) beftowe the fome of twoe hundred poundes about the Alteringe and Amendinge of the houfes and buyldin*ges* firft demifed vnto him by the de-fend*ant*: But faythe he knowethe that the deceaffed James Bur-bage did beftowe w^{th}in the tyme of the firfte ten yeares good ftore of money about the Alteringe and Amendinge of the houfes Demifed vnto him: yett not the full fome of twoe hundred pound*es* as he takethe yt: And faythe he knowethe not howe muche money was foe beftowed vppon the demifed *p*remiffs by the faid James Burbage: And more he Cannot depofe./

5./ To the vth Jnterr*ogatory* this depon*ent* faythe that for the fpace of the firfte ten yeares the Compl*ainantes* fath*er* kepte the *p*remiffs demifed vnto him by the defendt in good and Suffytient rep*ar*acions but afterward*es* in his lyffe tyme they fell to decaye and fome p*ar*te thereof was vnderpropped wth Shores: And fynce his deceafe that the *p*remiffs haue bene in the pl*aintiffes* poffeffion they have fallen into greater decaye and are vnder-propped wth more Shores: and foe remaynes yett vnrepayred: And will Cofte muche money to be putt in rep*ar*acions: but howe

muche he knowethe not for that he is not Carpenter nor woork-
man belonginge to that trade: And that he thinkethe the said
houses are soe ffallen to decaye for want of reparacions done in
tyme./ And more he Cannot depose./

6./ To the vjth Jnterrogatory this Deponent sayth that about
Michaelmas laste was twelue monethe he this deponent was in
Companye wth the Complainant and defendant at wch tyme yt
appeared vnto him this deponent that the Complainant had bene
an earneste sutor vnto the defendt for A newe lease of the houses
and groundes wch his late father James Burbage had by lease
from him the defendant. And then the defendt was Contented
to graunte the Complainant A newe lease for one and twenty
yeares of the said houses and groundes wch his father James
Burbage had yf soe be he the Complainant would paye vnto him
the defendant the thirtye poundes arrerages of Rent wch his father
James Burbage owght him at the tyme of his death put the houses
in reparacions, and paye him the defendant for the same
premiss twentye ffoure poundes Rent per Annum, And Suffer
the Theater then standinge vppon parte of the ground demised
vnto his father to stand for A playinge house but onlye one ffyve
yeares of his terme of one and twentye viz ffyve of the ffirste
yeares and after to converte the same to tenem^{tes} or vppon
reparacions of the other houses there and soe leave yt bestowed
after his terme ended for the defendtes benefytt. And he bounde
wth Suffytient suertye for paym^t of his Rent: wch the Complainant did Consent vnto, And then proffered his brother Richard
Burbage for his suertye to be bound for the paym^t of his rent
wch the defendant mislyked And therevppon they broke of Agayne
And soe parted. And sayth that yt was at the sygne of the
George in Shordiche that they had the said Communycacion of
Agreem^t touchinge the lease of the premiss and Couenantes and
that yt was about Michaelmas laste was twelue monethe that they
mett about the same. And the Christmas nexte after the said
Theater was pulled downe and Carried Awaye. And more he
Cannot depose touchinge any other Agreem^t betweene them./

7./ To the vij[th] Jnterr*ogatory* this depon*e*nt ſaythe that Ellen Burbage the late wyffe of James Burbage hathe not the good*es* and
Chattles w[ch] weare her ſaid huſbond*es* ffor he doethe knowe that
the ſaid James Burbage her huſbonde in his lyffe tyme made A
deed of guyfte of all his good*es* and Chattles vnto the Complain-
ant: w[ch] deed he hathe ſeene And there ffore he thinkethe ſhee hath
not in her hand*es* of her ſaid huſbond*es* good*es* and Chattles Suffytient to paye the defend*ant* the ſaid ſome of thirtye pound*es*
w[ch] her huſbonde owght vnto the defend*ant* for Rent and Arerages of Rent at the tyme of his deceaſe: And ſhee is accompted
A poore woeman not hable to Satiſſie her huſbond*es* Credyto[rs]./
But he knowethe not that ſhee the ſaid Ellen was by the p*laintiff*
and his brother p*r*ocured to take *lett*res of adminiſtrac*i*on of her
huſbond*es* good*es*, the good*es* beinge before ſecreatlye gayned by
the C*om*pl*ainant* into his and his broth*er*s owne hand*es* as is
alledged in the ſaid Jnterr*ogatory*./ to deceave the ſaid James
Burbage his Credito[rs]. And more he Cannot depoſe./

To the viij[th] Jnterr*ogatory* this Depon*e*nt ſaythe that the Theater
w[ch] was erected vppon p*a*rte of the demiſed p*r*emiſſes was buylte
by the C*om*pl*ainantes* ffath*er* and one John Braynes and not by
the ſaid James Burbage alone: for he hath ſeene the Accompt*es*
betweene them where*b*y yt appeared that the ſaid Braynes bore
halfe the Charge th*er*of and was a p*a*rtner wth James Burbage in
the p*r*ofytt*es* thereof: And more he Cannot depoſe.

9./ To the ix[th] Jnterr*ogatory* this Depon*e*nt ſaythe he knowethe not
what ſomes the C*om*pl*ainant* and his father haue gayned in there
ſeu*er*all tymes by meanes of the Theater: but they haue gayned
muche: And more he Cannot depoſe./

10/ To the tenth Jnterr*ogatory* this depon*e*nt ſaythe that he hard that
the Theater was in pullinge downe. And having A *lett*re of
Attorney from the defend*t* to forbid them: did repayre thyther
And did fynd there at the pullinge downe of the ſame and that
Comaunded and Countenaunced the ſame:/ one Thomas Smythe,

217

the Complainant and Peeter Streete the Cheefe carpenter And thother that weare there weare laborers and fuche as wrought for wages whofe names he perfectlie remembrithe not. And more he Cannot depofe./

11/ To the xj[th] Jnterrogatory this deponent faythe he is the defendtes tenant. And he hath alwayes found the defendt A very ffavorable and Confcyonable Landlord, And foe he is to all his tenantes beinge well delte w[th]all. And more he Cannot depofe

12./ To the xij[th] Jnterrogatory this deponent faythe that he knowethe the Complainantes ffather did in his lyffe tyme fayle the payment of his rent vnto the defendt for he knewe when at one tyme there was ffyftye poundes Rent owinge by the Complainantes father, And the defendant had muche troble wth the faid James Burbage about the fame: And the faid James Burbage placed fuche tenantes in fome parte of the houfes and buyldinges foe leafed vnto him by the defendt as the officers of that parifhe ffound muche falte wth the defendt for Sufferinge the fame, And the Complainant did and doethe Contynewe fome of thofe and fuche lyke tenantes there ftill: And more he Cannot depofe./

[Signed] John Goborne

Henry Johnfon of the parifhe of S[ct]: Leonardes in Shordytche in the Countye of middlefex Sylkeweaver of the Age of ffyftye yeares or there aboutes fworne and examyned the daye and yeare abouefaid depofithe and faythe/

1/ To the ffirfte Jnterrogatory this deponent faythe that the Complainantes father did in his lyffe tyme tender and deliuer vnto the nowe defendant the Draught of A newe leafe of Certayne houfes and groundes w[ch] he held of the defendt by A former leafe and the Complainantes father required the defendt to Seale the fame leafe w[ch] he tendered vnto him. but the defendt refufed to Seale the leafe tendered for that he faid yt was not accordinge to the fame Couenantes Conteyned in the ould leafe. And for that the faid Compl*ainantes* fath*er* (as the defendt then affirmed) was behinde wth the paym^t of p*arte* of his rent referved vppon the ould Leafe./ And that he knowethe the fame to be true for that he was pr*e*fent when the fame leafe was tendered by James Burbage to the defendt to Seale att wch tyme the faid James Burbage anfwered the defendt that whatfoeu*er* was Amiffe in the newe leafe was not longe of him but the fcryveno^r whoe drewe the fame. And more he Cannot depofe touchinge the fame Jnter*r*og*atory* for that he is not nowe at the tyme of this his examineac*ion* fhewed the newe leafe./

2./ To the feconde Jnterr*ogatory* this deponent faythe he hathe hard the faid James Burbage faye that the defendt was bound vnto him in the fome of twoe hundred pound*es* for the p*er*formance of Couenant*es* Conteyned in the ffirfte leafe made by the defendt to the faid James Burbage and he hath hard the defend*ant* acknowledge the fame to be true./ And hath hard the nowe Compl*ain*ant faye that he had that bonde in his Cuftodye and that he would put the fame in fuyte againfte the defendt./ And more he Cannot depofe./

3./ To the thirde Jnterr*ogatory* this deponent faythe he hath hard the defendt faye that the Compl*ainantes* father did at the tyme of his deceafe owe vnto him the defendt for Arerages of Rent the fome of thirtye pound*es*: wch fome of thirtye pound*es* ys yett owinge and vnpayd: And faythe that fynce James Burbage deceafe the Complainant hath confeffed the fame in this deponent*es* prefent*es*. And hath prom*i*ffed to paye the fame vnto the defendt Condiconally he the defendt would make him A newe leafe of the houfes and ground*es* his faid fath*er* James Burbage had of him by leafe. And more he Cannot depofe./

4./ To the ffourthe Jnterr*ogatory* this deponent faythe he thinkethe the faid James Burbage did not within the firfte tenn yeares (wch he held the demiffed prem*i*ff*es* of the defendt) beftowe the fome of twoe hundred pound*es* vppon and about the Alteringe and

Amendinge of the houſes and buyldingₑs demiſed vnto him by
the Defendt for that wᵗʰin the ſaid firſte tenn yeares he this
deponent hath hard the defₑndant fynd falte wᵗʰ the ſaid James
Burbage for that he had not performed his Couenant in that
poynt./ yett the ſayd James Burbage ſtill did ſaye that he had to
the vttermoſte. And more he Cannot depoſe./

5./ To the vᵗʰ Jnterrₒgatory this deponent ſaythe he knowethe that
the ſaid James Burbage in his lyffe tyme did not keepe the houſes
and buyldingₑs demiſed vnto him (by the defendt) in good reparₐ-
acions for in his tyme one end of the Barne did fale to ſuche
ruyne as that they weare Conſtrayned to vnderproppe yt wᵗʰ
Shores. And ſoe yt was remayninge at the tyme of James Burbage his deathe. And yet remaynethe ſoe: but vnderpropped wᵗʰ
more Shores then before: but he ſaythe he knowethe not what
yt will coſte to ſett the ſame wᵗʰ the reſte of the premiſſs in good
reparacions for that he hath but lytle Judgment in thoſe woorkₑs:
And ſaythe further that the ſaid Barne and thothₑr houſes are
ſoe ruinated for want of reparacions in dwe tyme./ And more
he Cannot depoſe./

6./ To the vjᵗʰ Jnterrₒgatory this deponent ſaythe that about Michaellmas Terme Laſte paſte was tweluemonethe the Complainant
one John Golborne and he this deponent mett at the defendtₑs
Lodginge (wᵗʰ the defendt) at the ſygne of the George in Shordytche aforeſaid at wᶜʰ tyme there paſſed betweene the Complainant and defendt diuₑrſe ſpeeches touchinge A newe leaſe of the
premiſſs to be made by the defendt to the Complainant for one
and twentye yeares: wᶜʰ ſpeeche and Communycacion was to this
or the lyke effecte viz the Complainant demaunded of the defendt
A leaſe of the houſes and groundₑs for one and twentye yeares
to commence after thexpiracion of the leaſe wᶜʰ had bene before
made vnto his ffather James Burbage: and that the Theater wᶜʰ
then was vppon partₑ of the ſaid groundₑs might for this terme
of one and twentye yeares remayne for A place to playe in as yt
was woonte: And in Conſidₑracion thereof he the Complainant

then promiſed to geue the defendt twentye ffoure pound*es* p*er*
Ann*um* for A yearlye rent for the p*r*emiſſs and would take vppon
him to paye the defendt the ſome of thirtye pound*es* w^(ch) the defendt Claymed for Arerages of Rent dwe in James Burbage his
lyffe tyme and would vndertake to putt the manſion houſes vppon
the premiſſs in re*p*a*r*acion./ And the defendt was Contented and
did accᵉpte of the Compl*ainantes* pr*o*ffer in all, excepte his demaund for the Theatre to ſtand as a playe houſe w^(ch) he miſlyked
w^(th) wherevppon the Compl*ainan*t requeſted the defendt that he
would Suffer yt to ſtand for A playe houſe but the ffyve ffirſte
yeares of the one and twentye yeares and afterward*es* he would
Converte the ſame to ſome other better vſe. viz into tenem^(tes) or
repayringe thother p*r*emiſſs demiſed vnto him and afterward*es*
leaue the ſame vppon the p*r*emiſſs for the defendt*es* benefytt.
w^(ch) the defendt then Agreed vnto And thcn demaunded of the
Compl*ainan*t Suffytient ſecurytie for the paym^(t) of his the Compl*ainantes* Rent duringe his terme of one and twentye yeares:
wherevppon he made p*r*offer vnto the defendt of his broth*er*
Richard Burbage w^(th) whome the defendt miſlyked and ſoe therevppon they lefte of and p*a*rted. And more he Cannot depoſe
ſaue onlye that there ſaid Com*m*unycacion was the Michaelmas
terme was tweluemonethe and the pullinge downe of the Theatre
was the Chriſtmas ffollowinge./

7./ To the vij^(th) Jnterr*ogatory* this deponnt ſaythe he thinkethe that
the ſaid Ellen Burbage menc*ioned in the Jnterr*ogatory* is A very
poore woeman and hath not in her hand*es* ſuffytient to Satiſfie
her late huſbond James Burbage his debt*es*: nor for his breache
of other Couenant*es*. And more touchinge the ſaid Jnterr*oga-*
tory this depon*en*t cannott depoſe ſaue onelye that he hath hard
that the Compl*ainan*t and his brother did take that Courſe mencioned in the Jnterr*ogatory* to defraud there fath*er*s Credyto^(rs)./

8./ To the viij^(th) Jnterr this depon*en*t ſaythe he thinkethe that the
deceaſed James Burbage did not of his owne p*r*oper Coſte and
Charge buyld and erecte the playe houſe called the Theater: ffor

he hath hard one John Braynes faye that he did defraye the better
halfe of the Charges thereof vppon Agreem^t betweene them:
And faythe he was A gatherer of the proffyttes therof vnder
James Burbage and John Braynes and knew they parted the
proffyttes betweene them: And more he cannot depofe./

9./ To the ix^th Jnterrogatory this deponent faythe that the Complainantes father and the Complainant haue gayned greate fomes
of money by the Theater: But howe muche he knowethe not:
And more he Cannot depofe./

10/ To the xth Jnterrogatory this deponent faythe he went to the
Theater when yt was in pullinge downe to charge the woorkemen
and the Complainant not to pull the fame downe for that yt was
not accordinge to anye Agreem^t or Communycacion of agreem^t
in his prefentes And beinge there he this deponent did perceaue
that the fame Theater was appoynted to be foe pulled downe by
the Complainant by his Brother Richard Burbage and one Thomas
Smythe: and one [Peter] Streete who was heade Carpenter that
gaue affiftance therein: And when he had foe Charged them not
to pull the fame Theatre Downe they the faid Complainant and
Thomas Smythe and [Peter] Streete the Carpenter tould him this
deponent that they tooke yt downe but to fett yt vpp vppon the
premiffs in an other forme and that they had Couenanted w^th
the Carpenter to that effecte and Shewed this deponnt the decayes
about the fame as yt ftoode there thereby Colloringe there de-
ceipte. And more he Cannot depofe faue onlye that notw^thftand-
ynge all there fpeeches they pulled yt downe and Carried yt
Awaye And more he Cannot depofe./

11/ To the xj^th Jnterrogatory this deponent faythe that he is the
defendantes tenant and faythe that his landlord Allen is A very
honefte and Confcyonable man very favorable to all his tenantes
not vfinge any of them in extremetye. And that he this deponent hath bene his tenant thefe thirteene yeares. And more he
Cannot depofe./

12./ To the xijth Jnterro*gatory* this deponent faythe he knowethe that James Burbage did in his lyffe tyme fayle in the paym^t of his Rent and in *per*formance of couenantes wth the defendt./ and the defendt hath Suffered muche Difquyetnes by occac*i*on thereof: for the faid James Burbage placed fuch tenant*es* in the Barnes and tenem^{tes} wch he held by leafe from the defendt as the officers of the *pari*fhe there haue ffound muche falte the*r*wth and haue geuen the defendt ill fpeeches for Sufferinge the fame. And the Compl*ainan*t ftill Contynewethe fuche lyke tenant*es* there for his *pr*offytt: And he knowethe the fame to be true for that he hath hard the defendt demaund his rent of James Burbage and Could not then haue yt, And he hath bene officer there and hath had fome of the *pari*fhners fynd much falte wth fome of thofe tenant*es*./ And more he Cannot depofe to his nowe remembr*a*nce./

[Signed] Henry Johnfon

*Idem. Depofit*i*ons ex parte Burbage 15 May, 1600.*

INTERROGATORIES

[In dorso]
Termino Trinit*atis*
xlij^{do} *Regni Regi*ne
*Eli*z*abethe*

Jnterrogatories myniftred fo*r* thexamynac*i*on of witneffes produced on the parte and behalf of Cuthberte Bur*b*adge Compl^t againfte Giles Allen defend^t

1. Jnprimis doe yo^w knowe the parties pl*aintiff* and defend^t and howe longe haue yo^w knowen them or either of them, And did yo^w not likewife knowe one James Burbadge father of the faid Compl*ainant* nowe deceafed.

2. Doe yo^w knowe that the faid Defend^t Giles Allen and Sara his wief aboute the thirteenth daye of April in the eighteenth yere of her ma^{ties} reigne did demife vnto the faid James Burbage cer-teine garden groundes lyinge and beinge in Hollywell in the

parifhe of Ste Leonard*es* in Shorditch in the Countie of Mid-
d*lefex* for what terme, rente, and vnder what Couenaunt*es* was
the fame leas fo made Declare yor knowledge herein, and how
yo^w knowe ye fame.

3 Doe yo^w knowe that the faid James Burbadge before thende of
the firfte terme of Tenne yeres menc*i*oned in the faid leas did
require the faid Defend^t to make vnto him the faid James a newe
leas of the *p*remiffes accordinge to the purporte and effecte of the
Couenaunte menc*i*oned in the forefaid leas, Did not the faid
James Burbadge tender vnto the faid Defend^t a newe leas readie
written and ingrofed wth labell*es* and waxe thereunto fixed, and
was not the fame agreable to the Couen^t in the faid firfte leas
menc*i*oned And did not the faid Defend^t then make fhewe that
he wolde deliu*er* the fame to the faid James Burbadge but fhifted
of the fynifhinge thereof, Declare yor knowledge herein and howe
yo^w knowe the fame/

4. Doe yo^w knowe that the faid Compl*ainan*t did aboute twoo yeres
nowe laft pafste & diuers tymes fince require the faid defend^t
[*and his wief* (stricken out)] to make vnto him A newe leas of
the *p*remiffes accordinge to the agreem^t menc*i*oned in the faid
firfte leas, Did not the faid Defend^t. denye to make vnto him
the faid leas, and what was the Caufe he the faid defend^t Did not
make the faid leas to yor knowledge or as yo^w Crediblie haue hard
Expreffe the truth hereof at large, and what yo^w knowe touchinge
the fame.

5 Did not Ellen Burbadge mother of the Compl*ainant* giue her
Confente that the faid Compl*ainant* fhould take downe, and Carry
awaie the tymber and ftuff ymploied for the theater or playhoufe
in the bill menc*i*oned Declare the truth herein.

6 Doe yo^w knowe that there was variaunce and Controuerfie aboute
eighteene yeres pafte betwene the Defend^t and one Edmond Peckham touchinge the title of the faid *p*remiffes, was not the faid

James Burbadge by reaſon of the ſame Controuerſie often charged
to finde men to keepe the poſſeſſion of the ſaid premiſſes from the
ſaid Edmond Peckham and his ſervauntes, and was not the ſaid
James Burbadge often arreſted and much troubled by reaſon of
the ſaide Controuerſie that he Coulde not peaceablie enioye the
premiſſes accordinge to his ſaid leas, Declare yoᵣ knowledge herein
and howe yoʷ knowe the ſame.

7 Did not the ſaid James Burbadge in his lief tyme for dyuers yeres
duringe his terme, diſburſe and beſtowe muche money aboute the
reparacions of the ſaid Tenemᵗᵉˢ to yoᵣ knowledge or as you
Crediblie haue hard, and to what value did the ſame money growe
Declare yoᵣ knowledge herein/

8 Hath not the ſaid Complainant ſithence the death of the ſaid
James Burbadge euerie yere beſtowed muche money in repayringe
of the ſaid Tenemᵗᵉˢ, and did not the ſaid Complainant this laſte
yere likewiſe beſtowe a greate ſome of moneye in reparacions of
the ſame to yoᵣ knowledge Expreſſe the truth herein and howe
much he beſtowed aboute the ſame

9 Did yoʷ knowe the ſaid Tenemᵗᵉˢ before and at the tyme theie
weare taken by the ſaid James Burbadg of the Defendᵗ, in what
manner and ſtate of reparacions were the ſame then in Concerninge the ſufficiencye of the buildinge of them, And are not the
ſame Tenemᵗᵉˢ nowe much bettred and lett for more rente then
theie then did Declare yoᵣ knowledge herein at large.

10 Was there not a decayed longe barne parcell of the ſaid premiſſes
demiſed to the ſaid James Burbage ſometymes in the tenure of
one Richardes, and Stoughton, and was not the ſaide barne at
the tyme of the leas made to the ſaid James Burbadge ruynous
and decayed, ſo as the ſame was fayne to be ſhored vpp vnto the
playhouſe called the Theater, when it was builte, and hath not
the ſaid James Burbadg and the nowe Complainant from tyme
to tyme repayred the ſame Declare yoᵣ knowledg herein

11. Whether were not yo^w pre*f*ente at A viewe and e*f*tymate made of *f*uche Dwellinge hou*f*es or ten*emementes* as were erected and builte, and other Co*ftes* be*f*towed vppon the *f*ame by the *f*aid James Burbadge taken the eighteenth daie of Julye 1586 by Bryan Ellam, John Grigges, Wil*l*i*am* Bothan, Wil*l*i*am* Clarke, Richard Hud*f*on and Thomas O*f*borne, howe longe before the *f*aid viewe or e*f*tymate *f*o taken was the *f*ame Co*ftes* in buildinge *f*o be*f*towed by the *f*aid Burbadge, and how much was there then be*f*towed by the *f*aid James Burbadge vppon the *f*ame buildinges to yor owne knowledge and were yo^w not pre*f*ente at the *f*ettinge downe of the *f*aid viewe or e*f*tymate written in A booke and Confirmed vnder the *f*aid parties handes, and was not the *f*ame A true *f*u*r*veye   Declare the truth herein at large.

12. Did not the *f*aid Brian Elham Wil*l*i*am* Bothan and Wil*l*i*am* Clark the *f*ame tyme affirme that theie had formerlie made A viewe of the *f*aid buildinges taken by them the twentith daye of November 1585, and had likewi*f*e Confyrmed the *f*ame vnder theire handes beinge written in A booke of Accompte, what did theye *f*aye the e*f*tymate came then vnto, and what doe yowe thincke or beleiue concerninge the truthe of the *f*ame   Declare vppon yor oathe.

DEPOSITIONS

Depo*f*ition*es* Capt*ae* ap*u*d We*f*tmon*aft*erium xv^to die maij A° Regni D*omine* Re*g*ine Elizabethe hunc &c   Quadrage*f*imo Secundo ex p*ar*te Cuthberti Burbage gen*eroſi* q^rtis ver*fus* Egidiu*m* Allen gen*erofum* Defend*entem*.

Richard Hud*f*on of the p*ariſ*he of S^ct: Albones London Carpenter of the Age of thirtye eight yeares or there a*b*out*es* *f*worne and examyned the daye and yeare aboue*f*aid depo*f*ithe and *f*aythe/

1./ To the ffir*f*te Jnterrogatory this depon*ent* *f*aythe he knowethe the Compl*ainan*t and did very well knowe his ffather James Burbage when he lyved./ And hath feene the defendt: And faythe he hath knowne the Complainant of A Child and more he Cannott depofe

2. 3. 4. 5. 6. 7.
8./ To the fecond, thirde, ffourthe ffyfthe, Syxte, Seaventhe and Eighte Jnterrogatories this deponent is not examyned at the requefte of the plaintiff

9./ To the nynthe Jnterrogatory this Deponent faythe he knowethe the tenem^{tes} nowe in the Complainantes poffeffion, And did knowe them for twentye yeares pafte in the Complainantes ffathers poffeffion vfe and occupacion and that then the fame tenementes weare ould decayed and ruynated for want of reparacions and the befte of them was but of twoe ftories hie./ And the fame tenem^{tes} are nowe muche better, And as he thinkethe they goe for more Rent then they then went for:/ And that he knowethe the fame to be true for that he this deponent did ferve his ffather in lawe Bryan Ellam when he Wroughte vppon the fame tenem^{tes} in the Compltes fathers tyme./ And knoweth that then there was muche money beftowed vppon repayringe the fame./ And more he Cannot depofe touchinge the fame Jnterrogatory for that he doethe not remember that he did knowe the faid tenem^{tes} before and at the very firfte tyme that the Complainantes ffather James Burbage tooke the tenem^{tes} of the defendant by leafe./

10/ To the tenthe Jnterrogatory this Deponent faythe he remembrythe that when he firfte wayted vppon his father in lawe Bryan Ellam wch is aboue twentye yeares fince there was An ould longe decayed Barne vppon parte of the premiffs demifed as he takethe yt to James Burbage. wch barne was very ruynous and decayed foe as then the fame was fayne to be fhored vpp vnto the Playhoufe Called the Theater: wch Barne the faid James Burbage and the Complainant haue bene fayne from tyme to tyme to repayre and Amend: wch he knowethe to be true for that he knewe his faid ffather in lawe Brian Ellam fhore vpp the fame vnto the

Playhoufe called the Theater, And he this deponent him felfe
hath fynce then wrought Carpenters woorke in and about the
same :/ But he doethe not well remember there names that then
dwelled in the fame Barne: yett hath Crediblie harde that yt was
one Richardes and Stoughton. And one Baker And more he
Cannot depofe./

11/ To the xjth Jnterrogatory this deponent faythe he was prefent at
A view and eftimate made of the Coftes beftowed by James Burbage in his lyffe tyme vppon the houfes and tenem^{tes} demifed
vnto him by Gyles Allen the nowe defendant. wch viewe was taken
the Eighteenthe daye of Julye in the yeare of ou^r lord god one
thoufand ffyve hundred Eightie Syxe by this deponentes faid
ffather in lawe Brian Ellam, John Grigges, William Bothan,
William Clarke, Thomas Ofborne and him this deponent, at w^{ch}
viewe yt did appeare vnto them the faid viewors that before that
tyme of there viewe there had bene beftowed vppon the premiffs
demifed to the faid James Burbage by him the faid James Burbage the fome of twoe hundred and fortye poundes as maye more
playnlye appeare by A rememberance thereof fett downe in one
of the faid James Burbage his Bookes of Accomptes wherevnto
is fubfcribed the faid viewors names and markes: vnto wch booke
for more certayntye of the truethe herein this deponent referrithe
him felfe./ And this Deponent faythe that he verelye thinkethe
that the faid Cofte wch then was by the viewors found to haue
bene beftowed vppon the houfes and buyldinges by the faid James
Burbage was beftowed fome three or ffoure yeares before the
viewe foe taken by the faid Bryan Ellame, John Grigges, William
Botham, William Clarke, Thomas Ofborne and him this Deponent: And faythe he was emongefte the refte prefent at the
fettinge downe of the faid viewe & eftimate wrytten in the faid
James Burbage his booke and confirmed there vnder all there
handes. wch he knowethe was Juftlie trulye and indifferentlye
furveyed by the parties Aforefaid afwell for the faid James Burbage as his Landlord Gyles Allen./ And more he Cannot depofe./

12./ To the xij^th Jnterro*gatory* this Depon*e*nt faythe that when they
mett togather to take the viewe the Eighteenth daye of Julye in
the yeare of ou^r lord god one thoufand ffyve hundred Eightie
Syxe he hard his faid ffather in lawe Bryan Ellame, William
Botham, and William Clarke affirme that they had fformerlye
made A viewe of the faid Buyldin*ges,* about nouember in the
yeare of ou^r Lord god one thoufand ffyve hundred Eightie ffyve
wch viewe they faid they had Confirmed vnder there hand*es* in A
booke of Accompte of the faid James Burbage And that as he
remembrithe they affirmed that the eftimate firfte by them made
came to twoe hundred and twentye pound*es* And more he Cannot depofe touchinge the fame Jnterro*gatories* to his nowe rememb*e*rance./

                           [Signed]   Rychard Hudfons

Thomas Bromfield of the p*a*rifhe of S^ct: Leonard*es* in Shordytche in the Countye of Midd*lefex* Bricklayer of the Age of
thirtye yeares or thereabout*es* fworne and examyned the daye
and yeare abouefaid depofithe and faythe./

1/ To the ffirfte Jnterro*gatory* this depon*e*nt faythe he knowethe the
Compl*ain*ant and defendt and hathe knowne the Compl*ain*ant
about Seaven years and the defendt about ffyve yeares, And
faythe he did very well knowe James Burbage menci*o*ned in the
Jnterro*gatory* father of the faid Compl*ain*ant./

2. 3. 4. 5. To the fecond, thirde, ffourthe ffyfte, Syxte Jnterro*gatories*
6/ this depon*e*nt is not examyned at the requefte of the pl*ain*tiff./

7./ To the vij^th Jnt*errogatory* this depon*e*nt faythe he knowethe of
his owne knowledge that the faid James Burbage did in his lyffe
tyme and for diu*er*fe yeares duringe his terme in his leafe of his
tenem^tes from the defendt Allen difburfe and beftowe muche money
about the rep*a*racions of the faid houfes and tenem^tes demifed
vnto him by the faid defendt Allen for this depon*e*nt faythe that
for eight yeares he this depon*e*nt wth others haue yearlye done

rep*a*racio*n*s vppon and About the fame tenem^(tes) at the Co*ſt*es of
the faid James Burbage for he ſtill payde the other woorkmen and
him this depon*e*nt for his woorke donne there. But the valewe
of his Charge beſtowed vppon and about the fame houſes and
tenem^(tes) he knowethe not Certaynlye./   And more he Cannot
depoſe./

8./ To the Eight Jnter*r*og*a*tor*y* this depon*e*nt ſaythe he knowethe
that ſythence the deceaſe of James Burbage the Compl*ai*nan*t* hath
euerye yeare beſtowed ſome money in repayringe of the ſaid
tenem^(tes) demiſed vnto his fath*e*r Jam*e*s Burbage. And this laſte
yeare he the Compl*ai*nan*t* lykewiſe beſtowed A greate ſome of
money in rep*a*racio*n*s of the ſame houſes and tenement*es* for he
beſtowed the buyldinge of twoe Chimneys in one of the ſaid
tenem^(tes), and repayred the houſes in diu*er*ſe places ſoe that they
be nowe in as good rep*a*racio*n*s as eu*er* they weare to this depon*ent*es knowledge and he hath knowne them theſe tenn or
eleven yeares./   And this depon*e*nt ſaythe that the laſte yeare he
this depon*e*nt for his p*a*rte earned of the Compl*ai*nan*t* for woorke
done vppon and about the ſaid tenem^(tes) ffyftye Shillinge*s* w^(th) his
laborers wages and the Stuffe w^(ch) the pl*ai*ntiff founde./   And
ſaythe that there was one other bricklayer that lykewiſe wrought
about the ſaid houſes and vppon the tenem^(tes) the laſte yeare but
howe muche his woorkmanſhipp and the pl*ai*ntiff*es* Stuffe came
vnto or was woorthe he knowethe not nor can eſtimate for that
he did not viewe the ſame. And more he Cannot depoſe./

9./ To the ix^(th) Jnter*r*og*a*tor*y* this depon*e*nt ſaythe he did not knowe
the houſes and tenem^(tes) before and at the tyme that the ſaid
James Burbage tooke them by leaſe of the defend*a*nt Allen, nor
in what ſtate of rep*a*racio*n*s they weare then concerninge the
Suffytiencie of the Buyldinge*s*: But ſaythe he hath knowne the
houſes and tenem^(tes) theſe tenne or eleven yeares and ſaythe that
they are now in as good and Suffytient rep*a*racio*n*s as they weare
at the firſte tyme of his this depon*ent*es knowledg and haue
bene continewallie ſynce then kepte in rep*a*racio*n*s by the ſaid

James Burbage in his lyffe tyme and fynce his deceafe by the
Complainant, for he this deponent hath earned of James burbage
before he Died for reparacions done in and about thofe tenem^{tes}
twentye markes or there aboutes : And this deponent faythe he
hath hard diuerfe ould men and woemen faye that when the faid
James Burbage tooke the faid houfes and tenem^{tes} of the defendt
Allen they weare houfes of Offyce as A Slaughter houfe and
Brewe houfe and lowe paulterye buyldinges. And that the fame
are nowe muche better then they weare and lett for more Rent
then they weare woorthe. wch happenethe by reafon of the reparacions and alteracions Donne vnto them by the faid James Burbage and the nowe Complainant./ And more he Cannot depofe/

10/ To the xth Jnterrogatory this Deponent faythe that he knowethe
the ould Barne mencioned in the Jnterrogatory, But that Richardes and Staughton mencioned in the Jnterrogatory did dwell in
the fame he knowethe not, nor that the fame Barne was ruynous
and decayed when James Burbage had his leafe of the premiffs
from the defendant Allen for yt was demifed vnto James Burbage before this deponent was acquainted wth the premiffs : But
when he this deponent firfte knewe yt he rememberethe the fame
Barne was fhored vppe wth twoe or three Shores from the Playhoufe Called the Theater : And faythe that w^{th}in this ten or
Eleven yeares the faid James Burbage and the nowe Complainant
hath from tyme to tyme repayred and kepte the fame Barne to
there befte endevor and the fame is nowe in reafonable good
repayre./ And more he cannot depofe to his nowe rememberance touchinge the faid Jnterrogatory

11. 12/ To the xj^{th} and xij^{th} Jnterrogatories this deponent is not examyned at the plaintiffes requefte./

[His mark] ⌐

Thomas Ofborne of the parifhe of ffanchurche London Carpenter of
the Age of ffortye twoe yeares or there aboutes fworne and examyned the Daye and yeare abouefaid Depofithe and faythe./

1/ To the ffirſte Jnterr*ogatory* this depon*e*nt ſaythe he knowethe the Compl*ainan*t and defend*an*t and hath knowne the Compl*ainan*t theſe eighteene yeares or thereabout*es* and the defend*an*t but A whyle./ And ſaythe that he did very well knowe James Burbadge deceaſſed mencioned in the Jnterr*ogatory* father of the Compl*ainan*t And that he did many tymes woorke for the ſaid James Burbadge about his houſinge and buyldi*ng*e*s* at Holliwell./ And more he Cannot depoſe./

2/3/4/ To the ſecond, third, ffourthe, ffyfte, Syxte, Seaventhe and 5/6/7/8/. Eight Jnterr*ogatories* this depon*e*nt is not examyned at the requeſte of the pl*ain*t*iff*./

9./ To the nynthe Jnterr*ogatory* this depon*e*nt ſaythe he did not knowe the tenem^*tes* (nowe in the Compl*ainan*t*es* poſſeſſion) before and at the tyme they weare takne by the ſaid deceaſſed James Burbadge of the nowe defend*an*t: but ſaythe that he knewe them for Eightene yeares paſte at wch tyme the ſaid James Burbadge had them in poſſeſſion./ and that then the tenem^*tes* weare in greate ruyne and wanted rep*ar*acio*n*s and ould buyldinges And the ſaid James Burbadge did about the tyme aforeſaid viz ſeaventeene or eighteene yeares agoe buyld his owne dwellinge houſe Almoſte all newe from the grounde and altered and Amended diu*er*ſe other tenem^*tes* wch he hadd there in his poſſeſſion but what eſtate he hadd in the ſame he knowethe not Certaynlye, but hath hard that he had A leaſe th*er*of from the defendt And that he the ſaid James Burbadge was to beſtowe A certayne ſome of money vppon ſuche tenem^*tes* as he had takne: And this depon*e*nt ſaythe that the ſaid James Burbadge in his lyffe tyme did buyld repayre and Amend diu*er*ſe of the tenem^*tes* wch he held, and beſtowed muche Coſte vppon them and made them muche better then they weare before and ſoe they are nowe./ but howe the rent is improued thereby he knowethe not./ And ſaythe he knoweth the ſame to be true for that he did woorke manye tymes wth the ſaid James Burbadge and dwelled neare vnto him and did ſee that he beſtowed muche coſte vppon and about the tenem^*tes* And more he Cannot

depofe touchinge the faid Jnterr*ogatory* to his nowe remem-
be*r*ance./

10/ To the xth Jnterr*ogatory* this depon*e*nt faythe that he well remembrithe the decayed longe Barne p*a*rcell of the p*r*emiſs in the
tenure and poſſeſſion of the faid James Burbadge wch Barne he
remembrithe was eighteene yeares paſte reddye to haue ffallen
downe. And the faid James Burbadge did then cauſe the ſame
Barne to be ſhored vpp, grouncelled, Croſſe beamed, dogged
togeather And ſoe ſtrengthned and repayred yt from tyme to
tyme duringe his lyffe tyme wch he knowethe to be true for that
he this depon*e*nt did healpe to doe the ſame and did often woorke
vppon that Barne and other the tenem^{tes} of the ſaid James Burbadges by the ſaid James Burbadge his appoyntment and at his
Coſte./ But that Richard*es* and Staughton menc*i*oned in the Jnterrogatory did dwell there this depon*e*nt remembrithe not, nor
knowethe what rep*a*racions the nowe Compl*ai*n*a*nt hath done
vppon the p*r*emiſſes ſynce the deathe of his father James Burbadge./ And more he cannot depoſe.

11/ To the xjth Jnterr*ogatory* this depon*e*nt faythe that he was p*r*eſent
at A viewe and eſtimate made of ſu*ch*e dwellinge ho*u*ſes or
tenem^{tes} as weare erected and buylte, (and other Coſt*es* beſtowed
vppon the ſame dwellinge houſes and tenem^{tes}) by the ſaid James
Burbadge in his lyffe tyme : wch viewe was takn*e* as he nowe
remembrithe the Eighteenthe daye of Julye one thouſand ffyve
hundred Eightie Syxe by one Brian Ellam, John Grigg*es,* Will*i*am
Bothan, William Clarke Richard Hudſon and him this depon*e*nt :
menc*i*oned in the Jnterr*ogatory*/ vppon wch viewe yt did appeare
vnto him this depon*e*nt and the parties aforeſaid that the ſaid
James Burbadge had wthin ffoure or ffyve yeares before that
viewe beſtowed vppon the houſes and tenementes (wch weare (by
reporte) demiſed vnto him by the defend*a*nt) the ſome of twoe
hundred and ffortye pound*es*./ And ſaythe that he this depon*e*nt
wth the reſte of the viewors did in one of the ſaid James Burbadge his book*es* of accompt*es* ſee A remembr*a*nce of that viewe

and eftimate fett downè in wrightinge vnto wch they the faid
viewors Subfcribed and fett to there mark*es* for better confirma-
c*io*n thereof And faythe that the fame was A true and Jndyffer-
ent furveye takne by the p*ar*ties aforefaid, And more he Cannot
depofe touchinge the faid Jnterr*ogatory* to his nowe remem*br*ance
but referrithe him felfe to the booke of Accompte where the fame
will more playnlie Appeare./

12./ To the xij^th Jnterr*ogatory* this Depon*e*nt faythe that at the viewe
takne the eighteenthe of Julye one thoufand ffyve hundred Eightie
Syxe he remembrythe he did heare the faide Brian Ellam, Willi*a*m Bothan and Will*ia*m Clarke affirme and faye that they had
takne A former viewe of m^r James Burbadge his buyldin*ges* and
Coft*es* bestowed vppon the p*r*emiffs, wch viewe they faid they made
about the twentythe daye of Nouember in the yeare of ou^r lord
god one thoufand ffyve hundred Eightie ffyve and that they had
Confirmed the fame vnder theire hand*es* in A booke of Accompte
of the faid m^r James Burbadge And that then the fame Came but
to twoe hundred and twentye pound*es,* And that he thinkethe yt
could be no leffe for that yt feemed there had bene greate cofte
beftowed vppon and about the fame by the faid m^r James Burbadge And for that they whoe weare viewors thereof weare
woorkemen of good Judgment in buyldinge and had wrought
vppon the fame for the faid James Burbadge at his Charge. And
more he Cannot depofe to his nowe rememberance./

[Signed]   Thoma,s Ofborne.

William ffurnis of the p*ar*ifhe of S^ct: Leonard*es* in Shorditche in
the Countye of Mid*dlefex* laborer of the Age of ffyftie Eight
yeares or there about*es* fworne and examyned the daye and yeare
abouefaid depofithe and faythe./

1/ To the ffirfte Jnterr*ogatory* this Depon*e*nt faythe he knowethe
the Compl*ainant* and defend*ant* and hath knowne the Compl*ainant*
about Eighteene yeares and the defend*ant* but A whyle, And

faythe he did knowe James Burbadge (the Compl*ainantes* fath*er*)
now deceaſſed./

2/.3/4./
5/6./ To the ſecond, third, ffourthe, fyfte and Syxte Jnterr*ogatories*
this depon*ent* is not examyned at the requeſte of the pl*aintiff*./

7./ To the vij[th] Jnterr*ogatory* this depon*ent* ſaythe that the deceaſſed
James Burbadge did in his lyffe tyme for diu*erſe* years duringe
his terme diſburſe and beſtowe muche money about the rep*ar*-
acc*io*ns of the tenem[tes] w[ch] he held of the defend*ant* and he
thinkethe to the valwe of twentye pound*es* and better. And that
he knowethe the ſame to be true for that he this depon*ent* hath
bene his tenant theſe ſeaventeene or eighteene yeares and hath
ſeene the ſaid James Burbadge and the nowe compl*ainant* ſynce
his deceaſe eu*er*ye yeare beſtowe ſome Coſte in repayringe and
mayntayninge in rep*ar*ac*io*ns the ſaid tenem[tes]./ Demiſed vnto him
by the defendt wth his manſion houſe w[ch] he lykewiſe beſtowed
greate coſte on, in newe buyldinge: and adioyninge another newe
buylte houſe vnto yt. And more he Cannot depoſe ſaue onlye
that he hath bene laborer there and ſerved the woorkmen when
the ſaid ould tenem[tes] haue bene repayringe././

8./ To the viij[th] Jnterr*ogatory* this depon*ent* ſaythe that the nowe
Compl*ainant* Cuthbert Burbadge hath yearlye ſynce the deathe of
his ffather James Burbadge beſtowed muche money in repayringe
of the ſaid ould tenement*es*, And this laſte yeare kepte one man
at woorke in repayringe the ſaid ould tenem[tes] ffyve dayes, and
after him an other Syxe weekes, and one other after hime ffyve
dayes more w[ch] this depon*ent* thinkethe Coſte the ſaid Compl*ain-*
ant about nyne pound*es* woorkmanſhipp and Stuffe./ all w[ch] he
this depon*ent* beinge tenant there and dwellinge in thoſe rent*es*
did ſee and therefore knowethe the ſame to be true And more
he Cannot depoſe./

9./ To the nynthe Jnterr*ogatory* this depon*ent* ſaythe he did not
knowe the ſaid tenem[tes] when the ſaid James Burbadge tooke the

fame of the defendt nor before./ but fayth that eighteene yeares
pafte or there about he this deponent came thyther to dwell: fynce
wch tyme he hath knowne the fame, and faythe that when he this
deponent firfte knewe the fame the faid tenem^tes weare very ould
and houfes of office, and his owne dwellinge houfe was but
ruynous and ould buyldinge and the faid James Burbadge did
buyld his owne houfe newe and an other nexte vnto yt and repayred and Amended the other buyldinges wch weare houfes of
office before, and converted them to tenem^tes and made them ten-
antable whereby the fame are bettered and are lett for more rent
then they then went: for mofte of wch alteracion and cofte beftowed there, was donne fynce he this deponent came thither to
dwell as tenant to the faid James Burbadge. And therefore
knowethe the premiffs to be true/ And more he Cannot depofe
touchinge the faid Jnterrogatory to his nowe rememberance./

10/ To the xth Jnterrogatory this deponent faythe that when he this
deponent came to dwell in the faid James Burbadge his rentes the
decayed longe Barne mencioned in the Jnterrogatory was in as
greate decaye as yt is nowe, for yt ftoode then Shored vpp againfte
the playhoufe called the Theater and nowe yt is but fhored vpp
from the ground, and the deceaffed James Burbadge did in his
lyffe tyme from tyme to tyme repayre the fame and foe hathe the
Complainant fynce his deceafe./ but he remembrythe not that
Richardes and Staughton mencioned in the Jnterrogatory had the
tenure thereof. And more he Cannot depofe touchinge the faid
Jnterrogatory to his nowe rememberance./

11/12/ To the Eleventhe and tweluethe Jnterrogatories this deponent
is not examyned at the requefte of the Complainant./

[His mark] X

William Smythe of Waltham Crofe in the Countye of Hartforde
gentleman of the Age of ffortye yeares or thereaboutes fworne and
examyned the daye and yeare abouefaid Depofithe and faythe

1/ To the ffirſte Jnterrogatory this deponent ſaythe he knowethe the Complainant and Defendant, and hath knowne the Complainant theſe ffyfteene yeare or there aboutes and the defendant but about three yeares And ſaythe that he did knowe James Burbadge mencioned in the Jnterrogatory nowe deceaſſed./

2./ To the ſeconde Jnterrogatory this deponent ſaythe he hathe ſeene An Jndenture of Leaſe whereby yt appeared that the defendt and Sara his wyffe did about the thirteenthe daye of Aprill in the eighteenthe yeare of her ma:ᵗᵉˢ raigne that nowe is demiſe vnto him the ſaid James Burbadge Certayne garden groundes lyinge and beinge in Hollywell in the pariſhe of Sᵗ: Leonardes in Shorditche in the Countye of Middleſex for the terme of one and twentye yeares yealdinge and payinge therefore yearlye duringe the ſaid terme ffoureteene poundes per Annum wᵗʰ prouiſoe in the ſame leaſe that the defendt wᵗʰin or at thend and terme of the firſte ten yeares in the ſaid Leaſe he the ſaid defendt ſhould make him the ſaid James Burbadge or his Aſſignes A newe leaſe for one and twentye yeares then to Commence at thend of the ſaid firſte tenn yeare graunted him in his ſaid Leaſe of the date of the Thirteenthe of Aprill in the Eighteenthe yeare of her ma:ᵗᵉˢ Raygne aforeſaid: And ſaythe that he remembrythe not the ſeuerall Couenantes compriſed in the ſaid Leaſe made vnto the ſaid James Burbadge. but for Certentye thereof referrithe him ſelfe vnto the ſaid leaſe now expired and remayninge in the Complainantes Cuſtodye And more he Cannot depoſe to his nowe rememberance./

3./ To the thirde Jnterr this deponent ſaythe he hathe harde the defendt diuerſe and manye tymes Confeſſe that the ſaid James Burbadge did in his lyffe tyme and before thende of the firſte Terme of Tenn yeares (mencioned in the ſaid firſte leaſe) require him the ſaid defendant to make vnto him the ſaid James Burbadge A newe leaſe of the ſaid premiſſs accordinge to the purporte and effecte of the Couenant mencioned in the ſaid former leaſe, And that he hard the defendt confeſſe that James Burbadge aforeſaid did tender vnto him the defendt A newe leafe reddye wrytten and ingroffed reddye to Seale accordinge [to] the couenant*es* and p*ro*uifoes conteyned in the firfte leafe   And he the defendt vppon the fame tender afked the faid James Burbadge and the fcriveno^r (whoe brought the fame leafe wth them reddye to be Sealed) yf they would geue him leaue to aduife of yt. wh*er*vppon they Anfwered no, then faid the faid defendt yf you will not geue me leaue I will take leaue and took the faid leafe and fynce then kepte yt in his owne poffeffion, and never Sealed the fame.   And that he knowethe the fame to be true but from the faid defend*antes* owne reporte.   And more he Cannot depofe.

4./ To the ffourthe Inter*rogatory* this Depon*ent* faythe that he knowethe the Compl*ainant* did about twoe yeares nowe lafte pafte or there about*es* and diu*er*fe tymes fynce then, require the faid defendt to make him A new Leafe of the p*remiffs* accordinge to the Agreem^t men*ci*oned in the ffirfte leafe, but the Defendt denied to make him any fuche leafe, alledginge that the p*remiffs* weare not bettered by James Burbadge accordinge to his Couenant, and that there weare Arerages of Rent behinde and vnpayde wch the faid James Burbadge did owe in his lyffe tyme./   But the defendt did tender the Compl*ainant* A newe leafe of the p*remiffs* wth Jmprouem^t of the rent and very ftricte and vnreafonable Couenant*es* Contrarye to the Agreem^t and the Couenant*es* in the firfte leafe made to James Burbadge, for wch Caufes the p*laintiff* refufed the fame./   And more he Cannot depofe touchinge the fame Jnter*rogatory* But for more Certentye thereof referrathe him felfe to the fame draught remayninge wth the defendt./

5./ To the ffyfte Jnter*rogatory* this deponent faythe that he knowethe the faid Compl*ainantes* mother did geue her Confent that the p*laintiff* fhould take downe, and Carrie Awaye the Tymber and ftuffe Jmployed for the Theater or playhoufe in the Bill men*ci*oned for fhee was there and did fee the doinge thereof and lyked well of yt and did alowe thereof.   And more he Cannot depofe./

6./ To the Syxte Jnterr*ogatory* this depon*e*nt faythe he hath hard the defendt and the faid deceaffed James Burbadge faye that longe fynce there was Controu*er*fie betweene the faid defendt and one Edmonde Peckham menc*i*oned in the Jnterr*ogatory* for and touch-inge the tytle of the p*r*emiffs by reafon whereof the faid James Burbadge reported that he was muche hindered and could not haue the vfe of the p*r*emiffs quietlye but was fayne to fynde men at his owne Charge to keepe the poffeffion thereof from the faid Peckham and his f*er*vant*es*:/ And more he Cannot depofe touchinge the faid Jnterr*ogatory*:/

7./ To the vijth Jnterr*ogatory* this depon*e*nt faythe he hath feene fome of the deceaffed James Burbadge his book*es* of accompt*es* in wch he hath feene twoe feu*er*all furveies made by feu*er*all woorkemen whofe names are fett downe to the faid furveies in the faid book*es* whereby yt appeareth that the faid James Burbadge did in his lyffe tyme beftowe vppon the p*r*emiffs the fome of twoe hundred and odd pound*es* accordinge to his Couenant befid*es* his yearlye expence in gen*er*all repayre of the p*r*emiffs: vnto wch book*es* for further and more certentye of the truthe therein, he referrethe him felfe./ wch book*es* are in the pl*aintiffes* poffeffion./ And more he Cannot depofe./

8./ To the viijth Jnterr*ogatory* this depon*e*nt faythe that fythence the deceafe of the Compl*ainantes* ffather he the Compl*ainant* hath yearlye beftowed fome Coft*es* about the repayringe of the p*r*em-iffs, and this lafte yeare to this Depon*entes* owne knowledge & fynce the removeinge of the Theater he the Compl*ainant* hath beftowed in repayringe the p*r*emiffs the fome of ten pound*es* or neere there about*es*. And more he Cannot depofe./

9./10/ To the nynthe tenthe, Eleventhe and tweluethe Jnterr*ogatories* 11./12./ this depon*e*nt Can faye nothinge more then he hathe all reddye depofed to his nowe rememb*er*ance./

[Signed] William Smythe

Randulphe Maye of the parifhe of S^{ct}: Leonard*es* in Shorditche in the Countye of Midd*lefex* Paynter of the Age of threefcore yeares or there about*es* fworne and examyned the daye and yeare abouefaid Depofithe and faythe./

1/ To the ffirfte Jnterr*ogatory* this depon*e*nt faythe he knowethe the Compl*ainant* and defendt and did knowe James Burbadge the Compl*ainantes* ffather./

2/.3./4/5/ To the feconde, third, ffourthe and ffyfte Jnterr*ogatories* this depon*e*nt is not examyned at the requefte of the pl*aintiffes*

6./ To the vjth Jnterr*ogatory* this Depon*e*nt faythe he well remembrithe that about eighteene yeares nowe pafte there weare fuy*tes* betweene the defendt Allen and one EdmondePeckham touchinge the tyttle of the Theater and land*es* in the deceaffed James Burbadge his poffeffion and by reafon thereof the faid James Burbadge was muche hindered and trobled and was often Charged to ffynde men to keepe the poffeffion of the p*remiffs* in Controu*e*rfie betweene Allen and Peckham and was once in danger of his owne lyffe by keepinge poffeffion thereof from Peckham and his fervant*es*./   And could not enioye the p*remiffs* peacablie and Quyettlye according to his leafe.   And that he knoweth the fame to be true for that he was then there.   A fervant in the houfe Called the Theater And knoweth that the faid James Burbadge lofte muche money by that controu*e*rfie and troble for yt drove manye of the players thence becaufe of the difturbance of the poffeffion And more he Cannot depofe touchinge the faid Jnterr*ogatory* to his nowe rememberance./

7./8./ To the vijth and viijth Jnterr*ogatories* this depon*e*nt is not examyned at the requefte of the pl*aintiff*./

9./ To the nynthe Jnterr*ogatory* this depon*e*nt faythe he did knowe the tenem^{tes} wch weare vppon the ground*es* demifed vnto the faid James Burbadge when he firfte had them demifed vnto him by the

defend*ant*, And faythe that then they weare very fymple buylding*es* but of twoe ftoryes hye of the ould fafhion and rotten, foe
that after the faid James Burbadge had them in leafe he was
fayne to pull downe fome of them and newe buyld them for his
owne dwellinge and to repayre the refte to his greate Charge to
keepe them vpp: And they are nowe better then they weare when
he tooke them by leafe and worthe more rent then they weare
then for the faid James Burbadge was fayne to deuide them and
Contrive them fytt for dwelling*es* where they before weare ould
houfes of office and fome of them open that Roges and beggers
harbored in them./ And more he cannot depofe to his remem-
b*er*ance./

10/ To the xth Jnterr*ogatory* this depon*ent* faythe that when the faid
James Burbadge tooke the pr*e*miffs by leafe from the d*e*ff*endant*
there was A decayed longe Barne p*ar*cell of the pr*e*miff*es* de-
miff*ed* vnto him fomtymes in the tenure of Richard*es* and
Stoughton menci*o*ned in the Jnterr*ogatory* wch Barne was then
very ruynous and decayed foe as the fame was fayne to be fhored
vpp vnto the Playhoufe Called the Theater when yt was buylt,
And the faid James Burbadge and the nowe compl*ainant* hath
fynce the firfte takinge of yt beftowed greate coft*es* vppon yt and
deuided yt and kepte yt vpp wthe rep*ar*acions, els he thinkethe yt
had fallen downe ffyfteene yeares Agoe./ And that he thinkethe
yt is rather better then worfe then yt was when the pl*aintiffes*
fath*er* tooke yt wth the refte of the pr*e*miffs in Leafe./ And more
he Cannot depofe to his rememb*er*ance./

11/12/ To the xjth and xijth Jnterr*ogatories* this depon*ent* is not examyned at the requefte of the pl*aintiff*./

[Signed]   Randovlph May

Oliver Tylte of the p*ar*ifhe of S^{ct}: Buttolphes London yoeman of
the Age of ffortye Eight yeares or there about*es* fworne and examyned the daye and yeare abouefaid depofithe and faythe./

1/ To the ffirfte Jnterr*ogatory* this Depon*e*nt faythe he knowethe the Compl*ainan*t and Defend*an*t and did knowe James Burbadge the Compl*ainantes* father nowe deceaffed./

2/3/4/5/ To the fecond, third, ffourthe, and ffyfte Jnterr*ogatories* this Depon*e*nt is not examyned at the requefte of the pl*aintiff*

6./ To the vj[th] Jnterr*ogatory* this Depon*e*nt faythe that he remem-brith that about Eighteene yeares fynce there was great varience and Controuerfie betweene the defendt Gyles Allen and one m[r] Peckham touchinge the tytle of the Playehoufe called the Theater: and faythe that when the faid Contrauerfie was betweene m[r] Allen and m[r] Peckham James Burbadge the Compl*ainantes* father did paye him this depon*e*nt and others wages for keepinge the pof-feffion of the Theater from the faid m[r] Peckham and his f*ervantes* whereby he faythe he verelye thinketh that the faid James Bur-badge was at great Charge:/ for he payde men wages for keep-inge poffeffion foe longe as the contrauerfie was betweene m[r] Allen and m[r] Peckham and m[r] James Burbadge was muche dif-turbed and trobled in his poffeffion of the Theater and Could not Quietlye and peaceablie enioye the fame./ And therefore the players for fooke the faid Theater to his great loffe./ And more he Cannot depofe./

7./ To the vij[th] Jnterr*ogatory* this depon*e*nt faythe that before the faid Theater was buylded he this depon*e*nt did dwell in A tenem[t] of the faid James Burbadge. And knowethe that the faid James Burbadge duringe his tyme did repayre the tenem[tes] he held of m[r] Allen often and many tymes and beftowed muche Cofte vppon them: but the valewe he knowethe not./ And more he Cannot depofe/

8./ To the viij.[th] Jnterr*ogatory* this depon*e*nt is not examyned at the requefte of the pl*aintiff*

9./ To the ix[th] Jnterr*ogatory* this depon*e*nt faythe that he did knowe the tenem[tes] before and at the tyme they weare taken by James

Burbadge of m^r Allen, And fayth that when he tooke them of m^r Allen they weare all very ould buyldinge*s* and of meane buyldinge and the faid James Burbadge after he tooke the *p*remiffs did re-edefie fome of the houfes and beftowed greate cofte*s* vppon the fame, And faythe that nowe the fayde houfes and tenemente*s* are A great deale better then they weare when James Burbadge tooke them of Mr Allen, And are nowe lett for more Rent then they weare then rented for. And knowethe the fame to be true for that he dwelled there when m^r James Burbadge tooke them, And more he cannot depofe./

10/ To the xth Jnterr*ogatory* this deponent faythe that there was vppon the *p*remiffs when m^r James Burbadge tooke the *p*remiffs of m^r Allen one longe decayed Barne *p*arcell of wch was fomtymes houlden for A barne Roome by one Richardfon dwellinge in Coleman ftreet London, and oth*er p*arte thereof houlden for A Slaughter houfe by one Stoughton, wch Barne when the faid Burbadge tooke yt wth the *p*remiffs was very Ruynous and decayed and foe weake that the faid Burbadge was fayne to Shore yt vpp vnto the playhoufe Called the Theater when it was buylte, And faythe that James Burbadge did in his lyffe tyme from tyme to tyme repayre and Amende the fame to keepe yt vpp, for when he tooke yt yt was lyke to haue ffallen downe and was foe weake as when A greate wynd had Come the tenant*es* for feare haue bene fayne to goe out of yte./ wch he knowethe to be true for that then he was A tenant in the fame And more he Cannot depofe./

11/12/ To the xjth and xijth Jnterr*ogatories* this deponent is not examyned at the *pl*aint*iffes* requefte

[His mark]   T

Idem. Depositions ex parte Burbage, 23 May, 1600.

INTERROGATORIES

[In dorso]
Termino Trin*itati*s
xlij^{do} *Regni Regine*
Eli*zabethe*./

[Note on upper left corner:]
the defend^{tes} wyttnefes ^{to}
be examyned on thefe./

Interrogatories myniftred to the witneffes produced by the defend^t to be examyned on the parte
of the Comp^l againft the faid defend^t

1 Item haue yo^w heard the faid Defend^t at any tyme demaunde of
the faid Compl*ainant* the fom*m*e of Thirtye poundes *pre*tended to
be due for arrerages of rente by James Burbadge the Compl^{tes}
father, and whether did the Compl*ainant* Confeffe the fame to be
due, and promifed to make paym^t thereof, vppon what Confidera-
c*i*on did the pl*aintiff* make fuche promife to paye the fame, where
when and vppon what occafion was that promife made and whoe
were prefent thereat befid*es* yor felf

2 Item whether haue yo^w at any tyme heard the Compl*ainant* entreate the faid Giles Allen to make him a newe leafe of the *pre*-
miffes nowe in queftion & when wher, at what tyme and how
longe fince were any fuch fpeeches vfed & who were then prefent
ther wth you What Anfweare did the faide Defend^t giue to the
faid Compl*ainant,* Did not the Defend^t deferr the makinge of the
faid leas from tyme to tyme, what was the meaninge or intente
of him the faid defend^t therein, And did not the faid Defend^t by
his owne appointm^t Caufe A paper booke of A leafe to be drawne
vpp, and did the faid Compl*ainant* agree or accepte of the fame
Draughte, if not what was the occafion that there was no agreem^t
betwene them Declare the truth of yor knowledge herein at large
and how yo^w knowe the fame.

3 Item Doe yo^w knowe or haue yo^w Crediblie hard that there weare
fpeeches of A newe agreem^t had betwene the Defend^t and the faid
James Burbage a little before the deathe of the faid James that
hee the faid James fhould haue A newe leas of the *pre*miffes
Conteyned in the former leas for the tearme of one and twentye
yeares to begynne after thende and expirac*i*on of the former

leas, for the yerelie rente of xxiiij^{li} was the faid agreem^t Concluded on betwene the Defend^t and the faid James Burbadge, and
whoe was prefente at the fame agrement (if any fuche were)
what reafon had the faid James Burbadge to agree to giue Tenne
poundes a yere more rent for the faid premiffes then he did in
the former leas, Declare yor knowledge herein and the reafon that
moued the faid James to make fuche agreem^t (if any weare)
vppon yor oathe.

4 Doe yo^w knowe that at or aboutes the tyme aforefaid there were
fpeeches of agreem^t had betwene the Defend^t and the faid James
Burbadge that the Theater fhould Contynue for A playinge houfe
for the fpace of ffyve yeres onelie after thexpiracion of the firfte
terme and not longer, and that after the faid ffyve Yeres ended,
yt fhould be Converted by the faid James and the nowe Complainant or one of them to fome other vfe and be ymployed vppon the
groundes demifed wherebie the benefitt and proffitt therefor after
that terme ended fhould remayne to the defend^t weare the fame
fpeeches agreed and Concluded vppon betwene the defend^t and
the faid James Burbadg, what perfons were prefente at that tyme,
What reafon had the faid James Burbadge to allowe of any fuch
agreem^t (if any weare) and did not the faid parties breake of theire
Agreem^t againe becaufe theie could not agree of fuerties, or what
was then done touchinge the fame agreem^t betwene them   Declare
yor knowledg to euerie pointe of this Interrogatory at large.

DEPOSITIONS

Depofitiones Captae apud weftmonafterium
xxiij^{tio} die Maij A° Regni Domine Regine Elizabethe nunc &c   Quadragefimo Secundo ex parte
Cuthberti Burbadge generofi q^{rtis} verfus Egidium
Allen generofum defendentem./

Henry Johnfon of the parifhe of S^{ct}: Leonardes in Shorditche in
the Countye of Middlesex Sylkweaver of the Age of ffyftye

yeares or there about*es* fworne and examyned the Daye and
yeare abouefaid Depofithe and faythe

1/ To the ffirfte Jnter*rogatory* this Deponent fayth he hath hard the
Defend*t* afke and demaunde of the Compl*ainan*t the fome of thirtye pound*es* p*r*etended to be dwe for Arerages of Rent by the
deceaffed James Burbadge And hath hard the Compl*ainan*t confeffe the fame to be dwe and p*r*omifed to make paym*t* thereof
vnto the Defend*an*t in Confid*er*acion he the Defend*an*t would
make him the pl*aintiff* A leafe for one and twentye yeares of the
houfes and ground*es* w*ch* his late father held of him before in
leafe, And in Confid*er*acion he the Defendt would p*er*mitt the
houfe Called the Theater to ftand for A playinge houfe for the
firfte ffyve yeares of the newe leafe w*ch* the Defendt was contented to doe. And the fame p*r*omife was made vnto the Defendt
at the Sygne of the George in Shordytche about Michaellmas lafte
was tweluemonethe in this Deponentes p*r*efent*es* and the p*r*efent*es*
of one John Golborne:/ And more he Cannot depofe touchinge
the faid Jnter*rogatory* to his nowe rememb*er*ance./

2/ To the feconde Jnterrogatory this Deponent faythe he knoweth
that the Compl*ainan*t hath many tymes labored and intreated the
Defendt to make him a newe leafe of the p*r*emiffs in Queftion for
this Deponnt faythe that many tymes when the defendt hath Come
vpp to London to receave his Rent*es* he this deponent hath bene
w*th* him payinge him certayne Rent and then he hath feene the
pl*aintiff* w*th* his Landlord payinge his Rent lykewife and then
fyndinge oportunytie the pl*aintiff* would be intreatinge the Defendt to make him A newe leafe of the p*r*emiffs in Queftion and
faythe yt is at leafte three yeares fynce he this deponent firft hard
the pl*aintiff* labor and intreate the defendt for A newe leafe and
that yt was at the fygne of the George in Shordytche that the
Defendt laye when he came to london to receave his rent*es* and
there the pl*aintiff* Solicited him for A newe leafe./ and the faid
Goulborne hath bene there p*r*efent and hard the fame afwell as he
this depon*e*nt: And the defend*an*t from tyme to tyme deferred

the makinge of any newe leafe fayinge vnto the plaintiff paye me
tharrerages of rent wch yor father owght me when he died and
performe the Couenantes that yor father performed not in his
lyffe tyme And then wee will talke of A newe leafe: And that
he thinkethe the Defendt deferred the makinge of A newe leafe
vnto the plaintiff of purpofe to drive him to Augment his rent
per Annum And to drive the plaintiff to paye the thirtye poundes
he claymed for Arerages and performance of other couenantes
And this Deponent faythe he hath hard that the Defendt did ap-
poynte and caufe A paper Booke of A leafe to be drawne vpp
But the Complainant did not agree and accepte of that drawght
becaufe as the plaintiff reported yt was vnreafonable penned and
drawne and for that the defendt would thereby haue Compelled
the plaintiff to haue affured the improued rent to Contynewe after
thexpiracion of his leafe then to Commence and contynewe for
one and twentye yeares. And more he cannot depofe touchinge
the faid Jnterrogatory for that he never Sawe the faid Draught
mencioned in the Jnterrogatory

3. To the third Jnterrogatory this Deponent faythe he knowethe that
    the Deceaffed James Burbadge was in his lyffe tyme A lyttle
    before his Deathe an earneft futor vnto the defendt for the ob-
    tayninge of A newe leafe of the premiffs: And faythe that there
    weare diuerfe fpeeches betweene the defendt and the faid James
    Burbadge touchinge A newe leafe of the premiffs (conteyned in
    his former leafe) for the terme of one and twentye yeares to com-
    mence after thexpiracion of the former leafe for the yearlye rent
    of twentye ffoure poundes: but he knowethe not that the faid
    fpeeches weare agreed and Concluded vppon betweene the defendt
    and James Burbadge: And more he Cannot depofe touchinge
    the faid Jnterr to his nowe rememberance faue onlye that the
    Defendt ftill defired the faid James Burbadge yf he would haue
    A newe leafe to encreafe his rent./ otherwife he would graunte
    non

4./ To the ffourthe Jnterr this Deponent faythe that he never hard
    of any fpeeches of Agreem^t betweene the defendt and the de-

ceaſſed James Burbadge touchinge the Contynewance of the
Theater for A playinge houſe for the ſpace of ffyve yeares onlye
after thexpiracion of the ffirſte Terme and not longer, nor that
after that tyme of ffyve yeares ended yt ſhould be converted by
the ſaid James Burbadge and the nowe complainant or one of
them to ſome other vſe and be imployed vppon the groundes
demiſed whereby the benefytt and profytt thereof after that terme
ended ſhould remayne to the Defendt./ And more he Cannot
depoſe touchinge the ſaid Jnterrogatory for that he never hard of
any ſuche conference as is ſpecified in the Jnterrogatory betweene
the ſaid defendt, James Burbadge Deceaſſed and Cuthberte Burbadge in his fathers lyffe tyme but ſuche ſpeeches paſte betweene
the nowe plaintiff and Defendt ſynce the deceaſe of James Burbadge the father but not Agreed vppon for that they brake of
becauſe they Could not Agree vppon ſuerties./

[Signed]   Henry Johnſon

John Golborne of the pariſhe of S^{ct}: Leonardes in Shordytche in
the Countye of Middlesex Marchaunt taylor of the Age of
ffortye twoe yeares or there aboutes ſworne and examyned the
daye and yeare aboueſaid depoſithe and ſaythe./

1/ To the ffirſte Jnterrogatory this Deponent ſaythe he hathe hard
the Defendt demaunde of the plaintiff the ſome of thirtye poundes
pretended to be dwe for Arrerages of Rent by James Burbadge
the Complainantes father. And vppon the Defendantes demaund
thereof the Complainant hath confeſſed the ſame and yealded to
paye the ſame in Conſideracion the Defendt would make him A
newe leaſe of the houſes, tenem^{tes} and groundes his father James
Burbadge held of the Defendt by A former leaſe in his lyffe tyme.
And that the plaintiff vppon occacion of conference wth the defendt of A newe leaſe and in Conſideracion of the defendtes
promiſe of A newe leaſe of the premiſſes the Complainant at the
ſygne of the George in Shoreditche about michaellmas laſte was
Tweluemonethe promiſſed paym^t of the ſaid thirtye poundes vnto
the Defendt, and that then there weare preſent beſides him this

Deponent one Henry Johnſon and one mʳ Thomas Nevile./ And more he Cannot depoſe./

2./ To the ſeconde Jnterrogatory this Deponent ſaythe that he hath diuerſe and ſundrie tymes hard the Complainant entreate the Defendt to make him A newe leaſe of the premiſſs in Queſtion, And that the laſte entreatye that the plaintiff made for the obtayninge of a leaſe of the premiſſs in this deponntes hearinge was at Michaellmas laſte paſte was tweluemonethe and there was then preſent the ſaid Henry Johnſon and mʳ Thomas Nevile, But the Defendt made the plaintiff this Anſwere vz that he would haue his arerages that he Claymed firſte payde him and then he would conferr wᵗʰ him about A leaſe and ſoe deferred yt from tyme to tyme And as he takethe yt he deferred the plaintiff becauſe he ment to be payde the Arerages aforeſaid and Converte the Theater from A playinge houſe to ſome other better vſe vppon the grounde./ And ſaythe that he hard that the defendt by his owne appoyntmᵗ cauſed A paper booke of A leaſe to be drawne vpp betwene him and the Complainant, but the Complainant did not accepte thereof for that (as the plaintiff ſayd) there weare very vnreaſonable couenantes therein conteyned And more he Cannot depoſe./

3./ To the third Jnterr this deponent ſaythe that there weare ſpeeches of An Agreemᵗ betweene the Defendt and the Complainantes father in his lyffe tyme and a lyttle before his Deathe wᶜʰ ſpeeches tended to this or the lyke effecte vz that he the ſaid James Burbadge ſhould haue of the defendt A newe leaſe of the premiſſs Conteyned in his former leaſe for the terme of one and twenty yeares to Commence after thende and expiracion of his former leaſe for the yearlye rent of twenty ffoure poundes per Annum wᶜʰ was ten poundes A yeare more then he payde before : but that Agreemᵗ was not Concluded vppon for that the Defendt then Aledged that the ſaid James Burbadge had not beſtowed ſoe muche money vppon buyldinge and repayringe the premiſſs demiſed vnto him as he was bound to beſtowe by Couenant : but the plaintiffes father aledged that the full fome was beftowed accordinge to his Couenant w^{th}in the firfte ten yeares of his firfte leafe./ And faythe that he hard the Complainantes father faye that he did proffer to geue the defendt the faid ten poundes A yeare more rent then was referued in the ould leafe for that he would haue the Theater to ftand for A playinge houfe for one and twentye yeares more whereby he might reape greate proffytt And for that reafon he profferred to rayfe his rent ten poundes per Annum./ And more he Cannot depofe./

4./ To the ffourthe Jnterrogatory this deponent faythe that he never hard that the faid James Burbadge and the defendt had at any tyme any fpeeches togeather touchinge the Contynewance of the Theater for a playinge houfe for the fpace of but ffyve yeares onlye after thexpiracion of his old leafe: But the defendt would fayne haue had the faid James Burbadge to haue Converted the faid Theater to fome other vfe vppon the premiffes demifed vnto him: wch the faid James Burbadge would not Agree vnto but tould the defendt that he would encreafe his rent ten poundes per Annum yf he might haue his leafe renewed for one and twentye yeares more after thexpiracion of the ould leafe and the Theater to Contynewe duringe that tyme for a playinge houfe:/ otherwife he would remoue the faid Theater from of the premiffs And take aduantage of the defendtes bonde wch he had made him:/ And that after the newe leafe wch he then entreated for weare expired he or the nowe Complainant would Converte the faid Theater vppon the premiffs to fome other vfe for the bene-fytt afwell of the defendt as for the leffee then in poffeffion: but vppon all that Conference nothinge was abfolutlie Agreed vppon becaufe the Defendt would not Confent to fuffer the fame Theater to contynewe foe longe for A playe houfe And faythe that when thefe fpeeches pafte betweene the defendt and James Burbadge he this deponent the faid m^r Thomas Nevile and the nowe Complainant weare prefent: And more he Cannot depofe touchinge the faid Jnterrogatory to his nowe rememberance.

[Signed]   John Gobvrne

AFFIDAVIT OF GYLES ALLEYN

Court of Requests, Miscellaneous Books, volume 122, 42 Elizabeth (1600).

[This book was found by me in the uncalendared Requests Proceedings, and later handed over to M. S. Giuseppi, Superintendent, on Dec. 7, 1909, to be filed among the Miscellaneous Books. It is a small book of original, signed affidavits, which were later copied into the register of affidavits by some clerk, who thereupon drew a line down through each of the originals. Unpaged.]

2° Junij [A° 42° Eliz., 1600.]

Towching the caufe at the fute of Cuthbert Burbage gent pl againft Gyles Aleyn gent def^t, the fayde Gyles Allen maketh othe, that neither he this deponent nor any other for him (to this deponent*es* knowledge) haue had any coppies of or are previe to or acquainted wth the depofic*i*ons of fuch witneffes as haue heretofore been examined in the faide caufe/. And he further depofeth, that theere are others to be examined on this deponent*es* behalfe who (as this deponent verily thincketh) are materyall witneffes to be vfed on his p*a*rte viz Richard Parramore efq^r whofe dwelling place this depont doeth not certenly knowe Robt Vigorus of ye middle Temple London efq^r, Thomas Nevill of Bricklefey in the county of Essex gent, Robt myles of ye parifh of white chappel wthin the fubvrb*es* of London Innholder & Rafe myles (his fonne) John Hyde who as this depon^t is enformed is of the p*a*rifh of St Dunftans in the Eaft in London grocer & Wm Gall who as this depon^t is enformed is of the p*a*rish of Alhalowes neere gratious ftreete in London fcryvener

[Signed]   by me Gyles Aleyn

[Entered also, without signature, in Affidavit Register, Requests, Misc. Bks., vol. 121, under above date.]

AFFIDAVIT OF CUTHBERT BURBAGE

Liber idem (a few pages later, unnumbered).

11° Junij [A° 42° Eliz., 1600]

Whearas in the caufe at the fute of Cuthbert Burbage gent pl againft Gyles Allen gent def^t, it was ordered the laft day of May laft paft that the faide def^t his Counfailo^r, Attorn*ey* & follic*itor* fhould furceafe & ftay & no further pro*ceede* in an acc*i*on of trefpas at & by thorder of her ma^{tes} comm*on* lawes, & not caufe the demurrer there tendred vppon the def^{tes} plea in that fute to be ioyned vp or entred vntill the hearing of the faid caufe, & other order taken & made to the contrary: The faid Cuthbert Burbage maketh othe that hee the faid def^t hath fince the faid order contrary to theffect thereof caufed the faid demurrer to be ioyned vpp and entered a rule thervppon for this deponent to ftand to his plea at and by thorder of the Comm*on* Lawe

[Signed]   Cuth Burbadge

[Entered also, without signature, in Affidavit Register, Requests, Misc. Bks., vol. 121, under above date.

See also suit referred to, Allen *v.* Street, Trinity, 1600, also the next document, the Court's order for arrest of Allen, and Allen's statement on the affair in his Star Chamber suit, Allen *v.* Burbage, 1602, and the examination of Lane, 1602.]

ARREST OF ALLEYN FOR CONTEMPT

Requests Proceedings, Uncalendared, 372.

Vndecimo die Junij Anno˙ R*egni* R^{ne} Elizabethe xlij°/

Quia Egidius Allen contempfit ord*inem* p*er* Confi*lium* fact*am* in caufa int*er* Cutbert*um* Burbage gen*erofum* qu*erentem* et p*redic*t*um* Egid*ium* Allen Def^t Geren*tem* Datum xxxj die Maij vltimo
per or-
dinem preterito.   Jdeo decret*um* eft nunc Bre*ve* de Attachiament*o* fieri direct*um* vicecomi*ti* Com*itatus* Effexie necno*n* Hugo*ni* Barbon gen*erofo* ad Attachi*andum* corpus dicti Egidii re*tornabile* Jmediat*er* &c

[Signed]   Jul: Cæfar:
[Master in Court of Requests]

[On lower part of leaf:]
vi*cecomiti* Eſſexie et
Hugoni Barbon
[For Allen's account of the execution of this order against him, see his
suit of Allen *v* Burbage, Star Chamber, 1602, *infra*.]

*Court of Requests Proceedings, 87/74. Depositions ex parte
Allen, 14 August, 1600.*

[These two depositions were taken in the country by commission. The
parchments of interrogatories, commission to examiners, and depositions
by Robert Vigerous and Thomas Nevill are attached to the three large
skins of pleadings in the suit of Burbage *v.* Allen, as already noticed.
Halliwell-Phillipps found this set of records, as above mentioned. See
his *Outlines*, I, 359.]

INTERROGATORIES

Interrogatoryes to be miniſtered to the witneſſes
to be p*r*oduced on the p*a*rte and behalf of Giles
Allen gentle*man* Defend^t againſte Cuthbert Burbage Complain*a*nte./

1./ Inprimis whether doe you knowe the p*a*rties Comp^{lte} and Defend^t
and howe longe haue you known them./

2./ It*em* whether was there not an agreament made betweene the
Comp^{lte} and the Defend^t to this effecte: that the Defend^t ſhould
make a newe leaſe vnto the Comp^{lte} of the howſes and groundes
which were formerlye Demiſed vnto Jeames Burbage ffather of
the Comp^{lte} for one and twentye yeares from and after the expiracion of that former leaſe and that the Comp^{lte} ſhould paie yearelye for the ſame the ſom*me* of foure and twentye pound*es*: And
whether was it not likewiſe agreed betweene them that the Theatre there erected ſhould Continue for a playinge place by the
ſpace of fiue yeares onelye, and that then it ſhould be Converted
to ſom*me* other vſe for the benifitt of the Comp^{lte} Duringe his
terme, and after for the benifitt of the Defend^t: And whether did
not the Comp^{lte} vppon that agreament p*r*omiſe the Defend^t to

paie him the ſomme of thirtye powndes which was due to the
Defendᵗ for rent, and to putt the howſes and buildinges in good
reparacions; and howe longe is it ſithence ſuche agreament was
made: Deliuer the trueth what you knowe or haue heard herein./.

3./ Item whether was it agreed betweene the Defendᵗ and the Compˡᵗᵉ
that the Compˡᵗᵉ ſhould take a newe leaſe of the ſaid howſes and
groundes for the terme of tenn yeares and that the Compˡᵗᵉ ſhould
giue a hundred powndes for the ſaid leaſe: and foure and twenty
powndes rente yearelye: or whether was there any ſuche agreament made betweene the Defendᵗ and the ſaid Jeames Burbage
Deliuer what you knowe touchinge this Interrogatorye: and at
what time any ſuche agreament was made,   And by what meanes
you had knowledge therof./.

[In dorso:]
Quinto die Junij Anno Regni
Regine Elizabethe &c xlij°/
fiant litere dicte Domine Regine directe Roberto Sand-
ford Arthuro Breather et Johanni Sammes generoſis vel
duobus eorum ad examinandum omnes teſtes ex parte
Virtute Ordinis Defendentis in forma iuris iurandi tam de articulis in-
fraſcriptis quam per predictum defendentem miniſtrandis
et ad certificandum eadem in octabis Michaelis proximis./

[Signed]   Jul. Caeſar.

[Addressed to:]
Thomas Alif ar
Arthur Breathes gen

COMMISSION TO EXAMINERS

By the Quene//

Truſtie and welbeloued we grete youᵘ well.   And ſende vnto youᵘ
hereincloſed certen Articles Interrogatories to be miniſtred to the
witneſſes on the parte and behalf of Giles Allen gentleman defendaunt againſt Cuthbert Burbage complaynant wherevppon we

truſtinge in yor approued wiſdomes, learning*es* and Indifferenc*es* will and deſire yo^u that by Aucthoritie hereof callinge afore yo^u in or name all ſuche witneſſes and *proves* as by the ſaid defendant ſhalbe no*min*ated vnto yo^u, ye then do duely ſubſtancyallie examyn them the ſaid witneſſes (by their othes in due forme of lawe ſworne) Not only vppon the content*es* of the ſaid Articles hereincloſed. But alſo vppon all ſuche other Articles wch by the ſaid defend^t ſhalbe exhibited vnto yo^u, Endevoringe yerſelves by all meanes poſſible to ſearche and try out the veritie of the *premiſſes* by yor ſaid exa*min*acions. And therevppon duely to certifie vs and or Counſaill by yor wryting*es* vnder yor ſeales in or Corte of Whitehall at weſtmin*ſter* in the vtas of St Michael the Archaungell next com*m*ynge, Of the verie true depoſic*ions* of the ſaid witneſſes likeas yo^u ſhall fynde by yor ſaid exa*min*acions To thintent that we by thadviſe of o^r ſaid counſaill may further do therein as the caſe rightfully ſhall requier. Not failinge hereof as ye tender or pleaſure and thadvauncement of Juſtice, Given vnder o^r Privie Seale at o^r Mannor of Grenewiche the fyveth day of Junie in the xlijth yere of o^r Reigne//

[Signed] Tho: Kerry.

[In dorso]
> The execution of this Commiſſion appeareth by a Certaine Schedule herevnto annexed.

DEPOSITIONS

Ex *parte* Def^t

> **Depositions** taken at Kelvedon in the Countye of Eſſex (before vs Arthur Breather and John Sam*mes* Gent*lemen* by vertue of a Com*m*iſſion to vs and others Directed out of her ma^{ties} Honourable Courte of Requeſt*es* on the *parte* and behalf of Giles Allen gen*tleman* Defend^t againſte Cuthbert Burbage gent*leman* Comp^{lte}) the fourteenth daie of Auguſte in the twoe and fourtith yeare of the Raigne of our Soueraigne Ladye Elizabeth by the grace of God of England ffrance and Ireland Queene Defend^{rs} of the faith &c

Robert Vigerous of Langham in the Countye of Eſſex Eſqʳ aged fourtye ſeauen yeares
or thereabout*es* ſworne and examined ſaieth
as followeth. vidzᵗ./

1./ To the firſte Interr*ogatory* this Deponᵗ ſaieth that he knoweth
Giles Allen gent*leman* Defendᵗ, And Cuthbert Burbage gent*leman*
Compˡᵗᵉ and that he hath knowne the ſaid Defendᵗ by the ſpace
of ſixe yeares: and the ſaid Compˡᵗᵉ by the ſpace of foure yeares./

2./ To the ſecond Interr*ogatory* this Deponᵗ Cannot Depoſe./

3./ To the third he ſaith that aboute foure yeares paſte the ſaid
Compˡᵗᵉ together with Jeames Burbage his father and the ſaid
Defendᵗ were in Communicaci*on* aboute the makinge and takinge
of a newe leaſe of the houſes and groundes and Theatre menci*on*ed in this Interr*ogatory* and at the laſte it was concluded and
agreed betweene all the ſaid p*ar*ties that the Defendᵗ ſhould make
a newe leaſe of the ſame to the ſaid Compˡᵗᵉ for the terme of tenn
yeares for and vnder the yearelye rente of foure and twentye
pownd*es* which (as this Deponᵗ remembereth) was an increaſe
of tenn pownd*es* rente more then was reſerved in a former leaſe
heretofore made to the ſaid Jeames & then expired or neare to
be then expired. And that at the enſealinge of the ſaid newe
leaſe ſoe to be had the ſaid Jeames and Cuthberte the Compˡᵗᵉ or
one of them ſhould paie vnto the Defendᵗ certaine arrerages of
rente reſerved vppon the ſaid former leaſe amountinge to the
ſomme (as this Deponᵗ verelye thinketh) of thirtye pownd*es*: All
which this Deponᵗ knoweth to be true for that he was of Counſell
with the ſaid p*ar*ties in the ſaid Agreament; and by all their
mutuall Conſentes was appointed and eſpeciallye named to drawe
penne and wrighte the ſaid newe leaſe accordinge to their ſaid
agream*ᵗ*. And this Examin*a*ᵗᵉ ſaieth that he did wrighte a
Draughte purportinge a leaſe to be made of the p*re*miſſes accordinglye, which beinge don*n*e he deliu*er*ed the ſame into the handes
of the ſaid Compˡᵗᵉ when he came to this Deponᵗᵉˢ Chamber to

Demaunde and ſee the ſame and paid him his ffees wᵗʰ promiſſes of further reward for his paynes aboute the effectinge of the ſame newe leaſe to be made wᶜʰ ſhould be a Satten Dublett howebeit he never had it.   But whether the Compˡᵗᵉ ſhould giue a hundred pownd*es* for the ſame leaſe or whether the ſaid leaſe tooke effecte or what other agremᵗ paſſed betweene the ſaid Compˡᵗᵉ and Defendᵗ this Deponᵗ by reaſon of his Diſcontinuance from the Temple knoweʹth not But he ſaith that he hath ſeene a Draughte purportinge a leaſe to be made of the ſame premiſſes wherein it is incerted that a hundred pownd*es* ſhould be paid by the Compˡᵗᵉ to the Defendᵗ, wᶜʰ Draught (as the Defendᵗ informeth this Deponᵗᵉ) was made or cauſed to be made by the Compˡᵗᵉ and by him brought and Deliu*er*ed to the Defendᵗ at his houſe in the Countrye.   And this deponᵗᵉ: beinge aſked by the ſaid Commiſſion*er*s yf he knewe vppon what Conſideracʲᵒn the ſaid hundred pownd*es* was incerted ſaʲd that he remembereth not the Conſideracʲᵒn mencʲᵒned in the ſaid Draughte: But he ſaieth vppon the firſte Comm*u*nicacʲᵒn had betweene the ſaid Compˡᵗᵉ and Defendᵗᵉ and the ſaid Jeames before this Deponᵗᵉ as is aforeſaid, the Defendᵗ did demaunde recompence at the hand*es* of the ſaid Jeames for that the Defendᵗ ſaid the ſaid Jeames had not beſtowed twoe hundred pownd*es* in the buildinge or repaʲrʲnge of the ſaid howſes accordinge to a Covenante mencʲoned in the ſaid former leaſe nor half ſoe muche or wordes to the like effecte: but whether the ſaid hundred pownd*es* was incerted vppon that Conſideracʲᵒn or noe this Deponᵗᵉ knoweth not: and more to this Interrogatorye he cannott Depoſe./

> Thomas Nevill of Brickleſea in the Countye of Eſſex gentl*eman* aged thirtye five yeares or therabout*es* ſworne and examined ſaieth as followeth. vidzᵗ./

1./ To the firſte Interrogatorye he ſaieth that he hath knowne Giles Allen gentl*eman* Defendᵗᵉ and Cuthbert Burbage gentl*eman* Compˡᵗᵉ by the ſpace of five yeares nowe paſte or neare therabout*es*./

2./ To the fecond Interrogatory he faieth that there was an agreemente had betweene them the faid Comp^lte and the faid Defend^te
for the howfes and grownd*es* wth the Theatre which were formerlye Demifed vnto Jeames Burbage the father of the faid
Comp^lte with an increafing of the rente from fourteene pownd*es*
by the yeare vnto foure and twentye pound*es* by the yeare w^ch
leafe fhould beginn at the expiraci*o*n of the ould leafe made vnto
the faid Comp^ltes father and fhould continue for the fpace of one
and twentye yeares: And this Depon^te further faieth that the faid
Defend^t was at the firfte verye vnwillinge that the faid Theatre
fhould Continue one Daie longer for a playinge place yet neverthe-
leffe at the lafte he yealded that it fhould Continue for a playinge
place for certaine yeares; and that the faid Defend^te did agree
that the faid Comp^lte fhould after thofe yeares expired Converte
the faid Theatre to his befte benifitt for the refidue of the faid
terme then to come; and that afterward it fhould remaine to the
onelye vfe of the Defendte: And further this Depon^te faieth that
the faid Jeames Burbage the father did acknowledge the fom*m*e
of thirtye pownd*es* menci*o*ned in this Interrogatorye to be Due
vnto the faid Defend^t for rente then behinde and vnpaied; And
that the Comp^lte Cuthberte Burbage did often times fithence
pro*m*ife paiment of the faid fom*m*e of thirtye pownd*es* at the en-
fealinge of the newe leafe: And he further faieth that the faid
Agreemente was made betweene the faid Comp^lte and the De-
fend^te nowe twoe yeares fithence or therabout*es* at michaelmas
terme nowe nexte Com*m*inge. And further to this Interr*o*gat*o*ry
this Depon^te cannot Depofe./

3./ To the third Interr*o*gat*o*ry this Depon^te cannott Depofe./

[In dorso:]

x° die Octobris Anno Regni R*e*gi*n*e Elizabethe &c xlij°

Jura*m*enta Retourned by Thomas Domiell

[The depositions were sealed, and signed by two commissioners across
the sealing strips of parchment, now gone, leaving only parts of their
names, thus:]

Art[hur Brea]ther   [John] Sa͂mes

Idem. Bdl. 242. Depositions ex parte Allen, 1 October, 1600, on Interrogatories drawn up June 5.

INTERROGATORIES

Jnterrogatories to be miniftred to the wittneffes to be produced on the parte and behalfe of Giles Allen gentleman Defend^t againfte Cuthberte Burbage Complainante./

1./ Jnprimis whether did Jeames Burbage father of the Comp^{lte} in his life time tender and Deliuer vnto the Defend^t a Draught of a newe leafe of certaine howfes and groundes which were formerlye Demifed by the Defend^t to the faid Jeames Burbage requiringe the Defend^t to feale the fame: And whether is the Draught nowe fhewed forthe vnto you the fame which the faid Jeames Burbage Deliuered vnto the Defend^t: And whether Did not the Defend^t refufe to feale the fame and for what Caufe to yor rememberance Did he foe refufe the fealinge therof?/./

2./ Item whether Doe you knowe or thinke in yor Confcience that the faid Jeames Burbage did within the firfte tenn yeares after the leafe made vnto him by the Defend^t beftowe the fomme of twoe hundred powndes aboute the alteringe and amendinge of the faid howfes and buildinges Demifed vnto him by the Defend^t: or what fomme of money did the faid Jeames Burbage beftowe to that purpofe within that time Deliuer the trueth what you knowe or haue Crediblye heard herein?/

3./ Item whether Did the faid Jeames Burbage keepe the faid howfes and buildinges in good reparacions: And whether are not the faid howfes and buildinges or fome of them nowe growen in great Decaye: And whether hath not the Comp^{lte} vnderpropped them wth fhores: And whether doe they not foe remaine: And what fomme of money will it cofte to fett the faid howfes and buildinges in good and fufficient reparacions Deliuer what you knowe or thinke in yor Confciences herein: And by what meanes as you thinke is it come to paffe that the faid howfes and building*es* are growen foe ruinous?/

4./ It*em* whether hath Ellen Burbage the late wife of the faid Jeames Burbage any goodes or Chattles in her hand*es* that were the good*es* or Chattells of the faid Jeames Burbage wherby the Defend[t] maie haue recompence at her hand*es* for the faid fom*me* of thirtie pownd*es* and the breache of other Coven*a*nt*es*: And whether is not the faid Ellen accounted a verye poore woman, and not able to fatiffie the Credito[rs] of the faid Jeames Burbage: And whether did not the Comp[lte] and his brother or one of them p*r*ocure the faid Ellen to take adminiftraci*o*n of the good*es* of the faid Jeames Burbage; the faid Comp[lte] and his brother or one of them hauinge before fecretly gotten the good*es* of the faid Jeames Burbage into their handes that therbye they might Deceiue the Credito[rs] of the faid Jeames Burbage Deliuer what you knowe or haue Crediblye heard herein?/

5./ It*em* whether was the Theatre (which was erected vppon p*a*rte of the grounde aforefaid built at the alone Chardges of the faid Jeames Burbage: or whether did not one John Braynes Defraie the one half of the Chardges therof vppon agreement betweene the faid Jeames Burbage and the faid John Braines that the faid John Braines fhould be partner wth the faid Jeames Burbage in the p*r*offitt*es* thereof: Deliu*er* what you knowe or haue heard herein?/./

6./ It*em* what fom*me*s of money haue the faid Jeames Burbage and the Comp[lte] in their feu*er*all times gayned by the meanes of the faid Theatre Deliuer the trueth what you knowe or haue Crediblye heard herein?/./

7./ It*em* whether did you heare the Defend[t] at any time Complaine of the bad Dealinge of the faid Jeames Burbage towardes the Defend[t] for the not paiment of his rente, or not repairinge of his howfes: And whether did you heare him foe Complaine before

fuche time as the faid Jeames Burbage did tender a Draught of a
newe leafe vnto the Defend^t or at the time of the tender therof:
And whether haue you not oftentimes heard the Defend^t finde
faulte wth the faid Jeames Burbage that he was a bad and troublefome tenante Deliuer what you knowe touchinge this Jnter-
rogatorye?/

8./ Item whether doe you knowe that the faid Jeames Burbage did
affigne his interefte and terme (in thofe growndes and buildinges
he held of the leafe of the Defend^t) vnto one John Hide: And
howe longe agoe to yor rememberance was the faid Affignement
made: And howe manye yeares of the faid leafe were then to
come and vnexpired at the time of the faid Affignement./

[*In dorso:*]
Quinto die Junij Anno Regni Regine Elizabethe &c xlij°./
fiant littere dicte Domine Regine directe Willelmo Aylif
vel duobus
eorum ad examinandum omnes teftes ex parte defend^t
Virtute Ordinis tam de articulis infrafcriptis quam per partem miniftran-
dis in forma iuris iurandi et ad certificandum eadem in
octabis Michaelis proximis
Rog^r Wilbraham

DEPOSITIONS

Depofitiones Captae apud Weftmonafterium primo
die Octobris A°: Regni D^{ne} Regine Elizabethe
nunc &c Quadragefimo Secundo ex parte Egidij
Allen generofi def^{tis} verfus Cuthbertum Burbadge generofum q^{rtem}./

Robert Myles of the parifhe of Whitechappell in the Countye of
Middlefex gentleman of the Age of threefcore and ffoure yeares
or there Aboutes fworne and examyned the daye and yeere abouefaid depofithe and faythe./

1/ To the ffirfte Jnterrogatory this deponent faythe he hath hard the
defendant faye that the Complainantes father did in his lyffe tyme

tender vnto him A draught of A newe leafe of Certayne houfes
and groundes formerlye demifed by him the faid defendt vnto
James Burbadge deceaffed, And that the faid James Burbadge
when he tendered the fame drafte did require the defendt to Seale
the fame, And that he the defendt did refufe to Seale vnto the
fame for that yt was not tendered vnto him at the tyme Agreed
vppon, and for that the Countenantes weare not therin fett downe
accordinge to there Agreem^t./   And more he cannott depofe
touchinge the faid Jnterro*gatory* for that there is no drafte of a
leafe nowe lefte to be fhewed vnto him at the tyme of his ex-
amyna*c*ion./

2./ To the fecond Jnterro*gatory* this depon*e*nt faythe he hath hard yt
reported that wthin the firfte ten yeares after the leafe made vnto
James Burbadge by him the faid defend*a*nt, he the faid James
Burbadge and his p*a*rtin*e*r or one of them did beftowe vppon the
houfes and buyldin*g*es foe demifed by the defendt vnto the *plaintiffes* fath*e*r the fome of twoe hundred pound*e*s or th*e*r aboute viz
about the Alteringe and Amendinge of the fame p*r*emiffs foe
demifed   And more he Cannott depofe touchinge the faid Jnter-
r*ogatory*

3./ To the third Jnterro*gatory* this depon*e*nt faythe that for any thinge
he knowethe to the Contrarye the faid James Burbadge and one
Braynes his p*a*rtn*e*r did duringe James Burbadge his lyffe tyme
keepe the faid houfes and buyldin*g*es in good rep*a*rac*i*ons   But
faythe he knowethe not howe the fame houfes and buyldin*g*es are
nowe repayred, or haue bene repayred fynce the deceafe of James
Burbadge, nor how they are decayed for that he hathe not bene
jn them aboue twice fynce the deceafe of James Burbadge./
And this depon*e*nt faythe that Syxe or Seaven yeares fynce there
was A greate longe Barne (p*a*rcell of the demifed p*r*emiffs)
vnd*e*rpropped and Shored: but he knoweth not that yt is foe
ftill for that he hath not feene yt of longe tyme, nor knowethe
what fome of money yt will Cofte to fett the fame in good and
Suffytient rep*a*rac*i*ons.   And more he Cannott depofe touchinge
the faid Jnterro*gatory*./

4./ To the ffourthe Jnterr*ogatory* this Depon*e*nt ſaythe he thinkethe
that Ellen Burbadge the wyffe of James Burbadge hath not in
her hand*es* Suffytient of her ſaid huſbond James Burbadge his
good*es* and Chattles whereby the defend*a*nt maye haue recompence at her hand*es* for the ſome of thirtye pound*es* and breache
of oth*er* Couenant*es*. for ſhee is accompted but A poore woeman
not hable to paye her huſbond*es* Credito*rs*./ And ſaythe that the
Compl*ainan*t and his broth*er* or one of them did pr*o*cure the ſaid
Ellen to take adminiſtracion of her ſaid huſbond*es* good*es* they
or one of them havinge before that ſecretlie gotten James Burbadge his good*es* into there hand*es* And ſoe th*er*by the Credito*rs*
are not Satiſfied otherwiſe he thinkethe Amongeſte them there
was left Suffytiente to Satiſfie all James Burbage his Credito*rs*./
And more he cannott depoſe

5./ To the v*th* Jnterr*ogatory* this deponent ſaythe he knowethe that
the Theater mencioned in the Jnterr*ogatory* was not only buylte
at the Alone Charges of James Burbadge. but one John Braynes
menc*io*ned in tꝯe Jnterr*ogatory* did defraye the one halfe of the
Charges th*er*of (or more) vppon Agreem*t* betweene James Burbadge and him the ſaid Braynes that he the ſaid Braynes ſhould
haue had from Burbadge A leaſe of the Theater vnder the lyke
Couenant*es* he the ſaid Burbadge had his houſes and ground*es*
from the def*endan*t And that he knowethe the ſame to be true
for that he was p*ar*tlie acquaynted w*th* there Agreem*t*. And hath
the bond*es* wherin Burbadge was bound to Braynes to p*er*forme
the Agreem*t*./ And more he cannott depoſe./

6./ To the vj*th* Jnterr*ogatory* this deponent ſaythe he verelye thinkethe that James Burbadge and Cuthberte Burbadge in th*er*
ſeu*er*all lyfes tymes haue gayned by the Theater aboue A thouſand mark*es*./ And more he Cannott depoſe./

7./ To the vij*th* Jnterr*ogatory* this deponent ſaythe he hath often hard
the defend*a*nt Complayne of James Burbadge his bad dealinge
w*th* him in not paym*t* of his rent./ And that the ſaid Defendt

did not Complayne but fynce the tender of the faid drafte of the
newe leafe./ And hath hard the defendt faye that James Burbadge was A troblefome tenant./ but he hard him not fynd falte
wth him nor Complayne of him for non repayringe of his houfes./
And more he Cannot depofe./

8./ To the viijth Jnterr*ogatory* this depon*e*nt faythe he knowethe that
the faid James Burbadge did affigne his Jnterefte and terme in
the p*r*emiffs demifed vnto him vnto one John Hide for a fome of
money./ And as he remembrithe yt is about ffyfteene yeres pafte
fythence the fame affignem^t made./ And there weare about fyf-
teene yeares to Come and vnexpired in the faid leafe at the tyme
of the faid affignem^t And more he Cannot depofe./

[Signed] By me Robart Miles

Raphe Myles of the p*a*rifhe of Whyte Chapple in the Countye of
Midd*le*f*ex* gent*le*man of the Age of thirtye fyve yeres or there
about*es* fworne and examyned the daye and yeare abouefaid depofithe and faythe

1/ To the ffirfte Jnterr*ogatory* this depon*e*nt faythe he hath hard that
James Burbadge the Compl*ainantes* fath*er* did in his lyffe tyme
tender vnto the defend*a*nt the drafte of A newe leafe of Certayne
houfes and ground*es* formerlye demifed by the defend*a*nt vnto
James Burbadge and that James Burbadge required the defendt
to Seale the fame newe leafe./ but what anfwere the defendt
made the p*l*aint*iffes* fath*er* when he demaunded to feale the fame
he knoweth not nor hath hard./ And more he Cannot depofe
touchinge the faid Jnterr*ogatory* for that the drafte of the newe
leafe mencioned in the Jnterr*ogatory* is not lefte to be fhewed
him neyth*er* hath he feene yt at any tyme./

2./ To the fecond Jnterr*ogatory* this depon*e*nt faythe that James Burbadge beftowed muche money in alteringe mendinge and repayringe the p*r*emiffs demifed vnto him by the defendt, but howe
muche he knowethe not, nor wheth*er* he beftowed that Cofte wthin

the tyme menc*i*oned in the Jnterr*ogatory*. And more he Cannott depo*s*e./

3./ To the third Jnterr*ogatory* this deponen*t* *s*aythe that James Burbadge in his lyffe tyme kepte the p*r*emi*ss* demi*s*ed vnto him in
rea*s*onable good rep*aracio*ns : but he knowethe not in what decaye
they nowe are for that he *s*awe them not of A longe tyme./ nor
wheth*er* the pl*aintiff* hath vnderpropped them wth Shores, nor
wheth*er* they be nowe remayninge vnderpropped./ nor what yt
will co*s*te to *s*ett the how*s*es in rep*aracio*ns for that he knowethe
not nor hath *s*eene howe they are decayed./ And more he Cannott depo*s*e touching the *s*aid Jnterr*ogatory*./

4./ To the ffourthe Jnterr*ogatory* this deponen*t* *s*aythe he knowethe
not that Ellen Burbadge hath any good*es* or Chattles in her
handes that weare her late hu*s*bond James Burbadge his good*es*
wherby the defen*dt* maye haue recompence at her hand*es* for the
*s*ome of thirtye pound*es* and the breache of other Couenant*es*./
And *s*aythe that Ellen Burbadge is accompted A poore woeman
not hable to Sati*s*fie her hu*s*bond*es* Credyto^{rs}./ And *s*aythe he
knoweth not wheth*er* the Compl*ainan*t and his broth*er* or one of
them p*r*ocured the *s*aid Ellen Burbadge to take admini*s*traci*o*n
of the good*es* of Jame*s* Burbadge they or one of them havinge
fir*s*te gotten the *s*aid James Burbage his good*es* into there hand*es*
thereby to deceave the Credito^{rs} of the *s*aid James./ And more
he cannot depo*s*e./

5./ To the vth Jnterr*ogatory* this deponen*t* *s*aythe he hath Crediblie
hard that the Theater menc*i*oned in the Jnterr*ogatory* was not
buylte at the Alone charge of James Burbage./ but that one
John Braynes defrayed the halfe of the Charge vppon Agreem^t
betweene them that Braynes *s*hould be p*artner* wth Burbage in
the p*r*ofytt*es* the*r*of. And that he hath *s*eene A bonde of Burbages to Braynes whereby yt playnelie appeareth that Braynes
had the moyetye of the p*r*ofytt*es* the*r*of in his lyffe tyme and
burbage was bound that he *s*hould enioye the *s*ame./ And more
he Cannott depo*s*e./

6./ To the vjth Jnterr*ogatory* this depon*e*nt faythe he thinkethe that James Burbadge and the Compl*ainan*t in there feu*e*rall tymes haue gayned by meanes of the faid Theater A thoufand mark*es* and better./ And more he Cannot depofe./

7./ To the vijth Jnterr*ogatory* this depon*e*nt faythe he hath hard the defendt Complayne of James Burbage his badd dealinge toward*es* him in not paym^t of his rent./ but not for the repayringe of his houfes./ But he rememb*e*rithe not wheth*e*r he Complayned of his badd dealinge before or after the tender of the newe leafe, but thinkethe yt was before the tender and at the fygne of the George in Shoreditche And that then the defendt found falte wth James Burbage and faid he was A bad and troblefome fellowe./ And fynce or before he hard not the defendt vfe the lyke fpeeches of James Burbadge./ And more he Cannott depofe./

8./ To the viijth Jnterr*ogatory* this depon*e*nt faythe he knowethe that James Burbadge did in his lyffe tyme affigne his interefte and 'terme in the premiffs vnto one John Hyde menc*i*oned in the Jnterr*ogatory*./ But he rememb*e*rythe not howe longe yt is fythence the fayd affignem^t was made to Hyde nor howe many yeares of the faid leafe weare then to come and vnexpired at the tyme of the faid Affignemen^t./ And more he Cannott depofe to his rememb*e*rance./

[Signed] *per* me: Raphe: Miles

APPEARANCE OF ALLEN

Requests, Misc. Books, vol. 109, fo. 8 (Appearance Book, 42 Eliz. to 7 Jas. I).

Nono die Octobris A° xlij^{do} [1600]

Egidius Allen gen*erosus* per*f*on*aliter* comp*a*ret coram con*cilio* R*e*g*i*ne virtute br*e*vis de Attachiam*ento* ad fectam Cuthberti Burbage

ALLEN *v.* BURBAGE

Queen's Bench, Easter, 44 Elizabeth (1602) membrane 257.

[The following pleadings incorporate the lease of Gyles Allen to James Burbage, April 13, 1576, here rendered into Latin. This document has not hitherto been printed or quoted from. Its existence was known to Halliwell-Phillipps who, in his *Outlines*, I, 349, refers to it as containing the same description of the leased premises as is found in the proposed but unexecuted deed of 1585. The latter is incorporated in Street's Answer in the suit of Allen *v.* Street, Court of King's Bench, 1600, printed in preceding pages.]

Adhuc De Termino Pafche Tefte J. Popham

Midd ff Memorandum quod alias scilicet Termino sancti Hillarij Anno regni domine Elizabethe nunc Regine Anglie quadragefimo tercio coram eadem domina Regina apud Weftmonafterium venerunt Egidius Aleyn armiger & Sara vxor eius per Johannem Tanner attornatum suum Et protulerunt hic in Curia dicte domine Regine tunc ibidem quandam billam suam verfus Cutbertum Burbage in Cuftodia Marrefcalci &c de placito Convencionis fracte Et sunt Plegii de prosequendo scilicet Johannes Doo & Ricardus Roo Que quidem billa sequitur in hec verba ff Midd ff Egidius Aleyn armiger & Sara vxor eius queruntur de Cutberto Burbage in Cuftodia Marrefcalci Marefcalcie domine Regine coram ipfa Regina exiftente de placito Convencionis fracte pro eo videlicet quod Cum predicti Egidius & Sara decimo tercio die Aprilis Anno regni domine Elizabethe nunc Regine Anglie decimo octavo per quandam Jndenturam suam factam apud Hallowell in Comitatu predicto predicto decimo tercio die Aprilis Anno decimo octavo supradicto inter prefatos Egidium & Saram per nomen Egidij Aleyn de Hallowell in Comitatu Middlesexia generofi & Sare vxoris eius ex vna parte & quendam Jacobum Burbage patrem predicti Cutberti per nomen Jacobi Burbage de londonia Joyner ex altera parte/ Cuius quidem Jndenture alteram partem Sigillo ipfius Jacobi Segillatam gerentem datum predicto decimo tercio die Aprilis Anno decimo octavo supradicto predicti Egidius &

Sara hic in Curia proferunt ex eorum vnanimis confenfu &
afcenfu pro & in Confideracione sume viginti librarum legalis
monete Anglie sibi in manibus ad sigillacionem Jndenture illius
per predictum Jacobum Burbage veraciter solute pro & nomine
finis vel prefolucionis Anglice income locaverunt & ad firmam
tradiderunt prefato Jacobo Burbage omnes illas duas domos vel
tenementa cum pertinentiis adtunc exiftentes in separalibus
tenuris vel occupacionibus Johanne Harryfon vidue & Johannis
Draggon Acetiam totam illam domum vel tenementum cum pertinentiis simulcum solo gardini Anglice garden grounde iacente a
tergo partis eiufdam adtunc exiftentis in occupacione Willelmi
Garnett Gardyner quod quidem Gardinum adtunc extendebat in
latitudine A magno muro lapidofo ibidem qui adtunc includebat
partem gardini adtunc vel nuper in occupacione prefati Egidij ad
gardinum ibidem adtunc exiftens in occupacione Evini Colefoxe
weaver & in longitudine ab eodem domo vel tenemento ad murum
Anglice A brickwall ibidem proximum ad agros Communiter
vocatos ffynnefburye fyldes/ Acetiam totam illam domum vel
tenementum cum pertinentiis vocatam siue cognitam per nomen
domus molendinarie simulcum solo gardini iacentis A tergo
partis eiufdem adtunc exiftentis in tenura vel occupacione predicti
Evini Colefoxe vel Affignatorum suorum quod quidem solum
gardini adtunc extendebat in longitudine ab eodem domo siue
tenemento ad predictum murum tegularium Anglice brickwall
proximum ad predictos agros Acetiam omnes illos tres superiores
locos cum pertinentiis proxime adiungentes ad predictam domum
molendinariam adtunc exiftentes in occupacione Thome Dancafter
Showmaker vel affignatorum suorum Acetiam omnes illos in-
feriores locos cum pertinentiis adtunc iacentes subter illos tres
superiores locos acetiam proxime adiungentes ad predictam
domum siue tenementum vocatam the Millhowfe adtunc exiftentes in separalibus tenuris vel occupacionibus Alicie Daridge
vidue & Ricardi Brackenbury vel Affignatorum suorum simulcum
solo gardini iacentis a tergo eiufdem adtunc extendentis in longitudine ab eifdem inferioribus locis vfque predictum tegularium
murum proximum ad predictos agros & adtunc etiam exiftentis

in tenura sive occupac*ione* p*r*ed*icte* Alicie Daridge Acetiam
tant*um* terr*e* & soli Anglic*e* soyle iacen*tis* & exi*ſ*ten*tis* ante om*n*ia
ten*emen*ta siue domos p*r*econce*ſſ*a quantu*m* adtunc extendebat in
longitudine a ext*er*iore p*ar*te p*r*edic*torum* ten*emen*torum adtunc
in occupac*ione* p*r*edic*torum* Johanne Harry*ſ*on & Joh*ann*is
Dragon ad stagnu*m* ib*idem* exi*ſ*ten*s* proximum horreo siue
Stabulo Adtunc in occupac*ione* prenobilis viri Comi*t*i*s* Rutl*and* &
in latitudine de p*r*edic*to* ten*emen*to vel domo molendinar*ia* ad
mediu*m* fo*n*tis exi*ſ*ten*tis* ante eade*m* ten*emen*ta/ Acetiam tot*um*
ill*um* magnu*m* horreu*m* cu*m* p*er*tin*en*t*iis* adtunc exi*ſ*ten*s* in
sep*ar*alib*us* occupac*ion*ib*us* Hugonis Richardes Jnhoulder &
Roberti Stoughton Butcher Acetiam p*ar*vam peciam soli adtunc
inclu*ſ*am cu*m* palo & prox*ime* adiungen*tem* ad p*r*edic*tum* horreu*m*
& adtunc in occupacione di*c*ti Roberti Stoughton si*m*iliter simul-
cu*m* & omnib*us* t*er*ris & solo iacen*tibus* int*er* p*r*edic*tos* interiores
locos po*ſ*tremo ante exp*r*e*ſſos* p*r*edic*tum* magnu*m* horreu*m* &
p*r*edic*tum* S'tagnu*m* viz extenden*tem* in longitudine a p*r*edic*to*
Stagno ad fo*ſſ*atu*m* vltra muru*m* tegulariu*m* proximu*m* agris
p*r*edic*tis*/ Acetiam p*r*edic*tus* Egidius Aleyn & Sara vxor eius
p*er* Jndentur*am* p*r*edic*tam* dimi*ſ*erunt conce*ſſ*erunt & ad firmam
tradiderunt p*r*edic*to* Jacobo Burbage tota rectu*m* titu*lum* & in-
tere*ſſe* sua que ip*ſ*i p*r*e*f*ati Egidius & Sara adtunc h*a*bebant vel
h*a*bere deberent de in vel ad terr*am* & solu*m* iacen*tia* int*er* p*r*e-
dic*tum* magnu*m* horreu*m* & horreu*m* adtunc in occupac*ione* di*c*ti
Comi*t*i*s* Rutl*and* vel a*ſſ*ign*atorum* suo*rum* extenden*tia* in longitudine A stagno predic*to* & A p*r*edic*to* Stabulo vel horreo in
occupac*ione* p*r*edic*ti* Comi*t*i*s* vel a*ſſ*ign*atorum* suo*rum* ví*que* ad
p*r*edic*tum* muru*m* tegulariu*m* proximu*m* p*r*edic*tis* agris/ Acetiam
predic*ti* Egidius & Sara p*er* Jndenturam p*r*edic*tam* dimi*ſ*erunt
conce*ſſ*erunt & ad firmam tradiderunt p*r*edic*to* Jacobo omnes suas
vacuas terr*as* iacen*tes* & exi*ſ*ten*tes* int*er* p*r*edic*tum* fo*ſſ*atu*m* et
p*r*edic*tum* muru*m* tegulari*um* extenden*tes* in longitudine A p*r*e-
dic*to* muro qui adtunc inclu*ſ*it p*ar*tem p*r*edic*ti* Gardini Adtunc
vel nup*er* in occupac*ione* di*c*ti Egidij Aleyn ad p*r*edic*tum* horreum
adtunc in occupac*ione* di*c*ti Comi*t*i*s* vel A*ſſ*ign*atorum* suo*rum*
Acetiam lib*erum* introitu*m* egre*ſſ*um & regre*ſſ*um ad & A p*r*edic*tis*

dimiffis premiffis & qualibet parte eorundem tam bene ad & pro
predicto Jacobo Burbage executoribus adminiftratoribus & Affignatis suis quam ad & pro omnibus & quibuflibet aliis perfona &
perfonis venientibus siue reparientibus ad premiffa antea demiffa
sive aliquam partem eorundem per tales vias quales adtunc
fuerunt vfe & occupate eifdem premiffis in iure predicti Egidij
quam etiam per tales pontes & vias quales adtunc fuerunt vel
poftea forent facti per predictum murum tegularium in predictis
agris omnibus & quibuflibet tempore & temporibus Convenienti-
bus adtunc impofterum durante toto termino Annorum adtunc
in Jndentura predicta conceffo abfque aliquo legittimo obftaculo
impedimento perturbacione vel interrupcione dicti Egidij heredum
vel Affignatorum suorum sive aliquorum eorum siue alicuius
alterius perfone vel perfonarum in eius vel eorum iure recto sive
titulo sive per eius vel eorum medium siue procuramentum/
omnia que quidem premiffa antea preconceffa adtunc fuerunt sci-
tuata iacentia & exiftentia in & prope Hallowell predictam
(exceptis & refervatis dictis Egidio Aleyn & Sare vxori eius &
heredibus & Affignatis suis & talibus aliis perfone & perfonis que
adtunc inhabitabant inhabitarent vel remanerent in Capitali Mef-
fuagio siue Tenemento ibidem vel in aliqua parte eiufdem adtunc
vel nuper in occupacione predicti Egidij & ad & pro tenentibus
dicti Egidij qui adtunc habitabant vel impofterum inhabitarent in
Hallowell predicta liberam libertatem portandi & hauriendi aquam
ad predictum pontem de tempore in tempus durante predicto
termino Jta quod illi reciperent comoditatem dicti fontis de
tempore in tempus inter eos equaliter super legittimam requificionem portare & soluere dicto Jacobo Burbage executoribus vel
Affignatis sius medietatem omnium talium onerum qualia ex-
penderentur Anglice layd out in & circa neceffariam repara-
cionem & emendacionem dicti fontis de tempore in tempus quoties
opus requireret durante Termino predicto Acetiam libera ingref-
fum & regreffum ad & pro dictis Egidio & Sara vxore eius &
heredibus Affignatis executoribus & servientibus sius & ad & pro
reuerendo in Xrifto patre Johanni Scorye adtunc Epifcopo here-
fordie Elizabetha vxore eius & servientibus & affignatis suis de

& a predicto magno gardino adtunc vel nuper pertinente dicto
Egidio in predictos agros per pontem & viam adtunc ibidem
vſitata et occupata omnibus legittimis tempore & temporibus
durante Termino Annorum in Jndentura predicta poſterius con-
ceſſo habenda & tenenda omnia predicta domos sive tenementa
horreum gardinum terram & omnia alia premiſſa preconceſſa
(exceptis preexceptis) dicto Jacobo Burbage executoribus &
Aſſignatis suis A feſto Annunciacionis beate Marie adtunc vltimo
preterito ante datum Jndenture predicte vſque plenum finem &
terminum viginti & vnius Annorum extunc proxime & imediate
sequentem & plenarie complendum & finiendum reddendo &
soluendo proinde annuatim durante termino predicto dictis
Egidio Aleyn & Sare vxori eius vel vni eorum & heredibus &
Aſſignatis predictorum Egidij & Sare quatuor decim libras legalis
monete Anglie ad quatuor feſta siue Terminos in Anno viz ad
feſta Nativitatis sancti Johannis Baptiſte sancti Michaelis Archangeli Nativitatis domini & Anunciacionis beate Marie vel infra
spacium viginti & octo dierum proximum poſt quodlibet eorundem
feſtorum per equales porciones/ Et predictus Jacobus Burbage
pro seipſo executoribus adminiſtratoribus & Aſſignatis suis convenit & conceſſit ad & Cum predictis Egidio Aleyn & Sara
heredibus & Aſſignatis suis & eorum quolibet per Jndenturam
predictam inter alia quod ipſe predictus Jacobus Burbage executores adminiſtratores vel Aſſignati sui ad eius vel eorum propria
Cuſtagia & onera predicta domos siue tenementa horreum gardina
& omnia alia premiſſa preconceſſa & omnes domos Anglice the
privyes predictis premiſſis siue alicui parti eorundem pertinentes
adtunc factos vel impoſterum faciendos in omnibus neceſſarijs
reparacionibus bene & sufficienter repararent manutenerent ſuſ-
tinerent facerent eſcurarent mundarent & emendarent de tempore
in tempus quando & quoties neceſſe requirerent Et eadem tam
bene & sufficienter reparata mundata eſcurata & emendata in fine
eiuſdem terminj viginti & vnius Annorum relinquerent & sur-
ſumreddirent eiſdem Egidio & Sare & heredibus & Aſſignatis
eiuſdem Egidij prout per Jndenturam predictam inter alia plenius
liquet & apparet/ virtute Cuiusquidem dimiſſionis predictus

Jacobus in tenementa predicta sibi vt prefertur dimiſſa intrauit
Et fuit inde poſſeſſionatus predictoque Jacobo sic inde poſſeſ-
ſionato exiſtente idem Jacobus poſtea scilicet decimo septimo die
Septembris Anno regni dicte domine Regine nunc vicefimo primo
Apud Hallowell predictam Aſſignauit tota intereſſe & terminum
Annorum sua que ipſe adtunc habuit ventura de & in tenementis
predictis sibi vt prefertur dimiſſa cum pertinentiis cuidam Johanni
Hide Civi & grocero londonie/ virtute Cuius predictus Johannes
Hyde in predicta tenementa prefato Jacobo vt prefertur dimiſſa
cum pertinentiis intravit & fuit inde poſſeſſionatus predictoque
Johanne Hide sic inde poſſeſſionato exiſtente idem Johannes Hyde
poſtea scilicet septimo die Junij Anno regni dicte domine Regine
nunc Tricefimo primo Apud Hallowell predictam aſſignauit tota
intereſſe & terminum Annorum sua que ipſe adtunc habuit ventura
de & in tenementis predictis prefato Jacobo vt prefertur dimiſſis
cum pertinentiis prefato Cutberto Burbage virtute Cuius predictus Cutbertus in predicta tenementa illa cum pertinentiis intrauit & fuit inde poſſeſſionatus Et predicti Egidius & Sara
vlterius dicunt quod licet ipſi ijdem Egidius & Sara omnes &
ſingulas Convenciones Conceſſiones Articula & agreamenta in
Jndentura predicta mencionatas ex partibus ipſorum Egidij &
Sare & eorum vteriuſque in & per Jndenturam predictam performandas obſervandas cuſtodiendas & perimplendas A tempore
confeccionis Jndenture predicte vſque finem & terminum predictorum viginti & vnius Annorum in Jndentura predicta superius
mencionatos bene & veraciter performaverunt obſervaverunt cuſtodiverunt & perimpleverunt secundum formam & effectum Jndenture illius/ proteſtando quod predictus Jacobus Burbage durante tempore quo idem Jacobus tenementa predicta sibi vt prefertur dimiſſa virtute dimiſſionis predicte sibi vt prefertur facte
habuit & tenuit & quod predictus Johannes Hide durante toto
termino quo idem Johannes Hyde fuit poſſeſſionatus de & in
tenementis predictis cum pertinentiis virtute Aſſignacionis predicte sibi per eundem Jacobum vt prefertur facte non tenuerunt
cuſtodiverunt & performaverunt aliquas Convenciones conceſſiones Articula & agreamenta in Jndentura predicta superius men-

cionatas & ex parte ipſius Jacobi dum ipſe poſſeſſionatus fuit de
& in tenementis predictis virtute dimiſſionis predicte & ex parte
ipſius Johannis Hide poſt aſſignacionem predictam sibi per predictum Jacobum vt prefertur factam & in & per Jndenturam
predictam per ipſos in forma predicta obſervandas performandas
& Cuſtodiendas secundum formam & effectum Jndenture illius/
Et proteſtando quod predictus Cutbertus poſt aſſignacionem predictam sibi per predictum Johannem Hyde vt prefertur factam
durante toto termino quo idem Cutbertus poſſeſſionatus fuit de &
in tenementis predictis sibi vt prefertur aſſignatis non tenuit &
Cuſtodivit aliquas Convenciones conceſſiones et agreamenta in
predicta Jndentura inter eoſdem Egidium & Saram & predictum
Jacobum vt prefertur facta mencionatas & ex parte ipſius Cutberti dum ipſe poſſeſſionatus fuit de & in tenementis predictis poſt
aſſignacionem predictam sibi per predictum Johannem Hyde vt
prefertur factam & per ipſum Cutbertum in & per Jndenturam
predictam in forma predicta obſeruandas performandas & Cuſtodiendas secundum formam & effectum Jndenture illius ijdem
Egidius & Sara in facto dicunt quod eodem Cutberto de tenementis predictis prefato Jacobo vt prefertur dimiſſis poſſeſſionato
exiſtente poſt aſſignacionem predictam prefato Cutberto per predictum Johannem Hyde vt prefertur factam & ante expiracionem
predictorum viginti & vnius Annorum scilicet primo die Octobris
Anno regni dicte domine Regine triceſimo sexto predictum mag-
num horreum & omnia predicta domus & edificia in Jndentura
predicta superius mencionata & prefato Jacobo per predictum
Egidium & Saram vt prefertur dimiſſa fuerunt magnopere ruinoſa
& in decaſu tam in defectu sufficientis coaperture & tegulacionis
Anglice tyling quam plauſtracionis Anglice dawbing Et predictum horreum & omnia predicta domus & edificia sic ruinoſa & in
decaſu in defectu sufficientis reparacionis & emendacionis eorundem ita remanſerunt & Continuaverunt ruinoſa & in decaſu A
predicto primo die Octobris Anno Triceſimo sexto supradicto
vſque finem & terminum predictorum viginti & vnius Annorum
per quod groſſum Maherremium horrei domorum & edificiorum
predictorum racione pluvie & tempeſtatum super eadem deca-

den*tium* total*iter* putrid*um* & va*f*tat*um* devenit Et sic ij*d*em
Egidius & Sara dicunt q*u*od p*re*di*ctus* Cut*b*ertus Convenc*i*onem
p*re*di*c*tam in*ter* ip*f*os Egidi*um* & Saram & p*re*dict*um* Jacob*um*
p*ro* se & A*ff*ign*atis* suis p*er* Jndenturam p*re*di*c*tam vt p*re*fert*ur*
fact*am* po*f*t a*ff*ignac*i*onem p*re*dict*am* p*re*fato Cutberto p*er* p*re*-
fat*um* Johann*e*m Hyde vt p*re*fert*ur* in eo q*u*od p*re*di*ctus* Jacobus
Burbage executores admini*f*tratores vel A*ff*ign*ati* sui ad eius vel
e*orum* prop*ri*a Cu*f*tag*ia* & on*era* dicta domos vel ten*em*en*t*a horreu*m* Gardiva ac omnia al*ia* p*re*mi*ff*a preconce*ff*a Ac om*n*es
domos Anglic*e* Privyes ei*f*d*em* p*re*mi*ff*is siue e*orund*em alique
p*ar*ti spectan*tes* adtunc fact*os* vel impo*f*ter*um* f*aci*end*os* in omni-
b*us* nece*ff*arijs rep*ar*ac*i*onib*us* bene & sufficien*ter* reparent manutenerent fac*er*ent e*f*curarent mundarent & emendarent de tempore
in tempus quando & quoties nece*ff*e requireret Et ea*d*em tam
bene & *f*ufficien*ter* rep*ar*ata e*f*curata mundata & emendata in fine
eiu*f*dem t*er*min*j* viginti & vni*us* Annor*um* relinquerent & sur*f*ur-
reddirent ei*f*d*em* Egidio & Sare & hered*ibus* & A*ff*ign*atis* ip*f*ius
Egidij se*c*und*um* formam & eff*ec*tum Jndenture p*re*di*c*te licet
sepius requi*f*it*us* non tenuit sed penit*us* infregit Et ill*am* ei ten*ere*
se*c*und*um* formam & eff*ec*tum Jndenture p*re*di*c*te penitus recu*f*a-
vit Et adhuc recu*f*at ad dampn*um* ip*f*orum Egidij & Sare ducen-
t*arum* librar*um* Et inde produc*unt* sectam &c./

Et modo ad hunc diem scil*ic*et diem M*er*curij p*ro*ximum po*f*t xviij
Pa*f*che i*f*to eodem T*er*mino v*f*q*ue* quem diem p*re*di*ctus* Cut*b*ertus
Burbage h*a*buit licenciam ad billam p*re*di*c*tam interloquend*um*
Et tunc ad re*f*pondend*um* &c C*o*ram d*o*mina Regina apud We*f*t-
mona*f*terium ven*er*unt tam p*re*di*c*ti Egidius & Sara p*er* Attorna-
t*um* suum p*re*dict*um* qu*am* p*re*di*ctus* Cut*b*ertus p*er* Thomam
Petre Attorn*atum* suum Et id*em* Cut*b*ertus defend*it* vim & in-
iuri*am* quando &c Et dicit q*u*od p*re*di*ctus* Egidius Aleyn & Sara
acc*i*onem suam p*re*di*c*tam inde ver*f*us eu*m* h*a*b*er*e seu manutenere
non debent Quia dicit q*u*od horreu*m* domus & edificia p*re*dicta
in Jndentura p*re*dicta sup*er*ius specificata p*re*fato Jacobo Burbage
p*er* p*re*dict*um* Egidi*um* & Saram (vt p*re*fert*ur* dimi*ff*a a tempore Confecc*i*onis dimi*ff*ionis illius v*f*que expiracc*i*onem p*re*-

di*cti* Te*rm*inj viginti & vni*us* Anno*rum* fue*runt* bene & sufficien*ter* rep*ar*ata & manutent*a* in omnib*us* neceſſarijs reparacioni-
b*us* de tempore in tempus dura*nte* Te*rm*ino illo quando & quoties
neceſſe fuit Ac sic bene & sufficien*ter* rep*ar*ata & manutent*a* in
fine eiuſdem Te*rm*inj viginti & vni*us* Anno*rum* relict*a* & surſur-
reddit*a* fue*runt* eiſdem Egidio & Sare iuxt*a* formam & eff*ectum*
Jndenture illius/ Abſq*ue* hoc q*u*od horreu*m* domus & edificia p*re*-
di*cta* in Jndentur*a* p*re*di*cta* sup*er*ius menc*i*onat*a* fuerunt ruinoſ*a*
& in decaſu modo & forma p*r*ov*t* p*re*di*cti* Egidius & Sara sup*er*ius
narrando allegaverunt Et hoc p*ar*at*us* eſt verificare vnde petit
Judi*cium* si p*re*di*cti* Egidius & Sara accionem suam p*re*di*ctam*
inde verſus eum h*a*bere seu manuten*ere* debeant &c./

Et p*re*di*cti* Egidius Aleyn & Sara dicunt q*u*od ip/i p*er* aliqua p*er*
p*re*dict*um* Cutbertum Burbage sup*er*ius pl*a*citand*o* allegat*a* ab
acc*i*one sua p*re*dict*a* verſus ipſum Cutbertum h*a*bend*a* preclud*i*
non debent Quia vt prius dicunt q*u*od horreu*m* domos & edificia
p*re*di*cta* in Jndentur*a* p*re*di*cta* sup*er*ius menc*i*onat*a* fuerunt ruinoſ*a* & in decaſu modo & forma p*r*ov*t* p*re*di*cti* Egidius & Sara
sup*er*ius narrando allegaverunt Et hoc pet*unt* q*u*od inquirat*ur*
p*er* p*a*triam Et p*re*dict*us* Cutbertus Burbage simili*ter* &c J*deo*
veni*at* inde J*u*rat*a* coram d*o*m*in*a* Regina Apud Weſtmon*a*ſteri*um*
die p*ro*xim*o* poſt Et qui nec &c ad recogn &c Quia tam &c
Jdem dies dat*us* eſt p*ar*tib*us* p*re*dictis ib*i*dem &c

[No judgment entered. This suit was begun in Hilary (Jan.–Feb.)
1601, and was here entered for trial in Easter, 1602. It was probably
stopped before coming to trial. Meanwhile, in November, 1601, Allen
had brought suit, on the same general matter of the Theatre, in Star
Chamber, and prosecuted it at the same time, until the summer of 1602,
when that case as well as this apparently failed. The Star Chamber proceedings here follow.]

ALLEN *v.* BURBAGE

Star Chamber Proceedings, 44 Elizabeth (*1601–2*), *A. 12/35.*

[Allen's suit in King's Bench against Street, 1599–1600, had been stopped
by order of the Court of Requests, first by injunction, 10 April 1600, and
finally by decree of Oct. 18, 1600, and thus failed. Then he lost the suit

brought in Requests by Burbage for relief against him in 1600, and the Court forbade Allen ever again to bring suit in any Court for the tearing down of the Theatre. This decree fell on Oct. 18, 1600, as recited in the Answer of the Burbages in the present suit. Then almost immediately, in the next term, Hilary, 1601, Allen sued Burbage in the King's Bench on the same matter under the subterfuge of breach of contract. This, too, could not but fail. Still determined on his course of annoyance and possible ruin to the new Globe theatre and the Burbage-Shakespeare company there, Allen next brought the following suit in Star Chamber, in November, 1601, still on the same matter, but under the shifted charges of riot, perjury, &c. This continued nearly to the close of 1602. That it likewise failed, finally ending Allen's litigation, is sufficiently indicated by Sir Francis Bacon's opinion upon it, quoted in the Demurrer of Hudson and Osborne, 12 June, 1602. The final decree is lost.

This suit was found by Halliwell-Phillipps, who quoted extracts from it in his *Outlines,* I, 360–61, 372. In a long uninformed article in the *Athenaeum,* Oct. 16, 1909, Mrs. Stopes, after using Halliwell-Phillipps, declared that he had not seen the pleadings in this suit, and claimed them as her "discovery"—only one of several claims by her to discoveries known to scholars.]

BILL

[Date, *in dorso:*]
Lune vicefino Tercio
Novembris Anno xliiij^{to}
Elizabeth*e* Regine
William Mill

To the Queenes moſt excellent Matie: ./

In moſt humble wyſe complayninge ſheweth vnto your moſt Excellent Matie: your highnes obedient and faythfull Subiect Gyles Allein of Haſeleigh in your highnes Countye of Eſſex gent*leman* That wheras your ſayd ſubiect together wth Sara his wyfe did heretofore by their Indenture bearinge date the thirteenth daye of Aprill in the eighteenth yeere of your highnes Raigne demiſe vnto one James Burbage late of London Joyner certen howſeing and voyde Groundes lyeing and being in Hollywell in the Countye of Midd*lesex* for the Terme of one and twentye yeeres then next following for the yeerelye Rente of foureteene pownd*es,* wherin

it was covenanted oɳ the parte of your fayd fubiect and the fayd
Sara to make a newe Leafe of the premiffes to the fayde James
Burbage or his affignes att any tyme w^{th}in the firfte Tenne yeers
vppon his or their Requeft for the terme of one and twenty yeeres
from the making hereof. And it was by the fame Indenture cove-
naunted on the parte of the fayd James Burbage That he or his
affignes fhould w^{th}in the fayd firft Tenne yeeres beftowe the fomme
of two hundred powndes in alteringe and amendinge of the buyld-
ings there (The value of the olde ftuffe therof to be accompted
parcell) In Confideracion of wch fomme of two hundred powndes
foe to be beftowed It was covenanted on the parte of your Subiect that it fhould be lawfull for the fayd James Burbage and his
Affignes att anie tyme w^{th}in the firft one and twentye yeeres
graunted, or w^{th}in the one and twentye yeeres by vertue of the
Covenante aforefayd to be graunted to take downe fuch Buylding
as fhould w^{th}in the fayd Tenne yeeres be erected on the fayd
voyde growndes for a Theater or playinge place, And afterwardes the fayd James Burbage did w^{th}in the fayde Tenne yeeres
(A Theater being then there erected att the Coftes and Charges
of one Braynes and not of the fayd James Burbage to the value of
one Thowfand Markes) tender vnto yor fubiect a Draught of a
newe leafe of the premiffes requiring yor Subiecte to feale the fame
wch yor fubiect refufed to doe, by reafon that the fayd Draught foe
tendred varyed much from the Covenantes in the former leafe,
And alfo for that the fayd James Burbage had before that tyme
affigned all his Intereft and terme in the fayd premiffes vnto one
John Hide and had alfo bene a verye badd and troblefome tenante
vnto your fayd Subiect. So that yor Subiect was in noe wyfe
bounde either in lawe or confcience to feale the fame, And afterwardes the fayd Hide conveyed all his Intereft and terme in the
premiffes vnto one Cuthbert Burbage the fonne of the fayd James
Burbage, whoe being defirous ftill to make gayne of the fayd
Theater fuffered the fame there to contynue till the expiracion of
the fayd Terme, Wherby the right and Intereft of the fayd Theater was both in lawe and Confcience abfolutely vefted in your fayd
Subiect, Wheruppon your Subiect feeing the greate and greevous

abuſes that grewe by the ſayd Theater intended to pull downe the
ſame, and to convert the wood and timber therof to ſome better
vſe for the benefitt of your Subiect wᶜʰ your Subiect had iuſt
Cauſe to doe, the rather for that yoʳ Subiect had noe other meanes
to be releived for thirtye powndes Arrerages of Rentes wᶜʰ the
ſayd James Burbage in his lyeſe tyme did owe vnto your Subiect
for the premiſſes, and for the breach of divers Covenantes in not
repayring the howſes and otherwiſe for that the ſayd James Burbage had in his lyeſe tyme made A deede of guift of all his goodes
to the ſayd Cuthbert Burbage and Richard Burbage his ſonnes,
whoe after the death of the ſayd James Burbage procured Ellen
Burbage his widdowe being a verye poore woman to take the
Adminiſtracion vppon her wᶜʰ was done to defraude your Subiect
and other Creditors of the ſayd James Burbage.   But ſo it is yf
it maye pleaſe your excellent Maᵗᵗᵉ: that the ſayd Cuthbert Burbage having intelligence of your Subiectes purpoſe herein, and
vnlawfullye combyninge and confederating himſelfe wᵗʰ the ſayd
Richard Burbage and one Peeter Streat, William Smyth and divers other perſons to the number of twelve to your Subiect vnknowne did aboute the eight and twentyth daye of December in
the one and fortyth yeere of your highnes Raygne, and ſythence
your highnes laſt and generall pardon by the Confederacye aforeſayd ryotouſlye aſſemble themſelves together and then and there
armed themſelves wᵗʰ divers and manye vnlawfull and offenſive
weapons, as namelye, ſwordes daggers billes axes and ſuch like
And ſoe armed did then repayre vnto the ſayd Theater And then
and there armed as aforeſayd in verye ryotous outragious and
forcyble manner and contrarye to the lawes of your highnes
Realme attempted to pull downe the ſayd Theater whervppon
divers of your Subiectes ſervauntes and farmers then goinge
aboute in peacable manner to procure them to deſiſt from that
their vnlawfull enterpryſe, They the ſayd ryotous perſons aforeſayd notwᵗʰſtanding procured then therein wᵗʰ greate vyolence not
onlye then and there forcyblye and ryotouſlye reſiſting your ſub-
iectes ſervauntes and farmers but allſo then and there pulling
breaking and throwing downe the ſayd Theater in verye out-

ragious violent and riotous fort to the great difturbance and ter-
refeyeing not onlye of yor fubiect*es* fayd fervaunt*es* and farmers
but of divers others of your ma^{ties} loving fubiect*es* there neere
inhabitinge. And having fo done did then alfo in moft forcible
and ryotous manner take and carrye awaye from thence all the
wood and timber therof vnto the Banckfide in the p*a*ri*f*he of S^t
Marye Overyes and there erected a newe playe howfe wth the fayd
Timber and wood, Whervppon your Subiecte in Hillarye Terme
following did com*m*ence an Acc*i*on of Trefpas agaynft the fayd
Peeter Streate in your highnes Courte at Weftmin*f*ter commonlye
called the kinges Benche for the fayde wrongfull entringe into
your fubiect*es* groundes and pullinge downe and taking awaye of
the fayd Theater, Howbeit the fayd Cuthbert Burbage malicioufly*e*
intending to vexe and moleft yor fubiecte in Eafter Terme followinge exhibited a Bill vnto yor highnes agaynft yor fubiect in yor
highnes Courte of Requeft*es* p*r*etending matter of Equitye for
the ftaye of yor fubiect*es* fayd fute att the Com*m*on lawe whervnto your fubiecte appeared and made Aunfwere, And afterwardes in Trinytye terme in the xlij^th yeare of yor highnes raigne
an order was conceived and then publifhed and pronounced by yor
highnes Councell of the fayd Courte by the Confent of yor fubiecte
that yor fubiect*es* fayd fute att the Com*m*on Lawe fhould ftaye
till the caufe in Equitye were heard in the fayd Courte of Requeft*es* which was appoynted to be in Michellmas Terme following yett foe that the Demurrer wch was formerlye ioyned in the
fayd fute betweene yor fubiecte and the fayd Peeter Streate might
be made vpp wch was expreflye graunted and allowed by the fayd
order vppon the fpeciall moc*i*on and defire of yor fubiect*es* Councell, whervppon yor fubiecte gave order to his Attorney to caufe
the Demurrer to be made vppe accordinglye./ But maye it pleafe
your excellent Matie the fayd Cuthbert Burbage myndinge further
to intrappe yor fubiecte and to circumvent him to his great Daunger as the fequell fheweth did verye malycouflye and fraudu-
lentlye after the fayd Order pronounced as aforefayd combyne
and practife wth one John Maddoxe then his Attorney in that fute
wth one Richard Lane the Regifter of the fayd Courte and by con-

federacye as aforefayd procured the fayd John Maddox to drawe an order (wch appertayned not to him to doe but vnto the Regyfter of the fayd Courte of Requeftes and likewyfe procured the fame to be entred and fett downe directly contrarye to that wch was delivered and pronounced as aforefayd by yor highnes Counfell of the fayd Courte, namelye that yor fubiect fhould not proceed to the making vpp of the Demurrer aforefayd. Therein verye high-lye abufing your highnes fayd honorable Courte and greatlye iniuringe yor fubiecte, Howbeit yor fubiect having formerlye given Order to his Attorney for the making vpp of the Demurrer nothing doubtinge but that fafelye he might fo doe being altogether ignorant of the fraudulent and finifter practife and confederacye aforefayd, And yor fubiectes Attorney havinge made vpp the fayd Demurrer yor fubiect made repayre home into the Countrye thinking all matters fhould reft in peace till the tyme appoynted for the hearing of the fayd Caufe. But the fayd Cuthbert Bur-bage purfuing his former wicked and vngodlye purpofe and feek-ing to plunge yor fubiecte in very greivous and inevitable mif-cheifs did the laft daye of the fayd Trynitye Terme by the practife and confederacye of the fayd John Maddoxe make oath in your highnes fayd Courte of Requeftes that yor fubiecte had broken the order of that Courte by making vpp of the Demurrer aforefayd, Whervppon your fubiect for that fuppofed Contempt was in the vacacion tyme then next followinge by the procurem^t of the fayd Cuthbert Burbage and by the confederacye aforefayd fetched vpp to London by a Purfevant to his great vexacion and troble (beinge a man verye aged and vnfitt to travell) and to his exceffive charges in his Journey and otherwife to his great difcreditt and difgrace in the Countrye, And yor fubiect then by the fayd Pur-fevant brought before one of the m^rs of your highnes fayd Courte did (by the fayd mafters order then made) become bounde vnto the fayd Cuthbert Burbage in a bonde of two hundred powndes to appeare in the fayd Court of Requeftes in the begining of the Terme of St Michell then next following to aunfwere the fayd fup-pofed contempt and to ftand to the Order of the fayd Courte vppon the hearinge of the Caufe. And afterwardes yor fayd fubiect at the fayd Terme appeared in the fayd Court accordingly, And the matter aforefayd being opened to yor highnes Counfell there your fubiect was thervppon by order of that Courte difcharged of the fupposed Contempt And afterward*es* in the fayd Terme of St Michaell at the day appoynted for the hearing of the fayd Caufe yor fubiect appearing in yor highnes fayd Courte and having divers wit- neffes there pre*f*ente to teftifie viva voce on the behaulfe of yor fubiecte, The fayd Cuthbert Burbage and the fayd Richard Burbage ftill per*f*iifting in their vnlawfull and malicious Courfes agaynft yor fubiect did by the Confederacye aforefayd then and there very fhamefully and vnlawfullye revile wth manye reproachfull termes yor fubiect*es* fayd witneffes and affirmed that they had formerly teftified in the fayd Caufe divers vntruthes, and threatned to ftabb fome of your fubiect*es* fayd witneffes becaufe they had teftified of the fraudulent deede of Guift made by James Bur- bage to the fayd Cuthbert Burbage and Richard Burbage as afore- fayd, By wch their furyous and vnlawfull threat*es* your fubiect*es* witneffes were then foe terrefyed that they durft not teftifie the truth on the behalfe of your fubiecte in the fayd Caufe. And further fo it is yf it maye pleafe yor excellent Matie That the fayd Cuthbert Burbage did verye malicioullye and corruptlye and contrarye to the Lawes and ftatutes of your highnes Realme fuborne and procure one Richard Hudfon of the parifhe of St Albons in London Carpenter and Thomas Ofborne of the pari*f*he of ffanchurche in London Carpenter to commit verye greivous and wilfull per*i*urye in the fayd fute in yor highnes Court of Re- queft*es* in diu*e*rs materyall poyntes concerninge the fayd fute The fayd Richard Hudfon teftifieing and depofing in the fayd fute on the behalfe of the fayd Cuthbert Burbage That he was pre*f*ent at a veiwe and eftimate made of the Coft*es* beftowed by the afore- fayd James Burbage in his lyefe tyme vppon the howfes and Tenem^tes demifed vnto him by your fubiect wch veiwe was taken the eighteenth daye of Julye in the yeere of our Lord god one thowfand five hundred eightye fixe by himfelfe and others And that then it did appeare vnto them That before that tyme The fayd James Burbage had beftowed vppon the fayd Howfes and

Tenem^tes the fomme of two hundred and fortye pound*es*. And
the fayd Thomas Ofborne in like manner teftyfieing and depofing
in the fayd fute on the behalfe of the fayd Cuthbert Burbage
That he likewife was pre*f*ent at the fame veiwe and that it did
then appeare that w^thin foure or five yeeres before that veiwe
taken there had bene beftowed vppon the fayd howfes and Tenement*es* by the fayd James Burbage the fom*m*e of two hundred
and fortye pownedes. Wheras in truth the fayd Richard Hudfon
was not pre*f*ent at any veiwe taken in the yeere aforefayd, but
onlye at veiwe taken in the three and thirtyth yeere of yor
highnes Raigne as by the Depofici*o*n of the fayd Richard Hudfon
himfelfe heretofore made in your hignes Court of Chauncery and
there remayning of record it doth evidentlye appeare neither had
the fayd James Burbage at the tyme of the fayd veiwe fuppofed
to be made the eighteenth daye of Julye in the fayd yeere of our
Lord God 1586 beftowed anye thinge neere the fomme of two
hundred and fortye pownd*es* wherof your Subiect hopeth he fhall
be able to make verye fufficient proofe. By which vnlawfull
practifes of the fayd Cuthbert Burbage your Subiect did then lofe
his fayd Caufe. And further fo it is maye it pleafe your excellent
maieftye, That afwell the fayd fute betweene your Subiect and
the fayd Streate As alfo the fayd fute betweene your fubiect and
the fayd Cuthbert Burbage were profecuted agaynft your fubiecte
by the malicioufe procurement and the vnlawfull mayntenance
of the aforefayd William Smyth (he t[he fayd] William vnlawfullye [bringing]e the fayd futes for th[e fayd] Cuthbert Burbage a[nd th]en vnlawfullye expen[din]g and layeing out divers
fommes of money in the fame for and in the behalfe of the fayde
Cuthbert Burbage [contrarye] to the Lawes and [ftatutes] of
this yor highnes R[ealme an]d to the greate [preiud]ice of your
fubiecte In Confideraci*o*n wherof and for that the Ryott rout*es*
forcible Entries confederacies abufe of Juftice maynten[ance and]
other the mifdem[eanors a]forefayd are contrar[ye to y]our
highnes lawes [ftatutes] and ordinances [made] and eftablifhed
for [the] quiet and happye governement of this your hignes
Realme and are not onlye ve[rye grei]vous vnto your fay[d

ſubiec]t but alſo verye de[leteri]ous in example to [others] yf ſuch and ſo fow[le m]iſdemeanors ſhould [eſc]ape their due and condigne puniſhment Maye it therefore pleaſe your excellen[t Matie] the *premiſſes* conſide[red to g]raunt vnto your ſu[biecte] your highnes moſt [graci]ous writt*es* of Su[bpoen]a to be directed v[nto] the ſayd Cuthbert Burbage, Richard Burbage, Peeter Streate Will*ia*m Smyth, [Richar]d Lane Richard H[udſon] and Thomas Oſbo[rne c]om*m*aunding them and [everye] of them therbye [on a] certen daye and v[nder] a certen payne therein to be lymitted *per*ſonallye to be and appeare before yo[ur high-nes] moſt honorable p[rivie] Counſell in your high[nes moſt] honorable Court [of Sta]rr-chamber to an[ſwer]e the miſde-mean[ors a]foreſayd. And yo[ur] ſayd ſubiect ſhall according to his bounden dutye daylye praye t[o Almig]htye god for your ro[yall] maieſties long lyfe [and pro]ſperous Raigne./

J. Jeffreys [attorney]

[During the years when the parchment of the above bill was rolled up, mice or rats gnawed through one side of the roll, making several holes an inch or more in diameter, when it is flattened out. Words and letters supplied in brackets, from the context, show where these defects occur.]

ANSWER OF THE BURBAGES AND OTHERS

Mercur*ii* 28 Aprilis
Anno 44° Elizabeth*e* Regine
William Mill

The ioynt and ſeu*er*all Demurrers, and Pleas of Cuthbert Burbage, Richard Burbage Peeter Streete and Will*ia*m Smyth fyve [sic] of the Defend^{tes} to ye bill of compl of Giles Allen gent Compl^t

The ſaid Defend^{tes} by proteſtaci*on* not acknowledginge nor con-feſſinge any of the matters in the ſaid Bill conteyned to be true ſayen. That the ſaid Bill of Compl^t exhibited againſt them and others into this moſt honorable Courte is verie vncerteine and inſufficient in the Lawe to be aunſweared vnto for diuers and fundrie fault*es,* and manifeft ymperfections therein appearinge fuch as by the Lawes of this Realme and orders of this honorable Courte they theis Defend^{tes} are not tied to make any aunfweare vnto. And namelie whereas the faid Complayn^t doth charge theis Defend^{tes} in his faid Bill for a Riott by them committed in pullinge downe of the faide Playe houfe called the Theater, and for takinge and carryinge awaye thence the woodde and Tymber thereon which Playe houfe was builded and erected vppon certeine groundes thentofore Demyfed vnto him the faide James Burbage in the faide bill of Complaint named by the Compl^t and his wife by theire Indenture of Leafe vnder theire hands and feales for the terme of diuers yeares then to come) The faid Compl^t havinge for that caufe in Hillarie terme next followinge the faid fuppofed Riott commenced an Acc*i*on of trefpaffe againft Peeter Streete, and the faid Cuthbert Burbage being two of the nowe Defend^{tes} in her Maties. Courte called the Kinges Benche at weftminfter. And the faid Defend^t Cuthbert Burbage being Affignee of the *p*remiffes, and being well able in good confcience and equitie to iuftifie the pullinge downe, vfinge and Difpofinge of the woodde and tymber of the faide Playe houfe, although in ftrictnes of lawe, by reafon of the Compl^{tes} owne wronge and breache of Covenaunte, he had noe fufficient matter to alleadge in barre of the faid acc*i*on, this Defend^t Cuthbert Burbage did for his releife and ftaye of the vniuft proceeding*es* of the faid Complayn^t in the faid acc*i*on exhibite his Bill of Compl^t vnto yor Matie before yor Highnes Councell in your honorable Courte of whitehall againft the faide Compl^t. Vnto which bill the nowe Compl^t appeared and aunfweared and this Defend^t Cuthbert replied, and diuers witneffes were examined on both fides, publicac*i*on graunted, and feuerall daies appointed for the hearinge thereof And vppon the open hearinge and full and deliberate debatinge of the faid caufe, it plainlie appeared vnto yor Maties faid Councell that the faid James Burbage had well and truelie for his parte *p*erfourmed and kepte all and fing*u*ler the Covenaunt*es* conteyned in the faid Indenture, and that the nowe Complayn^t in refufinge to feale A newe Leafe of the *p*remiffes tendred vnto

him by the faid James Burbage accordinge to A covenant in the
faid Indenture of Leafe on his the nowe Compl^tes parte to be
perfourmed contrarie to his owne agreement through his owne
wronge and breach of covenaunt in not fealinge the faid newe
Leafe vnto the faid James Burbage) fought to hinder him this
Defend^t Cuthbert havinge the intereft of the premiffes) to take
the benefitte of the faid agreement in the faid Indenture expreffed
in takinge awaye the faid playehoufe beinge made and erected by
the faid James Burbage at his chardge accordinge to the faid covenaunte.   Therefore it feemed vnto yor. Maties faid Councell that
there was good caufe in equitie to ftaie the nowe Compl^tes proceedinges in the faid Accion at the Common Lawe.   And therevppon it appearinge to your Highnes faid Councell the faid De-
fend^t Cuthbert for diuers reafons had iuft caufe to be releiued
in the premiffes   It was by yor Highnes faid Councell the 18th
daye of October in the two and fortithe yeare of yor ma^ties
raigne ordered, adiudged and decreed that the nowe Compl^t his
Counfello^rs, Attourneyes, and Sollicitors fhould from thence
fourth furceafe and ftaye and noe further profecute or proceede
at the Common lawe in the faid accion of trefpaffe foe commenced
againft the faid Peeter Streete for that caufe.   And that the faid
nowe Compl^t nor any for him, or by his confent, or procurem^t
fhoulde at any tyme then after commence, or caufe to be commenced any other accion or fuyte againft him this Defend^t Cuthbert or any his fervauntes, or Affignees for or concerninge the
pullinge downe of the faid Playehoufe, or for carrying awaye the
tymber thereof   And that this Defend^t Cuthbert fhoulde be at
libertie to take his remedie at and by the courfe of your Highnes
Common lawes againft the nowe Compl^t for not agreeing to feale
the faid newe Leafe accordinge to A covenaunte on the nowe
Compl^tes parte to be perfourmed in the faid Indentures expreffed
as (amongft other things) in the faid Judiciall Decree, and fentence of that Courte more at large it doth and maye appeare.
ffor which caufe, and for that the nowe Compl^t (if he had fuf-
pected or had fhewed any caufe of greife for any fraude, or indi-
recte practife, or dealinge (by him fuppofed to be vfed, or com-

mitted by any of the Officers of your Highnes faid Courte) in drawinge, or entringe of orders contrarie to thofe your Highnes faid Counfell had before pronounced or Deliuered in that caufe) or for any practife in any of them theife Defend^tes for procuringe the fame as he the faid Compl^t by his faid Bill of Compl^t doth falfely and vntruelie furmife) might at any time whilest the fame fuyte was dependinge in the faid honorable courte by Compl^t thereof made vnto your Highnes faid Counfell haue fuch fault*es* and mifdemeano^rs there redreffed and punifhed, and Juftice myniftred in that behalf And for that the Complayn^t doth offerre great fcandall, and abufe to your Highnes faid Counfell by callinge the fame matter againe into queftion, and in labouringe to haue the faid caufe, after fuch iudiciall fentence and decree paft againft the faid Complayn^t in the faid honorable Courte to be againe reexamined before your Matie in this Courte. Therefore and for diuers other defect*es,* fault*es,* and ymp*er*fections in the faid bill of Compl^t appearinge they theis Defend^tes doe demurre in lawe vppon the faid Bill, and Demaunde the iudgem^t of this honorable Courte, if they theis Defend^tes or any of them ought to make any other Aunfweare therevnto, and humblie praye to be Difmiffed wth theire reafonable coftes therein wrongfullie fufteyned

[Signed] Jo. Walter [Attorney]

ANSWER OF RICHARD LANE

Jur*ata* 28 Aprilis
Anno 44° Elizabeth*e*
Regine
     William Mill

> The Aunfwere of Richard Lane one of the defendant*es* to the vntrue and fclaunderous bill of complaint of Gyles Allen compl./

The faid def^t faving to himfelf now and at all tymes hereafter all advantages and excep*ci*ons to thincertenties and infufficiencie of the faid bill of complaint for Aunfwere and plaine declara*ci*on of

the trueth of fo much therof as concerneth him this def[t] fayeth
that true it is that there was A fute commenfed in her Ma[tes]
hono[r]able Court of Whitehall at weftmin/ter by one Cuthbert
Burbage complainant againft the faid Gyles Allen def[t] concerning
the ftay of A fute w[ch] the faid Allen had then dependinge in her
Ma[tes] Court of Kinges benche againft the faid Burbage or his
fervaunt towching the Playhoufe called the Theater in the bill
mencioned   In which Court this def[t] then and yet ferving as
deputie Regifter did to the beft of his vnderftanding, and wth as
much knowledge and diligence as hee could attende, and tooke
fuche briefe notes of Orders as from tyme to tyme her ma[tes]
Counfaill in the faid Court pronounced in the faid caufe without
anie affeccion to either of the fayd parties   Amongeft w[ch] vpon
the xxxj[th] of May in the xlij[th] yeare of her ma[tes] moft happie
reigne, the fame matter being moved and opened in prefence, of
m[r] fergeant Harris and m[r] Walter being feuerally of counfaill
learned wth both the faid parties, yt was therevpon (to the beft of
this defendantes remembrance) Ordered by confent of the faid
parties or their Counfaill, that the fame matter fhould be fett over
to be heard in the faid Court vpon the fyveth day of the ther next
terme, And in the meane time the def[t] fhould ftay his fute at the
common lawe and no further proceede therein, And it was alfo
then further Ordered that the faid Allen (makinge othe that he
was not privie to the depoficions publifhed and fetting downe the
names of the deponentes w[ch] hee intended to examine) fhould be
at libertie texamine the fame deponentes fo to be named vntill the
fecond day of the fayd next terme   And then the fame to be publifhed   As by A note remayning in A booke of remembraunces
then taken and kept by this def[t] appeareth.   Vpon the coppie of
w[ch] note fo conceaved, and deliuered by this def[t], The faid John
Madox named in the bill (being Attourney for the faid Burbage)
or fome of his clerkes or fome other on the behalf of the faid
Burbage, did drawe vp an Order at lardge towching the fame
caufe, and brought the fame fubfcribed and confirmed by one of
her ma[tes] faid Counfaill of the faid Court (As by the fame ready
to be fhewed vnto this hono[r]able Court may appeare) into the

Regifters Office to be entred, which accordingly was done. And this defendant further fayeth that if the faid John Madox or any other who had the drawing of the faid Order, did adde or diminifhe any thinge materiall to or from the fayd Order more or leffe then was pronounced yt concerneth him or them in theire othes and credit*es* and not this def^t who did nothing therein more then he had good warrant to doe as aforefayd. And this def^t further fayeth that the Atturneys of the faid Court of Whitehall (being fworne in theire places to obferve thorders and due proceeding*es* of the faid Court) have for the fpace of thirtie yeares laft paft to the knowledge of this def^t (for fo longe hee hath ferved as A Clerke in the fame Court) and longe before as hee hath hearde and doeth verelie beleeve to be true, vfed to drawe theire Client*es* Orders (being fworne to deale indifferentlie therein) And not the Regifter, As the faid Allen in his faid bill hath vntruely alledged efpeciallie fuch as doe concerne Decrees, or orders made for the graunting of Iniunc*c*ions for ftay of anie proceeding*es* at the com*m*on lawe difmiffions of caufes, deliu*ery* out of money or deliu*ery* of writing*es* or for theftablifhing of any poffeffion, and fuch lyke as are and be vfually confirmed before thentring thereof by and vnder the hand*es* or hande of fome of her ma^tes faid Counfaill of the faid Court, before they be entred into the Regifter And for thother ordinary rules and fhort orders, they are nowe vfually entred by the Regifter or his deputie w^thout any further circumftance or contradic*c*ion. And wheareas the faid compl*ainant* in his bill of complaint hath fclaunderouflye and vntruely fett downe, that the faid Burbage did very malitioufly and fraudulently after the fayd Order pronounced as aforefayd, combyne and practife wth the faid John Madox (his Attourney) and wth this def^t (the Regifter) and by confederacie procured the faid John Madox to drawe an Order, wch apperteyned not to him to doe; but vnto the Regifter of the faid Court, and likewife procured the fame to be entred, and fett downe directly contrary to that which was done and pronounced as aforefaid by her highenes Counfaill of the faid Court, namely that the faid Allen fhould not proceede to the making vp of the demurrer in

the bill menci*on*ed therein, very highelie abuſing her highenes
ſaid ho: Courte, and greatly Iniuring the ſayde Allen now plaintif
This defendant for plee and aunſwere therevnto, & every other
matter of miſdemeano[r], confederacie and combynaci*on* layde to
this def[tes] chardge in the ſaid bill ſayeth that hee is thereof and
of every p*ar*te thereof not giltie. Without that that this def[t] did
at any time directly or indirectlie practiſe, combyne or con-
federate wth the ſaid Cuthbert Burbage and John Madock*es* or
either of them, or wth any other p*er*ſon or p*er*ſons whatſoeu*er*
about the drawing or procuring of the ſaid Order to be entred
But did faythfully and ſincerely take the note of the ſayd order
as the ſame was pronounced to his beſt vnderſtanding in ſuch
forme as is before recited, And the ſame ſubſcribed as aforeſaid
was truely entred into the Regiſter accordinglie. And w[th]out
that that anie other matter or thinge in the ſaid bill of complaint
conteined towching or concerning this def[t], materyall to be aunſwered vnto, and not herein ſufficiently aunſwered, confeſſed and
avoyded, trau*er*ſed or denyed is true. All which matters this
defendant is readie to averre and proove as this hono[r]able Court
ſhall awarde And humblie prayeth to be diſmiſſed out of the
ſame w[th] his coſt*es* and chardges in this behalf moſt wrongfully
had and ſuſteyned./

[Signed] Smyth [Attorney]

DEMURRER OF HUDSON AND OSBORNE

Sabat*i* 12 Junij Anno
44 Elizabeth*e* Regine

Jouis 17 Junij Anno
predicto demur*atur*
p*er* Tho Oſborne

> The ioyncte and ſeuerall Demurrers of Rich-
> ard Hudſon, and Thomas Oſborne two of the
> defend[tes] to the Bill of Complaynte of Gyles
> Allen gent*leman* Complayn*ante*./

The ſaide defend.^tes by proteſtacion not acknowledginge nor con-
feſſinge anie of the matters in the ſaide Bill conteyned to be
true ſayen That the ſaide Bill of Complainte exhibited agaynſte
them and others in this honorable Courte is very vntrue and
ſlaunderous vncerteyne and inſufficient in the lawe to be aunſwered vnto for diuers and ſondrie faultes and manifeſt ymper-
feccions therin appearinge and ſuche as by the lawes of this
Realme and orders of this honorable Courte they theis defend.^tes
are not tyed to make anie aunſweare therevnto And namelye for
that the matters and ſuppoſed periurie in the ſaide Bill conteyned
wherewth they theis defend.^tes are or doe ſtande charged are
therin ſoe vncerteinlie and inſufficiently layed as they theis defend.^tes vnder the favor of this honorable Courte cannot and are
not tyed to make anie further aunſweare thervnto And theis
defend.^tes further ſaye That other of the defend.^tes in the ſaide
Bill of Complainte named havinge beene heretofore ſerved wth
proceſſe haue appeared and demurred vppon the ſame Bill whiche
demurrer beinge referred by the orders of this honorable Courte
to the right worſhipfull ffrauncis Bacon Eſquier, he vppon per-
vſall and conſideracion had of the ſaide Bill of Complaynte, hathe
already reported That the ſaide Bill is veary vncerteine and inſufficient and that noe further aunſweare needeth to be made
therto for whiche cauſes and diuers other matters and defectes
in the ſaide Bill appearinge They theis defend.^tes doe Demurre
in lawe vpon the ſaide Bill of Complaynte And prayen to be diſmiſſed oute of this honorable Courte wth theire reaſonable coſtes
and chardges by them in this behalf moſte wrongfullie borne and
ſuſteyned./.

[Signed] Jo: Walter [Attorney]

EXAMINATION OF RICHARD LANE

Star Chamber, Elizabeth, A 33/32.

primo Maij poſt
merediem: Anno
Regni Regine Elizabethe 44to./

Rec vj^s
T H

Interrogatories to be miniſtred to Richard Lane
on of the Defendantes at the ſuite of Gyles Allen
Complaynante.

1 **Inprimis** whither doe yo^u knowe that a bill was heretofore exhibited in her Maties Court of Requeſ*tes* by Cutbert Burbage
againſt the ſaide Complaynante for the ſtaying of a ſuite wch the
ſaide Complaynante had commenced in her Maties bench at Weſt-
minſter againſt one Peter Street for the pulling downe of the
playing place called the Theater./

2 **Item** whither doe yo^u knowe that it was ordered by the ſaide
Court of Requeſ*tes,* by an order made the laſt daye of May in the
Two and ffortieth yeare of her Maties Raigne, that the ſaid ſuite
betwen the ſaide Complaynante, and the ſaide Peter Street ſhould
be ſtayed, and whither did the ſaide Court then geue libertie, by
the ſaide order, vnto the ſaide Complaynant to ioyne vp the demurrer that was depending betwen the ſaide Complaynante, and
the ſaide Peter Street in the ſaide ſuite, or whither did the ſaide
Court reſtrayne the Complaynant from ſoe doeing,/

3 **Item** whither did yo^u enter the ſaide order trulie in ſuch mann*er*
as it was deliu*er*ed by the Court, and whither did yo^u deliu*er* a
true copie thereof vnto the Complaynant not altering or omm*it*-
ting anie thing that was then deliuered and pronounced by the
ſaide Court./

4 **Item** whither did yo^u vppon the ſaide laſt daie of May deliu*er*
vnto the Complaynante a Copie of an order dated the ſaide laſt
daie of May, and whither did yo^u therein ſett downe that it was
ordered by conſent that the Complaynant ſhould ſtay his further
proceeding*es* at the Comm*on* Lawe in the ſuite there depending
againſt Cutbert Burbage the Plf^t. in the ſaide Court of Requeſ*tes*
and whither did yo^u in the ſaide Copie make anie mention that

the Court had geuen libertie to the Complaynante to ioyne vp the aforefaide demurrer, or that the Court had ordered that he fhoulde not ioyne it vp, or did yo^u not altogither ommitt the fame./

5 **Item** whither did not the Complaynante come vnto yo^u the fame laft day of May in the afternone, and fhewe yo^u a note from his Councell, teftifying that the Court had by theire fayed order geuen him libertie to ioyne vp the faide demurrer, and whither did not the faide Complaynante then defire yo^u that the order might be foe entred, according as in trueth it was deliuered by the Court the fame daie and whither had yo^u receyued anie order of the faide laft day of May betwen the nowe Complaynant and the faide Cutbert Burbage vnder the hand of anie of the Mafters of the faide Court of Requeftes, before fuch time as the Complaynant came vnto yo^u and required yo^u to reforme the Copie wch yo^u had deliuered him as aforefaide./

6. **Item** whither did yo^u enter an order beareing date the faide laft daye of May, and therein amongeft other thinges fett downe that the nowe Complaynant fhould furceafe and ftay and no further profecute or proceede in the faide accion depending at the Common Lawe, and fhould not caufe the demurrer aforefaid to be ioyned vp, or entred vntill the heareinge of the caufe in the faide Court of Requeftes, and whither were yo^u procured or moued by John Maddox the Attorney of the faide Cutbert Burbage, and Cutbert Burbage, or either of them to enter the fame in fuch manner, and what fomme of money or other recompence did the faide Cutbert Burbage or anie for him, geue vnto yo^u, or anie other to yor vfe, for makeinge the faide entre, and for the Copie thereof./

7 **Item** did yo^u deliuer vnto the Complaynante a Copie of anie fuch order as is mencioned in the next precedent Interrogatorie, and when was anie fuch Copie firft deliuered by yo^u vnto the Complaynant and whither did yo^u geue anie knowledge vnto the Complaynante that the faide Court had ordered that he fhould not ioyne vp the demurrer aforefaide./

8 **Item** whither doe yo^u knowe that vppon the eleuenth day of Iune in the Two and ffortieth yeare of her Maties Raigne the faide Cutbert Burbage made oath in the faide Court of Requeſtes, that the nowe Complaynant had cauſed the demurrer aforeſaide to be ioyned vp, contrary to the order of the faide Court, and whither did not the faide Cutbert Burbage therevpon in the vacation then following, procure a Purſiuant to be ſent downe into the Cuntery for the Complaynante, and whither was not the Complaynante brought vp to London by the faide Purſiuant, and carryed before one of the Maſters of the faide Court of Requeſtes, and then enforced to enter into a bond of Two hundred poundes, to appeare in that Court the ffirſt day of Michaellmas terme following, to anſwere the Contempt, and allſo to ſtand to the order of that Court vpon the heareing of the faide Cauſe, or otherwiſe to haue been committed to priſon,/

9 **Item** whither did not the Complaynante appeare in the faide Court according to his faide bond, and whither was it not then opened vnto the Court, and teſtifyed by the Complaynantes Councell, that by the true order aforeſaide made the faide laſt daye of May the Complaynant had libertie geuen him by the faide Court to ioyne vp the demurrer aforeſaide, and that the Court was much abuſed, and the Complaynante much wronged by the practiſe of the faide Cutbert Burbage and the faide Maddox, and the Regiſter, in that behalffe, and whither was not the Complaynante therevppon diſcharged of the faide ſuppoſed contempt,/.

10 **Item** whither did not the Councell of the Complaynante make a mocion in the faide Court of Requeſtes, after the heareing of the faide cauſe betwen the faide Complaynant and the faide Cutbert Burbage to this effect, That the faide Cutbert Burbage was no aſſigne in Lawe or equitie vnto James Burbage deceaſed, (late ffather to the faide Cutbertt) of the faid Theater, and therefore not able to maynteyne anie bill in his owne name towching the ſame, and whither did not the Councell of the Complaynante

drawe a cafe accordingly and put the fame into the faide Court.
by lycence of the faide Court./

11 **Item** whither was it not ordered by the faide Court, by an order
dated the ffirft day of November in the Two and ffortieth yeare
of her Ma^{tles} Raigne vppon the motion of the Complaynant*es*
Councell, that the decree pronounced in the faide caufe betwen
the Complayn*a*nte And the faide Cutbertt Burbage fhould be
ftayed from figning, vntill the cafe aforefaide put in by the Complaynant*es* Councell towching the faide caufe fhould be further
confidered of, by her Ma^{tles} Councell of the faide Court./

LANE'S ANSWERS

Exam*inatio* Capta xj° die Maij A° *Regni Regi*ne
Eliz*abethe* xliiij^{to} Super *J*nterr*ogationes* ex*par*^{te}
Egidij Allen quer*entis* miniftrata*s*

Richard Lane of Courtenhall w^{th}in the Countie of North-
ampton gen*t*le*man* fworne and exa*mi*ned./

To the ffirft *J*nterr*ogatory* he faithe he thinckethe that there was
hearetofore a bill exhibited in her Ma^{tles} Courte of Requef^{tes} by
Cuthb*er*te Burbage p^{lt} againft the nowe p^{lt} then defend^t for the
ftayinge of a fuite wch the nowe Comp^{lt} had comenced in her
Ma^{tles} benche att weftmin*ſter* concer*ninge* the Theater And for
the more plainlie thereof this defend^t referrethe himfelfe to the
recordes of that Courte./

To the 2 *J*nterr*ogatory* he faithe that to his reme*m*brance ytt was
ordered by the Courte of Requeftes the laft of May in the xlij^{th}
yeare of her Ma^{tles} Raigne amongeft other thinges in prefence of
M^r S*er*geant Harris and Mr Walter beinge feu*er*allie of councell
on both p*a*rties and by their confentes that the fute att the Com-
*m*on lawe betweene Cuthb*er*te Burbage, and Gyles Allen fhoulde
bee ftayed, And that he this defend^t beinge deputie Regyfter
of that Courte received an order fubfcribed by one of her Ma^{tles}

Councell in that Courte to that effecte to wch order he referrethe himfelfe   And more faithe nott to this Jnterrogatory./.

To the 3 Jnterrogatory he faithe that to this defend^tes beft remembrance he this defend^t tooke a note of the faid order as yt was pronounced and thereof deliuered a true Coppie to the Comp^lt or fome other on the Comp^ltes behalfe w^thout addinge or deminifhinge anie thinge to or from the fame./

To the iiij^th Jnterrogatory he faithe that he this defend^t deliuered vnto the Comp^lt or to fome on his behalfe a note of an order dated the laft of May 42 Elizabethe Regine but whether the fame was deliuered the day of the date thereof or not this defend^t doth nott knowe.   Butt this defend^t faithe that yt was fett downe in the fame order as he remembrethe that the fd Comp^l fhoulde ftay his further proceedinges att the Common lawe in the fuite there depindinge againft Cuthberte Burbage the Comp^lt in the faid Courte of Requeftes.   And as touchinge the ioyninge vpp of the demurrer in this Jnterrogatory mencioned this defend^t doth nott knowe that he made anie mencion in his note touchinge the fame./

To the vth Jnterrogatory this defend^t faithe he doth nott remember that vppon the laft day of May in the xlij^th yeare of her Maties Raigne in the afternoone of the fame day or att anie other tyme that the faide Allen did fhewe this defend^t anie note from his councell teftifyinge that the Courte had by their faid order gyven him libertie to ioyne vpp the faide demurrer   Neither doth this defend^t remember that the Comp^lt fo defired that the Order might be fo entered [*But this defend^t faith that the Comp^lt came often tymes vnto him* (stricken out)] (wch yf the faid Comp^lt had), yett neuertheles this defend^t was to take noe notice thereof from his Councell, but to enter the fame as yt was pronounced by the Courte./ and as ytt was confirmed vnder the hande of one of her Maties Councell of the fame Courte./

To the vj^th Jnterrogatory he faithe that there was an order deliuered into the office to be entered by John Maddox or fome other

on the behalfe of the ſaid Burbage dated the laſt of May ſubſcribed by one of her Maties Councell of the Courte of Requeſt
purportinge the ſtaye of the ſute as in this Jnterro*gatory* is mencioned. wch he this defend^t afterward*es* cauſed to bee entered into
the Regeſter accordinge to his warrant, And as touchinge the
receyvinge of anie money or other recompence or promiſe of anie
from the ſaid Burbage or Maddox or anie in their behalfes other
then the ordinarie fees due to the Regiſter for the ſame this de-
fend^t denieth the receipte of anie money or other conſideracion
whatſoeu*er*.

To the vij^{th} Jnterro*gatory* he ſaithe that after the receipte of the
ſaid order ſo ſubſcribed as aforeſaid ytt was lawfull for this de-
fend^t to deli*uer* coppies to anie per*ſon* that woulde require the
ſame but howe manie Coppies or to whome the ſame were deliu*er*ed or when this defend^t doth nott remember; Neither doth
this defend^t remember that he this defend^t gave anie notice to
the p^{lt} otherwiſe then the order doth p*ur*porte./

To the viij^{th} Jnterro*gatory* he ſaithe that as touchinge the affid^t
in this Jnterro*gatory* mencioned he referrethe him ſelfe to the
booke of entryes, And as to the reſt of the Jnterro*gatory* he cannot c*er*tainlie depoſe/

To the ix^{th} Jnterro*gatory* he ſaithe that as touchinge the appar-
ance of the ſaid Allen he this def^t referrethe himſelfe to the booke
of apparances kepte in that behalfe. And as touchinge the diſ-
charge of the ſaid Allen his contemptes or anie other mocion made
or order taken in the ſaid Cauſe this defend^t referrethe himſelfe
to the bookes of orders kepte in that behalfe./

To the xth Jnterro*gatory* he ſaithe that he thinketh that there was
mocion made to theffecte ffollowinge viz that the ſaid Cuthb*er*te
Burbage was noe aſſignee in lawe or equitie vnto James Burbage
deceaſed late father to the ſaid Cuthb*er*te Burbage of the Theater
and therefore nott able to manteyne anie bill in his owne name

touchinge the fame. And faithe that by the direccion of her ma^{ties} Councell of the Courte of Requeftes there was a Cafe deliuered into the faid Courte vnder the hande of M^r S^rgeant Harris beinge of Councell wth the faid Allen wch this defend^t hath readye to fhewe to this ho. Courte.

To the xj^{th} Jnterrogatory he faithe that vppon the 5th of Nouember 42 Elizabethe Regine yt was ordered by mocion of the p^{ltes} Councell that the decree pronounced in the faid Caufe betweene the faid Comp^l and the faid Cuthberte Burbage fhoulde be ftayed from figninge till the Cafe aforefaid were further confidered of./
[Signed]   per me Ricardum Lane.